The Autism Discussion Page on Stress,
Anxiety, Shutdowns and Meltdowns

by the same author

The Autism Discussion Page on the Core Challenges of Autism
A Toolbox for Helping Children with Autism Feel Safe, Accepted, and Competent
Bill Nason
ISBN 978 1 84905 994 7
eISBN 978 0 85700 942 5

The Autism Discussion Page on Anxiety, Behavior, School, and Parenting Strategies
A Toolbox for Helping Children with Autism Feel Safe, Accepted, and Competent
Bill Nason
ISBN 978 1 84905 995 4
eISBN 978 0 85700 943 2

THE AUTISM DISCUSSION PAGE

ON STRESS, ANXIETY, SHUTDOWNS AND MELTDOWNS

Proactive Strategies for Minimizing
Sensory, Social and Emotional Overload

BILL NASON

Jessica Kingsley *Publishers*
London and Philadelphia

First published in 2020
by Jessica Kingsley Publishers
73 Collier Street
London N1 9BE, UK
and
400 Market Street, Suite 400
Philadelphia, PA 19106, USA

www.jkp.com

Library of Congress Cataloging in Publication Data
A CIP catalog record for this book is available from the Library of Congress

British Library Cataloguing in Publication Data
A CIP catalogue record for this book is available from the British Library

ISBN 978 1 78592 804 8
eISBN 978 1 78450 834 0

Printed and bound in the United States

SUSTAINABLE FORESTRY INITIATIVE

Certified Chain of Custody
Promoting Sustainable Forestry
www.sfiprogram.org
SFI-01268

SFI label applies to the text stock

Acknowledgements

This book and its companion books in the Autism Discussion Page series are the result of ongoing support and encouragement from the members of my Facebook page, Autism Discussion Page. All the people commenting, suggestions, sharing experiences and supporting each other have been an inspiration for my commitment to them and the page. Through the sharing of our posts across Facebook we can spread the information across all spans of the world, to thousands of people who otherwise do not have free access to such information.

Special thanks to my wonderful wife, whose love and support have encouraged me to complete this project. Without her patience and encouragement this book would have never happened. Also, gratitude for her patience for the time it takes for me to moderate our Facebook page day to day. In addition, thanks for the hours spent editing and proofreading the manuscript. Thank you, Lou Anne! Love you so much!

Most importantly, there are many special families and friends with autism who have enriched my life over the years. For all the families who have allowed me into their lives, thank you so much for sharing this journey with me! And last, for all the adults on the spectrum who have shared with me all their comments, suggestions, recommendations and experiences, thank you for providing me with the feedback and guidance to share your unique perspectives. Understanding your world allows me to communicate that awareness to the rest of the world. Thank you so much and keep advocating your perspectives!

Contents

INTRODUCTION

Welcome to the third publication in the Autism Discussion Page series. My name is Bill Nason and I am a retired mental health professional with over 35 years of experience in the field of developmental disabilities and autism spectrum disorders. Over the years, I provided psychological, consultant services to families, community settings, schools, mental health agencies and individuals with autism. In addition, I took part in numerous training seminars and speaking engagements, and volunteered for local autism support groups and coaching sessions with recreational sports programs for children with autism.

Approximately eight years ago I developed the Autism Discussion Page on Facebook. Over the years, I developed a variety of PowerPoint slide presentations that I used for speaking engagements. These presentations consist of a toolbox of strategies for helping children on the spectrum feel "safe, accepted and competent." My thought was to post these presentations on the Facebook page and lead some educational discussions around these presentations. I naively anticipated a membership of 300–400 parents, teachers and professionals who were interested in supporting those with autism. Little was I aware of the power and reach of Facebook and how fast the page would grow. Today we have over 175,000 members on the Autism Discussion Page, spanning the whole world and bringing together a host of parents, teachers, professionals and others who support those with autism. The page quickly turned into a three-hours-a-day commitment, with me writing two to three posts a day and responding to numerous comments, questions and messages. Today, the page provides a resource for thousands of parents, teachers, professionals and individuals with autism themselves, a place where we share knowledge, experiences, suggestions and support.

Autism Discussion Page book series

Approximately five years ago, with the encouragement of our page members, we expanded the information from the Facebook page into the Autism Discussion Page book series. At the time, the initial two-volume series was a collection of narrative articles posted on the page, organized into an easy-to-read toolbox of strategies for supporting those with autism. To date, we have sold over 25,000 copies of the books, and had excellent reviews from parents, teachers, professionals and individuals with autism. Many parents and professionals report that the two-book series is their major go-to resource for helping those they support. Instead of the books being labeled volume I and II respectively, they are usually referred to by their colors: blue and green.

1. *(Blue book) The Autism Discussion Page on the Core Challenges of Autism: A Toolbox for Helping Children with Autism Feel Safe, Accepted, and Competent* (Nason 2014a).

   This book provides an in-depth view of the four basic sensory, cognitive, social and emotional areas of vulnerabilities for individuals on the spectrum. There is a comprehensive view of each area of vulnerability with detailed guidelines on how to support the child through these challenges. When readers are finished, they will have a good understanding of how their children perceive the world, process information and act the way they do. The book takes you through all the sensory challenges that are common for those on the spectrum, how they process information differently, why they struggle so much socially, and how overwhelming their emotional world can be. From this awareness, it becomes easier to understand and accept those with autism, as well as help them regulate our world. Whether you are a parent, teacher, professional or someone on the spectrum yourself, this book will be of value to you.

2. *(Green book) The Autism Discussion Page on Anxiety, Behavior, School, and Parenting Strategies: A Toolbox for Helping Children with Autism Feel Safe, Accepted, and Competent* (Nason 2014b).

   This book covers some of the major challenges that children and families experience during their daily routine and how to address each challenge. We cover stress and anxiety, addressing behavior issues, co-occurring conditions, stretching comfort zones, harnessing strengths and preferences, parenting and discipline strategies, teaching empowerment skills, and a host of mentoring strategies for coaching your child in basic life skills.

3. *(Brown Book) The Autism Discussion Page on Stress, Anxiety, Shutdowns and Meltdowns: Proactive Strategies for Minimizing Sensory, Social and Emotional Overload.*

   This book analyzes the daily stressors that people with autism experience, the draining effects that tax their nervous systems and the resultant stress, anxiety, shutdowns and meltdowns. Trying to navigate a world that presents them with many challenges results in ongoing physical, mental and emotional drain, continually taxing their processing skills and leaving them vulnerable to sensory, social and emotional overload. Understanding these processing differences allows us to make modifications and accommodations to better match the expectations and demands of their daily routine to their processing abilities, thus making the world more autism friendly. This book will provide proactive strategies for minimizing stress, anxiety, meltdowns and burnout.

This third book expands on the information from the previous two books, focusing on topics that were of most interest to our members on the Facebook page (stress, anxiety, sensory issues, social challenges and meltdowns). Chapter 1 identifies autism as a bio-neurological difference, with a unique package of processing differences. If we understand, accept and respect these differences then support consists of modifying our world to better match the processing abilities of autism—not to cure, suppress or change people with autism, but to recognize, respect and foster their processing differences. Chapter 2 describes autism as an information processing difference, explaining what the differences are and how to help reduce the challenges these differences present.

Chapters 3 and 4 introduce the writer to how taxing and draining navigating their daily routine is for people on the spectrum. Given their sensory vulnerabilities and processing differences, many people with autism find that navigating our world is simply too fast and too overwhelming. This chapter presents strategies for slowing the world down, tuning down the intensity and respecting the processing needs of the individual. We learn what taxes their processing, drains their mental reserve and renders them vulnerable to burnout, shutdown and meltdowns. Chapter 4 presents and analyzes the seven major factors that render events taxing, how to appraise events for their processing strain and ways to minimize the mental and emotional drain. Both chapters combine to match the environmental demands to the processing needs of the individual.

Chapter 5 teaches the reader the difference between stress and distress. Stress is inevitable and manageable, but distress is the ultimate enemy to avoid. It explains how both stress and distress affect the person, overwhelming their processing and damaging their abilities. Strategies provide guidelines for minimizing stress and avoiding distress.

Chapters 6 and 7 review anxiety and how prevalent it is in autism. Chapter 6 gives a breakdown of the different types of anxiety, the primary sources of anxiety and strategies for minimizing it. Chapter 7 discusses specific coping strategies for managing anxiety during stressful situations. Although anxiety is a major co-occurring condition in autism, it can be managed effectively with both proactive, preventative strategies and coping skills for tackling anxiety.

Chapter 8 looks at the relationship between anxiety and rigid/inflexible thinking, showing how anxiety and cognitive/emotional rigidity go hand and hand. Rigid and inflexible thinking, obsessive thoughts and compulsive behaviors are often driven by anxiety. Strategies are offered to lessen rigidity and build greater flexibility.

Chapter 9 looks at those who experience severe anxiety associated with oppositional behavior and demand avoidance. To these individuals, the world is so frightening that they need to control everything happening to them and around them. This requires us to minimize all demands, let them lead, and become collaborative, working partners with them.

Chapters 10–12 discuss shutdowns and meltdowns (10), how to prevent them (11) and how to support individuals during meltdowns (12)—what they are, the differences between the two, ways to avoid them and proactive strategies for minimizing the turmoil when they occur. These chapters aim to make meltdowns understandable, predictable and manageable.

Chapters 13–16 go into more detail regarding the primary daily challenges of sensory overload (13), social challenges (14–15) and executive dysfunction (16). They explore how these three challenges represent the bulk of the stress and processing drain for those with autism, isolating out the specific challenges and providing strategies to proactively minimize their impact. Sensory sensitivities, defensiveness and overload are very common challenges for those with autism. Chapter 13 focuses on the different vulnerabilities and provides proactive strategies for minimizing these sensory challenges. Chapter 14 looks closely at the two primary social processing weaknesses (social context and perspective taking) and how they impact the difficulty relating with others and navigating our social world. Chapter 15 summarizes how stressful it is trying to fit in to our social world and the damage it can do to the self-identity and self-esteem of those with autism. Both chapters provide proactive strategies for equalizing the playing field socially and protecting the self-esteem of those struggling to fit in.

The book ends (Chapter 16) with the importance that executive dysfunction has for the autistic's day-to-day functional living and how it affects their ability to concentrate, plan and organize, execute and monitor "goal-directed" behavior, often the most restrictive neurological difference that prevents independent living. This chapter provides a list of strategies for each executive function, highlighting ways of compensating for these weaknesses and allowing the individual to function as independently and productively as possible.

The basic model of these books

These books work on a fundamental model that everyone strives to feel safe, accepted and competent. Over the course of my 35-plus years in the field, supporting people with many diverse needs, I finally realized a model of support that works for all human beings, regardless of differences. Once the person feels "safe, accepted and competent," he will grow and develop (see Figure 0.1).

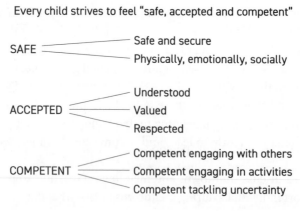

Every child strives to feel "safe, accepted and competent"

SAFE — Safe and secure / Physically, emotionally, socially

ACCEPTED — Understood / Valued / Respected

COMPETENT — Competent engaging with others / Competent engaging in activities / Competent tackling uncertainty

When these conditions are met, all children grow and develop.
Litmus test for measuring all strategies used with your child.

Figure 0.1: Basic model of feeling safe, accepted and competent

We are all striving to reach this state where we feel safe and secure, physically, emotionally and socially, as well as feeling accepted, valued and respected by others. Once we get there, then we strive to feel competent in what we do, relating with others and tackling new challenges and feeling confident. We all usually struggle in one or more of these areas, often feeling insecure and inadequate in our own relationships and abilities. However, we all have brief times when we feel safe, accepted and competent and feel as if we can take on the world and handle any challenge. We feel safe and engaged with others around us and confident that we can handle new challenges. Unfortunately, many children on the spectrum rarely have those moments of feeling safe, accepted and competent. They rarely feel accepted for who they are and what they can do. They experience frequent failure and ridicule for continually failing to fit in.

Throughout my career, I have never found a person, regardless of neurological profile, who does not thrive when we help them feel safe, accepted and competent. When the person is struggling with what we are providing, I first step back and ask myself in what way are our strategies failing to help the person feel safe, accepted and competent. This model gives us a criterion for evaluating appropriateness of services we provide. How do our strategies support the person (1) to feel safe (physically, emotionally and socially), (2) to feel accepted (understood, valued and respected), and (3) to feel competent in engaging with others, participating in purposeful activity and tackling new challenges? When progress is not occurring, usually we are missing at least one, if not more, of these three areas. When choosing a strategy, treatment or recommendation, always ask yourself, "In what way does this help the child feel safe, accepted and competent?" If it does not meet at least one of these factors, then question why you are doing it.

I have found that this model does no harm, respects the needs, differences, strengths and preferences of the person and builds a strong working partnership of support not change.

Things to consider

- *Person-first language.* There is currently controversy in how we address someone: "autistic" or "person with autism?" Those of us in the field have been indoctrinated with always using person-first language: "person with autism." It was more respect-ful to consider the individual a person first and autism as secondary. However, many autistic adults tell us they prefer to be addressed as "autistic," because autism is part of their identity and not a secondary condition. In this book, you will see references to "autistics" and "person with autism" or "person on the spectrum." I hope it doesn't offend anyone. I respect all of these references.

- *Male pronoun.* Most of the posts will refer to "him" as the person of interest. We use the male pronoun to include both males and females. It gets cumbersome and difficult to read when continually using him/her, he/she. The strategies can equally apply to any gender.

- *Children or adults.* Most of the discussions and strategies in this book apply equally to both children and adults. When the discussion is referencing children, please realize it also applies to adults. In addition, for children, most of the strategies will need to be implemented by parents and teachers. However, the person, as they age, must learn to provide these accommodations for themselves. Children with autism eventually become autistic adults. As early as possible, include the child in designing and implementing these procedures so they eventually learn do them on their own (when possible).

- *Prior knowledge.* Although this book can stand alone, it assumes that the reader has already read the blue book, *The Autism Discussion Page on the Core Challenges in Autism* (Nason, 2014a) or has a good working knowledge of the cognitive, sensory, social and emotional differences. Since many readers have already read the blue book, I have tried to expand on these topics, rather than rehash the material in the other two books. For those who haven't read the previous two books, I will frequently reference the book that provides more detailed information. The reader will be able to understand and benefit from the material regardless of prior reading.

- *Disclaimer.* As the author of these books I do not know your child, what his strengths and vulnerabilities are, and which strategies would be appropriate for him. Each of these strategies will need to be individualized to the needs of your child. I recommend that you seek guidance from those who have evaluated and know your child well. I am not prescribing any specific strategies for your child. Please seek professional guidance.

By reading these books you are taking your first steps into a very supportive, collaborative journey. I invite you all to join the thousands of people on the Autism Discussion Page (www.facebook.com/autismdiscussionpage), to learn, share and receive supportive guidance. Hope to see you there!

Chapter 1

BE TRUE TO THEIR NEUROLOGY

In the medical world, autism is often defined by the external behaviors (e.g. poor eye contact, repetitive ritualistic behavior, rigid adherence to routine, head banging, etc.) that the person exhibits. Little does it reflect on what the experience of autism is like and how it differs from that of people without autism. Usually, the cluster of traits that defines a child's autism is a list of behavioral descriptors: does not seek out interaction with others, prefers to spin toys rather than engage, tantrums when asked to shift gears, is upset with transitions, screams when touched by others, rocks constantly, on and on and on. Little do these behavior descriptors tell us how the child thinks, feels and experiences the world, what meaning these behaviors have for the child, or how we can help support the person.

Autism is more than a cluster of negative behaviors, lack of specific skills or a degree of deviation from the norm. Autism is a human condition, a neurological difference in processing that shows how the person experiences his world, how he or she perceives, processes and reacts to the world. Without gaining insight in how the person thinks, feels and experiences his surroundings, it is impossible to understand the cluster of behavior differences, the functional value the behaviors provide and how to reduce the challenges, stress and anxiety that people with autism experience.

All the so-called challenging behaviors (repetitive behaviors, need to control, avoidance of change, tantrums, self-abuse, aggression) are simply a reflection and expression of these processing differences trying to cope in a world that processes differently. To understand behavior, you must know how the person thinks, feels and processes the world, understand the internal meaning the behaviors have for the person and how these behaviors represent ways of coping with the often chaotic, confusing and scary world.

This book strives to present the reader with insight into some of the core processing differences that represent a different way of experiencing the world, which in turn often create overwhelming stress and conflict for those on the spectrum. By understanding these processing differences and the challenges they present, we can begin to make sense of all the behavior variations and gain a global perspective of how the person is thinking, feeling and trying to adapt to the challenges they experience. Instead of trying to suppress and change the behaviors that are survival skills for the person, we need to understand the neurological differences and how to match our expectations to their neurological profile.

We all are born with a set of neurological strengths and weaknesses that makes up our unique individual profile. The more we understand what our makeup consists of, accept and respect our unique profile and stay true to it, the happier and more successful we can be. The more we ignore or deny our strengths, weaknesses, needs and desires, the more stress and anxiety we experience and the more depressed and inadequate we feel. Our society values certain qualities (physical beauty, social confidence, flexibility, conforming to authority, etc.) that we compare ourselves to and try to model ourselves after. The more dissatisfied we are with ourselves, strive to be something that we are not and continually try to suppress our true needs and desires, the more anxious and depressed we become.

The truer to our neurology we are, the happier and more successful we become. Our neurological profile, if accepted and fostered to develop as patterned, will allow us to feel safe, accepted and competent. If society fosters our strengths, utilizes our preferences and desires and respects our vulnerabilities, our neurological profile will develop and strengthen as it was meant to do. Simply speaking, work with the person's unique profile rather than trying to work against their makeup to change them into something they are not meant to be.

Bio-neurological differences

Autism is a bio-neurological condition, not a mental illness. In the psychiatric literature, autism spectrum disorders are listed as a developmental disability, or neuro-developmental disorder. Many now argue that autism is not a disorder at all but a different human condition, with a different set of strengths and weaknesses. Our brains are wired differently, so we think, feel and experience the world differently.

Many autistic adults voice their concerns that much of their stress is not from their differences, but how society treats them. Having their condition labeled as a disorder connotes that their differences are symptoms, negative qualities that need to be suppressed and extinguished—that their human condition is an aberration, something that is broken, less human, needs to be fixed and looked down on. From this medical model, it leads us to erroneously believe that since autism is a psychiatric diagnosis—a medical disorder—it needs to be treated and cured. Many in the neuro-diversity movement argue that much of their stress comes from a society that does not understand and respect their differences, forcing them to change, to conform and be like others, to be non-autistic. The constant need to fake being normal, to suppress autistic behaviors, to conform, to fit in and be de-valued for who they are presents ongoing stress and anxiety. Fighting a society that views them as sick, needing a cure and treatment to appear normal leaves them stressed, drained, invalidated, frustrated and angry. The physical, mental and emotional damage that occurs from this lack of understanding, acceptance and accommodation presents tremendous stress, leading to post-traumatic stress disorder, burnout, depression, anxiety disorders and a host of other stress-related conditions. This is not from the autism itself, but from society's lack of acceptance and accommodation.

Autism is not about behavior

I dislike the way in which autism is diagnosed. It has always been about a cluster of behaviors. We reduce the human condition down to a set of behaviors or traits, which you either meet or don't meet. Diagnosing autism based on behavioral symptoms leads us to believe that if you change the behaviors, the person is no longer autistic. Autism consists of perceptual, processing and thinking differences—a different way of perceiving and experiencing the world. Nowhere in the diagnosis do you see all the sensory processing issues: difficulty reading context, struggles with processing multiple information simultaneously, difficulty filtering irrelevant details, the list of executive functioning challenges, attention to details and facts, emotional regulation issues, lack of flexible thinking, and other mental processes that still stand regardless of our focus on changing behavior.

This diagnosis based on behaviors leads to therapies to extinguish and shape behaviors, and drugs to suppress autistic traits. It ignores the many perceptual and cognitive differences that define autism and underlie all the social and emotional challenges they experience. Unfortunately, for many on the spectrum who do not exhibit the obvious autistic behaviors, their struggles go unrecognized. Autism is a human condition, not a behavior disorder.

The reason why our Facebook page and books are so popular is that we look at autism from the inside-out, trying to understand how the person thinks, feels and perceives the world. The page and books are devoted to giving parents, teachers and professionals a better awareness of how the person experiences the world in order to help support them and the challenges they experience. In doing so, we also accept, respect and validate the person so that they can feel safe, accepted and competent in being a person with autism. The only way that we can support all people is to stop labeling behavior and understand how the person thinks, feels and processes the world.

Autism is not a behavioral disorder, but a package of complex processing differences. It is a different human condition, not a set of behavioral symptoms. We need to assess the person's unique ways of perceiving, processing information and experiencing the world to better understand how to help them.

Possible alternatives for assessing autism

If we want to move away from diagnosing a cluster of behaviors, how else can we diagnose autism? How do we measure the underlying processing differences that truly define what the autism condition is?

There has been a lot of research lately isolating out processing differences (perceptual, information processing, executive functioning, etc.) that define more accurately the condition of autism.

Eventually, brain imaging will be accurate and inexpensive enough to visually see the neurology of autism and allow accurate diagnosis. There are simple assessment tools available to measure ability to read context, assessments to measure sensory processing issues, and tests for executive dysfunctioning. There are also scales for emotional regulation issues, rigid/inflexible thinking and pragmatic communication. All these test and scales isolate out different processing differences which would lead to better diagnosis and treatment rather than simply extinguishing and shaping behavior to look more neurotypical.

Sensory and information overload from difficulty filtering and rapidly processing multiple information simultaneously is probably one of the most definitive characteristics of autism. Observing the person in their natural settings could show these differences, but that usually takes too much time and effort for standardized assessments. However, many of these factors can also be artificially simulated by presenting specific processing tasks in a quiet area and then gradually introducing greater stimulation and complexity.

For example, the person may be able to make eye contact and converse well in a simple one-on-one interaction, but gradually increase the complexity of interaction to multiple people in flowing, open-ended conversations, and you will start to see the mechanical skills breakdown. This can be done for activities that require multi-tasking information, making decisions based on multiple options, evaluating context to isolate what stimuli are important to attend to and so on. These evaluations could be put into a standardized, multi-discipline evaluation that would isolate out processing differences that are often hidden. Like all good assessments, evaluations would include testing, observations and interviews.

Diagnosing needs to be more prescriptive, rather than simply descriptive. Currently, the diagnosis of autism often provides minimal clues on what treatments are needed to support the person's challenges. Often the parents leave the assessment feeling completely lost in what to do next. Good diagnosing should isolate out what variables are a challenge and point to strategies for supporting those challenges. From a comprehensive processing assessment, the clinical team could then develop a comprehensive support plan for assisting with each domain of challenges (sensory, information processing, executive functioning, social pragmatics, etc.).

Be true to their neurology!

We have been trying for years to "treat" autism by suppressing the behavioral symptoms while trying to shape people to look and act as neurotypical as possible. Many adults on the spectrum are now fighting back from years of trying to be something they are not, being forced to suppress what they are and having their self-identity stripped of dignity by constant negative feedback. They are burnt out from constant invalidation and struggling to conform to what others want them to be. They are often angry and hostile, or have given up in despair from constantly trying to fit in but hitting their heads against a brick wall.

This is not due to poor intentions of loved ones, teachers or the helping professions. We are intent on helping and supporting the children and adults to have happy and productive lives, but we always assume that means being like us—to value what we value and to look and act as typically as possible in order to fit in and be successful. These are noble goals but can be drastically harming.

The most happy and healthy people are the ones who are true to their neurology. Unfortunately, we usually do not know what that is. Neurotypical people, especially when young, are constantly trying to be something that they are not, trying to fit a popular vision of what is valued. It never works; eventually, reality sets in and we return to what we are meant to be. Usually as we get older, we become more comfortable about who we are and what we need to be happy—or we live a life of lies and despair, never reaching a model we aspire to.

Our neurology (how our brains are wired) sets the stage for our development. Some of us are more intellectual and detailed thinkers, while others are artistic or global thinkers. We are either fast-paced extroverts, sensitive introverts or somewhere in between. We all have our given learning styles, whether that is being visual, auditory or tactile learners. Some of us have great executive functioning skills, being focused and organized, while others are scattered, disorganized and stumble through life. Some people are very flexible and bounce through life with minimal conflicts, and others have difficulty adapting to any unwanted change in routine. Some of us are more anxious and emotionally reactive, and others are calm and steady.

We all are born with certain temperaments and neurological profiles. Except for some very early interventions, these characteristics do not change much. They have a defined path which we can foster and refine or ignore, deny and unsuccessfully try for years to change.

Autism is a bio-neurological makeup that is a bit different from ours (neurotypical). The way their brains are wired means they process information differently and experience the world differently than non-autistics. They cannot rapidly and intuitively process multiple information simultaneously and can become overwhelmed when pressured to try. They are fine-tuned to perceive details and sensory patterns much better than neurotypicals. They dance to a different drummer that has a defined beat.

There are people of many different styles of temperament and neurological profiles, all of whom when fostered along their given paths can develop into happy, healthy and productive people. We cannot make a creative artist or professional athlete out of nervous systems that are not programmed with these qualities. You can push, prod and spend fortunes on talented teachers, coaches and doctors, but you cannot make someone into something they are not wired to be. You can, however, create a very invalidated, broken and angry person by trying to force them into a mold that is not designed for them.

Being a soccer coach, at a very competitive level, I have seen the results of parents who try to shape their average child athlete into a superior competitor by paying for expensive trainers, over-practicing and providing intense pressure to become the best. They never come close to reaching that goal, and strip the fun and esteem from the children.

I once knew an experienced golf teacher who spent most of his time teaching average people how to hit a golf ball. The secret he used was not to drastically change the person's golf swing but to refine the swing they had to make it work better. People have different swings based on their temperament and physical makeup (neurology). Some people are hyper and have a fast-paced swing and some have calm, slow-paced swings. This tends to match their personality styles. Some have aggressive hitting styles and others have smoother, rhythmic swings. They all can learn to hit the ball straight by refining, not changing, their natural swing. When you try to radically change their swing style, everything tends to fall apart. Many golfers have quit the game over the frustration of trying to make their swing into something it isn't. You must take the profile you have, refine its strengths and let it grow and develop. All styles of swings can become effective if natural.

This is the same path for all of us when we try to deny what we are and what we're meant to be. We can have fun and be happy developing our internal package or we can be frustrated and invalidated by trying to change who we are. We cannot make ourselves into something we are not. We can pressure, force and prod and risk becoming frustrated, broken and depressed or we can define who we are (neurological path), foster our growth and promote our strengths. I assure you that your loved one will be happier, more productive and successful developing their neurological package then trying to deny and work against it. We need to embrace their neurological differences, redefine them as strengths and make accommodations for them to excel. Let's stop denying who they are and forcing them against the grain of their nervous system. Let's allow them to develop and feel strong in the makeup that they have and to grow into healthy, happy and productive people.

Happy or normal!

For many parents, how they embrace and adapt to autism goes through developmental changes. When first getting the diagnosis, especially at the young ages, parents are often overwhelmed, bewildered and stricken with grief for the child they have lost. This is a natural grieving process, one that each of you handles differently. Sometimes one spouse will go into denial while another spouse throws themselves intensively into researching every possible resource to help their child. At first, parents often seek out a possible cure to erase the "disease" that took away their child or spend the next five or more years trying desperately to extinguish or eradicate any obvious signs and behaviors that look autistic. The early behavior therapies were founded on the belief that if you look and act normal, you are no longer autistic. So, parents would focus their attention on eliminating behaviors that looked different, which somehow would magically transform their child into a "normal" (neurotypical), happy child. Success would be determined by how normal the child appeared.

For most parents, as time goes on and they move through the developmental stages of childhood, they realize that their children are not going to be cured and begin to appreciate them for who they are, accept their uniqueness and start to support the children to be as happy and independent as possible. However, we still spend enormous amounts of money and energy trying to model these children into something that they are not, often developing visions for the children based on what we value, rather than what they want.

We often focus more on the children's deficits and symptoms than on their strengths and preferences. Since their preferences are often odd or not age appropriate, we try to steer the children into more normal interests. What is different from the norm is obviously not worthy. What is closest to the norm is a worthy target. However, if you listen to children and adults on the spectrum, trying to be normal does not create happiness!

Trying to shape children and adults into something that they are not creates frustration and poor self-esteem, not happiness and fulfillment. When your brain is wired differently, and you experience the world differently and value things a little differently, it is against human nature to change that. Such a stance devalues the person, makes them feel unworthy, and puts them in a constant state of pretending and acting, suppressing their very "selves." Neurotypical people who feel uncomfortable with individuals who are different may feel better if autistics appear and act more neurotypical, but the individuals themselves feel invalidated, frustrated and emotionally drained.

Yes, when you are a stranger in a strange land, you must learn the customs and social rules needed to blend in and co-exist, without losing your identity, values, strengths and preferences. Minority cultures learn to adapt in a different land, but still value and celebrate their own culture and customs. The problem for most children on the spectrum is that they do not live in a family where everyone around them is from the same nature (autistic). Most individuals with autism are in isolation, developing in natural settings (family, schools, etc.), surrounded by others who experience the world differently from them. It is difficult to develop a strong sense of self and healthy self-esteem when everything around you is giving negative feedback and trying to change you. Anxiety, depression and despair are often natural by-products of suppressing your true self and conforming to something you are not meant to be. Even those who can pull this off, and "act" more normal report that it comes with great costs and frequently ends in burnout early in adult life.

In the 35 or more years I have been in this field, the children I have seen grow and develop into happy, healthy adults are those whose parents valued their uniqueness, placed less emphasis on changing them and put more focus on celebrating their differences and supporting their strengths and preferences. All children can grow in settings where they feel understood, accepted and valued for who they are, where their differences are not seen as faults or weaknesses but a different set of strengths and preferences.

For example, if a child needs to pace in circles because it helps him think, or rock back and forth to stay emotionally regulated, then these are strengths that need to be respected and valued, not behaviors to be suppressed and extinguished. If the child has a fixated interest in fans, trains, escalators or animation, then embrace and celebrate these interests and build functional skills around them. If the child starts to speak and learn new information through singing and music, then use this medium to build new learning experiences. Instead of trying to stop these fixations, embrace them. Become part of fixations, valuing what your child values and enthusiastically engaging with them. Value what he values and he will be attracted to you.

Every child will thrive and grow when those around them embrace and celebrate what they value. Instead of suppressing and extinguishing these differences, let them play out and foster them to grow. If the individual chooses to like dolls for their entire life, or certain fabrics, or movement patterns, or childhood animation, then this is their preference. If they are hyper-focused on plumbing, motors, baseball statistics, or whatever, foster these preferences and build strengths around them. If they need frequent breaks to stim and regroup, then see these as strengths that allow them to stay self-regulated. This makes them happy, relaxes them and gives them a sense of fulfillment. Isn't this what we really want for any of us? Yes, we need to teach life skills and learning to cope with the world around us but allow them the space and time to be themselves, value their differences and celebrate their uniqueness. Let them feel good about themselves, foster their strengths and develop their interests. You will find that at the end of the road, everyone is happier and more fulfilled.

Actualization not normalization

When advocating for your child, seeking help and teaching skills, be careful what your goals are. Autism was initially viewed as a disease, a horrible condition we needed to eradicate, that the autistic child was damaged, broken and needed to be healed. Autistic behaviors (self-stim, fixated interests, sensory seeking, etc.) needed to be suppressed and extinguished.

This brought on therapies to erase the autism and shape the child to be normal. If the child acted normally, he was less autistic, even cured. The person is left hating their autism, damning their neurology and striving to be "normal." This masking, pretending to be normal (neurotypical) leads them to further hate their autism. As the years roll on, they continually degrade themselves for trying but failing to meet these unrealistic expectations, further eroding their self-esteem and confusing their self-identity. The result is fatigue and burnout from trying to be someone they are not, leading to internalized self-hatred from the world's invalidating feedback.

Our goal should be to understand, accept and respect their differences and help them maximize their potential (actualize), not to suppress, change or cure them, not to deny their differences, but to maximize them to their potential. We should help them feel good about themselves, foster their abilities and clear a path for them to blossom into self-fulfilling, emotionally healthy individuals.

This means identifying what accommodations they need to break down barriers and open up accepting paths to actualize their potentials, to be a working partner with them, supporting their vulnerabilities and fostering their strengths and preferences. We need to see differences as potentials rather than defining them as abnormal and unworthy.

For most therapies and supports, ask yourself if you are using them to maximize the person's potentials as an autistic person or using them to suppress his autism and shape being normal. Are you supporting the child to maximize his true self as a worthy, self-fulfilling, autistic person or trying to make him normal, to change or cure him?

All children need to feel safe, accepted and loved for who they are, not who we dreamed for them to be. Yes, we need to make modifications and accommodations to reduce their challenges and teach them skills to maximize their potentials. But always accept and respect their true identities and foster their differences to maximize their potentials.

Remember, our goal should be to actualize, not normalize!

Acceptance and understanding

Learning from adults on the spectrum

It is useful to spend a few minutes talking about what adults on the spectrum have reported as being important for them. Since they live and breathe autism, it is important to listen to their voice. What are they telling us? Although many reports vary in what they experience, almost all report the following three conditions.

- Individuals with autism are constantly bombarded with sensory, social and information overload that is confusing and overwhelming. In this book, you will learn how chaotic, confusing and overwhelming our world can be for them. Because of their sensory challenges and processing differences, our world simply moves too fast, is overwhelming and therefore very draining for them. Trying to navigate through a world that processes differently can be impossible at times and very draining all the time. Through the rest of these chapters, you will gain an understanding of how overwhelming our world can be for them.

- Their constant struggles to fit in, meet our expectations and simply make sense out of our world make it difficult for them to feel "safe, accepted and competent."

- Their constant trying, but failing, to meet our expectations leaves them feeling anxious, insecure, unaccepted and inadequate.

Fitting a square peg into a round hole

Pretending to be normal, masking who you are and continually trying but failing to fit in all take a grave toll on autistics. This erodes their self-identities, increases social anxiety and often results in severe depression. These concerns are asserted by many adults on the spectrum who plead for others to listen to these needs and re-evaluate what we as parents, teachers and professionals are trying to do. They desperately want us to understand what they are experiencing, to accept and respect them for who they are and help support their differences, so they can live happily in our culture.

Changing the child is often like fitting a square peg into a round hole trying to press them into something they are not, what they can't become. To feel truly safe and accepted, a person needs to feel valued for who they are. We need to cherish them for who they are, not what we would like them to be. They need to feel understood, valued and loved for simply being them. We can support them, love them and teach them like any other child, but accept them for who they are. The more we try to change the child, the more we risk invalidating them, communicating that they are inadequate or unworthy. Unfortunately, in our early zest to change the child, often our support only communicates to them that they are broken, not worthy as they are, and need to be something they are not. We must be careful that when dragging them from one therapy to another, designing ongoing behavior plans, shaping behavior that often has little meaning for them, we are not invalidating their self-identity and telling them that they are broken and unworthy.

The children need understanding and acceptance first, then loving support to grow. We need to back up and first communicate unconditional love for who they are, accept and respect their differences and provide loving support to grow. This is no different from any other child. This does not mean that we avoid teaching them life skills and social niceties so they can regulate in our society and treat co-occurring disorders like anxiety, sensory disorders and medical issues. But when we are constantly trying to get them to suppress self-stimulation, we ignore processing differences and teach them to be something they are not, we risk invalidating their very existence, setting up a path leading to future turmoil and despair.

Invalidating feedback

"They either want to make me into something I am not...or refuse to understand my differences!"

Growing up on the spectrum often means years of invalidating feedback. When your behavior doesn't match the expectations of others, you often get labeled as lazy, stupid, rude, oppositional and defiant. When people do not understand your processing differences, they interpret your behavior as intentional and that you just need a good spanking and firm discipline. These children are constantly eliciting negative, invalidating feedback from others, no matter how hard they try. Eventually, the parents feel the same invalidations from the way others question their parenting skills, "If only she was stricter and disciplined, her child would not be that way." The comments that these children and parents hear can be devastating. Some of the common comments include:

"He enjoys being oppositional; he doesn't care." No child enjoys being oppositional. Children generally want to please and do care deeply, but everything they do is never good enough.

"What a rude kid; someone needs to teach him some manners." When your brain is overwhelmed and sends you into fight or flight mode, the last thing on your mind is manners. When the child cannot read the thoughts, feelings and perspectives of others, or the social rules of the situation they are in, they have no clue what "manners" are. They must rote learn manners through years of experience so that they become habit and have some meaning. We teach manners, one at a time through example, practice and highlighting what manners are. Believe me, if the child knew what do to and say they would much rather meet expectations and fit in with everyone else.

"He just needs a good spanking!" That is the worst thing you can do. Punishing does not teach the child what to do and only tells them that they are bad and broken. Spanking harms the child physically and emotionally, especially when they do not know what they are doing wrong or how to meet our expectations. Spanking only shows that not fitting in leads to physical harm, destroying their trust in you as well as their own self-esteem.

"Are you stupid! You get it, but you just don't want to do it." Unless you understand the processing difficulties and the executive functioning issues people on the spectrum have it is difficult to understand why they struggle with our expectations. They often do not know what is expected, cannot remember what to do, or cannot do it in the heat of the moment. Also, when pressure is on, and anxiety rises, their coping skills and problem-solving abilities tend to fall apart and leave them incapable of meeting expectations. Calling them stupid, lazy and oppositional only tends to further invalidate them and tear apart their self-image.

Years of invalidating feedback from their social world leads to incredible anxiety, isolation and depression. When we are constantly invalidated, we get to the stage where anger becomes action. The person is resistant to all help and is constantly in a defensive mode. They get sick of "pretending to be normal" (neurotypical) and trying to meet expectations, only to fail and be continually invalidated—never feeling safe, accepted and respected for who they are.

"Stop trying to fix me, change me and cure me!"

"This is me, understand me, accept and value me, and help support and guide me!"

We need to understand what their neurological differences are and be true to their neurology. We need to accept and support them, not constantly try to change them.

How to support these children

So where does that leave us? Does accepting and respecting them mean allowing them to abuse themselves or others, avoiding teaching them right from wrong, or not teaching social etiquette? Does it mean allowing them to stumble around, not learning how to take care of themselves or respecting others? No, not at all. However, it does mean understanding their processing differences and how they see the world, then accepting and respecting these neurological differences so that we are working *with* the children, not *against* them.

Once you understand and accept these differences then the following is easy.

First, understand the disability before trying to support and teach them. Understand the core differences of autism. When they are not meeting expectations, we need to observe, listen and understand where they are coming from before jumping in to guide and direct.

Do not assume intent to be oppositional or lazy; look deeper to understand how their vulnerabilities or our unrealistic expectations are influencing their performance. We first need to understand what autism is and how it is expressed in the child—how the child thinks, feels and experiences the world.

We need to start where the child is at, understand their experiences to know how to adequately support them. This means understanding the child's vulnerabilities and challenges. It is very important that we understand the unique sensory issues, processing challenges and emotional vulnerabilities that are expressed in the behaviors we are trying to change.

Next, we need to reduce the demands and stressors to level the playing field. We need to build in accommodations to support their vulnerabilities and reduce their stress. We need to develop a toolbox of supports to accommodate and lessen the sensory, processing, social and emotional challenges they experience to reduce the stress and anxiety they feel.

Next, we need to match the environmental demands and our expectations to their current skill level. When they are not meeting expectations, assume that either they do not know what is expected, or do not have the skills to meet expectations. From there, we either need to lower the demands by modifying the demands and providing greater assistance in helping them meet expectations, or teach them the skills needed to meet the demands. Through proactive supports, once you have matched the expectations and environmental demands to the current skill level, the child can relax and learn from you. This will go miles in helping the child feel safe, accepted and respected by us and teach the child that we are a working partner with them, not someone who simply wants to control and change them.

So far, we have talked about how to support the child by understanding and accepting their disability and how it is expressed in them, and building in accommodations to support their vulnerabilities to match our expectations to their current abilities. This will level the playing field, help them feel safe and accepted and to trust that we are a working partner with them. Next, we need to help them build skills to feel confident and competent in facing their challenges and tackling uncertainty. We need to move from helping them feel "safe and accepted" to feeling "competent and confident."

There are two fundamental premises for teaching and mentoring children on the spectrum:

1. *Start in the child's comfort zones and gradually stretch them.* When guiding and teaching we need to start where the child is at, build gradually, maximize success and keep it fun. We need to identify what the child's comfort zones are, respect them and slowly stretch them. We need to first meet them where they are at, provide small challenges that they can realistically handle and help them to feel safe following our guidance.

   Learning is intrinsically fun if you understand what is expected, can realistically meet expectations and can see the value in what you are learning. However, often we do not truly understand or choose to ignore what their comfort zones are and start to press too hard, demand too much and expect compliance to our direction. When we meet resistance, we blame the child and become even more persistent.

   Assume, the more resistant the child is the more inadequate they feel. Usually it means the expectations we are placing on them are greater than their current abilities, so the onus of change is on us, not them.

2. *Next, we need to build on their strengths and preferences.* Once we understand, accept and respect their neurological differences and built in supports to minimize their challenges, then we can focus our attention on fostering their strengths and preferences. We all have strengths and weaknesses, but we tend to spend too much

time trying to change their weaknesses rather than focusing on identifying and fostering their strengths and using their natural preferences to motivate learning. You do not build confidence and self-esteem by continually highlighting their weaknesses, as this only teaches them to feel broken and unworthy. Self-esteem and confidence come from highlighting and fostering their strengths and building on their preferences. This approach works with everyone, disability or not, child or adult.

In summary, if you help the child feel safe, accepted and respected they will be attracted to you. If you help them feel competent, they will truly follow your lead. Be a "working partner" with them to establish yourself as a "trusted guide."

Relax, you don't have to be right!

Many parents agonize over whether they are doing the right thing: the right therapies, diets, teaching, discipline and so on, as if there is a set of right answers they must live up to. Unfortunately, there are no set answers, agreed paths of teaching or prescribed courses of action. There are many options, with no set criteria for choosing which ones to take.

You don't have to be right, just try! Your love is not determined by how right you are, but the compassion behind how hard you try! There are no right and wrong answers, just guilt in "not acting." Move forward out of love, acceptance and respecting the child and don't worry about being right! The main axiom is "do no harm." Avoid advice that you intuitively feel will harm the child, even if given by a well-intended professional. No one knows your child like you do. Only try strategies that listen to and respect the child, help support his vulnerabilities and foster his strengths and preferences.

If you don't make mistakes, you are not trying hard enough! You are always treading unexplored areas—don't worry about being right! It hasn't been defined yet! Give yourself a hug! Deep pressure always helps!! Children who struggle the most need the greatest compassion. That doesn't mean that you don't get frustrated, defeated, embarrassed and angry as hell at times! They are natural feelings and come on strong. Let them come and go, don't hide them or feel guilty about them.

Don't beat yourself over the head from what you didn't do or think you have done wrong! When you act, you learn! If it's right, you keep it; if it isn't, you modify it or drop it. As professionals, we can give guidance, but these children are complex beings and most guidance is an educated guess. We must act and try, ask and listen to the child, and be observant to the results. Development is a long journey of stumbles and strides. Don't define yourself by your failures but by your persistence to keep trying until it works.

There are no definite answers to the challenges you and your child face. There are no "right" answers, only options to try and explore, modify and refine, all while loving, validating and enjoying your child. Your child is not keeping score! He feels the love and devotion, and the temporary expressions of frustration, anger and despair in your voice and face will not change that. You are human, exploring waters that have not yet been defined.

Do not let your indecisiveness and temporary setbacks hamper your efforts. You must fail to learn. "Fail to succeed!" Most importantly, take the time to slow down and love and enjoy your child for who he is! Unconditional love will never be wrong! When challenges arise, evaluate what you have in front of you, decide and act. If it is not right, learn from it and move on. If you do that, you are true champions!

Now, strap on your seatbelt, sit back and travel the journey with hope. The rest of this book will guide you in helping your child feel "safe, accepted and competent," navigating this journey with you. See the world through your child's eyes, be open to his perspectives and redefine his differences as strengths and preferences. You both will grow and develop together.

Chapter 2

AUTISM AS AN INFORMATION PROCESSING DIFFERENCE

Autism is a set of neurological, information processing differences that change the way information is registered, integrated and assimilated. Many contend that autism is not an illness or disorder but a set of neurological differences. Simply speaking, the brains of autistic people are wired a little differently from ours (neurotypical). Like all neurological profiles, autism consists of a host of strengths and weaknesses, many of which we shall review briefly in this chapter. People with autism tend to process information and experience the world differently from neurotypicals. Their processing styles are not better or worse, simply different. However, since our society is based on the neurotypical processing style, many of the autistic differences present multiple challenges and ongoing stress for those living in a world that is not designed for them.

Autism presents a difference in how information is taken in and processed to make sense of the world—how it is registered, integrated and processed. Once we know how autistics process information, we can more easily understand the sensory, social and emotional differences we see in autism.

To many with autism the world is often:

- confusing

- unpredictable

- overwhelming

- and scary!

This leaves them feeling vulnerable, insecure and anxious.

Throughout this book, we look at how many of these differences underlie why the world is so chaotic and confusing for those with autism, and leads to chronic stress, ongoing anxiety, frequent burnout and occasional meltdowns. Although it may sound discouraging, we will also discuss ways to make the world more understandable, predictable and easier for them to navigate, ways to accept their unique differences and enable us to become working partners with them and foster their strengths to build a safe quality of life. With understanding, respect and support from those around them, most individuals on the spectrum can live very happy and productive lives.

Processing differences

To understand the many social, emotional and behavioral differences, we must first understand processing differences in autism. Processing consists of how the brain registers,
attends to and organizes information. To understand these processing differences, it is
best to start with how the neurotypical brain processes information (see Figure 2.1).

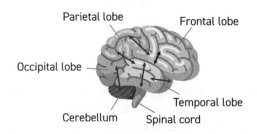

- Multiple brain centres with strong communicative pathways
- Provides simultaneous communication between brain centers
- Allows for rapid processing of multiple information simultaneously
- Over 80% of processing occurs intuitively at a subconscious level

Figure 2.1: Simultaneous processing requires strong communication between brain centers

Our brains consist of multiple centers that have interrelated but different functions.
These brain centers are connected by neurological pathways that allow these centers
to communicate simultaneously with each other. Some of the brain centers take in our
sensory input (what we see, hear, touch, etc.); others allow us to compare this information
with past experiences to apply meaning. Some areas provide us with an emotional reaction
to the experience, others allow us to appraise and evaluate what is needed, while other
centers help us formulate a behavioral response to what is expected. All these centers
simultaneously communicate with each other for smooth integration. For every daily
event we experience, our brains are taking in multiple information that is filtered and
funneled to the various brain centers. These centers communicate simultaneously and
instantaneously to provide us with an overall perception of what we are experiencing.
For most daily activity, this brain networking and integration occurs smoothly and often
subconsciously. The neuro-connections between the brain centers allow for simultaneous
communication and integrated processing to make sense of the environmental demands.

This network of strong neuro-connections allows us to rapidly process multiple
information simultaneously. It also allows us to integrate and smoothly process all
this information with minimal mental effort. Over 80 percent of information is being
processed at a subconscious level, without any conscious effort and below our awareness.
These well-integrated neuro-pathways allow us to process all this information intuitively
without us thinking about it. We quickly scan the information for a few facts and
immediately infer the overall meaning. We continually assimilate new information
and constantly re-adapt our responses to it. We smoothly process numerous pieces of
information, while focusing our attention on what is important at that moment.

For example, let's look at the simple act of driving a car. Driving requires us to rapidly process multiple information simultaneously, most of it at an unconscious level.

- We take in what we see occurring around us, immediately looking for danger both from our direct and peripheral vision, reading traffic signs, watching for movement of other people and vehicles.

- We also integrate what we are hearing (the sounds of other vehicles, people talking in the car, the radio blaring, etc.).

- In addition, we are receiving coordinated information from our hands and feet, from both the steering wheel and floor pedals, about the direction and speed of travel.

We usually process much of this sensory input subconsciously while multi-tasking, thinking about where we want to go, what we want to do, talking to others in the car or daydreaming about what is going to happen this weekend. We are taking in and rapidly processing all this information simultaneously, while modifying our driving moment to moment, on the fly, to stay within the lines, keep a safe distance from others, slow down and speed up as needed to avoid accidents. This requires different brain centers to perform their functions while simultaneously communicating and integrating this information with other brain centers. This network of well-synchronized brain centers allows us to process the multiple information simultaneously in order to successfully navigate complex daily living situations.

All this information is being integrated and processed very smoothly and effortlessly, most of it below our immediate awareness, with minimal mental effort. However, this varies significantly when the driving conditions change, for example when it is dark outside or the roads are icy. Because of the dangerous conditions, we must be consciously attentive to all the sensory input to avoid sliding off the road or into other vehicles. Driving now is much more effortful, both physically and mentally. Under these conditions, a long drive home can be very exhausting and mentally draining.

All this processing requires well-coordinated brain integration—smooth, simultaneous communication between all the brain centers to rapidly process, evaluate and respond to the immediate demands of the environment (see Figure 2.2).

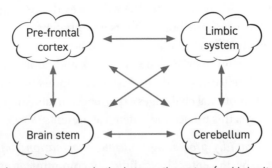

Smooth processing requires strong communication between the centers (rapid simultaneous processing)

Figure 2.2: Smooth processing requires strong integration of brain centers

In summary, the brain is a highly sophisticated network of brain centers communicating simultaneously through well-developed neurological pathways that connect these different centers. This integrated processing allows us to sense, think, feel and act simultaneously. This is called brain integration, the smooth synchronized communication and integration of multiple information. When the neuro-pathways are strong and organized correctly, we can process most of this information simultaneously and subconsciously with minimal effort.

Autism is an information processing difference

In autism, this processing is somewhat impaired by poorly developed neuro-pathways between the brain centers. Consequently, these weak connections (wiring) between the different brain centers interfere with simultaneous communication between the various centers. These weak neuro-connections are due to both underdeveloped, long-range connections between the brain centers, and in some cases, an over-abundance of poorly developed short-range wiring within individual brain centers (see Figure 2.3).

Theory of underconnectivity

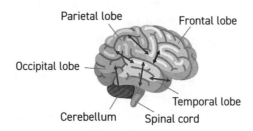

- Poorly developed neuro-pathways between brain centers
- Poor communication between different areas of the brain
- Difficult to rapidly process multiple information simultaneously

Figure 2.3: Autistic processing differences partly due to poorly developed neuro-connections

The weak wiring (long-range connections) between the brain centers interferes with rapid integration of the different centers. There is also evidence suggesting that the short-range connections within some brain centers are too dense, often overwhelming the centers with too much information to process. In both instances, the transmission of communication between the brain centers is weak and poorly integrated. As we will see later, this lack of well-integrated processing is responsible for many of the social, communicative and emotional challenges experienced in autism. For now, let's focus on two primary challenges this processing difference presents:

1. *Difficulty in rapidly processing multiple information simultaneously.* Simply speaking, the brain centers have difficulty communicating with each other to rapidly integrate all the information simultaneously. Since most of our dynamic

world requires us to integrate and process multiple brain centers simultaneously, the autistic brain is at a disadvantage.

2. *Delayed processing.* Instead of the brain processing this information simultaneously, it must consciously process the information sequentially, serially piecing the information together. Depending on the impairment of wiring and/or the amount of information bombarding the nervous system, this delay can take anywhere between ten seconds and hours. I have had some autistics tell me that sometimes it takes days for some information to get integrated and processed.

Relating with others

Let's look at an example of the important role our rapid processing of multiple information plays in our neurotypical daily living. The simple act of relating with another person requires the multi-tasking of an abundance of information and simultaneous communication between many brain centers. Our ability to rapidly process multiple information simultaneously is what allows us to effectively relate within our neurotypical world. To appreciate this rapid, integrated processing let's look at the multiple information that is required when interacting with another person.

1. While we are listening to what the other person is saying we are simultaneously reading their body language, facial expressions and nonverbal communication to understand their thoughts, feelings, perspectives and intentions—what are they thinking, how are they feeling, what is their perspective and, most importantly, what are their intentions? All this information needs to be processed, assessed and integrated in the background while we listen to what they are saying.

2. We also interpret what they are saying based on the social context that brings us together and our past experiences with that person—what situation are we in, what is the purpose of the interaction, what social rules apply to this situation and what experiences have I had with this person? We are subconsciously assimilating all this information with what we remember from the past and what we anticipate in the future. This information is also being simultaneously integrated with the information in step 1, all while we are attending to what the person is saying.

3. While we are listening to what they tell us, we are also formulating what we want to communicate back. Based on what they say and what we infer they mean (from steps 1 and 2), we are formulating how we will respond.

4. When it is our turn to talk, while concentrating on what we are saying we are also simultaneously interpreting their body language to read if they are attentive, interested and understanding what we mean. Do they understand me? Are they interested in what I am saying? Am I offending them?

5. This rapid processing, assimilating information and adjusting our reactions, helps us stay coordinated in this back and forth, reciprocal interaction. It allows us to

flexibly navigate through this complex dance of relating with another, constantly reading, assimilating and adjusting to a flux of dynamic information and open-ended communication.

6. All this processing also incorporates intuitive rules of engagement that allow us to initiate, maintain and repair breakdowns in communication, shift gears and flexibly navigate through the ongoing conversation.

Sounds exhausting, doesn't it? It certainly would be if we had to process all this information at a conscious level by "figuring it out." Instead, we are processing most of this information subconsciously and intuitively, with minimal effort. We typically listen to what they are saying while processing the rest intuitively and subconsciously. This allows us to interact smoothly with minimal effort. As we will see shortly, people on the spectrum cannot rapidly integrate and process all this multiple information simultaneously to read the thoughts, feelings, perspectives and intentions of others. They miss out on most of the information that is needed to smoothly relate.

When looking at this example of social relating and all the different information that must be processed simultaneously, it is not hard to see why relating is so difficult for people on the spectrum. They cannot integrate simultaneously the reading of body language, facial expressions, social rules of the situational context, and past experiences with the person, and infer the thoughts, feelings, perspectives and intentions of others. They are left guessing what is expected and are often out of sync with those with whom they are relating.

Many autistic adults say they have taught themselves how to read facial expressions and body language, to better understand the meaning of others. They have learned to listen to the words, then rapidly read the facial expression and then try to relate this to the context of the situation. However, this is a very labored process of consciously observing and then cognitively figuring out what the expressions mean. Even then, a simple act of smiling can have different meanings based on the context of the situation for which it is occurring. Subtle differences in similar expressions often will not be understood. Inevitably, when trying to incorporate the facial expressions with the person's body language, fluctuations and intonation in voice, they will miss much of the information and meaning.

Neurotypical people process this information intuitively, with minimal conscious awareness. When you must consciously figure it out, not only is it delayed but also very draining. We need always to be cognizant of how draining and frustrating interacting can be for autistics that we relate with. The amount of cognitive strain that is required for them is extreme.

Autistics also report that trying to regulate a conversation, to read the dynamic information flowing back and forth, with two or more people in a small group is almost impossible. Often by the time they have figured out what is being said and meant, and in turn decided how to respond, the conversation has moved on to another topic. There is simply no way to keep up. When they try, they are usually out of sync with the flow of the conversation. Many folks report that trying to regulate like this for a few hours might exhaust them for a couple of days. Please be aware of this when expecting your child to participate in group social events with other children.

Like a processor in a computer, our brain is a processor of information. Just as computers come with different speeds of processing, so do our individual brains. Some of us process information differently and faster than others. As you will see, the brains of people on the spectrum are more like the processors in a computer than the brains of neurotypical people. With autism, although there may be some structural differences in brain centers, it is the wiring between these brain centers that represents many of the differences in processing. It should be noted that the wiring within individual brain centers of autistics can be stronger and more skillful than those of neurotypical brains. This provides them with great skill in specific, concrete areas. However, the lack of rapid, simultaneous communication between the brain centers (poor brain integration) is what creates major challenges relating with others, planning, organizing and executing their daily routines, multi-tasking expectations and controlling emotions. Our fast-paced culture moves too quickly and is too intense for them to register, organize, categorize and assimilate the information.

Static versus dynamic processing

When it comes to processing multiple information simultaneously, it becomes important to distinguish between two types of information: static information and dynamic information (see Figure 2.4).

Static	Dynamic
Information that is concrete, constant and stays the same	Information that is vague, fleeting, free-floating and ever-changing
Facts	Requiring continuous evaluating, appraising, comparing, contrasting and assimilating
Details	
Procedural rules	Social processing
Perceptual patterns	

Autism is good at processing "static" information, but poor with "dynamic" information

Figure 2.4: Differences between static and dynamic information

Static information refers to information that is concrete, constant and absolute. Such information includes:

- *Facts and data:* historical events, details that are constant, logical and do not change.

- *Concrete details*, especially in what we see, hear, smell and taste (sensory detail). Autistics' perception of static detail is very keen and unbiased. Some have perfect pitch and photographic memories. They can pick out small, detailed imperfections that would go unnoticed by most of us. Many autistics can also notice perceptual patterns that many of us would easily ignore.

- *Procedural rules* (2 + 2 = 4) that are constant and absolute. These rules are predictable, absolute and do not change. Once you learn them, they stay the same.

- *Perceptual patterns* that are rhythmic, repetitive or follow a predictable pattern, such as music and art.

The processing of static information is usually a strength for autistics, often stronger than static processing in neurotypicals. Those with strong abilities can excel in the arts and sciences, data analysis, engineering and computer sciences. This is a very important processing strength for the advancement of society.

However, most of our fast-paced, social world is not static, but filled with "dynamic," very fleeting and continually changing information. Often the information from which we infer meaning is abstract, vague and invisible. This information is not constant and absolute, but continually changing. Because it is not static, rapidly processing this information requires ongoing appraising, evaluating, comparing, contrasting and assimilating of new information. Our knowledge of what we are experiencing and how we respond is continually changing and evolving based on new information that changes as situations unfold.

Most of our daily interactions and activities do not follow a constant, predictable pattern but are free floating and spontaneously changing from moment to moment. We continually assimilate new information, alter our perception and adjust our reactions to it. Nothing stays the same, nothing is concrete, absolute and constant.

Referring to our earlier example of relating with others, neither person may know where the conversation will lead from moment to moment, as it evolves from the continuous, free-floating exchange between the two parties. As we integrate and assimilate this dynamic information, we smoothly flow between topics, adjusting, modifying and adapting as needed. Most of our daily functioning is rapidly processing "dynamic" information, inferring meaning from vague inferences, often following invisible rules that vary based on the context of the situation. A given rule might apply in one situation but must be intuitively modified in another situation. No two events are exactly alike, and expectations change from one situation to another.

A person with autism is good at processing "static" information, but poor with "dynamic" information. Rapid processing of dynamic information simultaneously requires strong neurological connections between the brain centers for this information to be integrated, appraised, evaluated and then assimilated into what is already inferred. Our perception of what is occurring and expected is continually changing as we go along. This difficulty for people with autism makes life in our fast-paced, dynamic world hard to process. The parts of our life that are static, concrete, factual, absolute and constant are very attractive and often highly refined for those on the spectrum. Unfortunately, the rest of our dynamic social world of vague, ever-changing, fast-evolving patterns leave them lost.

As with all "thinking styles", the autistic way of thinking has both strengths and weaknesses.

Strengths include being good at:

- analyzing detail

- memorizing facts, statistics and other static information

- seeing sensory patterns, which is useful for the arts and music

- memorizing images (photographic memory) or perceiving notes (perfect pitch)

- computer sciences, mechanical and electrical detail

- tasks requiring concrete logical reasoning.

When it comes to very perceptive, detailed, oriented thinking, this static processing is advantageous. Their perception of static detail is very keen, which represents strengths in fields like physical science, computer technology and mechanical engineering where fine perception of detail, complex design and analysis of patterns are required. Any field that requires analyzing facts and details is usually a plus for many autistics.

Some autistics notice perceptual patterns and detailed designs that many neurotypicals would easily ignore. Another strength for many on the spectrum is that they can hyper-focus on fine detail, pick out imperfections in design and can be very sensitive to subtle sensory patterns.

Many autistics have very sensitive senses that allow them to see, hear and smell stimulation that is below the awareness of most neurotypicals. This can be both a curse and a gift. They can become overwhelmed by common lights, sounds and smells in our daily routine, which pass comfortably for many of us. However, in turn, their keen sensitivities allow them to enjoy very attractive sensory patterns that many of us filter out.

As with all processing styles, these strengths also come with general weaknesses. People with autism (static processing) often:

- struggle in situations that require rapid processing of dynamic information

- have difficulty multi-tasking and filtering out distracting information

- have problems seeing hidden, underlying social contexts and generalizing between situations

- have difficulty processing information that is vague with multiple meanings

- struggle with abstract reasoning that requires ongoing comparing, contrasting, reflecting and projecting (information that requires ongoing appraising and evaluating multiple options)

- have difficulty thinking on the fly—quickly shifting gears and flexibly adapting to change is difficult. They either will hyper-focus on specific, sometimes irrelevant details, or get distracted by too much information competing for attention.

When we look at the differences between static and dynamic processing styles, it is no wonder that many autistics are more comfortable with objects than people. Objects are more concrete, constant, absolute and predictable. People are very dynamic, relative and unpredictable. When you look at our fast-paced social world, you can see where their style of thinking makes social processing extremely difficult. Social processing is very dynamic, not static, requiring strong dynamic processing.

Most social thinking requires processing vague, invisible information that is inferred from the context of the social situation. This context is often filled with hidden meanings that change from one situation to another and vary from moment to moment. Without the ability to read, understand and predict the thoughts, feelings, perspectives and intentions of others, autistics are left literally interpreting what people say, rather than inferring meaning by reading between the lines. Thus, they are navigating an invisible maze, stumbling around trying to guess what is expected and how to react. This presents extreme uncertainty and unpredictability, resulting in high social anxiety.

Our world is very fast paced, with continual flux of rapidly changing information flooding our nervous system moment to moment. Our nervous system must sort out and integrate a host of dynamic information that:

- comes from many different sources

- is usually fleeting and fades quickly

- is often vague, with multiple meanings

- is difficult to interpret without rapidly understanding the context surrounding the information

- requires constant comparing, contrasting, evaluating, assessing

- needs us to continually appraise, integrate and adjust our thinking.

Our social world requires us to integrate multiple streams of information, filter out what is important, understand the "invisible context", rapidly categorize and appraise the meaning, and evaluate and execute how to respond. We must do all these processes simultaneously, requiring rapid processing and integrating multiple information. What is he saying? What does he mean? What are his intentions? What is expected of me? How do I fit in? It's all a guessing game. Most of our social culture requires strong dynamic thinking, which is a weakness for most of those on the spectrum.

How does a static brain adapt to a dynamic world?

Our dynamic world is patterned from the neurotypical processing style (dynamic processing). This means that somehow the autistics must learn how to navigate around all the dynamic information and expectations that our world presents—a world that is frequently chaotic, unpredictable and overwhelming. How can this be accomplished? How can a strong static processing brain adapt to a very dynamic flowing world?

Simultaneous versus sequential processing

Our differences in brain wiring result in two different ways to process dynamic information. Neurotypical people intuitively process all this dynamic information simultaneously. Many on the spectrum must process this information sequentially, piecing the information together to eventually see the whole picture. They literally have to connect the dots to define the plots that we read intuitively. What we process subconsciously, they must consciously figure out and piece together.

When the brain has good neuro-connections between the brain centers, it can process all the multiple information simultaneously, integrating it to form one overall meaning. This happens smoothly, usually intuitively and subconsciously. With all the information bombarding the nervous system, much of this information is processed below our level of consciousness, leaving our awareness to attend to the most relevant information. This smooth, simultaneous processing helps conserve mental energy to focus on the task at hand. When your brain cannot simultaneously integrate this information, it must sort through this information sequentially, consciously piecing together information. Thinking this through can be very taxing and mentally draining.

Delayed processing

This sequential, serial reasoning slows down the processing of information, often leaving the individual missing much of the rapidly changing information. Much of the information (words, actions, meaning, etc.) is too fleeting to be processed sequentially. The individual is often left with limited information that does not integrate well. Not only is information lost in translation, but also appraising information sequentially significantly slows down the processing. This leaves the person struggling to keep up with the speed of information.

Often, they only process pieces of the total amount of information, much of it coming and going before it is processed. So, when you are acting on only pieces of the information, your interpretation and resulting behavior often are out of sync with the rest of us. Consequently, socially the person is left confused and stumbling through daily interaction with others. Without the ability to rapidly process dynamic information, people with autism often get lost in the flux of information.

This delay in processing can vary from 10 to 30 seconds, or longer (sometimes several hours), depending on the situational variables, how drained the brain already is and the complexity of the information. When given extra time, the person can often process accurately, but will become confused and overwhelmed if pressed to process faster.

Research has shown that the average wait time for a child to respond to a question or request is a couple of seconds. After a few seconds, we repeat the request or increase the prompting. When we expect rapid responding from someone with processing delays, we create mass frustration. Each time we repeat the question or prompt before they have completed processing, they must start the processing all over again. As you can imagine, after we restate the prompt several times, the child becomes very frustrated. The child cannot process it fast enough and becomes overwhelmed. Children will often report that they will say "no" or "I don't know" because we are expecting a response faster than they can give it. They learn it is better to avoid committing by saying "no" or "I don't know." Consequently, these children end up being labeled defiant and oppositional.

Often complicating this delay in processing, some autistics think in pictures, not words. They must translate what is said in words into pictures to process and understand it. Next, they must re-translate what they have processed in pictures into a verbal response (words) to others. This further delays the processing.

How we can help

When trying to teach and relate with people on the spectrum we should be very conscious and respectful of this delay in processing. We need to speak in very concrete terms and give them added time to process what is said and what is expected. Tips for improving communication include:

- Talk in short sentences or phrases. Many have auditory processing problems.

- Be specific in what you are asking. Avoid vague language.

- Give time to process.

- Only give one step at a time.

- Verify that they understand. Do not assume they understand.

These strategies in no way are meant to be condescending. This delay in processing is not due to an intellectual disability, but simply a processing difference. The more we understand what autistics experience, the more we can change our communication to bridge these differences. When it appears that the person is uninterested, oppositional or indifferent, first assume this may well be a processing issue before interpreting their actions as rude or defiant, especially with children. Usually they either do not understand or misinterpret what you want. Try a different, more literal way.

Filtering

In addition to weak neurological connections between brain centers, autistics also have difficulty filtering out irrelevant information. Our (neurotypical) brains have a complex ability to filter out information that is not considered relevant. For example, if we are driving in a crowded area we are bombarded with multiple information (sights, sounds, conversations, sensory input from the gas pedal and steering wheel, etc.); to stay focused on the road and make immediate adjustments our brain must filter out the relevant from the irrelevant information. We can only attend to a limited amount of stimulation at one time. The rest must be filtered out in order not to distract attention.

If we are talking to someone at a large, noisy party, our brains must filter out or tone down all the background noise and activity so that we can focus on what the other person is saying and doing. If we could not filter out all the conversations, background music, movement of others around us, and other sights and smells, we would be too distracted to zone in on our conversation.

Often our brains are filtering out up to 80 percent of all information that is bombarding our nervous system. A very simple example of this process is sensory filtering. During your normal daily routine when you move your arm you do not feel the sleeve of your shirt move across your skin. However, once I direct your attention to it you can feel the fabric move on your skin. The nerves in our skin are picking up this sensation whenever the fabric moves across our skin. Thankfully, since this information is usually not important for us, our brains usually filter it out so it doesn't reach our conscious awareness. If we felt every little movement of clothing on our skin, we would be continually distracted. The same goes for background noises (fan, air conditioning, refrigerator turning on and off, ongoing noise of background traffic, etc.) which are bombarding our nervous system. This filtering occurs across all senses (sights, sounds, smells and tactile sensations), minimizing the information so that we can focus only on what is considered relevant.

For many on the spectrum, this natural filtering system is not as strong and functional. Their brains are often flooded with overwhelming amounts of detail to rapidly process. They must sort out what is relevant to focus on. If the stimulation is too intense, the brain becomes overwhelmed and panics. In addition, without the ability to adequately filter, autistics can often become distracted by the irrelevant information that is competing for their attention; hence the child who cannot focus on what you are saying because his attention is distracted by the flickering of light reflecting off your necklace or earring. Or, the child who is too preoccupied by an imperfection in your skin, hair or voice to attend to what you are saying.

Neurotypical brains immediately extract important details and simultaneously infer the big picture of what is expected. Those with autism must sort through a mass of details, relevant and irrelevant, to piece together the big picture. This flooding of irrelevant information further taxes and delays the processing, adding to the mental drain. As we will see in future chapters, this flooding can result in the brain shutting down its processing to avoid overload and becoming overwhelmed.

Information overload

In summary, we have discussed how the weak neuro-pathways connecting the various brain centers result in difficulty rapidly processing multiple information simultaneously and in delayed processing due to the need to consciously process sequentially what we process intuitively. In addition, the poor filtering functions often bombard the brain with too much information, making it difficult to sort out relevant from irrelevant information and often overwhelming the processing.

These differences (weak connections and poor filtering) mean that a much higher percentage of processing is at a conscious level, as autistics figure out what we process intuitively. This is very taxing and mentally draining. What we process with ease takes much more mental energy for people on the spectrum. This has major ramifications for their daily functioning. Many of our normal daily functions require more mental energy for autistics, which can tax and drain their nervous system. A typical day at school for a child with autism will be much more draining than it is for his neurotypical peers.

As we can imagine, these demands for rapid processing of multiple information, if not paced to the processing speed of the person, can result in information overload. Just too much information coming in too fast. When the brain gets overwhelmed, it becomes disorganized, which further compromises processing abilities and, if too overwhelming, sets the brain into fight or flight panic mode.

If the overload builds slowly, the brain will often go into "shutdown" mode. The brain will begin to shut off information from one or more of the senses to minimize the amount of information coming in. Usually you will see the child "space out," get that glazed look in his eyes, often stare off in space, and sometimes become mute and unresponsive. This is a protective mode and adaptive response the brain uses to defend against being overloaded and overwhelmed. When we see these signs, we need to back off all requests and interaction, reassure the child we understand and give him time to rebound.

If we continue to pressure, or the brain does not have time to shut down, and information comes in too quickly, the brain will panic, and the child may go into meltdown. The brain cannot process faster than it is programmed to. It is very important for us to respect these processing needs, not push the child faster than he can adequately process, and to back off when we see him starting to shut down. Allow him to pace the flow of information, take frequent breaks, and remember to break the information down for him to make it easier to process.

Supporting processing differences

Now that we have outlined the processing challenges for trying to navigate our fast-paced, dynamic world, let's look at strategies we can use to help bridge these differences. Try to remember you cannot force a brain to process faster or differently from how it is wired. We must respect the neurology, not work against it. Trying to force a brain to respond differently will only create frustration, brain drain and emotional turmoil.

Understanding goes a long way. The best way to earn the trust of children on the spectrum is to understand, accept and respect their processing needs. Understand the processing needs of the child and then match our demands to his processing abilities. Work with the child, rather than expecting him to match us. Tailor what we ask to how he processes and learns. If progress or communication breaks down, assume that we need to back up and change our approach (or communication), not require the child to change. Sometimes we may not be able to do anything about the overload, but the child knowing that you understand and support him can lower his anxiety, help him feel safe and establish trust that you will protect him. Assume, when the child is hesitant or struggling, that he is possibly overwhelmed. Acknowledge and show that you understand how the world is often chaotic, confusing and overwhelming.

Ways to help

- *Give the child time to process.* With delayed processing, it is important to give the child at least 10–20 seconds to respond (even longer for some children). If you keep repeating the prompt, before processing is completed, the child must start processing all over. This is very frustrating and exhausting.

- *Let the child pace the performance.* We cannot push a person faster than his brain can process. If we do, the brain panics and reacts in "fight or flight." I witness this all the time. We constantly try to speed these kids up, pushing them faster than they can process. This can be frustrating for us, since we process faster and naturally get impatient when we must slow down. But slowing down and letting the child pace his performance helps tremendously.

- *Shorten your words.* Provide very short, concrete directions. Use short phrases and sentences with only the main point. Many of the children have auditory processing problems. The longer the sentences and the more words used, the greater chance the information will get jumbled and lost. Only use the important words; get to the point.

- *Use visuals whenever possible.* Demonstrate (model) what you want. Give visual directions. Write out short instructions instead of relying on verbal directions. Words are fleeting, whereas written instructions are constant and can be easily referenced.

- *Break it down; slow it down.* Break tasks down into smaller parts and give children each step sequentially. If possible, give them a checklist to mark off as they do each step. Do not expect the children to multi-task. Allow them extra time but let them finish. It is important to finish one task before going to another.

- *Use visual templates.* Give outlines, laying out the important points so the child can categorize the information you give him. A simple outline will highlight to him what information is important, and give him mental files for categorizing, organizing and storing the information. Consider using worksheets, outlines and other templates that help the child organize and categorize important information.

- *Prepare by previewing.* If possible, preview the learning ahead of time, to provide a mental framework of what is being presented. Many of the children have difficulty sorting out the relevant information from the irrelevant. Previewing highlights the areas of importance to help direct their attention and gives them a frame of reference to organize the information.

- *Avoid mental drain.* Be cognizant of how draining the child's processing can be and provide frequent breaks to rebound and regroup. Do not wait until he gets taxed and overwhelmed. Allow for frequent breaks to maintain his energy reserve. We often press forward until the child is drained and agitated before giving him a break. We should be building breaks in before he reaches that point.

- *Know the early signs.* Most importantly, be aware of the early signs that the person is getting overwhelmed. Most children will provide behavior indicators that they are starting to get upset. When you see these signs, immediately stop the demands, give a break and provide support.

Using these measures not only tells the child that you understand what he is experiencing but that you are also respecting his needs, providing support and are seen as a trusted guide. All of us can handle our challenges if we feel safe, accepted and supported by those around us.

This chapter has provided a simplified summary of some of the processing differences in autism. We will see as we move along and talk about stress, social and emotional challenges, brain drain and meltdowns that these processing differences play a major role. Knowing about these processing differences allows us to better understand how autistics experience these challenges, helps explains many of the behavior differences we see and allows us to better understand, accept, respect and relate with autistics. We will continually remind the reader of these differences as we describe the challenges that present the most stress for those living with autism.

Chapter 3

BRAIN DRAIN FROM PROCESSING STRAIN

In the green book, *The Autism Discussion Page on Anxiety, Behavior, School, and Parenting Strategies*, (Nason 2014b), I provide the following scenario of Jimmy, a young boy in class, shutting down from processing overload. I will present it here as an introduction to processing strain and the taxing impact it has on the brain for many with autism.

Stop the world I WANT OFF!!

The world is spinning and bombarding too fast! I try, and try, until I cannot think any more. Help! My brain is drained, and my energy depleted. It is only noon and I must somehow make it through the afternoon. Recess is chaotic; let me hide to the side. I must somehow regroup and conserve, since I have little reserve. Like every afternoon I will have to "shutdown" to "shut out" the world. As I overload, my senses become heightened, hyper-sensitive, and impossible to tolerate. The sounds, the smells, the chaotic activity around me meshes into confusion. I must hold it together, and stay calm, as to explode would bring disaster. I will sit quietly but stare off. To be aware will overwhelm.

Like most every afternoon I will not remember what happened. It will be a blur. I will withdraw to maintain, and gasp for air to survive! I hurt all over but cannot cry! I feel panic as the bright lights blind my eyes, the voices overwhelm me, and the smells make me nauseous. I can barely feel my arms and legs, let alone use them effectively. I am falling apart as I hold it in. I will withdraw and hide, sit quietly in my chair and hope that everyone forgets I am there. I want to hide in a corner, wrap up in a blanket, and withdraw to survive. I pray there will be no snags, or added demands, and hope that the teacher does not call on me. I cannot distinguish between what is said, what I did, or what is happening around me. Please somebody! Stop the world and let me get off!

Always be aware that a full day at school can be very draining and overwhelming. The sensory bombardment, social strain, and academic demands can tax an already vulnerable nervous system. Our world presents too much, too fast, and too intense for many on the spectrum. Many have delayed processing issues that make processing slow and taxing. They must consciously "think through" much of what we process subconsciously and smoothly, with minimal energy. Slow it down, break it down, and give them a lot of breaks to rebound. Their energy supply drains fast, and they must have time to withdraw to regroup.

Many have sleep disturbances, dietary concerns, and anxiety issues that leave them with a low reserve starting out the day. If they had an exhausting time the previous day, chances are they still have not replenished to full reserve. Do not pressure, do not demand, and let them pace themselves. Develop a sensory diet scheduled set of sensory activities with plenty of breaks, and most importantly allow them to escape when needed. Give them a voice, and make sure they know how, and feel safe, to say "no" and "I need help." As a teacher or aid, help them feel safe in your presence, and trust that you understand. As the day wears on, be aware that stress chemicals accumulate, and the child will be drained. Do not pressure or ridicule, but support and reassure. In the mist of chaos, they need to feel safe and accepted, and know that they can count on you to support them. (p.238)

Mental energy

Everything that we do uses both physical and mental energy. As we go through the day, we expend energy, and slowly drain our reserve as the day rolls along. We eat and sleep to replenish our energy supply. This is like the automobile requiring gasoline to fuel it as you drive. You fill your car up at the beginning of a trip. How fast your car uses fuel will depend on how long you drive, how fast you drive, how heavy the car is, the size of the engine, how well the car is maintained, how rough the road conditions are, the weather and the driving habits of the person. If you are driving an old, out-of-tune, poorly maintained car, on hilly, muddy terrain, for an hour's ride, the chances are you will deplete your fuel at a faster rate.

This fuel range factor also applies to the human body (physical reserve) and brain (mental reserve). As we go through the day, we use up both physical and mental energy, both being determined by how full our reserve (tank) is at the beginning of the day, how maintained and prepared our bodies are, and how stressful our day is.

As with driving, we do not always start the day with a full tank. The amount of energy we start the day with will be determined by how draining the day before was, whether we had a good night's sleep, if we are healthy and not fighting off illness, and if we ate a good breakfast. If we are out of shape, in poor health, and/or anxious in general, then our nervous system (motor) is disorganized and running rough (out of tune and idling fast or slow). If we do not eat breakfast, or eat poorly, must rush because we are running late, run into a traffic jam getting to work, or have to return home because we forgot something, we are taxing our energy reserve before starting the meat of our day. Our nervous system is already frazzled and disorganized. As the day rolls on, the more disorganized and out of sync our nervous system becomes, and the more busy, stressful and mentally exhausting the day presents, the more taxed our system becomes and the more energy it depletes. The more taxed our nervous system becomes, the harder the engine runs, and the less efficient it is in handling current demands. Our concentration, cognitive abilities and coping skills begin to deteriorate. The immediate demands become harder to process, evaluate and adapt to. Without rest, food, and proper maintenance, the nervous system (engine) exhausts itself.

For people on the spectrum, the nervous system is more fragile, disorganized and anxious. Their nervous system has extreme difficulty processing the very hectic, chaotic flow of our daily routine. Their nervous system has difficulty rapidly processing multiple information, simultaneously. Our world simply moves way too fast, with too much information coming in too quickly for them to process. Instead of smoothly processing this information simultaneously at a subconscious level, they must process it sequentially, by consciously thinking about it, piecing this information together bit by bit. This slows down the processing and requires extensive mental energy to think through what we usually process without thinking about it. This taxes the nervous system and drains both physical and mental energy much faster. This means for the child at school, or adult at work, the typical day of processing normal daily expectations will require more mental energy than it does for those of us not on the spectrum.

This is the normal processing scenario for the person with autism. In addition, many autistics also have co-occurring disorders that further tax their fragile nervous system. For those who have extensive sensory processing issues, auditory processing problems and language processing difficulties, their processing of information is even more delayed and fragmented, further taxing the compromised nervous system (like the car that is out of tune, idling fast and misfiring constantly). Compounding matters, many people on the spectrum have other inhibiting factors such as poor sleep patterns, nutritional problems, weakened immune systems, constipation, seizure activity and high anxiety, which further tax the nervous system and deplete their energy reserve.

For those with severe sensory, language and information processing issues, the demands of our world are continually depleting an already constricted mental and physical energy reserve. Regulating through a normal day can be totally exhausting for them if they do not get a chance to withdraw, rebound and replenish their energy reserve. Research has shown that the average amount of stress chemicals in the nervous system of someone on the spectrum is much higher, even in a resting state, than a person without autism. Their nervous system is often anxious and on high alert, even in a resting state. When you add the difficulty the nervous system has simply processing normal daily activity, it becomes taxed and drained quickly, which reduces ability to process effectively, further taxing the energy supply. The stress chemicals continue to accumulate as the day goes on, until the system gets overloaded, shuts down and/or melts down.

Know your child's profile

Each child has his own unique profile of neurological strengths, weaknesses and vulnerabilities. His sensory, cognitive, social and emotional processing differences will make up the unique package of challenges that will add to his mental drain. By understanding his primary strengths and weaknesses, we can build in accommodations in the child's day to reduce the mental drain and minimize the stress. From this knowledge, we can begin to build in the proactive supports to help reduce the stressors that compromise the child's processing skills.

To help support your loved one, you must understand what sensory, processing, social and emotional challenges tax their nervous system. Also, what co-occurring medical concerns (sensory processing, visual and auditory processing problems, sleep or eating disorders, chronic digestive/immune system problems, anxiety and other mood disorders, seizure disorders and other chronic medical problems) does the child have that also compromise his nervous system and energy levels? Try to make a list of processing challenges with corresponding accommodations to lessen the stress and processing drain. Try to identify how these challenges impact the child in his daily routine and build in accommodations to minimize the stress. How can we tailor the demands, provide sensory tools (sunglasses, ear plugs, fidget toys, etc.), break tasks down into simpler steps and provide extra support to minimize the mental drain for the child? This becomes very important when trying to navigate the many daily activities at school, whether academic accommodations, sensory diet (a scheduled set of sensory activities), social supports, transitioning between classes, recess and cafeteria demands, struggles during gym class and staying organized during his daily schedule. There are too many sensory, social, academic and physical demands.

Finally, to keep the child's energy reserve from getting too compromised, we need to provide the child with frequent breaks during the day to regroup and rebound. Allowing the child to pull away from the daily demands and re-energize is so important for his emotional and mental stamina as well as his physical wellbeing. Such breaks can be as simple as taking 10–15 minutes every 90 minutes to rest in a quiet area, read or listen to favorite music, engage in soothing sensory activities or participate in strong physical activity to release stress chemicals. Each child is different, so it is important to know what unique activities help the child regroup and re-energize. By giving the child the chance to balance the demands of the day with breaks to re-energize, we are respecting the neurological needs of the child and making life much more successful for him. This delicate balance requires ongoing appraisal and monitoring of his energy level and processing abilities.

The spoon theory

The spoon theory is a disabilities metaphor story that provides a visual representation of energy levels and how events tax the energy reserve. Christine Miserandino developed this story to explain what it was like living with lupus, a chronic autoimmune disease. This simple model has been used by many disability groups to explain how the fragile nervous system leaves people with a limited energy supply.

Each spoon represents a unit of energy. You start the day with a limited supply of spoons. For Christine, these spoons represent the amount of physical energy she has in her reserve for the day. Because of her lupus, Christine has limited energy and must be selective in how she uses it to make it through the day. As she assesses what she needs to do, she has to subtract spoons for each activity, depending on how taxing the tasks are. Some days, depending on her physical condition, Christine may start with even fewer spoons, further constricting what she is able to do. Depending on how compromised her body is, a given event may require more spoons than at other times. She must prioritize what needs to be done and what she must let go. Each activity in her day requires giving up one or more spoons, until she is left with no more spoons. For example, she may have to skip showering to conserve her energy for eating and dressing. Christine must continually monitor how many spoons she has left and what the rest of the day will require. The more compromised she is, the less she can do. Some days she may be too physically exhausted to accomplish anything.

Although Christine used this metaphor to describe the restricting effects of lupus, many autistics use this spoon metaphor to represent the draining effects they experience living in our world. Whether you use the spoon metaphor, numerical points, or some other form of measurement, it is important to always be cognizant of how draining activities of daily living are, how much mental and physical energy you currently have and whether you are too compromised to continue as planned. The better we get at projecting ahead and planning the day, the less stress the child will feel and the more successful he will be. The better we get at monitoring the child's mental reserve, the better we can make adaptations to our expectations so as not to overwhelm him. Once the energy reserve reaches low levels, the child's thinking, reasoning and communicating deteriorate, leaving him vulnerable to emotional distress.

Gauging energy reserve

Although the spoon theory provides a nice metaphor for talking about energy use, many children might benefit from using a visual fuel gauge such as the battery charger they see on their cell phones. Also, many school programs use a simple color system to represent energy levels (green = good, yellow = compromised, red = low, danger). Figure 3.1 shows the energy gauge with corresponding spoons, color and percentage.

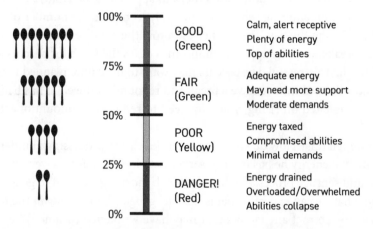

Figure 3.1: Use of fuel gauge to measure mental energy level

As discussed earlier, as the nervous system regulates throughout the day it uses up valuable mental energy. When you have processing issues (sensory, cognitive, social) like those on the spectrum, much of the processing that we do smoothly they must consciously work through, expending valuable mental energy. There is just too much information coming too fast. Simply trying to regulate an hour of interacting in group conversation (party, meeting, etc.) can leave them mentally drained, especially if they have had a chaotic day to begin with. What we take for granted takes extensive effort on their part.

Since processing his daily routine can be very draining, it is important that we monitor the child's mental energy throughout the day. How many spoons does he have left? Does he have what is needed for what we expect? We need to watch closely, listen carefully and respect the processing needs of the person. The more drained the nervous system, the harder it works, and the less effectively it can regulate. As processing is taxed, the child's coping skills become compromised. On days when the child is more organized and moving smoothly, he can tackle more. On days when he is obviously taxed and drained, we need to back off demands, conserve energy and give him more breaks to rebound.

Baseline (starting) level beginning the day

What is the state of your child's processing (energy level) at the beginning of the day? Did he get a good night's sleep? Did he eat breakfast? Is he feeling sluggish or ill? Did he have a hard time getting through his morning routine? Did he have a taxing evening the night before? These are all variables that will affect the child's baseline energy reserve (how many spoons he has) as he begins his day. Does he appear more anxious, stressed or labored in what he is doing? There are some days when he may be more taxed and less organized from the moment he gets out of bed. For both parents and teachers, it is important to know this energy level before starting the day. This helps us decide what activities and demands the child can handle without taxing and overwhelming him.

For a teacher, this information allows them to appraise if the child is already taxed and needs a break on entering school and possibly to reduce the number of demands placed on him during the day. The teacher monitors the child's energy level and backs off and gives breaks when he appears compromised. It's the same for parents at home. If the child has had a stressful day, parents may want to have little planned for the next day. The child will need time to have a break and rebound. If the child has had a rough evening and is agitated on rising, you may need to reduce the amount of activity for that day.

How do we tell this? How do we know what the child's processing abilities are and how much mental energy he has in his reserve? Let's look at Sally, a seven-year-old girl with autism and sensory processing disorder. Each morning we want to gauge how she is doing and what we can expect. What is her fuel gauge when waking in the morning? We may have to subtract any factors that may have weakened (drained) her nervous system. The three most common factors are (1) having an exhausting evening the night before, (2) lack of sleep, and (3) any physical illness or discomfort. Depending on the severity of these factors, you would subtract one spoon (or 10%) for each factor. For this example, let's assume that Sally had a social outing the night before, and did not sleep well. We might predict that her starting energy level is at six spoons or 80 percent charge.

If the morning routine goes well, everything going according to plan, then maybe Sally is leaving the house at about 75 percent, or six spoons. However, if there were snags to the morning routine (something went wrong, had to rush, etc.) and if she didn't eat breakfast, you may need to subtract an additional 10 percent, or one spoon, for each factor. This further drains her an additional 20–25 percent, or two spoons. Sally is now leaving the house with an energy level of only about 50–60 percent (four spoons).

Next, we need to consider the bus ride to school, which aggravates Sally's sensory issues: rough movement, the smell of exhaust, noisy/active children, peers bumping into her and so on. This, plus the chaos of walking into school and transitioning into the classroom can be draining, lowering her energy level by one or two spoons to less than 50 percent. Once her mental energy drops below half (50%), Sally begins to enter the "compromised zone" where mental energy is poor, processing becomes taxed and her coping skills begin to deteriorate. If you are using the spoon metaphor, Sally has already used up half of her spoons.

Once the child's energy level gets close to the half full mark, we want to allow her to pull back and regroup (re-energize) before she drops into the poor, compromising zone. The further we drain that reserve, the more taxing activity becomes and the less capable the child is to cope with the demands. Her processing skills start to deteriorate, energy drains faster and emotional regulation weakens.

It is important to catch Sally before she becomes compromised, give her a break to regroup and rebuild some energy reserve. Allowing the child to recharge before dropping below half full is important. Recharging is so much easier and occurs much faster than waiting until the nervous system is severely taxed, drained and fully compromised. Once severely compromised, the battery becomes inadequate and takes much longer to recharge.

Luckily, Sally's teacher has been working with her mom to monitor her energy level, pull back demands and give Sally sensory breaks to escape and regroup. Sally's mother sends a monitoring log to school each morning telling the teacher how the night and morning went and how organized Sally is coming in. The bus driver also lets the teacher know if any issues occur on the bus. On this day, Sally's teacher already knows that she has had a hard morning and is entering school already compromised. The teacher can see that Sally is more disorganized and agitated. She recognizes that Sally needs a break to regroup and recharge. She allows Sally to take a break, go to the sensory area and regroup, before entering the classroom to start the day. The teacher also realizes that Sally may be more compromised throughout the day and will need frequent breaks to regroup.

How the child refuels will be different from child to child. Some like to withdraw to a quiet area, some need physical activity and others like to read, listen to music or play with electronics. For many, simply escaping to a quiet area where they are alone and can self-stimulate can help them rebound. Each person has their own toolbox for regrouping. Simply pulling away from all demands and relaxing will reboot some kids. Others will need the addition of physical activity or soothing sensory stimulation to regroup.

Let's assume that every 15 minutes adds 10–15 points, or one spoon to the energy level, depending on the effectiveness of the strategy. Since Sally has already had a rough morning and depleted over 50 percent of her energy, the teacher gives Sally a 20-minute sensory break immediately on arriving at school.

The goal is to keep the child in the fair to good range throughout the day. My recommendation is pacing the day so that once the child begins to fall from the good to fair range you are already offering a break to recharge, staying within the optimum level of energy. Understanding how draining activities are and how much time is needed to recover is essential for maintaining a healthy energy level. Over time, it is important for Sally to learn how to monitor her own energy level and provide what is needed to recharge.

Waiting too long (yellow/compromised zone)

The mistake most people make is waiting too long before pulling back to recharge. We wait until we see the child becoming disorganized before beginning to think about giving a break. Often, we press on a little further hoping the child will learn to cope. As the child's energy level begins to drop into the compromised zone, three primary challenges occur:

1. The child's processing skills start to deteriorate, making the activity more difficult to process. Sensory issues become amplified, processing more fragmented and delayed, and judgement, reasoning and problem solving deteriorate.

2. Since the processing is more difficult it stresses the nervous system and drains energy even faster. An activity that typically represents a minimal drain when the child is operating on full charge may require moderate to severe drain if the child's battery is compromised. Hence, activities become more draining as the battery runs low.

3. The more depleted (compromised) the battery, the longer it will take to recharge. Once in the compromised zone, the child may take three times longer to recharge (a couple of hours) or a full day if the child is forced into the danger zone. Plus, once the child is in the danger zone we most likely will see a variety of challenging behaviors (opposition, acting out, etc.). Stress becomes distress, because the demands are greater than the child's abilities to cope with them.

Jimmy, the child sitting dazed in class at the beginning of this chapter, is in the compromised zone. By the afternoon, his battery has depleted and his processing is severely compromised. He cannot adequately process the expectations and is shutting down, trying to minimize the amount of stimulation coming in. Jimmy is doing his best to hold it together and avoid maxing out. Any simple demand or expectation at this point is too much for his depleted energy.

The teacher may not recognize that Jimmy is compromised because he is quiet and sitting still. He is being "good," although his nervous system is drained and overwhelmed. To avoid this state, Jimmy would need a well-designed plan to provide accommodations to lower the processing demands during the day, frequent breaks to recharge and a sensory diet to keep his battery operable. By reducing drain and providing breaks to recharge, Jimmy may be able to stay alert, receptive and organized for the full day.

The danger (red) zone!

Once the demands of the environment outweigh the person's processing abilities, the battery drains very quickly. A specific activity, which may be fine when the child is processing well, can become too demanding if his battery is compromised. Most teachers have experienced a child who comes into school already compromised, agitated and close to the danger zone. The child had such a poor night's sleep and rough morning that he is totally disorganized and depleted. For a child coming in like this, facing the daily demands of the classroom, it is like sending the helpless child into a battle zone. He can barely hold it together, let alone process any of the sensory, social and task demands of the classroom. This pushes the child further into the danger zone and places him under chronic stress. Like all operating systems, this ongoing stress will be detrimental to both the emotional and physical health of the child.

The best the teacher can do is allow the child to escape the classroom, withdraw all demands and allow him to sleep most of the day. If the child is not allowed to escape these overwhelming demands, he most likely will become agitated and either shut down (become unresponsive) or act out to escape the chaos. The child is better off not coming to school that day. It is simply too much processing for a helpless, depleted battery. If this stress and pressure occur regularly, even the thought of going to school becomes overwhelming in anticipation of the stress. The child then begins to refuse to go to school.

Once the child's mental energy becomes compromised and the demands (stimulation, expectations) become greater than his ability to process, stress chemicals (cortisol, adrenaline, etc.) rapidly increase. Anxiety increases, avoidance sets in and the child either withdraws, becomes oppositional or acts out to escape the overwhelming demands. All thinking, problem solving, communication and effective responding deteriorate. The child begins to respond reactively and defensively, with poor emotional control. Unfortunately, if not allowed to escape the stimulation and demands, the child will be pressed into fight or flight, which is traumatic for everyone.

Remember, these explosive outbursts are usually the result of others pressuring the child into situations where the demands are too overwhelming for him at that moment. This is not the fault of the person himself. Don't blame the child. We are the ones pressuring the child, not anticipating his processing needs, nor recognizing the early signs that he is struggling and not respecting the child's communication that he needs to escape, de-stress and recharge.

The child should never be pressed into the danger zone. We should recognize the early signs when the child is becoming compromised, pull back on demands (activities, expectations) and allow him to withdraw, de-stress and recharge. It is best to monitor the energy level, give frequent breaks to recharge and be cognizant of the processing demands of activities we are presenting. We should be accommodating for processing weaknesses, minimizing challenging demands, providing a sensory diet to keep the nervous system organized and giving frequent breaks to allow the child to de-stress and recharge. Under these conditions, the children feel safe and secure that we are not overwhelming them, that we are listening to their needs and allowing them to escape when needed.

Adult experiences

All the above concerns regarding mental energy and processing restrictions also apply to adults on the spectrum. Unfortunately, most adults do not have the same accommodations and assistance for supporting them. By the time the child leaves school, he needs to have a good understanding of his own vulnerabilities, how to accommodate for them and how to advocate for his needs. He must be able to understand how energized he is, when he is becoming compromised and how to escape and rebound when needed.

How to help? Minimizing stress and mental/emotional drain

1. Match demands to processing abilities.

2. Know which activities are most draining.

3. Provide recovery breaks.

4. Recognize early signs (behavior indicators).

5. Monitor processing drain.

6. Balance the day; stay in the green zone.

1 Match demands to processing abilities

When any engine is pressed to operate under conditions beyond its abilities, it will work harder and eventually wear down. It's the same with us. When we are placed in situations where the demands are greater than our abilities, we must extend our capabilities, placing great strain on our energy reserve. The more we understand the children's abilities and vulnerabilities, the greater support we can give them.

In Chapter 2, we discussed the processing differences that present challenges for autistics. Knowing the child's sensory sensitivities, processing challenges and social struggles, you can build in modifications and accommodations to better match the daily demands to the capabilities of the child. In school, the individual education plan (IEP) usually lists a host of accommodations to support the child's sensory, social and cognitive challenges. These accommodations are meant to lower overall demands, modify the demands, or provide added support in coping with the demands. This may include sensory accommodations (avoid noisy areas, use natural lighting, seating arrangements in the classroom, fidget toys, items to chew on, ear plugs, etc.), cognitive modifications (break tasks down, use visual strategies, preview learning, etc.) and social accommodations (minimize group interaction, provide peer mentor, coaching during play, social stories, etc.). The more we can match environmental demands (our expectations) to the child's abilities, the more smoothly he can process. Such a balance minimizes overload and unnecessary strain on the child's energy. He feels happy and competent, remains receptive and enjoys learning.

By understanding children's strengths and weaknesses, we can build in supports to accommodate for their vulnerabilities and focus on developing their strengths and preferences. By respecting the children's processing differences and making accommodations, we significantly lower the stress and processing drain that compromise the children. Instead of draining their energy struggling with overwhelming demands, they can use their energy for learning and navigating their day.

2 Know what activities are most draining

Even with accommodations, participation in daily living will expand energy and gradually drain energy reserve. It is important to understand what taxes the child and what events are the most draining. This allows us to understand which activities the child can easily handle, gauge how taxing an event will be and not pressure the child into events that overwhelm his processing skills.

Using our spoon model, we can rate how challenging common activities are for the child. Figure 3.2 provides an example list. Based on the child's sensory, cognitive and social challenges, you start to get a good idea of what activities are the most draining or overwhelming.

Easy	Moderate	Difficult	Overwhelming
Eating meal	Showering	Playing with peers	School assembly
Brushing teeth	Playing with sister	Shopping	Circus
Dressing	Doing chores	Homework	Parties
Playing with dog	Walking to school	Haircut	Large groups
Playing game	Brief outing	Unexpected event	Barking dogs
Preferred activity	Playing ball	Change	Dentist/doctor

Figure 3.2: Example list, using the spoon theory for ranking the draining potential of daily activities

Knowing how draining typical daily activities are gives you a good idea of how much activity the child (or yourself) can handle before becoming drained and compromised. For example, in the morning, if the child is going to use two to three spoons eating breakfast, brushing his teeth and getting dressed, you may want to skip taking a shower in the morning to save enough energy for the morning outing you have planned. If you have used up four to six spoons running a few errands, you may want to cut your community outing short as not to over-extend his reserve. Using that compromise becomes essential in helping the child stay regulated. Balancing these demands with recovery breaks can help optimize his energy reserve.

3 Provide recovery breaks

As the child goes through the day, we need to monitor the child's energy level and balance the number of demands with recovery breaks that allow him to withdraw from demands and recharge his battery (energy level). This allows the child to regroup and recharge for the next set of activities in his day, providing a healthy balance of breaks to regroup and rebound.

Recovery breaks consist of whatever helps the child pull away, rebound and regroup, giving him a chance to reduce the accumulated stress chemicals and to build up his mental energy. Recovery breaks often involve withdrawing to a quiet, isolated area, devoid of people and demands. Some people prefer to simply rest or nap. Some prefer to regroup by engaging in their favorite self-stimulation, which is used to help regulate their arousal level, release stress and recharge. Others prefer to withdraw into a favorite activity such as reading, music, or their iPad. Some individuals prefer to engage in physical activity (trampoline, walking, push/pull activities, etc.) to re-energize— hence the child who needs an hour on the playscape after coming home from school. All these activities allow the child to withdraw from all expectations, and give him time to recover and recharge his battery.

WHAT HELPS CALM AND ORGANIZE YOUR CHILD?

It is important to work closely with the child to identify and experiment with different coping strategies. For some individuals, engaging in physical activity helps them to release stress chemicals, organize their nervous system and re-energize. For others, physical activity will agitate and further drain them. Some children prefer more passive, self-involved activity (music, reading, stimming, napping) that allows them to totally escape the world and absorb themselves in calming, organizing distractions. Also, different techniques may work better at different stages. For example, short breaks for physical activity can keep a child regulated and receptive when in the fair to good zones, but when fully compromised the child may need to pull away from all demands/stimulation and be left alone for an hour or two. That is why it is important to keep the child regulated rather than trying to fall back and regroup once he is severely compromised. Also, remember, the more compromised the child, the more likely he may become resistant to taking a break or engaging in activities to calm and organize.

TYPE AND LENGTH OF BREAKS

The next factor to consider is determining how much break time or "regrouping time" is needed to recover and recharge for each level. The more draining the events, the longer the recovery time. The more drained the battery becomes, the more recovery time is needed to recharge. Breaks may only be 10–20 minutes when the battery is more than half full (optimum zones), several hours when fallen into the compromise zone and up to two days when pressured into the danger zone. Each person is different in how long they need to regroup. It is very important to balance the recovery breaks with daily activities to keep the child in optimum level, replenishing spoons as they are spent.

Minimize falling into the compromised zone and most definitely avoid the danger area. In the compromised zone, it will take the child much longer to recover. Even when the child has recovered from the stress it takes a considerable time to regroup and recharge.

You need to match the "regrouping" time to the battery drain level of the child (more time for lower levels). If the child is in the fair to good energy level, short breaks periodically throughout the day may be enough to keep him stable. If he drops into the "poor" energy level, you may have to double or triple the amount of break time you give him to regroup. Each child will be different. If you are unfortunate enough to drop into the danger area, you may be done for the day. It may take hours or even days for the child to regroup. In summary, we need to know where the child is at and balance the demands with rebound time to keep the child calm and organized.

Working with an occupational therapist, trained in sensory processing, can help develop a sensory diet to help calm, organize and keep the child regulated throughout the day. Some activities are very subtle, like chewing gum to stay alert, and others are more intense, like physical gross motor activity to release stress chemicals and re-energize. Some calming activities (rocking to music) may need to be used first to calm before allowing some gross motor activity to re-energize (or vice versa).

I have found that collaboration between parents, teachers, occupational therapists and the child is the best way to collectively identify what breaks should consist of and how long they should be. As the child gets older, we want to empower him to rate his own energy level and gauge when he needs to pull back and re-energize. We want him to be able to appraise how many spoons he has left and how many spoons (how much drain) an upcoming event will cost him. This allows him to judge if he has the reserve needed for the activity, and how much down time he will need to regroup. By the time he is in the later years of high school, it is hoped that he will be at the point of making these ratings and judgments on his own. It will become a major coping skill in adult life.

As can be seen, regulating the nervous system is very dependent on understanding the child's processing abilities and how much mental energy he has, and allowing him to re-energize as his reserve becomes drained. By keeping his fuel gauge in optimum range (ok to good), the child can more effectively regulate his daily demands.

4 Recognize early signs (behavior indicators)

It is very important that we recognize when the child is starting to get taxed and overwhelmed so that we can back off, lower the demands, provide assistance or give him a break to regroup. The early signs often consist of restlessness, more verbal or less verbal than normal, increased stimming, becoming quiet and withdrawn, argumentative and so on. When the child is dropping into the yellow, compromised zone you would expect to start seeing these early signs and provide assistance, use coping skills or back off and give the child a break. Even if the child finishes the activity with support, an immediate break would be warranted to allow him to rebound and regroup.

Once the child falls into the red, danger zone he is becoming overwhelmed and we run the risk that he will completely shut down, become noncompliant and/or act out. We need to immediately stop the demands, reassure the child that he is safe, and then give him time to regroup. It may take hours to rebound if we thoroughly taxed the child. Every support person in the child's life needs to know what the early signs are and how to support the child.

HOW TO KNOW WHEN THE CHILD IS COMPROMISED

Using the colors to identify processing states is common among regulation programs at school: green (good and fair level), yellow (compromised) and red (danger zone). Once you establish these levels, we need to match each level to behavior indicators for judging when the child is at a given level. You must be able to physically read the child; what he looks like and how he behaves at each level. For example, one child may be talkative and engaging in the green (good) zone; quiet, but still participating in the green (fair) zone; withdrawn and resistant in the yellow (poor) zone, and acting out, or shutting down completely in the red (danger) zone. We must know the behavior indicators to help us judge where the child may be at. Figure 3.3 gives an example of listing behavior indicators for the green, yellow and red zones.

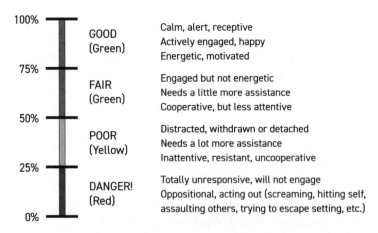

Figure 3.3: Behavior indicators corresponding to each energy level

These behavior indicators should be much more specific for you or your individual child. Usually those who live with or work closely with the child can identify early signs that the child is becoming drained or overwhelmed. Try to identify concrete behavior indicators for when your child is doing well, when he is compromised and when he is overwhelmed (danger zone). Be specific in defining the behaviors you observe; for example, the child is tapping his foot, instead of "agitated" or "nervous;" the child bites his hand, rather than "self-abusive." Many children are very subtle, where they may quietly hum to themselves, suck on a finger, engage in finger tapping or calmly rock. Sometimes self-stimulation like this can occur both when the child is regulated and when he is drained; however, the difference may be in the intensity in which he does the same behavior (rocks, hums or taps faster or in a more intense way). Ask yourself, what does my child look like and how does he act when he is in a good state and when he is compromised? Look for subtle cues like facial expressions, body language, tone or pace of speech, as well as specific behavior (rocking, pacing, refusing to engage.)

Some children do not show strong behavioral cues that they are becoming drained. They may sit quietly in class, look forward and appear normal for them, but be completely drained and close to shutting down. When questioned, they may show a delayed response, appear to be daydreaming or not respond at all. They may hesitate, but comply if pressured. When they pause, hesitate and delay responding, they may be having difficulty processing.

We also must be able to distinguish between happy/excited behaviors and those that are early signs of agitation, so that others do not mistakenly interpret the child as compromised. For example, people may see the child hand-flapping or humming as early signs of being compromised when these behaviors may signal that the child is content or excited. Children can look and react very differently when becoming compromised or overwhelmed. One child may become loud and oppositional when drained and another may become withdrawn and quiet. It is important to understand these behaviors for each child. It is best to include the parents, teachers and the children themselves when developing a list of these behavior indicators.

Over time, it is best to teach the child to recognize his own behavior indicators as well as physical cues (stomach ache, feels dizzy, head hurts, pressure in chest, shoulders very heavy, etc.). The person often does not recognize the behavior cues unless you point them out to him. If the child typically starts to play with his ears when he is becoming drained, then point this out when suggesting that he can take a break. Do not expect the child to necessarily feel that his body is becoming drained. Many autistics have impaired internal feeling for their body systems. They may not feel any different, with no obvious sensations. However, getting them to recognize the behavior indicators can help them to connect how their body is feeling when they are acting a certain way. The better the person becomes at recognizing his own cues, the more competent he can become in recognizing his own early signs and advocate for pulling back and regrouping. The key is that people need to respect the child's voice when he communicates that he is getting drained or overwhelmed and allow him to have a break and regroup.

Do not always assume that the lack of these behavior indicators means the child is doing well. Sometimes they are not showing their obvious indicators. This is where it is important to proactively monitor how draining the day has been, how much activity was expected and if they have had time to regroup. The best way to avoid being compromised is by balancing the day with times to recharge and not placing them in situations that may overwhelm them. It is better to be proactive and avoid draining the child, than waiting to see indicators that they are becoming overwhelmed. Usually, once we see these indicators it means we have expected more than they can give. Stop, take a break and regroup. By doing so, the child learns to trust that those around him understand what his needs are, respect when he is becoming drained and will support him when compromised. He will feel more competent in tackling daily challenges when he is not continually drained and overwhelmed.

5 Monitor processing drain

As we go through the day, we need to be aware of how much mental energy the person has at that moment, how taxing the expectations are that we are placing on him and what his behavior indicators tell us. We continually monitor these three variables to make sure that we are not overly taxing the nervous system (see Figure 3.4).

- How taxing has his day been so far (current energy level)?
- How taxing is the event coming up? What is being asked?
- What are his behavior indicators telling me?
- Does he need a break?

Figure 3.4: Four questions for monitoring energy level

If we truly want to be a working partner with the child, we need to be cognizant of his processing abilities and his current mental energy. At any time during the day we must monitor how taxed the child is or how much mental energy he has left. We must be aware of how draining the day has been and how much reserve he has left. Has he had breaks to regroup or has he moved from one activity to another without a chance to rebound? There are four variables to consider:

- *How taxing has his day been so far; current energy reserve?* Whether you are a teacher or parent you must be aware of how taxing the day has been, what demands he has experienced and how draining the new expectations will be for the child. If the child's day has been filled with frequent activity and expectations, then you can assume that his battery is being drained. Knowing what the child has experienced can help us decide if we can move forward, substitute a milder activity for those with higher demands, or avoid upcoming events. For example, if the child at school has been under greater stress (tasks demands, social expectations, etc.) in the morning, it may be wise to hold him back from the noisy pep assemblage (when students gather before a sports event) in the afternoon.

- *How taxing is the event coming up? What is being asked?* Activities will present a variety of stressful factors (sensory, social, task demands, etc.), some events being more draining than others. Going shopping all afternoon with mom may be more stressful than playing alone in the park. Think ahead before leading the child into an activity that may be over his head. Know what activities are easy for the child and which are more demanding. Match the expectations to the current processing abilities of the child. If the child is working on a full battery (energy level), then he may be able to handle more demanding activities. However, if he is somewhat drained, the activity planned may be too taxing for his compromised nervous system.

- *What do his behavior indicators tell us?* These indicators may be increased stimming, increased motor activity, being more verbal or less verbal, oppositional and so on. Each child is different. We must know the person's early signs of being drained and overwhelmed. Monitoring these behavior indicators can tell us when we need to lessen our demands, pull back on expectations and, if necessary, give a long break. Once into an activity, the behavior indicators tell us when we need to pull back and/or end the activity.

- *Does he need a break?* To avoid overload and maximize energy reserve, we need to insert recovery breaks throughout the day and try to avoid pushing children into situations that overwhelm them. We need to be a working partner with the children if we expect them to perceive us as a trusted guide. Not respecting their processing level will ruin their trust in our guidance. We will become someone to fear and avoid.

6 Balance the day

We need to balance the daily activity with frequent breaks. Try to avoid jumping from one activity to another that will quickly drain and compromise the mental energy. Keeping the child in the green zone (regulated) will make for a more successful and happy day. We also must be aware of the "delayed effect" where the child shuts down and holds it together while at school, or in the community, and then melts down as he gets in the car or arrives home. This is evidence that we need to find a way to reduce the stressors, minimize the drain and give breaks at school to keep from over-taxing the child.

For events that tax the child (high sensory demands, task performance expectations, strong social activity), we need to assume there is added stress and mental drain, requiring more frequent and longer recovery breaks. The battery needs recharging as energy is drained. Know when the child is in the compromised (yellow) zone and when he is hitting the danger (red) zone. In the compromised zone, as the child's energy is draining, his processing skills deteriorate, taking what little energy he has left to hold it together. You need to minimize the demands, build in extra support, and give the child a chance to rebound. Avoid the danger zone at all cost. The child is overwhelmed, very reactive and likely to melt down. At this stage, we need to immediately pull back all demands, let the child escape to a safe area, and allow him an extended period to regroup (sometimes an hour, up to several hours, and in worse cases, a day or two).

STAYING IN THE GREEN ZONE

The two greatest tools for minimizing mental drain are (1) knowing how draining common activities are and balancing them with frequent recovery breaks, and (2) knowing the early signs of stress and behavior indicators that the child is being compromised. Using the first strategy can help keep the child in the optimum range (green, fair to good zones), and understanding the early signs can help keep us out of the compromised and danger zones.

Referring to our battery metaphor, we broke our gauge into easily identified zones: "good" energy level (75% or above), "fair" (50–75%), "poor" (compromised 25–50%), and "danger" (25% or less). The first two are considered green zones, since the child has enough energy reserve to adequately process current demands. The poor/compromised zone (25–50%) is considered the yellow zone, and the danger zone (below 25%) is identified as the red zone. We want to minimize draining the child into the compromised (poor) zone, and at all costs, avoid the danger (red) zone.

This can be accomplished by respecting the child's processing needs, scheduling his activities not to overly drain him, balancing the day with recovery breaks and knowing when the child is compromised. The goal is to keep the child in the green zone where his energy level is adequate for his processing needs—understanding that it is not wise to drain the battery past 50 percent and that more breaks will be needed to regroup and recharge his battery. This means for most of us adults, we must let the child pace what he is doing and how fast he engages, as well as pull back once his battery is compromised.

This often means arranging your day based on how the child is doing, not forcing the child to match what you wish to schedule. The number one stressor for children is adults expecting them to match a desired schedule or pre-assumed expectations, often pressing them past their processing abilities. Although it can be hard to change, parents and teachers usually report that their lives are much easier and more comfortable when they let the child's processing needs pace the day. It takes time and patience to adapt, but parents and teachers can make that adjustment. The number one goal is to work with the child to keep him in the green zone, adequately charged, regulated and receptive.

PUTTING IT ALL TOGETHER: MAKING THE DAY SUCCESSFUL!

When planning the day, we need to take into consideration where the child is at (starting energy reserve), how draining the sequence of daily events will be, and how often the child needs breaks to regroup. We need to try to match the child's schedule to his energy level. For example, let's assume Jamie has had a good night sleep and ate a good breakfast, is not sick or worn out from the events last night, and is starting the day fairly charged and regulated. Realizing that each daily activity will present some mental drain, we need to balance her day with breaks to re-energize, trying to keep an optimum energy level.

Together, Jamie and her mother sit down and plan out her day. They talk about each activity, preview what she can expect and what is expected of her and discuss what tools she can use to help cope with any challenges. Jamie's schedule for the day is as follows:

Morning schedule
Breakfast (low demand)
Shower/Dressing (low demand)
Errands with Mom (high demand)
Break: read/listen to music

Afternoon schedule
Lunch (low demand)
Social group (high demand)
Grocery shopping (high demand)
Break: favorite movie
Dinner: pizza, favorite food

After having a shower, Jamie must go with her mom to run errands. Given that running errands is something that Jamie doesn't enjoy, that presents some novelty and possible sensory problems and that may last a while, we can assume that this activity is going to be draining for her. So, following these errands, her mother schedules in a good recovery, free-time break for Jamie to regroup and re-energize. She likes to rest, read or listen to music.

Following this break, they have lunch together and then it is time for Jamie's social group. Jamie enjoys the social group, but it is taxing since it requires her to regulate socially with several other children and it typically last 45 minutes. There is always a certain degree of novelty and possible sensory issues that can also add to the drain. In addition, Mom knows she will be pressed for time and needs to stop by the grocery store after the social group. Knowing that Jamie may already be drained from the group, Mom understands that this may compromise her. Jamie does not like shopping, as it can be sensorily overwhelming, plus she is already compromised due to the social group. To help Jamie regulate these challenges, Mom lets her listen to her iPod and play on her Gameboy while grocery shopping. They previewed ahead of time that Mom will end the shopping early if Jamie is struggling. As you can see, Mom was running the risk of depleting Jamie's energy level by doing two stressful activities back to back. As soon as they get home, they plan on letting Jamie watch a favorite movie to relax and regroup and have pizza (her favorite) for dinner. To make sure Jamie rebounds well for the next day, there are no other compromising activities for the rest of the night.

A caution for parents and teachers. Even if the events are pleasurable and exciting, they can still be very demanding, challenging the child's processing skills. We often make the mistake of cramming together two or three fun but draining activities, thinking that since the child enjoys the activities they will be less compromising, but they then compromise the child and result in a meltdown. Any long event or back-to-back events will increase the drain on the child's processing level.

In summary, trying to navigate a world that is meant for a processing style different from your own will be taxing for life. However, understanding what those differences are, what your strengths and weaknesses consist of, the challenges you face and how to balance your day can make the processing drain manageable. Knowing how to minimize stress, conserve energy, build in accommodations and avoid overload will help maintain healthy, happy living. Once children grow into adults, they need to have the self-care skills needed to recognize and appraise the processing demands of events they enter, advocate for accommodations they need and learn coping skills for tackling stress and anxiety. In the upcoming chapters, we will tackle these concerns and lay out a path for maximizing an autism-friendly life.

Chapter 4

APPRAISING THE PROCESSING DEMANDS OF ACTIVITIES

In the previous chapter, we discussed the draining nature that daily activities can have for those with autism. We discussed the need to balance their day with recovery breaks, monitor their energy level, watch for early signs of overload and pull back before they get overwhelmed. Recognizing what events challenge the child allows us to provide accommodations to minimize the processing strain, provide greater assistance to support the child and know when these events are too much for him to tackle. Being able to read the child's current level of tolerance, avoid taxing activities and balance the day with recovery breaks allows us to keep the child regulated and maximize a fun, successful day.

In order to balance the day to meet the child's needs, you need to know how to appraise events to determine how challenging they will be for the child (or for yourself if an autistic adult). To help balance the daily demands, you need to know your child's processing abilities and what he can tolerate so that you can predict how demanding an event will be for him. The seven variables in Figure 4.1 present the most common factors to consider when appraising an event. Each one of these factors is a common challenge that adds to the overall stress of activities. Of course, some factors will represent greater stress than others, and will vary from child to child.

For adults on the spectrum, it is also important to be aware of these factors, the role each factor plays and how to assess the overall processing drain of activities you engage in. From there, you can develop strategies to reduce these challenges and appraise your abilities for successfully coping with the demands. In addition, both parents and adult autistics can use this information to determine how much down time (recovery break) will be needed to regroup following the activity.

The more of these stressors an event includes, the more draining the activity will be

Figure 4.1: Seven stressful variables of events

Let's look at each challenge individually.

1. *Sensory challenges.* Sensory demands are often among the greatest challenges that activities present. Is it a loud, chaotic event with a lot of activity, lights and smells? Does the event insult your child's sensory sensitivities? Remember, your child may not be overly sensitive to any specific sense, but the accumulation of multiple stimulation (combination of noise, light, smells, people, activity, etc.) can be overwhelming. If so, this will represent a severe barrier to the event being successful. What accommodations (turn down the noise, wear ear plugs, wear sunglasses to filter out bright lights, etc.) can you build in to lessen the sensory demands?

    For example, grocery stores with all the bright lights, strong smells and noisy activity can be overwhelming. It might be better to shop at a slow time when there are fewer people and less congestion and overall chaos. Also, if the person has more spoons first thing in the morning it might be better to tackle shopping then, before his nervous system is more compromised later in the day. You might want to avoid very stimulating activities like going to the circus altogether. The combined sensory bombardment is often too overwhelming. Always be cognizant of how much sensory stress the event will present. Often when the child starts struggling, it is due to sensory overload.

2. *Degree of interest.* Does the child like or dislike this activity? If he hates the activity and does not want to be there, the event will be more draining for him. We often drag the child from one activity to another because we have errands to run. This can be hard for all children, but especially for those with autism. They struggle keeping their attention and participation in any event that does not hold interest and value for them. Their tolerance for enduring unpleasant activity is much lower. This is not willful opposition, but a brain wiring difference. So, be cognizant that pressuring the child into an event that has no value for him will significantly add to mental drain.

    This does not mean that activities that are highly motivating are not stressful. They often are, especially given the other six factors. We sometimes make the mistake of chaining too many fun events together, thinking that since the child is eager and excited it will not be overwhelming for him. First, any high emotion (e.g. excitement) will produce stress chemicals in the child. We have all experienced the child melting down in the middle of an exciting day and not realized that it is overwhelming for him. Second, the child may become very resistant to leaving an exciting event even if it is becoming overwhelming. He does not recognize that he is becoming overwhelmed and does not want to pull back. Now the additional stress of being pressured to leave is added to the already overwhelming stimulation. We often forget this and become surprised when suddenly, the child is in emotional turmoil. We need to gauge these activities and keep them short to avoid overwhelming the child.

3. *Novelty/Uncertainty.* Novel and unfamiliar events will present more uncertainty for the child. Uncertainty is very anxiety provoking for those on the spectrum, for several reasons. One, novel events require us to do more "thinking" our way through the activity, which will be very draining. Also, not knowing what to expect and what is expected of us requires constant appraising, monitoring and evaluating what we are doing to meet expectations. Therefore, "familiarity" is so inviting for those on the spectrum. It is predictable and understandable and requires minimal thinking.

   To lower the uncertainty, it is important to prepare the child ahead of time by previewing what he can expect to happen and what will be expected of him. Lessen the uncertainty by discussing ahead of time what he can expect to happen, what is expected of him, what challenges may be experienced and how to accommodate for them and what escape route is planned if the event becomes overwhelming. This will reduce the uncertainty, provide the child with a mental map of what will happen and increase his confidence in handling the event. When you preview how to handle challenges that may arise (e.g. temporarily pull back and regroup, go for a walk, back to the car, etc.) the child will be more likely to cooperatively use them. Do not throw unexpected snags or change the game plan in the middle of the activity. You can expect a meltdown.

4. *Degree of control.* The more control the child has over the event, the less draining it will be. The more control he has over what will happen, what he does and when he does it, as well as when he exits the event, the less anxiety he will experience. Having control makes it more predictable and less scary.

   We often go through events telling children what to do, where to go and what is expected, while giving them little control. This will significantly increase the mental and emotional drain. Try to include them in the planning and regulating of the activity, give them choices and allow them to pace what they do and how they do it. Be a working partner with them rather than simply instructing them what to do. Giving children a voice and collaborating with them is one of the best strategies for reducing stress, mental drain and possible meltdowns.

5. *Performance demands.* If the event presents any performance expectations this will add anxiety and mental drain. Putting the child on the spot to perform and doing something that is monitored or judged will be challenging, taxing and emotionally draining. If the event requires them to perform (do something, interact with others, etc.), even if they are capable of meeting expectations, it will significantly increase anxiety and mental drain. Autistic children (and adults) often have high task performance anxiety. Make sure to prepare them by previewing what the expectations are in advance and possibly practice the performance demands ahead of time. This will help prepare the child and lessen anxiety.

   Knowing what to do and being able to do it are two different things. We often tell children what they need to do and assume that they understand what to do and can do it in the moment. Children especially are not good at anticipating what is needed and appraising how well they can do it. Parents and teachers also make this mistake. Even if the child can perform what is expected, being put on the spot, in the heat of the moment, they may freeze or stumble due to anxiety.

When assessing events, look carefully at what is expected of your child, what he will be expected to do and assume that the more demands to perform the greater stress there will be, even if the child is excited about participating. The more performance demands there are, the greater the processing drain.

6. *Social demands.* Trying to relate and socialize with others is very taxing for people on the spectrum. It is very draining just conversing with one other person and can be overwhelming when adding multiple people. Adults tell me that after going to an important social event it may take them a couple of days of doing nothing to recover. The more people and the more expectations to relate, the more taxing it will be. Be aware of this stress when placing children in group play situations hoping they will learn social play skills. Keep the demands for interacting as minimal as possible and provide added support during group activities. Appraising the social rules, reading expectations of others and deciding what and how to engage can be very draining. Pressure to socialize will only result in the child becoming overwhelmed.

   This is also true for the more socially extroverted children. They have strong social interest, but poor social judgement. They will excitedly throw themselves into social situations, begin to struggle and melt down when things go wrong. They jump in with poor ability to appraise what is expected, find themselves in over their heads and panic with uncertainty. For parents, regardless of the social abilities of your child, always assume that the more social participation an activity presents, the more stressful it will be. Even if your child can successfully regulate the activity it will be very draining for him.

7. *Length of time.* Lastly, the length of time in the activity will help determine the extent of mental drain. With all the taxing variables there are in each event, the longer you must regulate these demands the more draining they will be. We often misjudge how long the children can handle events, over-extending their ability to hold it together and further compromising their coping skills. We wait until we see the child struggling before ending the activity. Worse yet, because we do not want to leave the event ourselves, we pressure the child to tolerate more. Although it is important to immediately pull back, or provide needed support when the child is struggling, it is better to end the activity before the child becomes drained. Otherwise, we are taxing the child too much, causing increased anxiety and ending the activities on a sour note. If you think 60 minutes is all the child can handle, keep the event no longer than 45 minutes. Keep it simple, fun and successful!

Given all these factors, the last thing to consider is how many of these factors the activity includes. Obviously, the more challenges the event holds for the child, the more taxing it will be. For example, going shopping will present sensory challenges, a strong degree of uncertainty, very little control and may be too lengthy for the child. If the parent is one who likes to stop and talk to everyone, social demands may add to the stress. Now you have multiple stressors, all together taxing the child. However, if the activity is familiar and predictable, with low sensory challenges and minimal social demands, it may be less draining. Remember, the more of these seven challenges an activity presents, the greater the mental drain and emotional strain the child will experience. It is the same for adult autistics. The better you can appraise upcoming events, the better you can monitor, accommodate for and avoid disastrous experiences.

Planning for success: build in accommodations to lessen demands

Once you appraise the seven demands an activity presents, you can identify accommodations to lower the challenges, especially for major sensitivities that will compromise the child. For example, if the activity is going to be noisy and the child is sensitive to noise, then the child may need to wear ear plugs to help mask the noise. When going to a family gathering, if your child cannot handle people talking to him or hugging him, you may want to notify others ahead of time not to hug or ask him questions. If the child is beginning a new group activity, it may be easier for the child to first sit back and watch from the periphery, and not actively participate, until he feels more comfortable. Or, he may benefit from a peer buddy or adult support to assist with peer interactions. If the activity will include some task performance expectations it might help to practice these expectations ahead of time to prepare the child.

If the child is expected to wait in line, sit quietly or tolerate boredom, you may need to include his favorite electronics to keep him occupied. Sometimes you can modify the event to reduce the processing challenges by inviting fewer people, turning down the noise and lighting, shortening the event, and so on, and other times you can provide added assistance (sunglasses for bright lights, a peer buddy to coach, etc.) to help support the child through the demands.

Figure 4.2 provides a sample worksheet for pre-planning events—what stressors will be present and what accommodations (supports) are needed to reduce the challenges.

This worksheet can be used to appraise and predict what barriers an event will pose and plan for accommodations to lessen the drain. It allows you to evaluate the seven processing demands, assess the potential challenges and design accommodations to support each challenge. Obviously, you cannot do this for every event that occurs. However, for those common and reoccurring events, it is beneficial in lowering the processing demands of daily living.

The first column lists the seven categories of stressors that we just summarized above. It systematically lists the major variables that produce mental and emotional stress. The second column lists specific challenges that may be experienced in these categories. It helps to isolate out and list specifically what challenges could be barriers. The last column has accommodations or modifications that we hope to build in to lessen the effects of the challenges. This column helps us modify or adapt the activity, so the event is less challenging, matching the event to the processing abilities of the child. Although this chart may seem cumbersome at first, you will quickly learn to appraise situations without the need of the chart. It also helps to use this chart with the child, together assessing and identifying barriers and supports. This chart allows the child to visualize how activities can be broken down and made more manageable. The more the child understands the stressors and how to reduce them, the more empowered and confident he becomes.

Event: Classmate's birthday party

Stressors	Specific challenges	Accommodations
Sensory challenges	Noise, chaotic activity	Ear plugs, sitting on the periphery
Degree of interest	Excited but anxious	Fidget tools
Novelty/Uncertainty	High uncertainty, new	Sitting on the periphery, playing on Gameboy, leaving early
Degree of control	Minimal control	
Performance demands	Sitting still and quiet during unwrapping	Previewing ahead of time, watching YouTube videos
Social demands		Checking off list of events
Length of time	High, unpredictable interactions	Having job to hand gifts with Mom's help
	Two hours, too long	Sitting on the periphery
		Arriving late and leaving early
		Escaping as needed

Figure 4.2: Worksheet for appraising stressors and planning accommodations

This example worksheet above includes a birthday party for 12 children at a classmate's house. As you can see, the event presents many challenges, including sensory sensitivities of the noise and hectic activity, extensive uncertainty, minimal control, sitting quietly during the unwrapping of gifts and ongoing social interaction, and it lasts far too long for this child's processing abilities.

Mom calls the friend's mother and gets an idea of the sequence of events that they have planned. This way, Mom can help prepare her son for what to expect and what will be expected of him. There is a lot of uncertainty since this is the first time he has attended a party. Together they watch some YouTube videos of birthday parties, unwrapping gifts and eating birthday cake. They talk about wearing his ear plugs to reduce the noise and sitting off to one side to minimize chaos. Mom also thinks that sitting off to one side will minimize uncertainty, give him some degree of control and reduce the amount of socializing for him. Mom knows he will have problems sitting still while the birthday boy unwraps gifts. She asks the parents ahead of time if her son can be responsible for handing the birthday boy the gifts to unwrap. This gives her son a role that keeps him sitting and staying in one place. Mom knows that staying two hours will be too much for her son. She decides to arrive late and leave early. This shortens the time and avoids the chaotic transition of everyone arriving and leaving.

Taking the time to appraise the processing demands of activities and then build in accommodations to lessen the drain will render activities more fun and successful.

However, since children's energy reserve and processing abilities fluctuate significantly depending on how their day has been going, it is important to match the activity demands to their immediate processing needs. It is better to cancel an activity if it may be too compromising for a child. The same applies to adults on the spectrum. Even though the activity may have been successful in the past, it may be too draining if processing skills are already compromised.

Chapter 5

STRESS AND DISTRESS

In Chapter 2, we briefly reviewed a couple of key neurological differences that present ongoing challenges and chronic stress for those with autism. In this chapter, I will distinguish between "stress" and "distress" so that we can learn how to avoid chronic distress. For the purposes of this discussion, stress occurs any time the demands of the immediate environment tax a person's processing abilities, but do not overwhelm them. The person can meet the demands, but this drains their processing abilities.

We have all been in situations where the demands greatly tax our processing skills. For example, a long, hectic drive in heavy traffic, bad weather or an unfamiliar setting can be taxing to our nervous system. Or a long day at work jumping from one crisis to another, multi-tasking responsibilities and juggling several roles; maybe a day filled with conflicting demands and unexpected snags; waiting to the last minute to write a term paper; hosting a holiday dinner or party.

Life is filled with events that tax our processing skills. We have what it takes to meet the demands, but they extend our abilities and drain our capacities. Any situations that require us to think, problem solve, execute and juggle multi-demands tax our processing skills. Any activity that is novel, presents unexpected snags or requires us to shift gears, change expectations and alter our actions can tax our processing abilities. We all have felt drained, dazed and frazzled when we are stressed. Our thinking, problem solving and emotions begin to weaken. We need a break, with minimal distractions to escape and regroup.

As our processing skills become taxed, they start to break down and deteriorate. When I first started doing lengthy speaking engagements, I was completely exhausted by the end of the presentation. After spending six hours lecturing, leading discussions, answering questions and mingling among numerous strangers, I was completely drained. There was too much focus, thinking and regulating conversations. As exciting and invigorating as it was, it took a lot out of me. My judgement and reasoning, as well as my sensory processing skills, were greatly compromised.

When I left the conference, I stopped at a convenience store in the hotel to get something to snack on while driving home. When entering the shop, my processing skills were compromised, and I had difficulty navigating the store. The background music was loud, a couple of kids were chasing each other through the aisles and a few customers were talking to the clerk. I had trouble integrating all the sights, sounds and smells. When I found the snack aisle, I had difficulty focusing on the items and deciding what to buy. My head hurt, and I was dazed and somewhat disoriented. I immediately realized that I was too overwhelmed to drive safely. My processing was greatly compromised.

I decided to stay and eat dinner at the hotel before driving home to allow my processing skills to regroup. Although the day's presentation went very well, and I thoroughly enjoyed it, the demands created ongoing stress on my nervous system. Any time your current situation demands continual appraising, thinking, contemplating, navigating and socializing, your processing is stressed, taxed and will eventually become drained.

For years, I coached two competitive soccer teams for a travel club. I had to juggle soccer practices four nights a week and multiple games at weekends. Those of you who have coached know that during a game you are constantly and simultaneously monitoring, assessing, problem solving and communicating. You also juggle an array of intense emotions (such as excitement, frustration, elation). At the end of a game I was often exhausted. I warned parents that following the game was not a good time to approach me with questions, suggestions or complaints about their child's playing time because my processing and emotional regulation skills were greatly compromised. I was too emotionally drained and might respond unfavorably. For a coach, competitive game situations can be both cognitively and emotionally draining. Very stressful! Regardless of how enjoyable or successful it is, any event that taxes your cognitive or emotional processing skills is stressful.

In these situations, fortunately I had the skills to meet what was expected, but the demands would completely exhaust my processing skills. To varying degrees, many daily situations can be stressful, and somewhat draining. Luckily for most of us, these events occur sporadically, not continually, with ample periods to pull back and recover. Unless the demands completely overwhelm our processing abilities, we usually bounce back rapidly, with minimal cumulative effects. Problems arise when we face ongoing stress with few opportunities to escape and rebound.

Many studies have shown how continual exposure to ongoing stress has detrimental effects on both our physical and mental health. Sleeping, eating, problem solving, thinking skills and emotional regulation all suffer. Chronic medical problems can develop as well as mental health issues.

Stress itself is not necessarily bad. In manageable forms it helps motivate us, improves productivity and helps us grow and develop. Yes, it taxes our abilities, but in small doses we recover nicely. Stress often means stepping outside our comfort zone, taking on new risks and tackling new learning. Often, stress can be exciting and even welcoming if we feel competent in tackling the challenges and have plenty of chances to rebound. The problem comes when stress is ongoing, continually draining our nervous system, or is too overwhelming. It wears us down, drains our abilities, taxes our immune system, changes our bio-chemistry and leaves us vulnerable to a host of physical and mental problems.

What if this processing drain happens every day, built into the fabric of our daily routine? What if once we step outside the comfort of our own home we walk into a confusing maze of uncertainty, unexpected snags, overwhelming sensations and confusing social expectations, where our brain cannot read the unwritten rules, implicit expectations and invisible context that help others navigate the maze? What if executing normal daily living needs requires extensive mental and physical energy, leaving us drained and exhausted? What if what we normally take for granted requires conscious thought, planning and analyzing?

Consider what it would be like continually guessing at what others are thinking, saying and expecting, often guessing wrongly and stumbling along out of sync with those around us. What if we cannot keep a mental map of what to do and when to do it, often misjudging time, forgetting things and missing appointments? Every simple, daily task takes much more time and mental energy, planning and executing, and our processing abilities are continually taxed and quickly crumble under multiple expectations. Even a good day that goes as planned is exhausting. Such is the life of many on the spectrum.

As is discussed throughout this book, the processing differences of those with autism leave them exposed to ongoing stress, which drains and taxes their nervous systems, further compromising their processing abilities. Our culture is based around how neurotypical people process information. For those with neurological differences, when the processing abilities are different, simply navigating through a typical day can be stressful and taxing. Since their processing abilities do not comfortably match the processing demands of our daily expectations, their nervous system is continually stressed, hyper-sensitive and easily taxed. When processing is not smooth, it has to extend itself, work harder and drain easier. People with processing differences must continually paddle up-river against expectations that are difficult for them. Even when they can successfully navigate the day, it can severely drain them.

Distress

Given that autism's neurological differences make living in our neurotypical world rough, daily living represents ongoing stress to their processing abilities. Stress is draining but manageable, as we will see, with appropriate support and accommodations. What we need to avoid is overwhelming stress, or what we will call "distress," which causes the greatest threat for those on the spectrum.

Whereas stress occurs when the processing demands tax our capabilities, distress occurs when the demands are greater than our processing abilities, and outweigh and overwhelm our skills. When the demands are too fast, too much and too difficult for us to process, they go beyond extending our abilities, to overwhelming our capacities, often flooding us with fear and panic and setting off a rush of stress chemicals (cortisol and adrenaline).

With stress, our processing skill may struggle but we can meet the expectations. Our abilities may have to work harder but can weather the tide, taxed but manageable. For most of us, the stress of our daily living will be draining, but tolerable. When our processing abilities match the demands of the environment, our systems may become strained, but rarely overwhelmed.

With the sensory vulnerabilities, processing challenges and social struggles of those with autism, many of the common daily experiences can be chaotic, confusing and overwhelming. Our neurotypical world presents too much, too fast for the processing skills of many autistics. As discussed earlier, rapidly processing multiple information simultaneously, and adjusting actions according to the ever-changing expectations (to go with the flow, quickly shift gears and reappraise what is needed), is often too overwhelming for those with autism.

When the demands overload the processing skills, stress becomes distress. In distress the brain feels threatened, insecure and anxious. Emotions flood, and panic, fight or flight set in. The brain becomes defensive and reactive to the threatening demands, with emotions overpowering thought and reason. It is when stress turns into distress that damage can occur to our nervous system. People with neurological differences, especially children, are constantly placed in situations where the expectations and demands are much greater than their abilities to effectively manage them. This is when stress turns into distress!

Stress = Abilities can handle the demands, just taxing and draining processing.

Distress = Demands outweigh abilities, overwhelming processing and coping skills.

Let's look at how stress and distress can occur in a child's routine at school. The child's sensory processing challenges may allow him to handle a small classroom with minimal noise, little visual clutter and reduced student activity. However, if this same child is placed in a classroom of 20 active children, the sensory demands may be too overwhelming, overpowering his processing skills and traumatizing his neurology. In the smaller classroom, the day may still be difficult (stressful), but manageable, still draining, but not overwhelming his capacities. However, in the larger room the sensory and social demands simply overpower his abilities, overwhelming his nervous system, creating a rush of distress and anxiety (increased cortisol and adrenaline). While the small setting presents manageable stress, the larger setting creates overwhelming distress.

The same is true for processing speed. A child with delayed processing skills may be able to handle the academic tasks of the classroom if his processing delays are recognized, respected and accommodated—tasks are broken down and presented visually and he is given more time to process. Hence, the academic demands better match his processing skills. However, without these accommodations, the academic demands may require him to process too much, too fast and may overwhelm the student's abilities. Like any system that is pressured to process too much, too fast, his processing system will freeze, shut down or break down if forced to stay in those conditions.

Socially, peer play is very difficult for most children with autism. Pressing them into group play is often too overwhelming. Well-intended parents often want so much for their children to socialize and make friends that they force them into group play situations (playground, clubs, sports, parties, etc.). The sensory overload and social processing demands are often too overwhelming for the children to adequately cope. The demands are too overpowering and above their processing abilities. The lack of social skills, inability to read subtle social cues and difficulty regulating multiple social demands prove too much. Certain distress! It is impossible for the child to cope.

It would be much better to assess what the child can handle and begin with simple, one-on-one interaction around a preferred interest that is much more manageable for the child. This can still be draining (stressful), but manageable. It stretches but does not overwhelm the child's capabilities. We make the mistake of assuming that what is good for age-related neurotypical peers is also good exposure for autistic children. A grave mistake.

This doesn't change as we get older. Daily living presents a host of sensory, social and processing challenges that can overwhelm the nervous system. Adult autistics with strong sensory processing challenges can become overwhelmed by the sensory, social and cognitive demands that we take for granted.

Take the simple act of grocery shopping. Many find the overall sensory demands (bright lights, strong smells, loud noise and confusing activity of others) too overwhelming for their processing abilities. Their ability to think, communicate and navigate the surroundings deteriorates under the distress. There is simply too much, coming too fast. Abilities start to shut down and panic sets in. The person must immediately escape or risk melting down (fight or flight response).

Most autistics who find shopping overwhelming attempt to remediate this distress by making accommodations that will reduce the overload. Some individuals will shop only at small stores during non-busy times. Some large grocery chains will allow people to call in a grocery list and have the items waiting for them when they come in. This way, they can meet at the service desk, pay for the groceries and leave. Others may have the items delivered directly to them. Online ordering has allowed some to avoid the stores altogether. Even though some of these alternatives are still stressful, they are manageable and not distressful (overwhelming).

Without awareness of their sensitivities and vulnerabilities we often unintentionally place children with autism into situations that overwhelm their sensory, social or cognitive abilities. When the expectations outweigh the child's abilities to cope, stress becomes distress (overwhelming). Even worse is when we intentionally pressure exposure because "they have to learn to live in this world," and throw them in to sink or swim, as if they have the abilities but choose not to use them or that throwing them into chaos will teach them to adapt. The brain cannot be forced to process information if it is unable to do so. It becomes overwhelmed, shuts down, or panics and melts down. The brain is in a defensive, reactive, survival mode, not responsive to new learning. It is not a learning opportunity.

What situations result in distress? As discussed in Chapter 2, their neurology makes it difficult for autistics to rapidly process multiple information simultaneously. Their brains can become overwhelmed when placed in situations where multiple information or stimulation is too much for them to process. Examples include going to the circus where there are numerous sensations (noise, lights, smells, activity, etc.), or group social situations with multiple conversations and interactions to process. It is too much for the brain to filter, sort out and process. There are also situations where the information/stimulation is coming in too fast for them to process and respond to. An example would be driving in busy traffic, where the rapid processing and quick, on the fly decision making required is too fast for their processing skills. In these situations, the person may have the abilities to process the demands if they had more time.

Another example is the child who can adequately perform math problems when given more time, but panics when pressured to complete them in half that time; or when the teacher requires children to write out their answers but they struggle with writing.

Their fine motor challenges do not allow them to think and write at the same time. They simply cannot do it. They may know the correct answers, but cannot write them down. With accommodations (giving verbal answers or typing out responses), the child can express what he knows. Simply match the expectations to the child's abilities.

Our social world is another good example. We are continually pressing autistics to make accurate social decisions when they cannot read the hidden social rules, invisible context and the perspectives or intentions of others who are required to make such judgements. When placed in these situations where the information is either too much, too difficult or coming too fast, distress will be inevitable.

Unfortunately, when the brain is placed in situations of distress, the person's thinking, problem solving, communication and coping skills all begin to deteriorate, causing the brain to panic and reactively try to escape (fight or flight). The brain will either begin to shut down (withdraw and shut off processing), actively try to escape or lash out to protect itself. However, since the child has lost all reasoning and coping skills, the means he uses to escape are often disruptive to both himself and others. Unfortunately, in these situations, we blame the child for being oppositional and disruptive, as if they are choosing to be "bad" and can do better if they so desire. This is simply not the case!

Most distress comes from others pressuring the person into situations that overwhelm their processing abilities.

Please remember that. When the person is struggling, most likely it is our overwhelming expectations that are causing the problem. Do not blame the person. It is we who need to:

- lower the expectations (demands)

- provide greater assistance to support the person

- withdraw the demands.

Do not force participation.

Spiraling reaction to distress

The brain doesn't like being placed in situations that overwhelm it. Like all living systems, it will tend to avoid situations that make it insecure, fearful or painful. It immediately imprints the situation that causes the distress and will anxiously react to anticipation of being placed in that situation again. If the child is overwhelmed by being dragged into the grocery store, then the anticipation of going back will make the brain defensive and reactive. The fear of doing something (anticipatory anxiety) can be greater than the actual experience itself. Just the thought or mention of it occurring soon can heighten the brain's fear of the event, rendering the event itself even more distressful.

The more we put these children in overwhelming situations the more anxious and resistant they are entering future situations. Just the thought of it may overwhelm them. The child will attempt to avoid the situation at all cost. Hence, this is another reason not to continually pressure exposure to distressful situations.

This can be especially important for teachers to remember at school. If the child is pressured into activities that overwhelm him too frequently, he can begin to avoid all similar learning situations. If learning is overwhelming and distressful, then anticipatory anxiety will lead the child to resist other learning tasks. Alternatively, the child will associate the person (teacher) with the distress and be fearful of following that person's direction. Distress breeds fear and avoidance, which become a reason to avoid distressing situations at all costs.

Distress from ongoing stress

Stress can be tolerable if it is regulated to avoid overload. The neurological differences will present frequent stress. Stress can become distress if pushed past the point the person can tolerate. Coping skills decrease as the system becomes drained. When the environmental demands outweigh the processing abilities, the nervous system becomes taxed from the system being continually overloaded. Like an engine that is out of tune and running rough, the nervous system must work harder, taxing its capacities and further compromising its processing abilities. A nervous system that is constantly stressed will wear down, become fragile, leaving itself vulnerable to further stress. As many adults with autism testify, this constant drain on the nervous system results in chronic stress and anxiety, leaving it vulnerable to breakdown.

Like all systems that are being taxed, it can handle short-term exposure to stress, but will start to deteriorate under ongoing exposure. The system needs a break to cool down and rebound. What once was manageable stress, with continued exposure, will eventually break down processing and coping skills. The stressors become overwhelming and distressful. What once was manageable "stress" is now becoming "distress."

Exercising is a great example. When we exercise within our tolerance level, stretching but not overwhelming, our physical abilities grow. Stressful, but manageable. However, if we press ourselves to exercise too long, past our tolerance levels, our body starts to break down, risks injury and loses strength and tolerance. We become weaker. This is often called "over-training"—training too hard, damaging the body.

Ongoing exposure also affects our sensory, social and cognitive processing. With continued exposure to stress, our processing abilities become taxed and eventually drained. What was once manageable is now distress. The person's thinking, communication and coping skills deteriorate and can no longer meet the environmental demands. Our expectations may be fine at first, but continued exposure may overwhelm the person. He can handle and keep it together only so long. Over-extending the demands will eventually weaken his abilities, rendering the demands overwhelming and distressful.

If an event is sensory stressful (a lot of noise, odors, bright lights), the child may be able to cope with the demands only for so long, then his sensory tolerance weakens and the event becomes overwhelming.

The same goes for social exposure. Many children with autism have strong social interest, but poor social abilities. You can assume that any social event will be stressful, if not distressful for autistics. Most social events, if they last long enough, can become distressful. Events that seem manageable, even enjoyable at first, can turn to disaster once the processing skills become drained. "What happened? He was having fun!" Even though they wanted to participate and were enjoying it, the longer the exposure, the greater the stress.

Even in manageable situations, stress chemicals accumulate and eventually become distress. The same is true for kids who are addicted to video games, but often get frustrated and disruptive as the stress of navigating the game accumulates the longer they play. It is all very manageable at first, but over-exposure leads to distress.

We must understand what the child can safely tolerate and not tax him too much. Knowing and respecting the child's tolerance is important in not overloading him. I have witnessed too many children pushed into distress by well-intentioned adults pushing their tolerance levels. It is better to end the event early before the child reaches his tolerance level. This keeps learning successful and fun. End on a good note, with the child feeling good about the experience. Waiting until he becomes overwhelmed risks creating negative associations that will develop future avoidance.

In our zeal to teach skills, we often tax children's abilities too much by demanding they stay in learning/therapy sessions too long or jumping from one session to another without breaks to regroup. Learning is taxing. Even if these children have the capabilities, their abilities deteriorate as their processing drains. As we will see in the next chapter, all daily activities present varying degrees of stress. The more we pressure children into ongoing social and task performance demands, the more taxed and drained they become. Even good skills deteriorate under ongoing stress.

In summary, the two primary situations presenting "distress" are when the children are presented with demands that overwhelm their current abilities (sensory overload, social overload, emotional overload, etc.) and when they are faced with continual stress, without a means of escape, that drains and exhausts their processing abilities. In most cases, distress is avoidable. Usually it is the result of others pressing the person into situations that overwhelm them; this is especially true for children who are at the mercy of an overpowering adult. Children have the least ability to advocate for and defend themselves.

Reactions to distress

Behaviorally, each individual is different in how they express distress. When faced with overwhelming demands, the brain must act to protect itself from overload. The person will use his own coping skills to mediate stress, which often consist of self-stimulation (rocking, hand wringing, hand flapping, repetitive vocal noises, etc.) to block out stimulation and regulate anxiety. A child may become giddy, get up and move, and even repeatedly approach the source of stress. The stress chemicals mobilize the child into activity to mediate anxiety.

If the distress continues, the next tendency is to escape the overwhelming situation. If the brain cannot successfully escape the distress, it may begin to shut down. If the build-up of stress chemicals is slow enough, the brain tends to shut down to reduce the amount of stimulation coming in and avoid overload. The brain may shut down sensory channels to minimize stimulation and withdraw from incoming demands. Thinking, judgement, reasoning, communication and coping skills quickly deteriorate. The brain withdraws in attempt to shut out the overwhelming stress.

The person may look dazed, non-communicative and unresponsive. All brain functions deteriorate to pull away and withdraw for protection. Some children will close their eyes, lay their heads down and sometimes even fall asleep. It is very important that we back off all demands (no requests, instructions, questions, prompting, etc.). Move the individual to a quiet area if possible, or lower the sensory demands (reduce lighting, quieten noises, minimize activity around the person, etc.).

Do not try to counsel, reason or engage the child in dialogue. His auditory processing collapses, resulting in difficulty processing language. Your talking only adds to the chaos. Reassure the child that he is safe, give him space and let him withdraw to regroup and rebound.

On the surface, the person may look fine, appear calm and totally shut down if no one is pressing him. This is the child who becomes overwhelmed with the sensory, academic and social demands of the school day, but holds it together by shutting down and checking out. He is calm but dazed and unresponsive to learning, in a withdrawn state to avoid overload. However, the stress chemicals that have accumulated will come out in an emotional charge once the child leaves school. Parents frequently experience this delayed effect. The child is fine at school, but emotional outbursts occur once home or in the car coming home.

If the stress chemicals build too quickly and overpower the brain's ability to cope, it will panic, setting off the fight or flight response. The brain doesn't have time to withdraw and shut down, thus panics in fear and reacts instinctively to escape or fight the source of distress. This is what is commonly called a "meltdown." The child is extremely reactive, may impulsively run to escape, lash out at anyone or anything within reach (that is perceived as a threat) or turn the rage internally by hitting and biting himself or slamming his head and body against objects. This rage serves two purposes: to release the accumulated stress chemicals and to escape the overwhelming stimulation that is overloading the brain. The person has lost all judgement and reasoning abilities and self-control and is reacting instinctively.

We will discuss shutdowns and meltdowns, how to prevent them and ways to best respond to them in more depth in later chapters. The main point here is to underline how draining, exhausting and emotionally damaging distress can be.

Temporary regression

Many children with autism may react to ongoing stress with regression in functional skills. They may regress in all areas of functioning, start having toileting accidents, problems sleeping, eating concerns or lose communication skills. In turn, you can expect to see an increase in the autistic traits. They may show an increase in self-stimulation, ritualistic behavior, social withdrawal or compulsive behavior. Emotionally, they may withdraw or become more reactive, with increased irritability and acting out.

Children in distress will often show regression in the learning objectives they are working on. Usually this regression is temporary, while they are exposed to the ongoing stress, but it can last for some time afterwards, until the nervous system has had time to rebound. It is very important during these times that we recognize that the child is in distress, and that we investigate and identify the source of stress, reduce the demands if possible and assist the child in coping with the stress.

If we do not recognize and reduce the stress, or worse, continually pressure the child into overwhelming distress, the brain can become extremely defensive, insecure and anxious, always apprehensive, hypervigilant and on guard for the next unexpected assault on the nervous system. The child may shut down, become disengaged, passively compliant and emotionally detached. Or, they may react in the opposite way, becoming emotionally reactive, resistant and oppositional (more on this topic in Chapter 9).

If the world is too overwhelming, after years of constant stress and distress, the person may burn out, give up and withdraw into self-isolation. The effects of ongoing stress, distress and overload create conditions very similar to post-traumatic stress disorder.

How to help! Matching environmental demands to processing abilities

At the beginning of the chapter, we defined distress as any situations where the demands and expectations overwhelm the processing skills of the individual. Stress occurs when the demands tax the person's abilities, but distress happens in situations that overwhelm their processing skills. To help maintain both physical and emotional health, it is important that we avoid creating distressful (harmful) situations and reduce overall stressful conditions that continually tax the person's processing abilities. Since stress is inevitable for people on the spectrum, it is important to learn how to reduce and manage stress to avoid overload and eventual burnout.

The two best preventative strategies for avoiding distress are to:

- match demands to processing abilities to avoid overwhelming distress

- keep exposure to stress within tolerable levels.

Match demands to processing abilities

Identifying and understanding the person's processing differences, as well as his vulnerabilities, allows us to build in accommodations to better match the environmental demands to the person's capabilities. For many individuals with autism we need to slow the world down, lower the intensity and make the world more predictable. We must better tailor our expectations, how information is presented and the way we relate with the individual to match their skillsets. Instead of ignoring their neurology, we need to respect their processing differences and make accommodations to match our expectations to their abilities.

Matching expectations and supports to the person's processing differences first starts with identifying the core sensory, cognitive, social and emotional differences that make the world so chaotic and overwhelming. We must identify the individual's unique processing profile (sensitivities, vulnerabilities, strengths), use it to match our expectations, and provide support to bridge these differences. Such strategies usually consist of (1) modifying our expectations or reducing environmental demands to match current abilities, (2) providing assistance to help the individual master the demands, and (3) teaching coping skills for tackling stress.

For example, if the child is sensitive to loud noises, bright lights and strong odors, we need to reduce the intensity of the settings he is in, provide tools (ear plugs, sunglasses, etc.) to help mask the stimulation, provide coping strategies to help manage the stimulation (fidget toys, self-stimulation, relaxation procedures, etc.) and avoid situations that completely overwhelm him (sensory overload). The world will always be taxing in a sensory way for those with autism, but we can learn to make accommodations, better manage sensory intensity and avoid sensory overload. This reduces the brain's defensiveness, hypervigilance and reactivity, allowing it to relax and be receptive to learning. We will discuss this in more detail in Chapter 13.

We also need to identify and understand how the child processes information, how to present information (e.g. break it down, slow it down, make it visual and concrete, preview new learning, etc.) and the best way for the child to communicate what he knows (orally, written, pictorially, demonstrating, etc.). Matching teaching methods to the child's learning style will reduce overload and maximize learning. When the person feels competent in tackling the demands, learning is fun, and the brain is receptive to learning.

The same is true for socializing. There are numerous social processing differences that make relating in the neurotypical world extremely overwhelming (see Chapter 14, Social Challenges). We need to understand the social processing differences (difficulty processing facial expressions and body language, understanding context and social cues, and reading thoughts, perspectives and intentions of others) so we can make ourselves clearer, and can verify and clarify understanding and match our interactions to their relating style. We must realize that interacting is very taxing and not overload their social tolerance. In addition to sensory overload, social challenges present one of the greatest stressors for those on the spectrum. Navigating our social world is exhausting, if not overwhelming for most individuals on the spectrum. Unfortunately, parents and teachers often are not aware of how taxing socializing is, and frequently pressure the children into too much socializing.

As much as we can modify and accommodate for processing differences, there will still be situations that are too overwhelming for the person. These situations need to be identified, respected and avoided at all cost. Stress is inevitable, but most distress (overwhelming situations) is avoidable.

Keep exposure to stress within tolerance levels

The second important strategy for minimizing distress is understanding and respecting the person's tolerance levels to stress. Stress is inevitable, ongoing and manageable if we recognize and respect the person's tolerance level. Keep within those limits, pull away before they become drained (and overwhelmed) and provide frequent breaks to rebound.

When the environmental demands extend and tax the processing abilities, the nervous system becomes drained from being overworked. Like an engine that is out of tune and running rough, the nervous system under stress must work harder, taxing its capacities and further compromising its processing abilities. When continually stressed, the nervous system will wear down, become fragile, leaving itself vulnerable to further stress. As many adults with autism testify, this constant drain on the nervous system results in chronic stress and anxiety, weakening processing abilities, which can lead to the system breaking down or shutting down.

In order to prevent damage due to chronic stress, it is imperative that we:

- identify which events are the most stressful for the child

- understand what the child's tolerance levels are (how long he can be exposed before becoming drained)

- keep exposure within safe limits

- allow the child to pace exposure and intensity of stress.

For someone living in a foreign culture, trying to process, understand and adequately respond to the unique expectations of that culture is very taxing and draining. If I was magically placed on a different planet with a population that processed information and related differently, I would be lost and handicapped because my processing differences would not meet the demands of that environment. That doesn't mean that I would be broken, just different. However, these differences would mean I'd struggle to regulate in a world not designed for me.

I would have to learn to adapt, first by trying to understand how they processed information and how it was different from how I processed. I would have to learn how to interpret their customs, utilize my strengths and accommodate for my weaknesses. I would need to identify what environmental demands did not match my processing abilities and then determine how to either change the demands to match my skills, advocate for accommodations that allowed me to meet expectations and avoid situations that overwhelmed me. This is no different from autistics who are living in a neuro-typical culture.

We need to help the autistic person—who is like the stranger in a strange land— by accepting his processing differences, providing modifications and accommodations to lessen his challenges and striking a balance that does not tax and overwhelm him. Unfortunately, as I describe all the various cognitive, sensory, social and emotional challenges autism presents, it tends to provide a negative and seemingly hopeless picture for those on the spectrum. It doesn't have to be. However, it is important to identify all the different ways in which autism's processing style can present multiple challenges for the individual. Each person has a different profile of strengths and challenges. Once we identify the person's profile of differences, we can build in accommodations to lessen each of these challenges and better match the environmental demands to the processing needs of that person. Notice how I do not mention "changing" the person—not at all. We must recognize, understand and respect the processing differences, essentially accepting the person's neurology (autism), change our expectations, modify demands, build in accommodations and help teach coping skills for dealing with inevitable stress. It is a process of bridging the two cultures so that autistics can be true to their neurology, feel safe and accepted for who they are and receive help in better matching the demands of society to their unique processing abilities.

Summary: managing stress, avoiding distress

1. First and foremost, it is important that people feel safe, accepted and valued as they are, with all their strengths and differences. As we will discuss later, feeling the need to suppress their autism to "fit in" presents ongoing stress which damages their self-identity and self-esteem (see Chapter 15, The Costs of Fitting In).

2. Identify and respect their vulnerabilities and work together to build in accommodations to lessen the stress. Identify when and where the environmental demands outweigh their processing skills and modify the stressors, provide assistance to support them through the demands, and avoid situations that overwhelm their processing abilities (see Chapter 3, Brain Drain from Processing Strain).

3. Be a working partner with the children, giving them a voice, listening to and respecting their sensitivities and advocating for their needs. Even when it is difficult to bridge some differences, it is so comforting to know that those around them understand and validate their concerns and are trying to help them cope with the challenges.

4. Avoid criticizing, denying and humiliating individuals who are struggling with expectations. Assume they are doing the best that they can, given the situation they are in and their ability to deal with the demands. Assume that they would do good if they could, show that you understand and then immediately help to modify the demands to lessen the stress.

5. Be cognizant of how stressful the daily routine is. Balance the day with frequent recovery breaks between taxing activities. Slow down the routine, allow the child to pace his activity load and escape and recover when drained (see Chapter 3, Brain Drain from Processing Strain).

6. Minimize sensory overload by modifying the environment (turning down stimulation), providing adaptive tools (ear plugs, sunglasses, fidget toys, etc.), avoiding overwhelming situations and providing an escape route when activities become overwhelming (see Chapter 13, Sensory Overload).

7. Recognize and respect how stressful socializing is for those with autism. Keep within their comfort zone and respect their tolerance level. Give them plenty of breaks to recover and allow them to pace their social participation (see Chapter 14, Social Challenges).

8. Teach the child coping skills for dealing with stress (pull away, take breaks, deep breathing, positive statements, self-stimulation, preferred activities, etc.). We cannot avoid all stress, so we need to learn strategies for coping with it (see Chapter 7, Coping Skills).

9. Promote sleep and plenty of exercise. Exercise is one of the best preventative strategies for minimizing stress. From an early age, promote daily exercise that will help regulate anxiety and stress.

10. Manage stress but avoid distress. Identify what the child's sensitivities, comfort zones and tolerance levels are and avoid situations that overwhelm him. Monitor closely, look for early signs of distress and have a set plan for escape and rebound (see Chapters 11 and 12 on preventing and responding to shutdowns and melt-downs).

11. Make sure to focus on fostering the person's strengths and preferences. Accommodate for sensitivities and weaknesses, but focus most attention on developing the person's strengths and interests.

12. Remember that for young children, it is important for parents, teachers and others to advocate for the accommodations that they need, but as they get older, teach them to identify and advocate for their own needs, to feel good about their strengths and differences and to feel empowered to advocate for what accommodations they need. Adults need to have good awareness of what stresses them, how to avoid, reduce and manage stress and how to balance their processing needs with the daily demands of their environment.

The bulk of this book will provide positive, proactive strategies for making the world more user friendly for those with autism, remove unrealistic expectations, respect and accommodate their differences and assist them in managing the inevitable stress they will experience.

What adults with autism tell us
Shutdowns

Temporary shutdown and regression can occur during ongoing stress. When the nervous system is totally exhausted from overwhelming sensory and social demands, the individual may withdraw, shut down and isolate for days to weeks at a time, sometimes unable to get out of bed, perform daily self-care or interact with others. Some people lose the ability to speak or advocate for themselves—a complete lack of volition. Most stressful situations seem to be events with strong sensory stimulation (sensory overload) and any social events that require them to interact and relate with others (social overload). Many report that they experience brain fog and extreme fatigue.

Many individuals experience this overload on a continual basis, especially at work and school, leaving them exhausted and unable to function for the rest of the day and every weekend; they often miss school or take time off from work because they are incapacitated. Most autistic adults report that they need time alone for extended periods, either to nap or engage in a relaxing activity, in order to regroup and rebound. Shutdowns will occur at any age when the daily or situational demands become too stressful and completely drain the brain's processing.

Burnout

Whereas shutdowns are a reaction to immediate stress and distress, "burnout" occurs over years of constant exposure to stress and distress, much of which occurs from continually trying to fit in and "be normal" (neurotypical). Autistics can have years of being pressured into situations that overwhelm them, overload their capacities and deny their neurology; they suppress their autism and "fake it to make it." We will look at this in more depth in Chapter 15. Burnout can occur not just from social stress but also from years of accumulated distress due to being pressured into situations that overwhelm their processing abilities. Society has not respected their autistic differences, there has been constant pressure to fit a neurotypical mode, and they have been taught to deny and suppress their own differences. Continually working against their neurology, they find that their processing system eventually breaks down and collapses.

What does burnout consist of? One of the most important but less talked about vulnerabilities in autism is executive dysfunction. The executive functions are our abilities to focus, think, problem solve, organize, motivate and execute a plan of action. These brain functions essentially help orchestrate most of the brain's abilities into coordinated action to meet daily demands. We will discuss each one of these functions in more detail in Chapter 16, Living with Executive Dysfunction.

Executive functioning weaknesses are very challenging for many with autism. The constant stress of processing and navigating our neurotypical world is continually draining and exhausting. Ongoing taxing of the executive functions wears them down, making them weaker and even more vulnerable to stress. Like a battery that is continually drained, it becomes weaker and more difficult to recharge, eventually wearing out or taking longer and longer to rebound.

What does burnout look like? You can expect to see erosion in all areas of executive function, with the child becoming unable to concentrate, think, organize, motivate and execute a course of action. Basically, there is a shutting down of all functions that are essential to meeting daily needs.

Adult autistics report that when burnout sets in, they are unable to bring themselves to face most of the expectations of daily living. Some cannot go to work, interact with others, take care of the household needs and meet their own self-care needs. In many instances, they need to pull away and isolate themselves from the external world, avoid any demands and allow their brains to withdraw, regroup and heal over time. Their sensory systems become very sensitive or they shut down. They cannot handle family obligations or cope with socializing outside the home. They simply lose the ability to "act," minimizing any and all functions requiring organized action.

As we will discuss in the next chapter, most self-reports of burnout come from years of trying to be "normal," denying their autism and suppressing their natural tendencies, from navigating a world that is too fast, too chaotic and too overwhelming for them. They have been pretending to be someone they are not, losing sight of who they are and what they need, trying to meet unrealistic social expectations and forcing themselves to fit a mode that goes against their basic neurology.

This can start in childhood, where they learn early on that they are broken, unworthy and need to deny their autism, suppress their basic tendencies and mask their differences. Usually by late teens, after many years of masking their autism, pretending to be normal and exposing themselves to ongoing stress, the toll it takes on their self-identity, self-esteem and organizational skills leaves them feeling broken, helpless and angry.

High anxiety and depression are common co-occurring disorders for many young adults with autism. As we will see in later chapters, this state of constant stress, anxiety and denial does not have to be the outcome. Once we understand, accept and respect the person's neurology and differences, allow them to appreciate and feel good for who they are, stop trying to force them to be something they are not, modify our expectations to match their differences and provide accommodations to make our world easier to navigate, chronic stress, shutdowns and burnout are less likely.

In summary, since stress is inevitable for autistics living in our culture, we can help them experience less distress, minimize overload and avoid burnout. First, we need to understand, accept and respect people with autism, allow them to feel valued and accepted for who they are and not who we would like them to be. All individuals need to feel worthy for who they are and not feel the need to pretend to be someone different. The masking, pretending and denying their own unique qualities creates a massive drain on their neurology, eventually resulting in poor self-esteem, anxiety, depression and burnout.

Next, acceptance paired with true support to help match societal demands to their processing abilities will significantly lower stress. We need to listen to adult autistics who speak out and share how they experience the world and what they need to live peacefully. For years, their voices have been ignored and devalued, as if we know more about them than they know about themselves. As a society, we need to work with them to design a world that is more autism friendly, to identify accommodations and proactive supports that highlight their strengths while minimizing their weaknesses. We need to work with the individual to create a profile of supports that will minimize distress and overload, modify expectations to match processing abilities, make the world more user friendly and maximize their processing strengths and talents.

The rest of this book will focus on building proactive strategies for supporting people with autism to actualize their potential—not trying to change them or devalue, deny or suppress their autistic needs but accepting them for who they are and embracing their unique differences. This will improve the lives of all of us.

Chapter 6

AUTISM AND ANXIETY

Anxiety is the most frequently co-occurring disorder for those diagnosed with autism. This is understandable given the fragile nature of their nervous systems and the amount of stress experienced from trying to navigate a confusing, often unforgiving world. Studies have shown that autistics, even in a resting state, have much higher levels of stress chemicals (cortisol and adrenalin) than neurotypical individuals. This general state of anxiety and apprehension leaves their nervous system on "high alert" and in a defensive state. Unfortunately, individuals with high anxiety are hyper-sensitive to any uncertainty, exaggerate simple stressors and overreact to minor snags. They also have greater incidents of obsessive/compulsive behavior, rigid/fixated adherence to routines and rituals, oppositional resistance and a host of other avoidance behaviors due to chronic anxiety that permeates their day. Anxiety is often the underlying physical trigger to strong emotional reactions and behavior outbursts.

The core cognitive, sensory, social and emotional processing differences leave the nervous system constantly paddling upstream against a rapid current that continually drains and overwhelms their capacities. This ongoing strain weakens the nervous system and leaves it anxious and on guard to any cognitive, sensory, social or physical challenges that may quickly crop up. Since the world is often chaotic and confusing for those with autism, being continually on high alert taxes the nervous system, leaving it more anxious and insecure. In the green book, *The Autism Discussion Page on Anxiety, Behavior, School, and Parenting Strategies* (Nason 2014b), I summarized the following seven forms of anxiety common to many on the spectrum:

1. *Sensory/informational overload:* becomes anxious in settings that present strong sensory stimulation, or informational processing demands.

2. *Anxiety of uncertainty:* fear of anything new or unfamiliar, seeks sameness; can be controlling and oppositional.

3. *Social anxiety:* interacting with others, participating in social events; fear of not knowing how to act or fit in. The stronger the desire to fit in, the greater the anxiety.

4. *Performance anxiety:* perfectionism and fear of being wrong; asking them questions or prompting to do something. Any demand for performance puts them "on the spot."

5. *Anticipatory anxiety:* becomes anxious over an upcoming event; either good or bad. May ruminate/perseverate on an upcoming event.

6. *Diffused generalized anxiety:* an ongoing, pervasive anxiety that is not connected to a specific event. Seems to always be apprehensive and insecure.

7. *Separation anxiety:* has to be next to mom or dad at all times. Becomes highly anxious when parent leaves their sight.

The level of anxiety and how debilitating it is will vary extensively from one person to another but will most likely occur in one or more of the above categories. (pp.43–44)

Sensory issues and anxiety

Most people on the spectrum have varying degrees of sensory processing problems. These can range from over- or under-sensitivities, distorted or fragmented sensations, poor integration of all the senses, and sensory modulation issues. For those on the spectrum, sensory processing is not a fine-tuned integrated system like it is for many neurotypical people. As neurotypical people, we have a well-refined filtering system that allows our brains to filter out (turn down) most of the background sensations (noise, sights, touch, etc.) that are not important for us to attend to and focus on the information we wish to take in. For many on the spectrum, their filter is not working well and lets in too much, often competing, stimulation, distracting the person from attending or overwhelming them. Their brains are bombarded with stimulation that can overwhelm and set off a panic, fight or flight response.

Many people are hyper-sensitive to noise and light, being able to pick up the slightest sensations and frequencies that others would never register. Common sensations that we often ignore are impossible for them to avoid. Many daily sensations (e.g. the phone ringing, smell of dinner cooking, sunshine flickering through the blinds) can be far more intense than they are for us. Artificial smells like perfume can be nauseating, and common fabrics can feel painful. Where our brains quickly habituate (become used to) ongoing stimulation, for many on the spectrum these sensations always demand attention.

To make matters worse, their sensory processing is poorly wired and can short-circuit moment to moment. One minute their hearing may be smooth and synchronized, and the next moment the hearing is interrupted with loud squeaks and squeals or jumbled up in fragmented noises, or the auditory channel might cut out altogether with no warning. The same disruption can occur in one or all senses. The brain is always hyper-alert and on guard for any sensory assault that is unexpected and sends them into panic. It must sort out all the competing background noise to focus on what it needs to. This can be very draining and overwhelming.

The brain is in defensive mode and can react with panic to any unexpected changes. The more sensory noise (multiple sensations) a setting has, the more likely the brain will become drained and overwhelmed. When the brain starts to become overwhelmed, it becomes anxious and processing deteriorates. Unfortunately, sensations become further heightened, setting off a panic response. Often the person loses his ability to talk or think. The body sensations can be painful and the flood of anxiety unbearable. All sensations and emotions become jumbled together into a negative spiral. Since the person can never really predict when this sensory bombardment might happen, the brain is always on high alert and defensive for the next unexpected sensory assault.

What can we do to help?

Although the underlying problems with this neuro-connectivity have not yet been adequately identified, there are ways that we can help the brain relax and feel more secure.

1. *Reduce sensory bombardment.* Turn down the sensory noise in the setting (make it more sensory friendly), especially background noise, bright lighting and artificial smells. For teachers, try to avoid wearing strong perfumes, deodorants, hairsprays and other odors that may irritate the child. Try to minimize bright lights and, if possible, avoid fluorescent lighting which hums and flickers for the sensitive child. Try to avoid large, reflecting jewelry that may distract the child when he is listening to you. Also, be aware that clothing with bright, colorful patterns can also be distracting. Classrooms often have every inch of their walls filled with bright, colorful posters, pictures, schedules and other visual clutter, which can be distracting and overwhelming. Smells from the markers, paints and pastes can be nauseating. When you combine all these sensory issues in a classroom, the child is often overwhelmed and must shut down to minimize sensory overload. Have an occupational therapist at school assess the classroom for possible adaptations that will reduce sensory overload.

    Parents also must be cognizant of their child's sensory vulnerabilities and be ready to modify the sensory challenges in settings the child frequently enters. Some events like the circus, sports day and concerts may have to be avoided entirely. Get used to trying to predetermine what sensory challenges any upcoming events will present so that accommodations can be built in.

    Adults with autism must learn to assess situations for sensory challenges, and advocate for modifications in settings such as work and school to match their vulnerabilities. Adults must be aware of how drained they are and how much stimulation they can handle as to avoid sensory overload. Where they go, what they do and how long they stay in an event need to be continually monitored.

2. *Mask what you cannot modify.* When the intensity of stimulation cannot be reduced, find ways to mask the sensations. Sunglasses, brimmed hats/caps, ear plugs, MP3 players and electronic distractors (games, phones, etc.) can be used to help mask the ongoing stimulus overload. Provide the child with a sensory toolbox that includes the items he may need if stimulation becomes too intense.

3. *Develop coping skills for managing anxiety.* Design coping skills to keep the child's nervous system calm and organized during times when the environment poses challenges for him. In the classroom, or at work, these may include fidget items, air

cushions, standing tables, ball chairs, bungy cords on legs of chairs, so the child can feed himself forms of ongoing calming and organizing stimulation to stay regulated.

Most autistics use self-stimulation to keep themselves calm and organized. As the environment starts to become overwhelming, the person may engage in sensory stimulation (humming, rocking, hand flapping, etc.) to help block out external stimulation and regulate the anxiety. Self-stimulation should not be stopped or discouraged since it is a coping skill to keep the child from becoming overwhelmed. Sometimes the person can block out stimulation by distracting the brain's attention with a favorite book or electronic game.

4. *Provide a sensory diet.* Occupational therapists, trained in sensory processing challenges, can evaluate and design a sensory diet that can help regulate the nervous system and reduce sensory sensitivities. Sensory challenges can be wide ranging in type, scope and intensity (hyper-/hypo-sensitivities, fragmented senses, modulation issues, problems integrating senses, etc.). Sensory processing therapy and a well-designed sensory diet (a schedule of sensory activities throughout the day) can be instrumental in minimizing these sensory challenges.

5. *Pay attention to the activity level in settings.* The more people, unpredictable activity and variety of noise, smells and visual changes, the greater drain on the brain. Look for ways to reduce the overall activity and stimulation, especially where the person is expected to actively participate. Turn it down and shorten the amount of time expected to stay in that setting. Make the setting less stimulating and more predictable. Preview what is going to happen and what can be expected and brainstorm how to keep activity to manageable levels. The person may need to sit off to the side and avoid some of the activity to manage the chaos. Being a passive observer is less draining than being an active participant where the expectations are higher. The expectation to actively participate greatly increases anxiety, further augmenting the person's sensory sensitivities.

6. *Make stimulation predictable and controllable.* The more unexpected and unpredictable the stimulation, the more anxiety it creates. If the person knows what is coming and what to expect, his brain is better prepared to tolerate it. Also, if the person has some control over the intensity of the stimulation (can turn it down or turn it off) then his brain is less anxious. Sometimes this is a very effective tool that we often forget to use.

7. *Have predetermined escape routes.* Always give the person a means of escaping the stimulation (setting, event) when it becomes too overwhelming. This may consist of going temporarily to a quieter area to rebound and regroup, going for a walk, going back to the car for a few minutes or completely leaving the event. For parents and teachers, discuss this escape plan with the child ahead of time so he feels secure that he can exit and avoid being overwhelmed. This drastically lowers anxiety as he knows in advance that he can immediately escape when needed.

8. *Support during overload.* Always provide acceptance and support when the child becomes overwhelmed. Show that you understand he is overwhelmed, back off all demands, lower the stimulation and try to get the child to a calm setting to rebound. Minimize your talking and try not to touch the child unless he welcomes it. Keep everyone safe and reassure the child that he is safe with you. Remember, minimize your interaction to avoid adding to the chaos. Respect that the person is overwhelmed, cannot process and reason well and possibly is unable to communicate. Simply reassure and let him know you are close by if he needs you. Avoid scolding, pressuring or punishing the child for being overwhelmed. He needs to feel safe and accepted, not criticized. He feels embarrassed, guilty and horrible enough from how he reacted. Criticizing him only increases his anxiety and promotes further overload.

9. *Consider medication.* Others have reported that certain medications (e.g. selective serotonin reuptake inhibitors) can have a damping effect on sensory sensitivities. Some parents have reported that neuro-feedback helps to organize the brain better to handle sensory overload (although this has not been proven).

In summary, we need to identify the person's sensory challenges, adapt the environment as best as possible, provide tools for filtering the stimulation (e.g. sunglasses) and teach coping strategies for escaping situations that overwhelm the nervous system. These sensory issues can be managed but most likely will continue to present challenges for the person's lifespan.

As with social challenges, sensory issues are complex and varied (sensitivities, perceptual distortions, fragmented perception, synesthesia, sensory defensiveness, etc.) A comprehensive discussion of sensory challenges and strategies to support them is well beyond the scope of this book. The blue book, *The Autism Discussion Page on the Core Challenges of Autism* (Nason 2014a), looks in-depth at sensory challenges and ways to modify, accommodate and help treat sensory challenges.

Fear of uncertainty

People with autism continually find the world very confusing and unpredictable. There are so many unwritten social rules, vague meanings, invisible contexts and underlying expectations, which they cannot read; their daily world is often confusing, unpredictable and difficult to navigate. They have difficulty connecting the dots to define the overall picture of what to expect and what is expected of them. They are frequently left guessing at what is expected, and often guess wrongly. Even when they misstep, they frequently do not know how and why, leaving them confused, hurt and angry. This can lead to a strong fear of uncertainty, and avoidance of many daily activities. This anxiety will often lead to a strong desire for sameness and rigid adherence to familiar rituals and routines. In addition, these children will need to control all activity around them to make the world predictable and safe.

The best way to help reduce this anxiety is to make the world more understandable and predictable for them. The more we can make the vague and invisible more concrete and visible, the more predictable the world will be for them. In the green book, *The Autism Discussion Page on Anxiety, Behavior, School, and Parenting Strategies* (Nason 2014b), I list the following guidelines for making the world more understandable:

1. *Build structure to daily routine.* The more structured, and predictable, the daily routine is, the less uncertainty there is for the child. When he knows what is coming up next, and how his day is going to flow, there is less anxiety. Unfortunately, many of our family lives are very scattered and disorganized, with little predictable pattern. This can cause severe anxiety for children on the spectrum. Using visual strategies like written checklists and picture schedules can help make the world clearer and more predictable.

2. *Routine "habits" use less energy.* Keeping familiar routines throughout the day also allows us to skate smoothly through our daily activities without much cognitive effort. We do many routine activities without thinking about them. We do these daily tasks out of habit with little effort. This frees up our mental energy for more important matters. The same is true for our children on the spectrum. Since the world is often chaotic and confusing, keeping the simple routines consistent allows children to know what to expect and to perform them with minimal effort. This helps reduce both uncertainty and cognitive effort. This adds predictability and certainty to their world.

3. *Define a path to provide a map.* Many kids on the spectrum go through the day essentially lost, with little concrete direction to lead the way. Since they cannot read the invisible rules that help us make sense of our world, they often do not know what to expect, or why they are doing what they are doing. Like all of us, if we do not know how to navigate in our immediate world, we feel anxious. If possible, provide visual (pictures, written) schedules so the kids can *see* what is coming up next and what they are doing. This provides predictable order to their day. These visual schedules provide a nice detailed path to follow. It lets them know what to expect and when to expect it. This alone can drastically reduce anxiety.

4. *Prepare by previewing!* We often lead children into tremendous, unnecessary uncertainty by not previewing for them what is going to happen. We move them from one event to another without much preparation. To reduce uncertainty, it is important that we prepare the children before entering events, by previewing (1) what they can expect, (2) what is expected of them, (3) how long they are going to last, and (4) what is coming up next (afterwards). Lay things out very concretely so the child clearly understands what he is walking into. This helps to reduce uncertainty and anxiety.

5. *Describe as you do.* Since the children often do not understand the invisible rules, and especially the thoughts, feelings and perspectives of others, it is

important for us to describe what is happening (what they don't see) as they go through the day. Increase understanding by filling in the empty holes from what the children miss. Give the information to complete the understanding. If we are walking through a foreign country, it helps to be with someone who can describe and interpret for us. So, when doing something together, verbally describe what is happening, why it is happening, and highlight what is invisible. Be the social interpreter for your child.

6. *Don't assume; clarify and verify.* We often assume; since we know, they know! Or, since the child is bright and verbal, he automatically understands. This is a bad mistake to make. The child often cannot read the invisible assumptions we make. To maximize understanding, first clarify very literally what to expect, and then verify that he understands.

7. *Ease transitions; prepare for change.* For many children, their brains have difficulty rapidly shifting gears. They do much better if we make out a concrete schedule for what is coming up, and they have warnings or reminders when one activity is ending and another is beginning, especially if the current activity is a strongly preferred activity. To ease transition difficulties, try to (1) ensure that the child always knows what will be coming up next (watch TV, then bath), and (2) give the child five-, three- and one-minute reminders that the current activity is going to end (watching TV), and he will move to the next activity (bath). A few minutes before the end of the TV show, say, "Johnny, remember once the movie ends we are taking your bath." This way the brain is prepared for what is coming up next, and the reminders help bridge the transition.

8. *Have a plan B.* When a favorite activity is canceled abruptly, the child can explode. For activities, especially preferred activities, that may be cancelled or postponed, discuss a plan B. "If it rains and we cannot go swimming, then we can go bowling instead." This way the child already is prepared for what may happen, and what will happen instead. This works well for common activities that are dependent on weather or factors that you cannot control.

In summary, help reduce anxiety by decreasing the "uncertainty" in your child's life. Provide predictability to his daily routines, use visual strategies (schedules, directions, etc.) to define a path to follow, prepare him by previewing ahead of time, provide information as you go, verify that he understands, and prepare him for change! It may exhaust you, but it will drastically reduce his anxiety.

In all seriousness, these strategies may seem overwhelming at first. Do not try and learn these strategies all at once. Use one strategy at a time until it becomes "habit" for you (remember, habits use little energy, because you do them without thinking about it). Build in one strategy at a time until the whole sequence you do out of habit, without thinking about it! Don't worry, when you forget, your child's reactions will remind you. (pp.49–51)

Social anxiety

If it is difficult for autistic people to read the thoughts, feelings, perspectives and intentions of others, to rapidly grasp the social context that gives meaning to an inter-action and to understand the invisible social rules that govern the relating, our social world naturally creates strong anxiety. What comes intuitively for neurotypical people must be consciously "figured out," moment to moment, by those on the spectrum. It is very draining and taxing for the brain to have to continually analyze social context.

All this happens when trying to relate with one person at a time. Add several others to the conversation and the brain becomes overwhelmed. Remember to keep interaction with the autistic person short and simple and minimize social burnout. Do not force ongoing social engagement, especially if it involves placing social demands on the person. When relating with autistics, always communicate acceptance and understanding, since this is a grueling process for those on the spectrum.

There are many difficulties that lead to strong social anxiety:

- Difficulty understanding vague, abstract language, multiple meanings, innuendos and subtle inferences.

- Inability to read the thoughts, feelings and perspectives of others.

- Difficulty processing the social context (the social rules and expectations common to that event) that gives meaning to the interaction. What is appropriate in one social context is not in another.

- Problems reading what is meant and what is expected. The person is left guessing from confusing information.

- Inability to read between the lines to grasp the underlying meaning.

- Difficulty regulating the fast paced, back and forth, give and take of dynamic interaction.

- Inability to process the multiple interactions in group conversations.

- Problems with interpreting mean that actions are often out of sync with expec-tations, resulting in negative feedback from others.

- Being misinterpreted as rude, indifferent or oppositional.

- Being taken advantage of, made fun of and bullied.

- Burnout from trying to copy others and masking their true selves.

- Strong anxiety and depression from years of trying to fit in but constantly failing.

The inability to adequately work out what to expect and what is expected of them makes social situations confusing, unpredictable and highly anxiety provoking. They are never sure if they are getting it right or understanding why they got it wrong. They stumble around a social world without a map to navigate.

How to reduce social anxiety

1. Use literal, concrete language, spelling out exactly what you mean. Avoid vague language, multiple meanings, innuendoes and sarcasm. It is difficult communicating with neurotypicals because communication is full of ambiguous, hidden and vague meanings.

2. Do not assume understanding, clarify what you mean and then verify that the child understands. Also, make sure you clearly understand what he is saying. We often misinterpret what autistics mean. Verify that you understand.

3. Slow down the pace of interacting, giving the child time to process and formulate what to say. Depending on his auditory processing skills, it may take him longer to grasp what is said, interpret what is meant and then formulate what to say back.

4. If communication breaks down, assume misunderstanding either on your part or his, not indifference, rudeness or opposition.

5. Try to avoid large group activities that will require regulating interactions with multiple people simultaneously. These are very draining, if not impossible.

6. Help the child to connect the dots to understand the context he is entering. Point out underlying social rules and expectations, help interpret the perspectives and intentions of others and paint a picture of what he is experiencing. Neurotypicals usually have a social map (understanding what to expect, what is expected of them and how to act accordingly) to guide them through the social event. Autistics do not have this social map to navigate situations. Be a social interpreter for your child.

7. Give the child a preview of what to expect and what is expected of him before entering social situations. Help provide a mental map to increase understanding, lessen the confusion and guide actions.

8. If possible, scope out the social event/activity ahead of time, getting a picture of what will occur, what challenges to anticipate and how to modify, support and coach the child through it. Try to avoid throwing the child blindly into social events with little preparation or guidance.

9. If possible, role-play and practice any social scripts, social rules and common expectations that may make the activity smoother.

10. Build in accommodations to lessen anxiety, keeping the activity short and providing an escape once situations become overwhelming.

11. Provide awareness training for peers in how to relate with the child, how to interpret his behavior and how to help him feel safe and accepted. Often the negative reactions peers give are due to not understanding the child's differences, what they mean and how to bridge them. Peers need to meet the child halfway,

learning as much about how to relate with him as the child learns how to relate with them. Learning needs to occur both ways.

12. Always respect the child's tolerance and ability to regulate a social event. Allow him to feel safe communicating that he is scared, overwhelmed or needs help to process. It is better to end an event early on a successful note than stretch it to the point at which the child becomes overly taxed and overwhelmed.

There are many supports and strategies for helping children with autism navigate the social world, learn relating skills and help others learn to better relate with their autistic loved ones. A discussion about these strategies is well beyond the scope of this book. For those who want a comprehensive review of social strategies, I refer you to the blue book, *The Autism Discussion Page on the Core Challenges of Autism* (Nason 2014a), where I provide a thorough discussion on how to make the social world more understandable, predictable and easier to navigate.

Respect the child's social interest

Parents and loved ones often strive for their children to be social, extrovert and enjoy relating with others. However, social interest varies extensively between autistics. Many have strong social interest and desire to fit in socially. What they yearn for is so difficult to obtain. They copy and imitate others, often losing their own identity in the process. They continually stumble because they are out of sync with others and never grasp the back and forth, fluid dance of relating with others. They keep beating their heads against the wall trying and failing to relate in our social world. By the time they are teens they are filled with social anxiety, trying to fit in but never "getting it." Often, the stronger the social interest and desire to fit in, the greater the social anxiety.

There are others on the spectrum who have little desire to socially connect, to relate for the simple sake of relating. It's not that they do not like people, they just do not enjoy emotionally relating with others. They simply do not have the desire or the need. They are more interested in the beauty of objects, facts, details, patterns, how things work, art, music and the sensory beauty of auditory and visual patterns. These individuals learn how to co-exist with others, navigate their social world to meet their needs, but do not welcome ongoing social activities. These individuals often have less social anxiety. Since they are not attracted to socializing, they do not feel the emotional pains of not fitting in. Their frustrations will come more from others trying to make them more social, but not from a deep urge to be emotionally connected with others. They are not as anxious trying to navigate and fit in with the social and emotional nuances of relating. In my experience, these individuals are more comfortable with their autism and can use their perceptual and intellectual strengths and interests to develop fulfilling lives. They are usually more comfortable with their differences because they do not yearn to be like us socially and emotionally. Try not to force them to be social butterflies, and respect their preferences.

Ongoing negative social feedback

Trying to navigate our world of invisible social rules, vague language, hidden meanings, nonverbal communication, different perspectives and hidden intentions often leaves people with autism guessing, misreading and out of sync with others. The uncertainty of our unpredictable society naturally breeds anxiety. What is expected, what do they mean, how do I act, what do I say? It's taxing, draining and anxiety provoking.

In addition to this uncertainty, another great source of anxiety is the ongoing negative feedback from others around them. Growing up autistic often means years of invalidating feedback. When your behavior never matches the expectations of others, you get labeled as lazy, stupid, rude, oppositional and defiant. When people do not understand your processing differences, they interpret your behavior as intentional and just needing a good spanking and firm discipline. These children are constantly eliciting negative, invalidating feedback from others, no matter how hard they try. Others often refuse to understand the processing differences and try to scold, shame and command these children, and demand they change. The children learn early on that their autistic differences are bad, broken and need to be suppressed.

From the earliest years, our emphasis is often on teaching the child to be as normal (neurotypical) as possible. We constantly try to change them, demanding that they suppress their autism, stop self-stimulation and odd behaviors; we dictate what they should value, force them to be more social and continually make them pretend to be normal. This has several negative impacts for the person. It teaches them that they lack value, are broken and need to change. It creates poor self-esteem, weak self-identities, pervasive anxiety and depression.

Suppressing behaviors like self-stimulation and odd fixations requires conscious effort, is cognitively draining and emotionally taxing. Self-stimulation is a natural mechanism for reducing anxiety and regulating the nervous system. Many ritualistic, repetitive behaviors are very adaptive coping mechanisms. Attempts at suppressing these behaviors will only increase anxiety and eventually lead to autism burnout. Trying to change behavior without understanding and respecting the functions it serves is very dangerous.

Constantly trying to teach and train the child to talk, think and act normally provides ongoing invalidating feedback that they are broken, not worthy and need to change. This can lead to the child striving to suppress his autism, pretending to be normal and faking who he is.

The more we try to "change" these children, the more we risk invalidating them; communicating that they are inadequate or unworthy. Unfortunately, in our early zest to change children, often our support only communicates to them that they are broken, not worthy as they are, and need to be something they are not. We must be careful when dragging them from one therapy to another, designing ongoing behavior plans and shaping them to appear less autistic that we are not invalidating their self-identity and communicating that they are broken. This ongoing negative feedback leads to pervasive anxiety and depression.

We need to back up and first communicate unconditional love, then accept and respect them for who they are and provide loving support for them to grow. This is no different from any other child. It does not mean that we avoid teaching them life skills and social niceties so they can regulate in our society, or that we don't treat co-occurring disorders like anxiety, sensory disorders and medical issues. But when we are constantly trying to get them to suppress self-stimulation and we ignore processing differences and teach them to be something they are not, we risk invalidating their very existence, setting up a path to future turmoil and despair.

Task performance anxiety

Task performance anxiety occurs whenever a request, command, demand or instructional prompt is placed on an individual. Whenever we are put on the spot to act or perform, it can create anxiety for most people, especially if others are watching, evaluating and judging our performance. However, for many kids on the spectrum, this anxiety is much stronger and more debilitating. They freeze when pressured to perform, which is often misinterpreted as being noncompliant and oppositional, and sometimes they act out if pressured to comply. There are many factors that lead to this anxiety:

1. Difficulty understanding what is being asked of them, resulting in lack of confidence in how to act. Also, often people do not communicate expectations in ways they understand.

2. Delayed processing, where they need to act before adequately processing what is expected. They may say "no" because they know that the others want an immediate response. It is safer to not respond than to act without adequately understanding.

3. Difficulty appraising what is needed and how to do it.

4. Strong fear of failure from not meeting expectations in the past.

5. Poor ability to judge what is "good enough," resulting in a strong need to be perfect (perfectionism). They will often refuse to try rather than look incompetent.

6. Their strong social anxiety about relating with others makes them very nervous when others place demands on them. Most task performance demands are initiated through interaction, which they may struggle with from the start. Meeting the expectations of others makes them feel very vulnerable.

7. Poor hand—eye coordination, auditory processing difficulties and motor planning problems can inhibit adequate performance, creating strong anxiety when asked to perform.

Task performance anxiety can range from moderate to very severe, resulting in children who resist even the simplest of demands (pathological demand avoidance). Here we will discuss general task performance anxiety and ways to minimize the anxiety. We will talk more about extreme demand avoidance in Chapter 8, Anxiety and Rigidity.

Imperative versus declarative language

The greatest tool for reducing performance anxiety is changing the way you communicate with the child—the language you use. Steven Gutstein, the founder of Relationship Development Intervention (RDI), a therapy approach for people with autism, has been instrumental in introducing us to the impact that our language has on increasing engagement with children on the spectrum. RDI highlights the important differences between "imperative" language and "declarative" language.

Imperative language refers to statements that are meant to elicit a specific response. These include questions, directives, instructions, prompts and other instructing/questioning type statements. They are meant to direct and control. Imperative language tends to put people on the spot, requires a specific answer and causes social and performance anxiety in people who have difficulty interacting. Direct communication to act requires the person to rapidly process what is said, what is meant and how to respond, and to execute the response. This rapid processing and executing creates strong anxiety in many with autism. What did they say? What did they mean? How do I respond? Will it be right? This all creates anxiety, further inhibiting their already compromised communication.

For the child:

- Questions, prompts, directives put me on the spot!

- I feel pressured: "What do they want?" "What do I say?" "What do I do?"

- My initial response is to "*freeze!*"

- Then I want to escape or avoid the situation!

- When put on the spot, I get anxious and find it hard to respond.

- If they keep pressuring me, I get overwhelmed!

- If they invite me to speak, but do not force it, I can relax, find the right words and enjoy talking.

We want so badly for our children to speak that we try and pull it out of them. We are constantly prompting, questioning and almost demanding that they speak. The anxiety that this creates can inhibit the child from speaking or makes "speaking" an undesirable action that is demanded of him.

Imperatives are for directing, rather than relating. They put people on the spot and often make them anxious. When others are primarily imperative, we wish to avoid them. People with autism feel anxious about relating to begin with. When we primarily use questions, prompting and directing, they wish to escape the interaction. Imperative language tends to push them away, rather than invite relating. They shut down or become oppositional.

Alternatively, declarative language refers to statements not meant to produce a specific response, not prompting, directing or instructing. These include sharing your thoughts, feelings and ideas about something, describing events, sharing experiences and knowledge, and other interaction that is non-demanding. This language is non-directive and does not produce performance anxiety. For example, "I like the color blue" does not require a response but often invites the other to also share, "I also like the color blue," or, "I like red!" This is communication to relate and share, not to direct or instruct. Steven Gutstein found that autistic children feel freer to relate when we are not questioning, prompting or directing them to.

When two neurotypical people are relating, their interactions tend to be 80 percent declarative language and 20 percent imperative language. They spend more time sharing thoughts, feelings and perspectives than questioning, prompting and directing. However, when neurotypical people and autistics are relating, it tends to be the opposite—about 80 percent imperative and 20 percent declarative. Since the person with autism tends to struggle with conversing, the neurotypical person will try and maintain the interaction by asking more questions to draw a response from the person. Unfortunately, the very language that we are using to help the autistic person interact is the language that makes him the most anxious. Instead of making it easier to relate, we are making it harder.

Most of my experience with this is with children on the spectrum. I watch children freeze up with anxiety when adults question and prompt them but relax when I rephrase everything in declarative language. When I relate with declarative language, share experiences instead of prompting and directing, the children relax and relate a lot easier. Unfortunately, most teaching techniques commonly used with children on the spectrum are imperative. We prompt, direct, instruct and pressure performance. This approach not only inhibits learning, it also discourages relating. Learn to rephrase what you say to share your thoughts, feelings and perspectives, rather than prompting and directing. You will see the child begin to open, relate and share more. Learn to rephrase your imperative statements (directives) as declarative (non-directive) statements and watch your child respond. Figure 6.1 provides examples of the different types of declarative statements. Figure 6.2 gives examples of how to rephrase imperatives as declarative statements.

Using declarative language allows people to respond in their own way. It promotes relating by sharing thoughts, feelings and perspectives. Also, it takes the pressure off, reduces anxiety and makes communicating easier. Sharing your thoughts, feelings and experiences promotes perspective taking. This allows the child to relax and pattern his own thoughts and responses.

Types of declaratives	Examples
• Describing	I like...
• Commenting	I wonder if...
• Sharing how you think or feel	You seem...
• Giving your perspective	That makes me...
• Narrative statements	That's a pretty...
• Reflecting	We are...
• Announcements	You look...
• Praise, encouragment	That was fun!
	I predict that...
	I bet you are good at...
	We rock!
	Yuk! This is awful

Figure 6.1: Types and examples of declarative statements

Imperatives (questions, prompts and directives)	*Declaratives* (comments, descriptions, thoughts and feelings)
What color is your shirt?	What a pretty shirt. I love red!
What is the matter?	Boy, you look upset
Eat your food	I love mash potatoes
John, help me pick up…	I could use help with this
STOP YELLING!	Wow! That hurts my ears!
Do it this way	This might work
Can you do this?	I bet you are good at this
	Declaratives invite rather than direct. Declaratives foster relating (experience sharing). Imperatives are instrumental.

Figure 6.2: Rephrasing imperatives as declarative statements

A different way of teaching: we-do (mentoring) versus instructional teaching

With children on the spectrum, we usually teach by prompting, instructing, questioning, prodding and directing—what is called instructional teaching. We try to force it on them and pull it out of them. We question, prompt and direct them to "do it." Direct prompting puts them on the spot, demands a response from them, often causing them to freeze and shut down. It makes learning no fun, and something to avoid. Usually the adult is instructing (prompting) the child to do something. The child is put on the spot to perform (usually by himself with the instructor watching). If the child is right, he is reinforced with praise (and other rewards). If the response is incorrect, the instructor corrects and prompts the child to do it again. This is called instructional teaching, which is a common way to teach, especially with autistic children. Figure 6.3 is a visual diagram of the process of instructional teaching.

TRADITIONAL APPROACH TO TEACHING

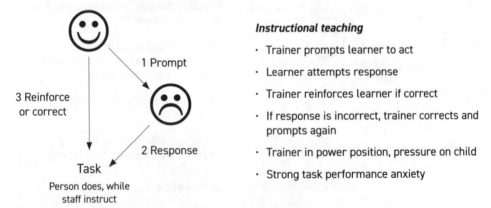

Instructional teaching

- Trainer prompts learner to act
- Learner attempts response
- Trainer reinforces learner if correct
- If response is incorrect, trainer corrects and prompts again
- Trainer in power position, pressure on child
- Strong task performance anxiety

Figure 6.3: Visual diagram of instructional teaching

Performance anxiety is very strong for children on the spectrum. Placing them in a position to perform puts them on the spot. This often produces extreme anxiety that weakens their ability to think and perform. They can freeze and stumble their way through it, which taxes their cognitive abilities. The normal teaching procedures of the instructor prompting/directing a specific response from the student can be very upsetting for a child with autism. Even if the child knows the right answer, just being prompted to respond will make it hard for him to produce it. His fragile processing skills fall apart under pressure to respond. The child may stay with it for a while, but his coping skills eventually cave in. With repeated "task performance" learning, the child eventually learns to dread such therapy and teaching.

One of the best ways to lower task performance anxiety is by using we-do teaching (mentoring). The teacher becomes a mentor, rather than an instructor. Instead of using the instructional model, with we-do teaching the mentor and learner do the task together. The learner engages with the mentor, who models, guides and frames the learning to take the pressure off the performance and maximize success by doing it together, bridging the learning. They are working partners, sharing the experience, and the lack of pressure minimizes anxiety. Figure 6.4 provides a visual diagram of we-do teaching. In RDI, Steven Gutstein calls this apprenticeship teaching, with the learner being an apprentice to a more experienced teacher.

Whether you are a parent, teacher or therapist, mentoring by doing with the learner and sharing the experience together will reduce task performance anxiety, create a stronger bond between mentor and learner and make learning more fun!

What if the child doesn't feel comfortable engaging in we-do activities? When the child is very anxious and doesn't trust to follow the lead of the mentor, it is best to start off by engaging in the child's preferred activities together, letting the child lead, allowing him to mentor the adult. The child controls the activity, feels more competent and learns to share the engagement. Once the child feels more comfortable engaging with the mentor, then the mentor can begin to build in variations and provide greater guidance, thus teaching the child to feel able to follow the lead of the mentor. You must first be a working partner with the child to be viewed as a trusted guide.

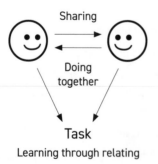

- Learning through "doing with," working alongside a mentor

- "Doing it together," sharing the experience, while the mentor models, guides and scaffolds the learning

- Takes the pressure off, minimizing anxiety

- Through guided participation, the mentor tranfers skills to the learner

Figure 6.4: Visual diagram of we-do teaching

Anxiety around choices

One of the tools often used for promoting a sense of empowerment (control) is by giving children choices. However, choices can create great anxiety for some children on the spectrum. Below is how one mother described her experiences on our Facebook page. This is followed by a list of factors creating anxiety that we included in response.

> Since you are discussing anxiety, I thought I would tell you about an issue with anxiety that was difficult to figure out. With anxiety, parents are often told to offer a choice as a way of reducing anxiety and gain compliance. With my son, we discovered that choices were causing anxiety. My husband and I examined our son's behavior and discovered by giving my son choices to go out to eat and offering different places or going to the movies or the mall, he became anxious. He didn't want to be left behind but he wasn't sure that he wanted to go either. What made it worse was throwing in incentives for going. The choice was easier if he loved the place. It was difficult to figure out because choice is often used as a solution. Now we don't offer a choice, we get ready to go and my son will ask, "Where are you going?" When we tell him he will grab his shoes and either come with us or stay with his older siblings. We have been able to reduce the meltdowns that way.

AUTISM DISCUSSION PAGE

Giving choices can create great anxiety for children as well as adults. Listed below are some of the factors that produce anxiety during decision making.

1. Choices require evaluating options to find out which one is the best option. Depending on the cognitive development of the person, they may not have the skills for comparing, contrasting and appraising the options. They will freeze with anxiety. Suggestion: Helping the child make a list of the pros and cons can be useful. Also, doing it together takes the heat (responsibility) off the child.

2. Worrying about picking the one best option causes anxiety. The more options, the greater the anxiety. Suggestion: Start with only two choices, one a preferred option and the other a "yucky" (obviously negative) option. This makes the decision obvious. Then gradually move toward a preferred choice and neutral choice and then two preferred choices.

3. Task performance anxiety can come from making the decision by themselves. Children often get anxious when put on the spot. The responsibility is too much. Suggestion: At first, make it a shared experience where the two of you weight the pros and cons and make the decision together. That way the responsibility is shared and not solely on the child. Over time, fade out your assistance.

4. The idea of picking one option and losing the other can also create anxiety. Many kids over-exaggerate the temporary effects of making the decision, as if the decision binds them forever. Suggestions: Start by giving choices of which one (of two options) they have or do first. Then they can have or do the second option next (or the next day or time offered). This way they are not losing anything, just choosing the sequence in which to do them. The child doesn't feel that he is permanently giving something up and that decisions are temporary.

5. Like all anxiety, the children often over-exaggerate the importance of the decision, worrying about making the wrong decision. Suggestion: Help the child appraise (1) why the is choice important, (2) what the consequences are of not choosing a given option, (3) how likely it is that the consequence will happen, and (4) how horrible it would be if the consequence (loss of option) did happen. Try to help him reason that the decision really isn't that important. Then make the decision an experiment to test the hypothesis that the child had predicted (did the perceived consequence happen, was it that bad?).

6. Some children freak out because they see their decision as being permanent and they are stuck with the choice forever. Help them see that most choices are only temporary, that some decisions can be changed, and the same choices will be offered again the next day, week and so on.

7. Some choices are not good or bad, simply options where there is no "one right choice." This is often hard for their rigid, black and white thinking. Suggestions: This can usually be helped by evaluating pros and cons and by giving this choice frequently, so the child has future chances to try the other options.

For all the above, it is important that you give frequent options, starting with two-choice decisions, throughout the day. Make the two choices very concrete and obvious—for example, the choice of which two shirts to wear, which of two snacks to have, which two videos to watch, the order of what to do first. Throughout the day, provide frequent exposure to making choices. Sometimes it helps to keep a journal of decisions to review at the end of the day (how hard the decisions were, if the choice was a good one, did the world collapse when he didn't choose the other option, how he tackled the decisions). This helps the child see how the world is filled with options and choices, how making choices can be fun and that choosing one thing over another does not result in a big catastrophe.

General strategies to reduce anxiety

In addition to tackling the specific types of anxiety, it is important to build in general strategies for lessening overall anxiety. Although anxiety is inherent in the autism condition, it can be managed effectively. First and foremost, the person needs to eventually learn how to appraise his environment, accommodate for his vulnerabilities, create a balance between adapting to the world around him and being true to his autism (respecting his neurology), understand his own comfort zones and limitations and stay within them.

For children, these factors need to be built in proactively by the adults supporting them, but as the children grow into late teens and early adulthood, they need to take over these strategies for themselves. They need to understand their own autism, neurological differences, strengths and weaknesses. They also need to be able to appraise their settings to advocate for the accommodations they will need to better match the environmental demands to their neurology (accommodate for sensory sensitivities, minimize social overload, create safe settings, etc.). They will have to realize what they need to maintain a healthy balance of struggling to fit in while maintaining their autistic self-identity, to respect and appreciate their own differences and learn to co-exist in a world that is not easy to navigate. In the early years, parents and teachers are responsible for identifying and supporting these vulnerabilities, respecting their neurological differences, fostering their strengths and preferences and helping them grow healthy attitudes about their own autism.

In the book, *The Autism Discussion Page on Anxiety, Behavior, School, and Parenting Strategies* (Nason 2014b) I outline some guidelines for organizing the nervous system to minimize anxiety. They are worth repeating here:

1. *Diet.* A healthy diet is very important for keeping the nervous system strong and organized. Many children have food intolerances, allergies, and problems processing proteins, sugars, preservatives, food colorings, and other additives. Also, with food sensitivities and selective preferences, it is often hard to provide a well-nourished diet. Although difficult to follow, establishing a good diet is important to organizing the nervous system.

2. *Sleep and rest.* Sleep is also important for regulating the nervous system and keeping the immune system effective. Approximately 50 percent of children on the spectrum have sleeping problems. If the nervous system is not getting enough sleep, it will be taxed and easily fatigued, slowing down an already impaired processing system. The more drained the nervous system, the higher the anxiety. Also, because their nervous systems are often stressed throughout the day, it is important for people on the spectrum to take frequent breaks to rebound and re-energize. Their nervous systems drain quickly and need frequent breaks to reorganize. As their nervous system becomes taxed, their processing abilities deteriorate very quickly.

3. *Exercise and physical activity.* Movement and physical exertion are paramount to an organized nervous system. This increases serotonin, which organizes the chemistry in the nervous system, keeping it calm, alert, and organized. Exercise will also help stabilize sleep and mood. It releases stress chemicals from the nervous system, reduces anxiety, decreases depression and increases mood. Physical exertion is one of the best tools for regulating anxiety.

4. *Sensory diet.* Provide a sensory diet that calms, alerts, and organizes the nervous system. Providing the nervous system with calming stimulation (deep pressure, calming music, slow rocking, etc.) can sooth the nervous system when over-aroused. In turn, when the nervous system is under-aroused and sluggish,

providing it with alerting stimulation (swinging, physical exertion, chewy and spicy foods, fast-paced music, fidget items, etc.) can keep it alert and organized. Keeping the nervous system at an optimal level of arousal is important to lessening anxiety. Sensory diets are usually assessed and designed by occupational therapists. Sensory input can be used throughout the day as a proactive strategy to keep the nervous system calm and organized and then sensory techniques can be used during stressful events to minimize the anxiety they elicit. For a more thorough discussion of sensory issues and using sensory diets please refer to our blue book, *The Autism Discussion Page on the Core Challenges of Autism* (Nason 2014a).

5. *Favorite activities.* Engaging in preferred activities can be very organizing to the nervous system. Focusing attention on reading, music, walking, or other favorite activities increases dopamine (the feel-good chemical) which helps calm and organize the nervous system.

6. *Relaxation techniques.* Using techniques such as meditation, mindfulness, yoga, muscle/tension exercises and imagery a couple of times a day can help release stress chemicals and help the nervous system rebound.

7. *Back to nature.* Being outside in the country, away from the artificial lights, noises, and sounds, can help the nervous system rebound. Also, the sensory patterns of nature (sights, sounds, and smells) can be very organizing to the nervous system. Living in the country often gives people on the spectrum a chance to escape the overwhelming artificial stimulation of the city.

8. *Self-stimulation.* Self-stimulation, in the form of repetitive, rhythmic sensory patterns can help regulate the nervous system by alerting it when under-aroused or calming it when overwhelmed. It also can be used to block out other uncomfortable stimulation. Whether it be movement, vocal or tactile patterns, the controlled rhythmic patterns calm and organize. Self-stimulation is often the go-to tool for managing anxiety. It is portable, always available and very effective in regulating anxiety—a very important tool for those on the spectrum.

9. *Supplements.* Supplements can be used to change the chemistry of the nervous system and reduce anxiety. They are frequently used to increase digestion, strengthen a weak immune system, or directly reduce anxiety. The discussion of supplements is way beyond the scope of this book, but they have been used successfully for combating some of the co-occurring medical conditions creating anxiety.

10. *Medications.* Lastly, but only in combinations with above strategies, medications can be given to reduce severe, chronic anxiety. Anti-anxiety medication and anti-depressants have been used effectively with many on the spectrum. These, however, often come with side effects and should be used with caution. Use medications only as a last resort after first trying the above strategies. Whenever possible, medications should be used as a temporary tool until more proactive

strategies can be supplemented. Medication use with children is often overused and mostly approached with caution; close monitoring and frequent consultation with a physician is required. Children with autism vary in their reactions to medications. Many are very sensitive to medications and can have strong negative reactions. Results are very individualized, so trials on several medications may be needed to find the right medication for you or your child. Try to avoid using multiple medications simultaneously and discontinue medication if you do not see a significant positive effect. (pp.45–47)

Each person has a different nervous system, with different neurological vulnerabilities. Combining as many of the above strategies as possible will help organize and strengthen the nervous system, leaving it less vulnerable to anxiety. All these strategies will help manage anxiety, but not eliminate it. Anxiety is part of the autism condition but can be managed to be less debilitating.

Cognitive behavior therapy for anxiety

All of the above recommendations are proactive strategies for stabilizing the nervous system to minimize anxiety. Next, we need to look at the underlying cognition (thinking) behind much anxiety. In the green book, *The Autism Discussion Page on Anxiety, Behavior, School, and Parenting Strategies* (Nason 2014b), I discuss how anxiety is often the result of how we cognitively appraise situations.

ANXIETY: DISTORTION OF TWO APPRAISALS

Cognitively, anxiety is often the result of two distorted appraisals. How we perceive the potential threat of an event, and how competent we feel in tackling it, will determine how anxiety provoking it is for us. How we cognitively appraise our experiences drastically affects how anxiety provoking they are for us.

Anxiety is often caused by two faulty cognitive distortions: (1) appraising the situation as being a greater threat than it truly is, and (2) appraising yourself as being incapable of handling it. The further these two appraisals are apart, the greater the anxiety. If we exaggerate the actual threat of the situation, and underestimate our ability to tackle it, our anxiety will increase. When we have poor ability to read situations to accurately appraise the event, we tend to exaggerate the potential threat. In addition, if we experience a lot of failure, we tend to feel inadequate in tackling new challenges. Thus, many children on the spectrum experience strong anxiety entering task performance and new situations. For example: a young child is scared to pet the neighbor's small dog for fear of being bitten. Even though the dog is harmless and unlikely to bite, the child over-exaggerates the chances of the dog biting and feels helpless in protecting himself if the dog does bite.

COGNITIVE TREATMENT STRATEGIES

To lessen anxiety, cognitive strategies often work on teaching people to more realistically appraise the actual threat of the event and their abilities to handle the situation. Let's look at both appraisals separately:

1. *Appraising the threat of a situation.*

    i.   Learn to change your appraisal to the "feared" event by having repeated, non-punishing exposure to the situation, so that you learn that it is not as threatening as you thought.

    ii. Learn to "question and test out" your faulty belief systems that over-exaggerate the threat. There are two questions to explore: what is the probability of the threat occurring in the first place (how likely is the threat going to happen), and how bad would it be if the threat occurred (realistically looking at what it would be like if the worse result happened)? This strategy can only be used effectively for those with strong cognitive abilities. For those with more severe impairments, the primary strategy is to use the repeated, non-punishing exposure. For example, if the child who fears the neighbor's small dog has strong cognitive abilities, he could watch the dog with others and learn that the dog is not likely to bite, and if the dog does attempt to bite, it will not be that bad. This, paired with giving the child repeated exposure to successfully petting the dog, will show the child he can do it without being anxious. If the child is more cognitively impaired, we could only use the step to lessen the anxiety: providing frequent attempts at petting the dog without being bitten.

2. *Appraising ability to handle the situation.* At this step, we want to teach the child that he can effectively master the situation. We would teach the child what to do, so that he can successfully tackle the event. We would provide repeated practice, so he feels more competent in tackling the challenge. With the example of the dog, we could teach the child how to approach the dog slowly, and pet the dog gently, so the dog does not get scared and bite. This way the child learns to feel more competent tackling the potential threat of the challenge.

By pairing the two steps together, the person learns to more realistically evaluate the situation as less threatening, plus learns that he is more competent in dealing with the challenge than he first thought. You can lessen anxiety by effectively dealing with step 1 or 2, or both together.

Since anxiety will always be present for many people on the spectrum, part of lessening anxiety is to learn to feel competent in the face of it. Many children on the spectrum panic as soon as they begin to feel a little anxious. They can learn to not panic when feeling a little anxiety, by experiencing repeated exposure of successfully mastering the situations causing the anxiety. To do this, the child needs to learn how to cope with anxiety, and then feel himself successfully mastering their anxiety with these coping skills.

In these situations, the child must feel the anxiety, so that he can feel himself master it with the coping skill. So, tackling of anxiety consists of two parts: (1) providing gradual exposure to the stressful event, while (2) using coping skills to master the anxiety being felt. That way the person learns that these situations are not as threatening as first thought, and that he is more competent in dealing with them. The more practice he gets in tackling stressful situations, the more accurate he becomes in appraising the actual threat of situations, as well as his ability to handle the stress. He then becomes confident in tackling future situations. (pp.56–58)

The importance of a "constant"

We all have constants (little objects, pieces of clothing, a favorite photo, power card, self-stimulation, consistent routine, rituals or certain arrangements) that allow us to feel safe in the mist of uncertainty. Some may call these security blankets; they are items (little trinkets, plush animals, doll, etc.), rituals and activities that help us feel secure. For many people with autism, because of sensory issues, social anxiety and information processing differences, our social world is filled with uncertainty, insecurity and anxiety. For them, sensory overload, social confusion and unexpected change present an ongoing world of uncertainty and unpredictability.

For those on the spectrum, having a "constant" provides them with just that—a constant in the sea of uncertainty, something that is familiar, predictable and anchors them in the here and now. They help keep sameness and familiarity in the sea of flux around them. Often this is something that is small and portable that they can always carry. It can frequently help them from becoming overwhelmed because they can use the constant to anchor them and distract themselves by focusing on something they feel secure with. As with self-stimulation used to regulate their nervous system, constants are used to provide a stable source of support in the face of uncertainty.

Constants can make it easier to face the social anxiety, help children feel more secure when entering social situations, allow them something to cling to when anxiety hits, and to stay connected to themselves during the uncertainty. Many people on the spectrum have used the phrase "losing oneself" in the mist of uncertainty and social anxiety. This can be a frightening experience when they no longer feel anchored or connected to the world around them. Latching onto their "constant" can keep them anchored, secure and help them navigate the uncertainty.

It is important to be aware of our loved one's constants—their security blankets—and make sure we do not strip them of these anchors. These constants are the glue that can hold the children (and adults) together during times of stress and social anxiety. Just because these items (little toy, super power figure, Pokémon, etc.) may seem unusual or childish to many of us, they can be lifelines for those on the spectrum. In turn, we want to create as many constants as possible to help make the chaotic and confusing world more manageable for them.

In summary, anxiety is inherent in autism and stems from autistic people trying to regulate in a world that is not design for them. Identifying what types and sources of anxiety they experience can allow us to build in supports for reducing these anxieties. In addition, combining the general strategies for minimizing overall anxiety with teaching coping skills for tackling anxiety will make the anxiety more manageable. We look more closely at teaching coping skills in the next chapter.

Chapter 7

COPING SKILLS

As we have discussed, stress is inevitable and anxiety very common for people with autism. Because of their neurological differences, the strain and drain on their nervous system leaves them vulnerable to distress and anxiety. Even with well-intended accommodations and proactive strategies, stress will be inevitable all their lives. Those with high anxiety, even with support, will experience some degree of ongoing anxiety for most of their lives. Although inevitable, the stress and anxiety are manageable with accommodations to lower the unnecessary demands, self-care strategies (diet, sleep, exercise, relaxation, etc.) for strengthening the nervous system and coping skills for tackling anxiety when it happens. As the children become older, it is imperative that they learn coping skills for managing both stress and anxiety. They must become empowered to identify and avoid distress, as well as advocate for the accommodations they will need, and learn coping skills to manage and minimize both stress and anxiety.

Throughout this book, we have discussed preventative strategies for minimizing both stress and anxiety, but each person will need a set of coping skills for managing stress, anxiety and emotional overload as they occur. Being prepared for stress with a toolbox of concrete strategies helps the person feel more competent in managing stressful situations when they arise. Since people with autism will face situations of uncertainty, confusion and anxiety throughout their lives, it is important that they feel secure in knowing what to do to manage them.

Not knowing what to do leaves people with autism fearful in moments of stress. They feel incapable of tackling the challenge, and anxious, insecure and panicky in anticipation of the stress. Once they begin feeling anxious, their fear turns into panic, augmenting the stress and anxiety and leaving them more vulnerable to ongoing anxiety. They become on guard, and hyper-alert for any situations of uncertainty. Anxiety stifles them, the anticipation of stress freezes them and they go to great lengths to avoid any and all situations that could be stressful.

Knowing what to do and feeling competent doing it when stressed can minimize anxiety and increase confidence in tackling stressful situations. When you feel prepared and competent facing stress, you do not panic when feeling anxious. You face it, manage it and work your way through it. You learn not to fear it, realize it is temporary and that you can manage it. The more prepared you are with concrete scripts for what to do, the more competent you feel tackling stress.

We discussed the importance of preparing for upcoming events by previewing what the child can expect to happen and what is expected of him. In addition, we always include what barriers (challenges) may occur and how to handle them. These include techniques for managing stress during the event and ways to escape if the stress becomes overwhelming. Knowing that the child has tools to help tackle the anxiety, and knowing that he can pull back and escape if stress becomes overwhelming, will drastically reduce the anxiety of feeling helpless. The more stressful situations the child successfully masters, the more confident he feels tackling future occurrences. The more competent he feels tackling stressful events, the less anxious he feels facing them. He is less likely to panic and overreact.

Calming strategies

One of the best coping skills is learning techniques for calming the nervous system as it becomes stressed. Keeping themselves calm and regulated when exposed to stressful situations can help autistics work their way through them. Listed below are some common techniques used for regulating both stress and anxiety.

1. *Self-stimulation.* Probably the most potent and frequently used methods by autistics is self-stimulation. As discussed earlier, stimming is any repetitive, rhythmic sensory stimulation (usually movement or vocalizations) used to block out overwhelming stimulation, release stress chemicals and regulate arousal (anxiety). This may include rocking, hand flapping or hand wringing, pacing, bouncing, humming, chanting, singing or repetitive vocal noises. Self-stimulation is often used to calm when excited or stressed, manage anxiety and regulate sensory input. Many seek movement when anxious (rocking, flapping, pacing, tapping, etc.). It is important to recognize that increased stimming often means the person is stressed and we need to allow the individual to use the stimming to regulate themselves. In the blue book, *The Autism Discussion Page on the Core Challenges of Autism* (Nason 2014a), I discuss at length the importance of self-stimulation, how to encourage it and how and when to discourage disruptive self-stimulation (e.g. self-injury, infringing on rights of others, etc.) by substituting more adaptive self-stimulation. Always be respectful that self-stimulation will be needed to regulate anxiety.

   Many autistics keep small sensory objects to fidget with to help alleviate anxiety during stressful events. These include items to manipulate with their fingers (twist, twirl, flick and rub), items to squeeze with their hands, and pieces of fabric to rub between their fingers. Chewing is also a great form of self-stimulation for regulating anxiety. Children will often use chewery (rubber necklaces) or rubber items to chew on when stressed, which can help to release the stress and alleviate anxiety.

2. *Deep pressure, proprioception.* Deep pressure stimulation calms the nervous system and proprioception (tension to joints and tendons), releases stress chemicals and helps organize the nervous system. This can be self-applied or, in the case of young children, applied by another person (e.g. parent, teacher).

This usually consists of applying deep pressure massage or squeezes. Self-calming deep pressure can include massaging the palms of the hands together, self-hug squeezes, and rubbing the tops of the thighs. Weighted vests are also commonly used to help calm the nervous system. When at home, people can use deep pressure sandwiching, which consist of lying on a couch or bed and having someone press their bodies with a large pillow or bean bag. Some adults will lie between their box springs and mattress and children often like lying under the couch cushions. Others lie on the bed and have their partner lie on top of them. Chapter 12, Supporting Meltdowns, describes in detail a variety of deep pressure and proprioceptive calming strategies.

With proprioception, the person is providing tension to the joints and tendons. Proprioception releases stress chemicals and helps regulate the nervous system. Common strategies include chewing gum (chewing and biting provide strong proprioception) and providing resistance to the ankles, wrists or fingers. One common technique is crossing the ankles and intertwining the feet. From this position, the person presses the feet together to provide resistance into the ankles and feet. Any resistance to the joints will provide proprioception. Simply pointing your toes out in front of your feet provides strong input into the ankles. Similarly, making a fist and bending your hands up or down will provide strong input to the wrists.

Another easy technique for people to use in the moment of stress is providing input into their fingers. The fingers have many joints that can be combined to provide strong input. Wrap one hand around the fingers of the other hand. Simultaneously squeeze and twist all the fingers together in a rhythmic pattern. This pressure and twisting of the finger joints provide strong proprioceptive input. All these techniques can be done anywhere, at any time. They are easy self-calming tools that can be used during times of stress and anxiety.

In Chapter 12, we also describe a variety of deep pressure and proprioceptive techniques that parents can easily do with their children. As the children age, they will need to learn self-calming tools.

3. *Physical activity.* Any gross motor activity will help reduce stress and regulate anxiety. Going for a walk, doing wall push-ups, jumping jacks or full body stretches can all provide temporary relief, give the person a chance to rebound and help organize the nervous system to be better prepared for mastering stress. Any push, pull, lifting, or carrying can provide immediate help when stressed. A daily routine of exercising is a valuable tool for minimizing stress and anxiety, but temporary activity (e.g. going for walk, wall push-ups, etc.) can be used in the heat of the moment to help manage stress.

4. *Deep breathing and muscle relaxation.* Learning deep breathing and muscle tension relaxation can be a great help in staying calm. Using controlled breathing can help keep the nervous system calm and organized, and muscle tension relaxation can help keep the body relaxed. The book, *Relaxation: A Comprehensive*

Manual for Child and Adults with Autism and other Developmental Disabilities (Groden, Weidenman and Diller 2016), outlines comprehensive relaxation procedures. We usually teach the person to do a full set of deep breathing and relaxation exercises before events and then use short modified versions if needed during stressful situations.

5. *Favorite activity.* When someone is exposed to stressful situations, engaging in a favorite activity can help them to tolerate the stress until the event is over. Listening to music, reading, writing, coloring, engaging in favorite electronics (video game, YouTube, etc.) or occupying oneself with a favorite toy or game will help distract and focus attention on a preferred activity. Adults will frequently use headphones to listen to music or simply to suggest to others that they are preoccupied and do not wish to interact. This helps mask and block out stimulation, distract attention and minimize interaction with others.

   For small children, counting and reciting the alphabet can help focus attention and reduce anxiety. Many children like to sing songs or chant favorite nursery rhymes. Incorporating their favorite interest or cartoon/video character is effective. Discussing how their favorite action hero would deal with the situation can empower them to tackle stressful events. "What would…do in this situation?"

6. *Positive self-statements.* Reciting positive self-statements to yourself can help block out negative thoughts and provide temporary confidence that you can tackle it. "I can do this." "Breathe slowly, stay calm." "I'm ok, we're all ok." Positive self-statements remind the child that he is safe and can master the stress. For older children and adults, it is good to pair a confirmative statement of reassurance with a concrete directive of what to do. "I am ok, take a deep breath and ask for help." Positive statements also draw the person's attention out of the emotional/reactive centers of the brain into the thinking part of the brain.

7. *Constant (security blanket).* A constant is any object that represents familiarity and security. It may be a small stuffed animal, action figure, picture of a loved one, favorite locket, power card, almost anything that represents security for the person. If it is small and portable, the person can keep it with them and hold on to it during times of stress. Many parents and teachers try to make children abandon these constants (e.g. must leave them home when coming to school). This is a mistake. A simple constant can be a strong support when facing stress throughout the day.

8. *Take a break, ask for help.* Understanding when to pull back and take a break is so important for people with autism to learn. This includes building in frequent breaks during stressful events to regroup and rebound as well as taking a break when they feel themselves getting overwhelmed. Escaping by going to the bathroom, going for a walk, withdrawing to a quiet area or temporarily going to the car to calm are common ways to take a break. Autistics should always be prepared to temporarily withdraw from situations to avoid overload and maintain

tolerance of stress. Before entering events, always identify the safe means of escape that are available to the person.

In turn, also teach children how to ask for help. "When in doubt, ask for help." Knowing who they can approach and how to ask is important for reducing their anxiety. It is essential that they feel safe to ask for help when in distress. Knowing who and how to ask for help and trusting that they have an escape route if they need to pull back can help the children feel more confident about facing stressful situations. The more competent they feel, the less anxiety they experience.

Practicing coping routines

There are a variety of self-management tools that people can use to calm and regulate themselves. Every person is different and we each have our own calming strategies. For children, it is important to practice several strategies. Over time they may have two or three preferred techniques that they rely on.

Since these children usually have poor emotional control, it is important first to practice these strategies when calm, not in the heat of the moment. Start as early as the child can follow your lead and do them with you. It is important to find some calming strategies that you can do with your child—doing them together allows you to guide the child through the techniques. Over time, by following your lead, the child will eventually begin to use self-calming strategies.

Instead of using these techniques when the child is upset in the heat of the moment, practice them when the child is calm. Do not expect the child will be able to use these during stressful times at first. Pick two or three strategies that seem to work for the child and practice them until they become routine and familiar.

Choosing calming strategies

It is usually best to stick with a few techniques that the child can learn to feel comfortable and confident using. However, some strategies may work better in some situations than others. Techniques such as exercise, reading and deep pressure stimulation may be good strategies to use at home, but will not be portable enough to use in community activities. Also, some strategies (like doing full relaxation routines) may work well when the person can remove themselves to a quiet area but cannot be implemented easily in a stressful situation. Stimming, deep pressure palm squeezes, finger compressions, positive self-statements and fidget toys are portable and easy to use in the heat of the moment.

Often a child will have favorite sensory channels that they go to when stressed and upset. Use the child's preferences to guide what he uses. If the child seeks out and enjoys deep pressure, then use one of the techniques for applying deep pressure. If he seeks out tactile manipulation, then use fidget toys, fabric to rub, soft items to squeeze and so on. If he seeks out oral input, then chewing gum can be a good tool. Children who like to move can use movement (walk, bounce, dance, pace, etc.) to help regulate themselves.

Always start with the children's preferred interests and build them into coping strategies. They are more likely to use activities that they enjoy.

Young children may not be able to do calming routines by themselves. They may need an adult to assist them in calming. Many sensory strategies require a second person to apply the stimulation (e.g. deep pressure) to the child (see Chapter 12, Supporting Meltdowns, for detailed procedures). Engaging the child in simple repetitive, rhythmic rocking, dancing, singing, chanting and stretching often helps regulate the child as well as most deep pressure techniques. However, care must be taken to only use techniques that the child is comfortable with. Do not force any techniques on the child. Make sure to respect any sensory sensitivities (e.g. tactile defensiveness) and stop any technique if the child shows any signs of stress.

Role-play and practice coping routines

Before attempting the coping skills in the heat of the moment, teach and practice them when the child is calm. Role-play and practice the strategies together. Many parents make the mistake of trying to teach these techniques when the child is stressed and overwhelmed. No new learning can take place during heated times. Practice them daily, when everyone is calm. I usually begin by coming up with three common situations that are anxiety provoking or stressful for the child. Decide which coping skill would help for each event. Then, role-play the situations and practice using the coping skills for each situation. Discuss any anticipated problems that may arise and practice using the coping skills to manage the stress. Parents and child can switch roles and have fun practicing the coping skills. Parents can even role-play situations they find stressful to show how they would use the coping skills.

When practicing the coping strategy, try to role-play situations that are most familiar for the person. For children, parents should do the coping strategies with them, modeling the techniques, doing them together, coaching them along. Have fun, talking about how they make you feel and when to use them. For example, if using deep breathing, the adult should sit facing the child, so they can model slow, deep breaths. The child paces himself to the adult's breathing. Otherwise, most beginners breathe too fast and not deeply enough. Also, once the child begins using them in real-life situations, the adult should continue to do the coping strategy right along with the child, coaching and guiding as needed. It is also good for the child to see the parent doing the strategies when stressed, "I am starting to get nervous (upset, stressed, etc.). I better stop and take a few deep breaths."

Real-life situations: start with gradual exposure

As mentioned above, do not begin using these techniques during stressful moments until the person has established the routines through practice. Once the techniques become learned routines, they are easier to use in the heat of the moment. However, even if the routines are well practiced, do not expect them to be used during times of intense stress.

Often the person is too overwhelmed to try using newly developed techniques in these situations. It is best to keep it simple at first to maximize success. Start by using the techniques during events that are only mildly stressful.

Once learned, look for opportunities (real-life situations) during the day that are good for practicing the skills—times when both of you are calm and can successfully use the techniques. Briefly pause and practice the technique. Whether it be taking a few deep breaths, doing palm squeezes or squeezing a stress ball, use them frequently and randomly throughout the day to practice the skills during real-life situations.

Before using the skills during stressful times, determine what situations to start with. While collaborating with the child, build a hierarchy of common situations from least to most stressful. I usually recommend three categories: mild, moderate and highly stressful. The low stress situations increase the probability that the child can use the coping strategy successfully. This helps build confidence that using the coping skill will work. Start simple, maximize success and build feelings of competence.

Remember, highly stressful situations inhibit judgement, reasoning and self-control, rendering success unlikely. Once the child builds mastery using the techniques during mild stress, move on to moderately stressful events. Only up the ante if the child remains successful in mastering the situation with the newly acquired coping skills.

Remember to do the techniques right along with the child, modeling, guiding and tackling stress together. The child usually feels safer doing them with you, especially if you two have practiced them together. Start by setting up brief situations where the coping skills will be needed. Prepare the child by previewing what he can expect to happen, what is expected of him and what may be stressful, and practice the coping skills before entering the event. Once in the event, identify possible stressors and practice using the strategies together. Look for early signs that the child is becoming stressed or simply pick a few times to briefly use the copings skills. This helps introduce the child to using the skills during real-life situations. Again, start with mild situations to maximize success.

You will have to remind the child when to use the strategies. Once in events, even when the strategy has been discussed beforehand, the child is often too distracted to recognize that they are beginning to feel stressed and to remember to use their strategies. Make sure that if items are needed (fidget toy, power card, etc.), the child has them with him to be immediately available. Periodically during the event, calmly coach the child in using his strategies. Also, when the child begins to appear stressed, remind him to use his coping skills. He may not want to at first. Do not argue or pressure the child. Talk about it afterwards and keep coaching at future events. Keep the guidance positive, working with the child, rather than forcing him.

After the events are over, sit down with the child and discuss how it went, highlighting moments of success. You want to ingrain memories of feeling confident using the coping skills to master anxiety. It will take time and repeated exposure for the child to learn how and when to use the strategies to master stress and anxiety. Remember, if the situations become too overwhelming for the coping skills, then teach the child to pull away from the event to take a break, ask for help or end the activity. These strategies will help in many situations, but there will always be events that are too overwhelming to stay in.

Learning to use calming strategies to minimize anxiety takes time and the child will have to practice in order to feel competent using them in the heat of the moment. Stay patient, practice frequently and continue gradual exposure to using them in daily situations. It helps if the parents use the coping skills themselves during times of stress to demonstrate for the child that these techniques also help them. It is important that the learning is fun and not pressured. Try not to get angry or express frustration when this is not going well. The event may have been too stressful, or the coping skill may not be good for that situation. Also, you may have waited too long before encouraging the coping skill, as the child was too stressed to successfully use it. Always investigate to see what went wrong and what needs to be changed. Possibly start with less stressful situations, back up and practice more or use a different coping skill. Stay patient, keep it fun and the child will eventually learn how to use his own coping skills for managing anxiety.

Chapter 8

ANXIETY AND RIGIDITY

Rigidity and anxiety go hand in hand!

Our world requires flexible thinking to navigate the fluctuations in rules, expectations and daily snags that are present each day. When the brain is wired for either/or, all-or-nothing, black and white thinking, our world represents ongoing anxiety and insecurity. Such a thinking style naturally breeds anxiety in our culture. The world is full of changes, uncertainty, vague meanings and unclear expectations. Anxiety is inevitable!

Rigidity plus anxiety represents opposition and the need to control everything around you. This leads to conflict and confrontation from those near you and creates an atmosphere of fight and control at all costs. Unfortunately, the more rigid and confrontational we are with the child, the more opposition and fight we arouse. In the end, the child is blamed for the discord, even though the adult's inability to meet the child's rigidity with flexibility is often just as responsible. The more rigid the child, the more flexible the adult must be. A rigid and inflexible child meeting a rigid and inflexible adult is a disaster.

Flexible thinking

One common characteristic of autism is cognitive and emotional rigidity, or lack of flexibility. Before we look at rigid and inflexible thinking, we should first define what flexible thinking is. Our world of dynamic flux requires us to go with the flow, bounce between contradictions, shift gears when needed and change our perspective based on conflicting information. We realize that our world is not fixed and absolute, but relative and dynamic. Expectations change based on different contextual information, requiring us to assimilate new information and modify our perspective and behavior accordingly. Look around you. The more flexible the person, the happier they are. Being able to flexibly shift gears and modify expectations to match environmental demands, the less anxious and more emotionally stable we are.

Flexibility requires three cognitive abilities:

1. Ability to see past the concrete and read the overall meaning (context) of events. Seeing the big picture requires the flexible ability to read the invisible social rules and expectations, hidden agendas and underlying goals of given events. Although there are common rules and expectations for similar events (e.g. birthday parties), no two events are the same. Each birthday party will have its own flavor based on the people, place and time it is occurring. Each event is different, including similar but different expectations.

2. Flexibility also requires the ability to read the thoughts, feelings, perspectives and intentions of others, compare them with yours and modify expectations to meet the needs of everyone in the event. There is an ability to understand and accept that others have different perspectives and expectations.

3. Flexibility requires that our beliefs and expectations are not absolute, but flexible, open to new, sometimes conflicting, information. Our view of the world continually evolves based on new developments we experience. Our emotional security is not dependent on everything staying the same, but easily adapts to changes in expectations and is not blind to evidence that contradicts our current beliefs.

The neurotypical brain processes from general to specific. Our brains are wired to see past the details to infer the overall picture. We quickly look past the individual details for the invisible relationships between the parts. We seek out the underlying meaning to help us define the individual parts. By reading the underlying meaning, the overall picture does not change based on minor variations in details.

A wedding is still a wedding, even though the place, people, time and ceremony change. There are common expectations that occur at most weddings, although many procedural details vary. The neurotypical brain immediately looks beyond the immediate details and reads the common meaning to provide glue to the details. When we enter a new bank, we scan over the concrete details specific to that bank (physical layout, formation of lines, differences in forms, etc.) to see the general purpose and functions. This helps us navigate the differences in specifics to accomplish our goal of banking.

For many autistics, the whole is defined by the sum of its parts. If you change a few minor details, the whole may fall apart. For some, changing the arrangement of furniture in a room renders it a different room. Or a familiar person changes their hairstyle or glasses and they are not recognizable any more. To understand that superficial changes in detail do not change the overall picture requires the ability to see beyond the details for the underlying meaning.

This difficulty results in severe anxiety for many with autism, because their view of the world collapses when things vary, and events do not go as expected. It is difficult for them to flexibly appraise events and assimilate the new information into the overall picture. In the face of changing information, they may panic from the unexpected snags. When faced with evidence that conflicts with their current beliefs, they may deny the new information and hold rigidly to their initial perspective ("It has to be this way!").

Another important factor for flexibility is the ability to understand different options, alternative approaches and different perspectives. When you can see the overall picture, understand the context and what is expected, you can look for different options, ask for different perspectives and evaluate alternatives when things are not working. When you cannot read between the lines and understand the overall picture, it is difficult to recognize and accept alternative options and that others have different perspectives. With rigidity, the person gravitates to one right way of doing something and wants to hold on to that approach, even in the face of contradictory information.

Not accurately seeing the big picture leads to people feeling insecure and anxious. There is too much uncertainty. Consequently, rules, regulations and expectations need to stay very black and white, with one correct answer. Panic sets in when autistic people are forced to abandon their secure belief and evaluate other options.

Flexible thinking also requires the ability to gauge relativity, to read gray areas and understand that most rules, situations and expectations are not absolute. Not much in our lives is absolute, either/or and all or nothing. Most rules and expectations flexibly vary from situation to situation, different activities and among different participants. Rules and expectations are general in nature, only meant to be suggestions to guide our behavior. They are meant to be relative to the situation and demands within them.

Driving is a great example. Driving within the speed limit often allows for driving within 5–10 miles an hour over the posted speed. Many people make a "rolling stop" at stop signs when no one is around to yield to. We do not always use our indicators when switching lanes and making turns, especially when those actions are obvious. These rules are general guidelines for regulating behavior, not absolutes that are followed blindly.

Most actions/performances do not have to be perfect to be "good enough." If you are playing baseball, getting a hit once every three times at bat is considered a good batting average. When taking a test, what is considered good enough or excellent work varies extensively from test to test and instructor to instructor. How long do you need to study to get an "A" on a test? This is a question that cannot be accurately predicted. It would depend on how well you comprehend the material, and how well you judge what information is needed. You do not have to be a perfect driver to keep a driver's license. Some drivers are better than others, but most are "good enough" to keep their license. Most rules and regulations are designed to be bent and not followed blindly.

Our world is filled with vague, unwritten expectations. How do we go about making these relative judgements? To appraise expectations, monitor how well we are doing and modify our actions accordingly, we must be able to read between the lines, consider what is "good enough," and understand when expectations change and shifting gears is required. We must infer what is expected and allowed and then measure our performance to that. Making these inferences from multiple information and then flexibly adapting them to different situations requires the understanding that expectations are relative and not absolute.

For kids with inflexible thinking, everything is very literal, black and white, either/or, all or nothing. Rules are absolute with little middle ground. They have difficulty realizing that expectations are relative to what the situation warrants. Having difficulty gauging the relative importance of rules and expectations within the context they are in leads to extensive anxiety. The world is not consistent and absolute. Telling a white lie to not hurt someone's feelings still makes you a liar. Bending rules and minor transgressions are often allowed and expected in given situations. When, where and with whom these transgressions are allowed, and sometimes expected, is lost in the sea of confusion.

Lastly, people who are flexible can accept things not being as initially expected, roll with simple snags and continually modify how they are reacting to events around them. We do not panic when things are not as expected or when we hit minor snags, and can usually shift gears, change our expectations and modify our behavior accordingly. When you do not have flexible thinking, events not going as expected, rules not being rigidly adhered to and simple snags can result in extreme frustration, absolute denial and even panic. When you experience this turmoil multiple times a day, every day, your safety and security are fragile. Anxiety is inevitable.

Rigid/Inflexible thinking

When people with autism cannot read between the lines, understand the hidden, unwritten rules and appraise expectations, their behavior is often out of sync. When they cannot adequately connect the dots to define what is needed, the world becomes confusing, chaotic and overwhelming. They rigidly hold on to rules and routines as constant and absolute, in attempts to keep their world predictable and reliable. Without these rigid rules and routines, their world crumbles. Their security is rigidly dependent on every detail staying the same. Sameness, constants and absolutes are needed to reduce uncertainty and minimize anxiety. Simple changes in routines can leave them lost and panicky.

This inability to read between the lines and connect the dots results in very concrete, literal interpretations that are absolute and resistant to change. Their thinking is very rigid and inflexible, with little tolerance for variability. Rules, regulations and expectations become very black and white, right or wrong, with little room for variation. They may demand that people follow the rules exactly as stated, police others to stay within the rules and refuse to accept changes in expectations.

As can be imagined, our world of variations and fluctuations creates strong feelings of insecurity and anxiety. Uncertainty produces panic. Many of these children with inflexible thinking may need to control everything around them to keep the world predictable and in their control. They hold on to their rigid beliefs and expectations, become very demanding, refuse to follow the lead of others, and actively resist any attempt to change their beliefs or course of actions. Any pressure to the contrary may elicit extreme meltdowns. As you can expect, the child feels safer with concrete, very consistent rules and expectations that remain the same and are predictable.

Black and white thinking

When the world must be good or bad, right or wrong and either/or, there is little room for much variance in between. These children have difficulty seeing the relatively gray area between the two extremes. They need the world to be very concrete and absolute, with minimal relativity to second guess. Unfortunately, our world is not concrete and absolute. Most rules, regulations and expectations are variable and flexible from one event to another, requiring us to appraise what is needed based on the context of the situation.

Sometimes we can tell a white lie if it may hurt someone's feelings, bend a rule to navigate a snag and avoid telling our boss he is wrong. We do not need to tell everyone exactly what we think and give advice (e.g. "You are overweight and need to go on a diet") to those who are not seeking it. For children, it may be expected to tell naughty jokes with friends, but not to adults, and alright when out on the playground but not in the classroom. All these social road maps are difficult for them to navigate. When you cannot grasp the dynamic flex of changing context and expectations you hold tightly to black and white, all-or-nothing rules and boundaries. "Please mean what you say and say what you mean and keep it that way forever!"

This inflexible thinking also affects their emotional life. Emotionally, they frequently live in the world of extremes, often showing exaggerated emotional reactions. When happy, they are ecstatic and when upset, they are devastated. There is little room for the full range of intensities. It is as if they have an off and on switch with no volume control. They can show no response to seemingly reactive events, or overreact to minor frustrations. They can adamantly resist sudden, simple changes in expectations. Since they have difficulty reading the relative importance of snags, even minor snags can send them into panic. They do not realize that feeling a little anxious is natural and motivates us to either try harder or change our course of action. Feeling a little anxiety is interpreted as a major threat with a need to panic.

Decision making can be a daunting task. Answers must be all right or all wrong, with little room for variations. Either you are good or bad, perfect or a failure. Consequently, many autistics have difficulty recognizing and accepting multiple ways of doing things; there must be only one right way. "Don't give me multiple options. I want to know the one correct answer."

This may carry over to their expectations for their own performance. Since the kids have difficulty reading expectations, they have trouble reading when their performance is "good enough." When expectations are too vague or variable, then the only performance good enough is perfection. The performance needs to be perfect, all correct, no errors or mishaps. One mistake becomes a failure.

This is the child who will tear up a drawing and start again if he needs to erase a simple error. Or, a child who panics when he does not make a basket every time he shoots the ball. I once had a child who kept shoveling the snow on his driveway because the light snow was falling on spots that he already cleared away. He would keep going back over and over what he had already shoveled. The job was not complete because there was still snow on the driveway. He couldn't grasp that a little bit of snow would not hurt anything, that his work was good enough.

Inevitably, the rigid/inflexible child can be frustrating for parents and teachers because it is very difficult to get children to change their minds, see a different perspective or try a different way. They will demand that their way is the right way and actively fight against you. Continued pressure on our part will only lead to a meltdown.

The more anxiety the greater the rigidity

This rigid and inflexible thinking can lead to strong anxiety and a host of behavior challenges. Rigidity is strongly correlated with anxiety. The more anxiety the child has, the greater the rigidity, and that rigidity will create greater anxiety. One drives the other. The more rigid the child, the more oppositional, demanding and controlling he can be. Uncertainty is very scary for him and he often resists following the lead of someone else. Hence, children usually must control all interactions and activities they engage in to make them safe and predictable. Let down the control and the world becomes very threatening.

Common characteristics of these children include:

- Rigidly seeking predictable, static routines and activities.

- Actively resisting change, unless they are creating it. Overreacting emotionally to any snag or unanticipated change.

- Needing to control all activity and interactions, dominating the activity.

- Avoiding uncertainty and lessening chaos by controlling everything they possibly can.

- Resisting following the lead of others—often labeled as oppositional and intentionally defiant.

- Rigidity often results in a variety of compulsive, repetitive, ritualistic, self-absorbed, self-stimulation and active resistance when things do not go their way.

These children can be very difficult to parent and teach because they will activity fight against your instruction. They will actively resist following your lead, question your authority and demand things be their way. Again, like most characteristics of autism, this rigidity can vary significantly in intensity, from mild resistance to very severe avoidance of anyone trying to control or direct them. In Europe, they are informally using an additional co-occurring disorder called pathological demand avoidance, since these children have a unique emotional and cognitive profile.

As expected, this cognitive rigidity can lead to a variety of the behavior traits common to autism (self-stimulation, rigid routines, difficulty shifting gears, overreacting to small snags, obsessive compulsive behaviors, and meltdowns).

Resistance to change

As could be expected with increased anxiety, the more rigid the child the more resistance he is to change. These children feel so insecure and inadequate that all uncertainty represents a threat to their security. This has nothing to do with cognitive intelligence. You can see this strong rigidity in some of the very intellectually capable children. This adherence to rigid beliefs, rules and rituals helps to reduce the chaos and confusion. However, these children are rarely happy.

This rigidity serves as a defense mechanism to reduce uncertainty and anxiety. However, their inability to follow the lead of others greatly limits their ability to learn and grow. It creates constant friction with those trying to support and guide them. Adults often try to control them by typical discipline, punishment and forced compliance, but this usually fuels greater resistance. We must take the mindset that the more resistant and oppositional the child is, the more unsafe and inadequate he feels. He may act in a superior way and be demanding, but he is scared and feels very inadequate.

Defensive brain versus receptive brain

When the world is chaotic, confusing and overwhelming, the brain becomes anxious and insecure. It feels unsafe and is hypervigilant for the next unexpected assault. Therefore, anxiety is very prevalent in autism. Unexpected changes, unpredictable reactions and sensory overload all present ongoing anxiety. When placed in situations that are chaotic, confusing and overwhelming all of us become anxious, frightened and extremely reactive. The difference between neurotypical people and those on the spectrum is that for the neurotypical person these overwhelming situations are infrequent, and we recover quickly after the threat subsides. Our fight or flight response recovers quickly once the threat is over.

Many on the spectrum, since the world is always unpredictable and overwhelming, experience very frequent threatening situations and their brains often take much longer to rebound. This persistent state of anxiety and apprehension creates a brain that is defensive and reactive, always on guard for the next potential assault, and never understanding when the next sensory threat, social misunderstanding, miscued response, negative reaction from another or unexpected snag will occur. The brain is on high alert and is hyper-focused for any potential threat. This puts the brain in an escape/avoidance mode—an apprehensive defensive mode that anxiety generates. Just like all of us when anxious and defensive, the brain will impulsively overreact to minor threats, snags which often create strong emotional reactions. Over the years of facing numerous threatening assaults, the brain becomes habitually stuck in defensive mode.

The defensive brain is spending so much energy trying to protect itself that it often has little left for learning. When we don't feel safe, accepted and competent, we have one eye widely open for any possible threat and one foot turned away to quickly escape if needed. Safety is the brain's priority. It will take precedence over learning. We must feel safe and secure to be receptive to learning. When defensive, the person is always tip-toeing into new situations, very apprehensive about threats and ready to run or fight to escape the uncertainty. For some children, this anxiety is often expressed as extreme opposition and defiance in an attempt to control everything around them and feel safe. Or they may withdraw into shutdown, passive avoidance and learned helplessness.

Why the need for rigidity?

Emotional security comes from predictability. When the world and our relationships within it are consistent and predictable, we feel emotionally secure. The more chaotic and unpredictable our world, and our relationships within it, the more insecure and anxious we feel. From my conversations with those on the spectrum there are three primary inconsistencies that make the world unpredictable and scary:

1. *Sensory experiences.* For those with problems with sensory hyper-sensitivities, fragmented and distorted perception and sensory overload, the world is often very chaotic, unpredictable and scary. The nervous system is on guard and defensive when they cannot trust that their senses will give them a consistent picture of the world. All their inner experiences and adaptive behavior are dependent on their sensory input being consistent and predictable. When that is disturbed, they are anxious and insecure.

2. *Consistency and predictability to our routine.* It is essential to their sense of security to know what is coming up next and be able to predict and prepare for it. Without this, the world becomes chaotic and unpredictable. Routine and consistency in knowing what will occur and what is expected of them lie at the heart of their security. When the world is chaotic, they seek out rigid routines that bring order to the chaos. The more inconsistency and chaos, the higher the anxiety and the more rigidity the child will require.

3. *Social inconsistencies.* The most important threat to the person's security is the inconsistency and unpredictability of their social world. Nothing is more confusing and unpredictable for autistics than socializing. Our social world is regulated by vague, unwritten, and invisible rules and expectations, which are often lost for those with autism. They are continually placed in situations where they are guessing at what is expected and how others will respond. When the responses of others are often unpredictable and harsh, every step they take is against a backdrop of uncertainty and anxiety.

So, when the child rigidly demands that things stay the same and responds consistently every time, he is seeking predictability to his world. Without this consistency, his world of security falls apart. When little snags, changes in routine or differences in his response create strong emotional reactions, remember that his map of the world has just collapsed, leaving him feeling anxious and vulnerable. Therefore, it is important to provide structure to the child's routine and consistency in to our expectations and reactions. When he seeks rigid routines, repetitive patterns and continual reassurance, he is trying to bring order to his world.

The more predictable and reliable the world, the more confident and competent we all feel. The more our behavior is consistent and predictable, the more they can trust in following our lead. But remember that this security is always fragile when you live in a world of ambiguity and inconsistencies. When you cannot effectively read the world around you, you are always vulnerable to unexpected changes and inconsistencies in reactions from others. Hence, the ongoing anxiety and need for rigidity for many on the spectrum.

Try to remember that the more oppositional and resistant the child becomes, the more confused, vulnerable and inadequate he feels. It is not our job to lay blame and "command and demand," but provide familiarity, predictability and help him feel safe and secure in our presence.

Rigidity and comfort zones

Since our world is often chaotic, confusing and overwhelming, these children tend to fear uncertainty. Uncertainty creates anxiety, which motivates them to escape and avoid the uncertainty. In doing so, they often build themselves rigid comfort zones to protect themselves. These comfort zones narrow their world down into familiar and predictable patterns that help them feel safe and secure, providing a buffer from the dynamic uncertainty our world presents and minimizing anxiety.

To help these children feel safe, we must understand what their comfort zones are and respect them. The children hold very rigidly to these comfort zones. Stepping outside them usually presents strong anxiety, so the children actively resist attempts to do this. Once they define their comfort zones, children often rigidly hold on to them at all costs. They will actively fight anyone who tries to push them past these boundaries. Their sense of safety and security is rigidly defined by these boundaries.

This has nothing to do with cognitive functioning. Some of the brightest children on the spectrum have more rigid comfort zones than the less capable children. These children go into panic mode very easily when presented with new situations or expectations that do not match these comfort zones. They will actively resist anyone who rigidly expects them to "suck it up" and do it anyway. For most of these children, avoiding uncertainty is of the upmost importance to their security.

The mistake that many of us make is not understanding what the children's comfort zones are and then unintentionally pushing them past these safety nets. If we try to pressure or push them, they often freeze and panic, become resistant or shut down. However, once we understand what their comfort zones are, learn to respect them and then slowly stretch them, the children can learn and grow like everyone. You cannot learn unless you feel comfortable and confident tackling the challenges facing you. If the child is pressured past these comfort zones, the brain is defensive and in survival mode, rather than receptive to new learning. If this happens frequently, the brain is apprehensive to all new learning, ready to panic with minimal uncertainty. Learning how to identify, respect and gradually stretch their comfort zones is a major tool in mentoring kids on the spectrum.

Types of comfort zones

We must first identify and respect the child's comfort zones if we are going to establish trust with them. Our greatest mistake is either not understanding what their comfort zones are, or ignoring them and pushing the children too fast and too far, causing severe anxiety and pushing them further away from trusting us. Again, their total foundation of safety and security is dependent on these comfort zones. Identifying and respecting them is essential to building trust in being safe and accepted with us.

In the green book *Autism Discussion Page on Anxiety, Behavior, School, and Parenting Strategies* (Nason 2014b, pp.62–64), I discuss five common comfort zones that must be respected to minimize stress and anxiety: sensory, social, emotional, cognitive and uncertainty, and we revist them here.

Sensory

We need to be familiar with what the child's sensory preferences and vulnerabilities are, what overwhelms him, what stimulation alerts him, and what comforts and soothes him. The child may be hyper-sensitive (sensory avoiders) in some areas, and a sensory seeker in other areas. He may have sensory issues that set off "panic," which must be respected and accommodated for. Because of their sensitivities to bright lights, loud noises, strong smells and various touches, the world can be very overwhelming and scary for these children. We need to be keenly aware of what their sensitivities are and help soften the sensory bombardment they experience.

Accommodations usually consist of (1) lowering the intensity of stimulation around the children by reducing noise, lights and smells and allowing them to escape situations that overwhelm them, (2) providing adapted supports to mask stimulation that cannot be reduced, such as ear plugs, sunglasses, and (3) providing items that can help distract and divert attention away from stimulation (books, music, electronics, etc.). When a child is uncomfortable in any situation, first look to see if there are any sensory issues that may be irritating him. This is often the first place I look when trying to figure out why someone is being resistant.

In turn, these children will also have sensory preferences that they are attracted to, seek out and which can be used to engage them. These preferences can be used to build learning experiences around. If the child is attracted to colors, a teacher can build coloring, brightly colored pastes, paper and pencils into the lessons at school. If the child loves rough-housing and swinging, a parent can use rough-housing (run and crash, wrestle together, tumbling races, etc.) and swinging activities (pushing the child on a swing, picking him up and swinging him around, swinging on a glider swing together, etc.) to build into social play with him. Building these sensory preferences into learning and play initially motivates the child and helps maintain his attention. Also, pairing the new learning with pleasurable stimulation helps encode the new learning into memory. Engaging the child in sensory play activities helps solidify the social bonding through sharing pleasurable moments together. Tapping into these sensory preferences not only attracts the child but also helps him feel safe and connected with you.

Sensory preferences can also be used to calm and organize the child. For example, deep pressure stimulation often helps calm some children, as well as slowly rocking together. Quiet music, soft singing, pleasant smells, soft lighting can be effective tools for calming a child. In turn, using alerting stimulation can also be used when the child is sluggish and under-aroused. In the blue book, *The Autism Discussion Page on the Core Challenges of Autism* (Nason 2014a), I provide a detailed discussion on sensory preferences and using them to calm, organize and engage the child.

It is important to define what the child's sensory comfort zones are: what is he attracted to, what does he avoid, what calms him and what alerts him? Understand and respect his sensory sensitivities and utilize his sensory preferences to engage him.

Social

Social anxiety can be very strong for people on the spectrum. Since they have difficulty reading social cues, understanding unwritten social rules and co-regulating interaction, these children are often apprehensive and anxious interacting with others. Since over 80 percent of new learning comes from social learning (watching, copying and following the lead of others), it is important that we identify the interaction style that works best with your child—the style of relating that helps him feel safe, accepted and engaging.

Does your child respond best to an animated, jolly approach, or to a slow, gentle approach? Does he respond best to words or better when using fewer words and more gestures and visual cues? How does he respond to touch? Does your child crave and connect best with physical contact, or avoid it with a passion? Does he relate better side by side, where eye contact is minimal or facing you to reference your facial expressions? How much does he need to control the interaction to feel safe? Is he ok with you sharing the control or does he do better with you following his lead? Does he like sharing pleasurable emotions with you or prefer you to be flat and unemotional? Will he allow you to actively participate in his play or only allow you to passively observe from the side?

There can be several different comfort zones for the child: (1) the personal interaction style he feels most comfortable with, (2) the amount of social stimulation he can handle at one time before being overwhelmed, (3) the type of social activity (one on one, group of two or three, larger group activities) he can comfortably process; and (4) the level of participation (passively watch, follow along, actively participate, or lead) the child can comfortably handle.

What is your child's level of social interest? It is a myth that autistics do not desire to connect with others. Social interest varies extensively between them. Some have strong interest, but struggle relating with others. They want to be around others, have friends and be involved in many social activities, but struggle with the reciprocal give and take, reading the thoughts and needs of others. Not understanding these subtle rules, they try and dominate the interaction and control the activity, leading peers to reject them.

These children are often willing to throw themselves into social activities which they cannot handle, experience rejection, get upset and possibly become aggressive if things do not go their way. Parents may think, because the child is strongly interested, they should throw him into a variety of group activities unprepared for the social skills needed to survive—that somehow, he will learn as he goes. He jumps in over his head with minimal skills to survive.

As we discussed earlier, some children are introverted, have minimal interest in relating and are happier in individual endeavors. That is their comfort zone and we should respect that. Trying to push them into social events and friendships will overwhelm them.

How much social activity can your child tolerate? Usually the three main factors to evaluate are: (1) what type of activity is your child most comfortable with (small clubs, sports, one-on-one play, online groups, etc.), (2) what type of relating can he regulate (one on one, a few people at a time, adults or peers) (3) how structured does the activity need to be (very structured game with black and white rules, adult-led to facilitate interaction, or loosely organized, like playing at the park), and (4) how long can he handle participating in such activity before becoming drained and overwhelmed (30 minutes, one hour, etc.)? Understanding your child's comfort zones with socializing can be instrumental in minimizing anxiety and ensuring successful relating.

Emotional

This comfort zone has to do with the general flexibility in emotionally adjusting to variability, novelty and change around them. It includes how your child experiences and handles his own emotions. Many children have very poor emotional regulation. They get upset very easily, escalate very quickly and take a long time to calm down. They often fear their emotions and can become overwhelmed very easily. They go from 0 to 100 quickly, often in situations that present minimal frustration. It is important to know how your child responds to his emotions, and what are the best ways to calm and soothe him.

In addition, some of the children are very scared of the emotional reactions of others. If others are upset, agitated or being criticized, the child may act as if the emotional reactions are his. He becomes upset at any intense emotion coming from those around him. The people important in your child's life need to know what helps him feel safe emotionally, and what to avoid in keeping him feeling safe.

Cognitive

Autism is an information processing difference. Every child on the spectrum has difficulty processing multiple information simultaneously. Much of what we process intuitively, at a subconscious level, children on the spectrum must process consciously. This can be very taxing and mentally draining. The children each have different thresholds on how much and how fast the information can come before they hit "information overload." Many children have delayed processing and need to have information presented visually, sequenced out in small portions at a time, and need to be given more time to process it.

Many children have auditory processing problems and do better with visual information (pictures, written directions, demonstrations, etc.). If the teaching doesn't match their processing style, then they will often pull back and shut down. It is important to know how much information your child can process at one time, what his best learning style is, how often he needs breaks to rebound, and what strategies help calm and organize him for learning. We must protect the child from becoming mentally drained and overwhelmed. Know how to give it, how much to give, how fast to give it, to keep learning fun.

Uncertainty

This comfort zone has to do with the child's ability to handle uncertainty, not overreact with panic, and rebound quickly once agitated. The more rigid and inflexible the children are, the greater degree of familiarity and control they need. Children with weak flexibility need strong structure with a very predictable routine. Uncertainty scares them extensively and they will panic when things don't match their expectations. They do not feel competent tackling the normal snags that occur in their daily routine. They will demand to control everything around them to feel safe.

So, it is important to define what degree of certainty must be built into your child's life for him to feel comfortable. What type of uncertainty, novelty and new learning can he handle? Does he need rigid routines to feel safe? Does novelty scare him? Does he need to lead everything to feel secure? What degree of certainty does he need to feel safe and secure? It is important to know what rituals and routines help him feel safe and secure, and how much you can stretch him at one time.

These children may have a variety of other comfort zones that are very important to them in feeling safe, accepted and competent. You as the parent can best identify these comfort zones and advocate for others to know and respect them. It is very important that as a parent, and strongest advocate for your child, you define your child's comfort zones so that all people working with him can understand what your child is comfortable with, what his fears are and how to help him feel safe, accepted and competent. It is very important that you give teachers, therapists and any support people this information and then demand that they respect the child's comfort zones. If you don't, everyone will be guessing at what is appropriate for the child, often demanding that he conforms to their expectations, and pushing the child into panic or shutdown mode.

Stretching comfort zones

For your child to grow and develop, once you define and respect your child's comfort zones, it is important that you teach him to feel safe stretching them. The biggest mistake we make in respecting the child's comfort zones is allowing them to rigidly hold on to them. The comfort zones help the child feel safe and accepted, but stretching them helps him to feel competent. The longer the child stays in his comfort zone, the harder it is to get him to stretch it. The longer he avoids stretching, the more rigid the comfort zone becomes. So, helping the child learn and grow is a constant balance between respecting the comfort zones, while continually stretching these zones.

Principles of stretching

Effective stretching consists of the following stages:

1. Start simply, in the child's comfort zone. Maximize success by starting where the child is at, with what he feels comfortable with. Build feelings of security in engaging with you.

2. Begin adding a little stretching at a time. We call this the "just right" challenge, baby steps that provide just enough variation (stretching) to present a little uncertainty, but not enough to overwhelm the child (elicit avoidance).

3. Frame the new learning, providing assistance and support to help the child tackle the uncertainty. Do it together, sharing the experience to maximize security. Frame the activity and scaffold the new learning to maximize success. Allow the child to experience the challenge (uncertainty) to feel the mastery.

4. Keep it simple, maximize success and build gradually. If the child starts to become overwhelmed or resistant, pull back, rebuild comfort and continue with smaller steps.

As the child masters repeated steps of stretching (learning) he builds greater confidence in tackling new uncertainty (as well as greater trust in following your lead). "Mastery" becomes attractive and builds strong motivation for further learning. Tackling uncertainty becomes fun and inviting. Doing it with you establishes great trust in following your lead as a mentor; there is greater trust, better confidence and more fun.

Mentoring children on the spectrum consists of guiding them to safely stretch their comfort zones, eventually feeling more and more confident in stepping outside them. The secret to stretching is to add just a small amount of new challenge ("just right" challenge) at a time, so that the child feels the challenge, but not so much that it overwhelms him, thus setting off his fight or flight panic response.

How much can you comfortably stretch, allowing the child to feel the challenge, but small enough for him to comfortably master? This is accomplished by two factors: only adding a little challenge at a time, and providing guidance and support to maximize success in mastering the new challenge. As the child experiences numerous trials of successfully stretching his comfort zone, he begins to feel more confident in taking risks and more trusting of following your lead when stepping outside his comfort zone.

By engaging in the activity with the child, you are framing and guiding the activity to maximize success while allowing the child to feel the mastery of stretching. While adding little bits of uncertainty (new learning) and providing guidance, you help the child feel safe in the face of the uncertainty, allowing him to feel competent in tackling the uncertainty. The feeling of "mastery" is attractive and motivating for further learning. Repeated exposure to mastering uncertainty becomes fun and inviting when success is experienced. Also, by framing the activity for success, presenting only enough new learning to stretch without overwhelming and then immediately pulling back when observing signs of distress, you enable the child to feel safe and trust in following your lead.

This obviously sounds simpler than it can be, especially with children who are very scared of experiencing any uncertainty and do not feel safe at all with engaging with others. It can take many sessions, repeated attempts and frequent modifications to become skillful at being a mentor for an autistic child.

Avoid overwhelming the child

It is very important not to stretch too fast or too much at a time. We often push too much, too fast in zealous attempts to accelerate learning. We bounce the child from one activity to another (social activity, therapies, school, etc.), continually attempting to provide as many learning opportunities as possible. Some therapies have instilled this in parents, saying that children need 40 hours of training a week, and do not give them down time otherwise they will regress into their own world. Teaching, training and therapy can be very taxing and draining for these children. They need small doses at a time, with recovery breaks in-between. Trying to pressure ongoing stretching (learning) can result in cognitive and emotional burnout. Less can produce more productive learning. Presenting frequent but short learning opportunities, with ample breaks to rebound, keeps learning safe and fun.

Each child is different when it comes to how much exposure they can tolerate without becoming drained and burned out. Remember what we learned in the chapters on processing—we need to respect the child's vulnerabilities and mental energy levels and give him plenty of breaks to rebound and regroup. It is quality of learning, matching the child's neurology, that is important. We need to keep stretching within the boundaries of the child's processing capabilities and avoid overwhelming him. By continually taxing the child, we make learning negative and something to avoid. Regardless of how much exposure and learning you provide, the child is not learning when he is no longer receptive. Even if the child is compliant, he is not assimilating new learning when taxed.

Stretching too much and too fast will create distress, instill distrust and promote avoidance of us. This may traumatize the child over time. Your primary objectives should be to help identify, respect and support the child's comfort zones, build in accommodations and strategies for reducing the sensory, cognitive, social and emotional overload, make the world more understandable and predictable and teach effective skills for tackling future challenges. By identifying the children's profiles (strengths and vulnerabilities in each area – social, sensory, cognitive, social and emotional) and tailoring the environmental demands to these comfort zones, the children start to feel safe and accepted enough to lower their anxiety and become receptive to learning. Only then can they begin to trust the world and people around them, feel safe enough to risk and stretch their comfort zones and begin to develop the competence and confidence to tackle new challenges. The brain must feel safe to exit the defensive mode and become responsive to new learning.

When the child is not doing well, assume he may feel unsafe, insecure, overwhelmed and inadequate. More than likely we are placing him in a situation where the expectations are greater than his perceived abilities for dealing with them. Back up, temporarily lower the demands, offer more assistance and provide greater support. If we do this, the child experiences greater success, feels more confident tackling challenges and learns to trust in following our lead. Even then, expect that some children (especially those with pathological demand avoidance) will take a long time to break through the rigid defensiveness and develop trust in following your lead. Patience, understanding and acceptance, while allowing the child to pace and control the new learning, will eventually get you there. The brain gradually becomes less defensive and more receptive.

Teaching flexible thinking

In addition to stretching comfort zones, to reduce generalized anxiety, we must also work on teaching flexible thinking. First, we must be cognizant that this rigidity is not just a thinking style, but also an emotional defense against the uncertainty of the chaotic world these children live in. The children seek sameness, predictability and concrete, black and white, absolute answers. Since our world is not black and white, but filled with variability and ambiguity, almost everything that is not constant is scary. When walking through life always confused about what to expect and what is expected of them, the children are inevitably anxious and insecure. It is no wonder that they seek out things that are absolute, hold rigidly to black and white rules and rituals, and resist any change to those givens. They rely on these constants staying the same to bring order to the chaotic and confusing world around them. They do not want relativity and variability because such inconsistency shakes the very foundation of their safety and security.

How we can help

We can use the same principles of stretching we described above to teach greater flexibility. Start where the child is at, keep it simple, build gradually and maximize success.

1. First, we must identify and respect the child's comfort zone, including the rigid beliefs, routines and rituals that help the child feel safe. We need to identify and respect how the child perceives the world and what rules he currently uses to make sense of the events around him. Start with trying to meet the child's needs by minimizing ambiguity and variability, reducing uncertainty and initially accepting the rigid rules, rituals and routines that help provide order to his life.

    If he needs to have the furniture in the room arranged the same way, it is important to respect that; likewise, if he needs to have the same toothpaste, engage in a repetitive ritualistic routine, or needs to sit in the same spot at the dinner table each day. Start by validating and respecting the rigid patterns that help him feel safe. Acknowledge and show that he needs these to bring predictability to his world. By doing so, the child trusts that you are a working partner with him and he will be more likely to feel safe following your lead as you begin to stretch his comfort zone.

2. Next, slowly teach flexibility by gradually building small variations into the child's day. Make little modifications to the child's routine. Gradually present different options, different ways of doing things, alternative ways of tackling problems and simple snags to build greater flexibility. Start in areas of the daily routine that are not currently a compulsive need for security, where variability can be easily built in to provide greater flexibility to the day. Take a different route to school, read a different book at bedtime, provide different options for an evening snack, and so on. Take small steps, keeping it very simple and building flexibility gradually.

This helps both the parents and child to experience mild differences in when, where and how things occur. Again, avoid major compulsive routines that you know will disturb your child.

3. Once you have gained experience with building in minor changes, then you can begin working on routines that hold greater importance for the child. Make a hierarchy of the least to most likely routines to cause major anxiety if changes occur, from the least anxiety provoking to the most. Start at the bottom (least anxiety provoking) and build simple variations in them (change a step in the sequential order, add or modify an element of the activity, who he does it with, etc.). First, make very simple, small changes, that are barely recognizable and do not shake the child's confidence too much. It is what we call the "just right" challenge—there is just enough uncertainty that might make the child uneasy but not enough to panic him.

    For example, let's consider a child who likes his environment to be orderly and rigidly arranged the same way. He might also have a lot of compulsive little rituals and routines that he does each day and gets upset if these routines are interrupted. This child also melts down frequently when simple snags happen during the day. In looking at all three issues— compulsive arrangements, rigid rituals and freaking when snags are presented—the parents feel that starting with the compulsive orderliness is easier than tackling the other two. Remember, keep it simple by only stretching one variable at a time.

    While discussing the child's need for the living room always being arranged in the same way, the parents identify what minor changes constitute "just right" challenges. For example, the child notices, but probably can handle, the pillow being on the opposite side of the couch more so than moving furniture in the room. The parents proceed to make little changes in arrangements at different times during the day, such as changing the plates at dinner, mom and dad switching seats at the table, using a different towel during bathing, moving the position of his toy chest to make room for a new preferred toy.

4. Depending on the age, cognitive abilities and rigidity of the child, you can collaborate with the child in determining the hierarchy and deciding which steps to start with. While using the hierarchy of least to most anxiety, you and your child can work together, previewing what the changes will be ahead of time, having them help you create the variations and giving them logical reasons for making the changes.

    You also can have fun playing the "change game," first having the child make a change in routine and see if you recognize it and then you make a change and see if he can identify it. Then, move to planning together what the next changes will be, to see if dad will recognize it. Once the child sees this as fun, make an agreement that you need to make one simple change a day, or a week, and plan them out ahead of time. Start pinpointing simple changes in your day that often go unrecognized.

Talk about how these changes can be good, some even exciting. The child begins to see that his life and security do not change based on structural changes in his settings. Keep building in simple changes to both the arrangement of his setting and to his daily routines. This way he continues to experience that simple changes do not disturb the basic patterns of his day, that minor variations in his setting and routine do not change what he is doing.

5. Lastly, keep it simple and build gradually. Depending on their anxiety and flexibility, some children can move faster than others. Keep the changes within the "just right" challenge so as not to overwhelm the child. If you guess wrong, simply back up and break the change down into simpler steps. Keep the stretching easy, with minimal distress.

6. Gradually, one at a time, build in greater variability throughout the child's day. This will take time. Don't hurry or stretch too fast. The child's emotional reactions will help guide you. Stepping outside his comfort zone is very difficult. As discussed, this is a very gradual process of continuing to stretch the comfort zone, simple steps at a time, over a long period. This may create mild anxiety, but not enough to overwhelm the child. The child also learns that mild anxiety is nothing to be afraid of. Helping the child tackle and overcome these simple challenges builds greater confidence in tackling new situations. Over time, the child learns that the challenges are not as devastating as he first thought (less threatening) and repeated success at tackling such challenges builds greater competence and confidence for future challenges. He begins to realize that the world is not absolute, nor does it have to be.

Other strategies for teaching flexibility

1. *Provide structure, without rigidity.* Using a visual schedule, either written or pictorial, is a common way to provide a predictable routine for children. However, if you stay with the same schedule every day the child can become rigidly dependent on that routine. You can do two things to build in flexibility. First, your schedule can build in general categories of activities, such as "household chore", and then the child can pick the chore (dust, clean the mirror, vacuum, etc.) to do each day off a picture or household chore menu. One day he can pick to dust, clean the mirror or vacuum. He can do the same for leisure activities (video game, reading, games), school work (math, reading, etc.), physical activities (riding bike, playscape, playing ball), and community outings (meal out, movie, park, etc.).

   For each day, the general routine of the day stays the same; for example, the evening routine might include leisure activity, household chore, dinner, physical activity, homework then leisure activity. Within this schedule, the specific activities are chosen from a menu of choices. This way the structure of the day stays the same, but there is variability in the activities.

Another, more advanced, scheduling for older children is to not have a set structured schedule but to sit down at the beginning of each day, or when first coming home from school, and write a schedule for the day. This is not set, but determined each day, previewing what will occur and when. This way, the current day is predictable, but each day varies. Even if you have a very structured daily routine, flexibility can be built in by making pre-discussed changes, adding and subtracting events that will be different each day. By doing this, you are keeping a familiar pattern to the child's day, but building in flexibility.

2. *Dealing with snags.* Changes in general can really shake their security. Unexpected changes to a set mental expectation throw their world off course. Previewing the change ahead of time often helps. However, sometimes these unexpected snags are inevitable. Parents can help teach this flexibility by making it an objective to focus on for several weeks.

Each time you plan or schedule to do something, talk about what snags or unexpected changes may occur, such as a detour because of construction, a store being closed, a restaurant not having his favorite dessert, an event taking too much time. Talk about possible alternatives if such snags occur. Then, while attending the event, highlight any changes that were not expected. This exercise gets the children used to assessing upcoming events for possible snags and preparing for them.

Many kids on the spectrum only see the expected path that is their mental set. It is good for them to preview that things do not often go as expected and we must shift gears and negotiate these unexpected variations. Discussing the possible snags and then highlighting any variations while in the event helps them to see that their mental path is not always exactly the way they planned it to be. The more they preview and are prepared, the less anxiety there will be.

After the event, discuss how these snags may have created an initial shock, but were successfully navigated and everything was fine. We really need to highlight these snags, so the child builds a memory bank of tackling daily challenges.

The next step is to build planned snags into one or two activities a day. Let the child know what the snag will be and then discuss how to navigate around them. When the child is ok with these, then tell the child a snag will occur but not what it will be. Once the snag happens, try to navigate through it. The last step is telling the child a snag will occur sometime today and let's see if he can, with your help, work out an alternative on the spot. You may need to stay with each step for repeated trials, but tolerance will improve.

For common events that often get delayed or cancelled, have an alternative plan (plan B). Help the child plan out plan Bs for when snags happen throughout the day. If the baseball picnic gets rained out, we will go to a movie instead. If the store doesn't have what we want, we will go to this other store instead. This helps reduce anxiety and teaches the child that there are alternative ways of doing things when one does not work. Many adults on the spectrum tell me that they create many plan Bs for common snags they experience. If they are doing something new, they try and anticipate what snags may occur and develop a plan B for them. "If this happens, I will do that." This helps alleviate anxiety. Try to get your child used to previewing events, what he can expect, what snags may occur and possible plan Bs.

Lastly, to help teach the child how to emotionally react to snags, highlight times during the day when you experience snags (changes in plans, expectations or minor mistakes) and then model how you recover. You may purposefully make mistakes and show an initial emotion, take a deep breath, then think your way through it. "Oh no! I dropped the sugar!" "That's ok, I have more in the cupboard." Let the child view how you have initial reactions, but navigate around them. Next, plan simple snags into his activities and coach him through them.

3. *Teach "same but different."* Next, start teaching the concept of "same but different" by building in simple variations in daily routines. Slightly modify how you do things, and when and where you do them. Teach variability and different ways of doing things. Take a different car when driving to school, sample ice cream at different places or find different ways to tackle a problem. For many rigid children, doing things the same way each time becomes crucial to their security. Try to continually stretch their comfort zones by adding variations to what you are doing and how you are doing it, so children realize that their daily patterns stay the same even though there are minor changes to what and how they are doing it.

    Other examples include changing the order of the steps of your routine, switching what you do first, sitting in a different spot at the dining room table, going in through a different door at the mall and so on. This is teaching the child the principle of "same but different," that their basic daily patterns are staying the same, just with minor variations. You want them to learn not to panic when there are simple variations.

4. *Teach multiple options.* To combat either/or, all-or-nothing thinking, build in numerous learning opportunities by highlighting possible options during your typical daily routine. As you approach daily decisions, pause and consider what options are available and how to appraise them. Use a strategy I call "think out loud." Identify the task or decision and what the goal is, and look at all available options. Even if the child is nonverbal, receptively they understand with repetition. Think out loud and talk it through. When time is available, have fun identifying and then trying out each alternative so the child experiences how you appraise and evaluate options. Talk about how there can be several good options with no one right way of doing it. There can be several options that meet the same goal. If you run into a snag with one, try another.

These are just a few of the strategies for teaching flexible thinking. We discuss many more ideas in the blue book, *The Autism Discussion Page on the Core Challenges of Autism* (Nason 2014a). Since anxiety and rigidity go hand and hand, supporting the child's anxiety and fears can provide the backdrop for teaching greater flexibility.

Reasons for resistance and opposition

Many children on the spectrum have problems with following the lead of others and are often viewed as oppositional. This is frequently seen as "intentional" noncompliance, and the child is often labeled as having oppositional defiant disorder. These children must control all activity and interaction, lead the activity their way and refuse to follow the lead of others. If we press the issue, they may act out to re-establish control. This reaction can occur if they do not get something that they want, are pressured to do things they wish to avoid, and whenever someone is trying to lead what they are doing.

Listed below are some of the reasons why a child on the spectrum will be resistant, and which strategies to use to support them. Your child's resistance may be driven by one or several of the reasons here. Often resistance comes from lack of understanding what is expected, inability to meet expectations, others pressuring too fast, and inhibiting anxiety. Each child's resistance must be analyzed to identify what underlies the avoidance. In addition, the suggestions below are general guidelines that must be individualized for each child. They will not work with all children and each child will respond differently. I am not recommending strategies for specific children. This should be done in conjunction with input from significant others and guidance from professionals associated with the child.

Reason 1: Processing problems

Because of the variety of processing problems (sensory sensitivities, delayed information processing, auditory processing difficulties, etc.) many children on the spectrum become overwhelmed easily and feel safe only when they are controlling and leading everything they are engaged in. Uncertainty scares them, so they need to control everything to maintain predictability to their world.

Suggestions:

- Respect and accommodate for sensory sensitivities and use a sensory diet to calm and organize the nervous system.

- Break tasks down into smaller parts; make them concrete with visual strategies; provide information in small bits that are clear and concrete.

- Let the child pace the activity and learning.

- Respect, avoid and accommodate for situations that tend to overwhelm the child.

- Teach the child coping skills for dealing with overload.

- Respect the child's comfort zone and give avenues to escape situations that overload them (break card, say "no", ask for help, etc.).

Reason 2: Difficulty understanding what is expected

Children on the spectrum have difficulty appraising what is needed, so they are either anxious entering new situations or dive in without understanding what is needed (then act out when they struggle). These children do not know what to expect and do not know what is expected of them. They need the world to be very predictable.

Suggestions:

- Preview, clarify and verify: prepare the child before going into situations with what they can expect to occur, what is expected of them, how long it will last and what will come up next. Also, anticipate any problem areas and how to handle them (e.g. withdraw and regroup when overwhelmed). Don't assume the child understands, but clarify and verify that they understand.

- For new situations, while knowing the child's vulnerabilities, try to make modifications and accommodations to reduce the impact. Again, preview these ahead of time.

- During activities/tasks, think out loud! Provide a narrative of what is needed, and how to do it. This can help guide and coach the child through the tasks.

- Use visual schedules to help provide predictability and understanding.

- Ease transition by preparing ahead of time: "Johnny, when this TV show is over you will take a bath." Then provide five-, three- and one-minute reminders before transitioning between tasks: "Johnny, in three minutes we will need to put the Game Boy away and have your snack."

Reason 3: Safer to avoid

From a history of constantly being placed in situations where the demands are greater than their skills to handle them, the children have learned that it is safer to escape and avoid any activity that is not initiated and led by them. So, they must control all activity.

Suggestions:

- Understand the sensory, cognitive and performance issues of your child and always look at how the demands can be lowered and presented differently, or provide more support to make them match the current skill level of the child.

- Respect the child's apprehension and approach stretching slowly.

- Let the child pace the activity to match his processing skills.

- Do the tasks/activities as "we-do" activities (do them together, helping each other out) to frame and scaffold the activity and maximize success. Match the demands to the child's skill level and do them together to support the child through it.

Reason 4: Task performance anxiety

Many on the spectrum have strong task performance anxiety. So, when we ask them to perform, they will resist unless they know that they will be perfect at doing it. Because of their black and white, all-or-nothing thinking, unless they feel completely competent (which is often just in their preferred, self-directed activity), they will pull back and resist. It is an all-or-nothing response, resisting any activity that will take some time to learn.

Suggestions:

- Understand the child's comfort zone and stretch this slowly.

- Start where the child is at; keep it simple, build one step at a time and maximize success.

- Find the "just right" challenge and stay within it. Providing too big a challenge may overwhelm the child.

- When possible, do the activity together (we-do activity) so you take the pressure off the child, thus lowering the task performance anxiety.

Reason 5: Difficulty initiating tasks

Some children have a hard time initiating a task. They simply cannot get themselves started. This is due to weak executive functioning (brain wiring). They need you to "jump start" them.

Suggestions:

- Assist them in starting the activity, then fade out the assistance as they get going.

- If the children with executive functioning issues cannot remember multi-step directions, provide visual prompts for each step. Give written directions and a written outline (worksheet) to lead them from one step to the next. Be nearby to redirect and assist as needed.

Reason 6: Lack of motivation

Many children on the spectrum have low motivation to do things that are not exciting for them.

Suggestions:

- Increase motivation by following non-preferred activity with preferred activity. Use an activity that they enjoy to reinforce completion of the other activity. First do homework, then watch TV.

- Catch them being good! Provide three times more praise and positive attention for being cooperative than negative attention for being resistant (scolding, coaxing, etc.). Minimize attention for noncompliance.

- Build in token systems, star charts, sticker programs and so on, if needed to increase motivation.

- Some children are resistant when tasks are boring. Try and build new learning around their strengths and interests to increase motivation.

Reason 7: Easier to say no than to do

Some children have learned that it is easier to resist any demand or instruction than it is to engage! Often any statement that is interpreted as a demand will elicit a negative response. (Warning: the third and fourth suggestion points below should not be used by highly resistant and aggressive children.)

Suggestions:

- Pick your battles. Reduce 80 percent of all "requests," demands and directions. Telling them, or asking them to do things, will elicit an automatic no! They will resist all imperative statements (questions, prompting, instructions, directions, requests). It just gives them ammunition to be noncompliant.

- Use more declarative language to invite engagement. For example, "Wow…I could really use help with this!" or "I bet you are better at this than me!" rather than "Billy help me do…" Invite without asking. It allows the child to feel himself volunteering to help, and being in control under his own volition.

- Provide no negative emotion to refusal. The main things to avoid when your child is resisting are strong emotion, getting upset and any scolding, negotiating, coaxing or bribing. The children will feed off the negative emotion (it helps them feel powerful) and attention that we give counseling, scolding and coaxing. However, if you choose to respond to noncompliance, do it with little emotion, and with minimal talking.

- For requests that the child must do, use the following. (Do not use with highly resistant/aggressive children and individuals with pathological demand avoidance).

  - Get the child's attention, face to face, at eye level.

  - State the prompt in short, clear, concrete language.

  - Give the child ten seconds to respond (longer for delayed processing).

  - Repeat the prompt in firm manner, using the same language.

  - If there is still no response, continue to stand your ground, saying nothing but repeating the same statement every 30 seconds.

  - For some children, increase the assistance with physical guidance (unless it agitates them more), or simply wait until they are ready to respond.

- Once the child responds, provide support as needed and reinforce all co-operative participation.

- Often these children respond negatively to positive praise (the opposite of most children). They read "praise" as you manipulating them to do things. So for these children, do not praise performance, just let mastery be motivating.

Reason 8: Resistance gets them what they want

Because of our wish to avoid a fight, many children have learned that by resisting, people back off and withdraw the demands in order to avoid a tantrum or destructive behavior. By doing this, we often get to the point where we pacify the child, so he will not become aggressive. We coax and bribe the child to do things. Consequently, the child learns that by being noncompliant and acting out, he can manipulate the people around him to give him what he wants and to escape and avoid everything he does not wish to do.

Suggestions:

- Build in the proactive strategies above to match the demands to the child's current skill level.

- Use a visual schedule so the routine is consistent and predictable for the child, with preferred activity built into the schedule every two or three activities.

- Do the activities as "we-do" activities as much as possible. Provide support and praise as you go along.

- When the child is resistant, do not argue, negotiate or justify your request at that time. Take away the battle and let the consequences teach the behavior. Tell the child, "You are too tired to do it right now. That's ok, you let me know when you are ready, and I will help you." Show no emotion, simply back away and ignore noncompliance. However, make it clear that the child cannot do any preferred activity until he follows through with the routine task.

- If the child complains, simply remind him that it is his choice and you are there to help him when he is ready.

- Be very clear in the expectations and consistent in following through with consequences until the child becomes responsive again.

As you see, there are different reasons why children on the spectrum are oppositional. However, assume that the child is doing the best that he can, given the situation he is in and his abilities to deal with it. Also, assume that the more oppositional he is, the more incompetent the child feels. Focus on helping the child feel competent, and responsiveness will increase. We tend to focus too much on forcing compliance, when we need to be assisting these children by taking away the fight, lowering the demands (at least at first), providing increased supports, and focusing on what they are doing right. Help them feel more competent, and they will follow your lead.

Chapter 9

ANXIETY, OPPOSITION AND DEMAND AVOIDANCE

As we pointed out in the last chapter, anxiety and rigidity often lead to a host of behavior challenges usually clustered under labels such as resistant, oppositional, defiant, manipulative, aggressive and destructive. To these children, the chaotic and confusing world, with all its ambiguity and inconsistencies, leads to chronic anxiety. These children do not have good mental maps for navigating our social world, thus are left guessing at what is expected. They are constantly pressured into situations where they cannot read the expectations and have to guess at what is needed. Unfortunately, when they are left guessing at what is expected, they often guess wrong. Anxiety for these children can range from mild to severely debilitating. Their coping skills for handling the anxiety also can vary significantly. However, most will show a variety of resistant behaviors to escape and avoid the conditions that lead to their uncertainty.

Pathological demand avoidance

There is a movement in Europe to recognize a small subset of autism that is extremely resistant to any and all daily demands as well as following the lead of others. Anxiety is so severe that these people are apprehensive in all daily activity and must control everything happening to them and around them. This behavior profile within the autism spectrum has been labeled pathological demand avoidance (PDA). These children are usually bright, very social (but lack good relating skills), creative, good at role-playing and pretending, and good at manipulating their way out of daily demands and expectations. Although PDA is not yet an official diagnosis, it is steadily gaining acceptance and it is to be hoped that it will be included as a subset under the description of autism spectrum disorders. It is not the intent of this book to provide a comprehensive description of PDA, but readers can easily find current books and websites devoted to this profile by googling the term. Also, not all autistic children with severe avoidance and anxiety have PDA (due to other defining symptoms) but the suggestions below, based on my experience, should apply to any autistic child with severe anxiety and avoidance.

For children with severe avoidance, anxiety overwhelms every aspect of their day. Their world has to be just right, entirely predictable and totally under their control for them to feel safe and competent. Fear of uncertainty and strong feelings of inadequacy render them constantly anxious, insecure and resistant to all influences of others. They need to control everything around them to keep it predictable and aligning to their expectations.

For most of us, the children's behavior can seem very unpredictable. You can be offering the child something that they like or a preferred event and still get strong resistance, demands and aggressive behavior. No matter what you try, it doesn't work. Even when allowed to lead and control, they still might melt down at the least little snag. Why? Why would the child melt down when he is given what he wants or allowed to do what he desires? Listed below are the seven most common reasons.

1. *Fear of uncertainty.* These children need to know exactly what to expect and what is expected of them. Preview events ahead of time to provide a mental map of what is going to happen, how long it is going to be and what is expected of them, especially if it is a new, unfamiliar event. The more novel, unfamiliar or vague the event is, the more anxiety and chances of melting down there will be.

2. *Unexpected events.* The children's security is based on the understanding and predictability of their immediate world. What is occurring around them must match their expectation. Unexpected changes collapse their sense of safety and security. Even if what you present is something that they desire, if they were not expecting it and were not mentally prepared for it, their fragile security falls apart. This can happen if there is a snag in what is expected, something is postponed or delayed or if there is a small variation to a familiar activity. When the course of events does not occur as expected, the whole picture collapses. This can happen even in events that seem to be going along just as expected. However, if some small part is different and not according to expectation, the child can immediately react as if the whole event has fallen apart.

3. *Need to control.* These children fear uncertainty and need to control everything to make it predictable and safe. They do not trust in following the lead of the adult and resist any attempt from us to direct, instruct or lead them. Even if the event is something they like and is previewed adequately, if they are being directed by someone else, they will get anxious. So, when the child is resistant, first look to see how much control you are exerting over the activity. Ask yourself, if you were the child, would you feel in control of what is happening? This is very hard for adults because we want to be in control and lead. We want to guide, direct and instruct. But the more we try, the more resistant the child becomes.

4. *Must initiate the event.* These children often show an immediate negative reaction to anything initiated by others. Even if the children can pace and lead the activity, if it is not initiated by them, they will still feel anxious. If it wasn't their idea and initiated by them, they may still resist. This resistance will occur even if what you are requesting is something the child likes. When initiated by someone else, it is not safe.

5. *Performance anxiety.* You do everything above, let the child do what he wants, let him lead, preview expectations ahead of time and let him dictate every element of the event and he still freaks! Why? These children have strong task performance anxiety. It makes sense that when we place an expectation on them, they feel

strong performance anxiety and feel "put on the spot." So, we place minimal demands and let them control and they still get upset!

What gives? Whether the expectation is placed by others or themselves, it still represents performance anxiety. If their performance is not going as planned and matches their expectation, they will become highly anxious and lose control. Usually they have a very strong fear of failure and perfectionism. When a little slip-up occurs, they fall apart. Making things worse, these children are often very poor in appraising what is needed and how to monitor their performance. They often jump in, feeling they can do it and at the first snag or problem, fall apart, blame others, become demanding and sabotage the much-desired event. Feeling inadequate and a failure sets them up for increased anxiety the next time.

6. *Strong social anxiety.* The more people there are, the more the child must regulate during the event and the greater the anxiety. Problems reading the nonverbal communication of others, understanding the intentions and perspectives of others, reading the invisible social rules of the situations and understanding what others expect make interacting very unpredictable and stressful. This is hard enough when they are just relating with one person, but greatly falls apart if it is a group event. Birthday parties, holiday get-togethers and other group activities can be a disaster. Too much uncertainty, vague expectations and unpredictable actions and the child becomes overwhelmed.

7. *Sensory overload.* Since many of these children have sensory sensitivities and problems integrating multiple sensations, the greater the sensory stimulation (noise, sights, smells, movement and activity), the more overwhelmed they become. The more involved the activity (people, activity, expectations), the more sensory integration is required. There is simply too much coming in too fast. Also, the more anxious the child becomes, the more sensitive he is to the stimulation around him.

What happens for the child? If any of these seven elements are present, anxiety will increase. The more variables that occur, the greater the anxiety. If something occurs unexpectedly, the child does not know how to respond, what to say or what to do. If the child cannot control everything and direct exactly what is going on, then the uncertainty becomes frightening and overwhelming. Adults may try making everything as desirable as possible for the child, but they cannot control all these variables.

These children are consistently inconsistent. They may do fine one time and completely melt down the next. They may appear to be having fun and then instantly fall apart. They may be enjoying your company one minute and kicking and hitting you the next. Our anxiety and emotions escalate and so do theirs.

Such is the life for autistic children with severe anxiety and/or PDA. They are the most fragile and vulnerable of children. They are also the most frustrating for parents and teachers to support. Every typical parenting and teaching strategy falls apart. Every single person around the child, as well as the child himself, feels entirely inadequate.

The intent here is to outline some of the rigid comfort zones (need for predictability, control, perfect performance and minimal social regulation) that come into play in each daily activity for the child. In analyzing each negative outcome, we must look at these seven variables and appraise which ones create the problems, and design strategies for helping to lessen their impact. We must then learn to appraise events ahead of time to see how each of these seven variables will come into play and how we will accommodate for them. The more we understand the comfort zone of the child and what variables shake this comfort zone, the more we understand why the child is resisting and how we can support him.

Just remember, when the tide turns and the child is falling apart, his world is crumbling, he is becoming overwhelmed and he immediately panics. The more resistant the child, the more scared and inadequate he feels. A tidal wave of emotions overwhelms the thinking part of his brain and all hell breaks loose. These children are trying to cope as best as they can.

Think for one minute. If your sense of safety and security was so fragile and dependent on these seven variables being predictable, every daily activity would be frightening. Be patient with both the child and yourself. These are very difficult challenges that test the best of us.

The anxiety of uncertainty; how do they cope?

Because the world is very chaotic and unpredictable for individuals on the spectrum, uncertainty is the child's worst enemy. Since they often cannot read the context of situations, the unwritten rules of conduct and the perspectives of others, our social world is unpredictable and anxiety producing. This fear of uncertainty often results in one of two ways of coping:

1. Typical autistic children welcome and seek out concrete rules and expectations that set boundaries and provide a mental map of when and how to act. For these children, rules are welcomed and rigidly needed to make the world predictable and to minimize anxiety. However, once these rules are established, the child needs them rigidly followed. He also needs everyone else to follow them consistently, otherwise his predictable world collapses, but at least the use of rules and clear expectations establishes predictable boundaries and lowers their anxiety.

2. In contrast, for those with PDA, external rules and expectations create severe anxiety. For the highly anxious, severe avoiders, rules and expectations produce an innate fear. The threat of uncertainty leads them to fear following the lead of others and resists any concrete expectations and boundaries. Rules immediately elicit opposition. Any attempt by others to guide and direct them elicits an immediate "no", even if it is in their favor. These children are so insecure and anxious they must control all activity and interaction around them. Any expectation or direction produces fear and immediate avoidance.

Like most children on the spectrum, children with PDA have the same fear of uncertainty, but more intense and more generalized to most daily demands. In addition, their persistent anxiety doesn't allow them to feel secure following the rules and expectations that others place on them. They must control everything around them to feel safe and secure. They feel too vulnerable to follow the lead of others. It is not just when someone is asking something of them, but all expectations, even those that are easy to meet—any expectation, easy or difficult.

Directions and expectations bring inherent anxiety from the responsibility of meeting these expectations. They often make their own rules and rigidly hold to them. They will resist and adamantly fight any attempt to follow the expectations of others. So, it is not just the immediate requests of others, but also the expectations of the normal daily routine that can create fear and opposition. These children, often cognitively bright, are driven by generalized anxiety and are on high alert for any expectations they will have to meet.

Children with PDA are often the most oppositional (driven by anxiety) and exhibit some of the most challenging behaviors. They are fragile and to maintain their sense of security it requires a very delicate balancing act of allowing them to control most of their daily activity and guiding their development.

As you can see, there is a real dimension to how children on the spectrum deal with their fear of uncertainty. On the one end are the children who crave clear, concrete rules and expectations to make the world more understandable and predictable, and on the other end, the children who are so anxious and rigid that they actively resist any rules and expectations and must control all interaction and activity occurring around them. How children cope with the fear of uncertainty (crave rules or resist them) will dictate their level of anxiety and social/emotional relations with others.

For the children for whom resistance is a functional response to their core vulnerabilities, the common strategies listed in the eight reasons in Chapter 8 often work well. However, those individuals with extreme anxiety will resist many of the above-mentioned strategies, because their fear of following the lead of others is so severe that it threatens their core emotional survival. The whole world becomes a battlefield and most attempts to help them are met with extreme resistance.

It is all about control!

Because the world is frequently confusing and overwhelming for those autistics with severe anxiety and/or PDA, their brains are often in a reactive, defensive mode. When the brain is in the defensive mode it has one thing on its mind: "safety." It feels threatened and all uncertainty represents a threat to its safety. Safety takes priority over learning. Until the brain feels safe it is not in a state of readiness for learning. When the brain feels threatened it sets off hormonal changes that heighten the senses, increase the adrenaline and put all systems on high alert for possible fight or flight action. Research also shows that for the neurotypical brain once the threat is over, systems rebound quickly and we fall back to a calm state until the next perceived threat occurs. However, for many on the spectrum, this rebound takes much longer and the brain stays hyper-alert for the extended future. Even in the relaxed state, the stress chemicals for people with autism are still much higher.

Children with high anxiety and rigid inflexible thinking are most often working in the reactive, defensive mode. When in this state, the brain seeks to control all that is around it to make the world more understandable and predictable, lessening the threat and lowering the anxiety. The child will try to control all interactions and activity to feel safe and will often actively resist following the lead of others because of the threat of uncertainty. If the anxiety is high, the child will be actively oppositional and resist all force that we apply. We must recognize that the need for control is required for the brain to protect itself and this is not the willful intent of the child. Increased pressure to comply will be met with extreme resistance and violence if need be. The child simply has no choice.

As parents, teachers, caregivers and professionals, we need to recognize this need for control as being an innate part of the child's brain functioning (wiring) and realize that the child's need to control is the only coping skill that he has available. It is not a bad thing, but a coping skill for feeling safe, both physically and emotionally.

Unfortunately, we often meet resistance with increased pressure to comply. This "command and demand" mode will rarely work and only fuels the flames and makes the brain more reactive. This is a natural neurological response from the brain, and we cannot force the brain into more uncertainty and insecurity. It is hard wired to revert to control or explode.

What does this mean for us? First, we need to recognize that when in a defensive mode, the brain seeks avoidance of anything it is not controlling. Therefore, we must not take this need to control as a power struggle with us, but recognize it as a survival technique to feel safe and secure. Once we can recognize this, it should lower our anger and frustration. Second, we need to give the child as much control as possible, so the brain feels safe. We need to meet rigidity with flexibility, recognizing that we need to initially make sure the child feels safe before we attempt to teach. Meet the child where he is at and collaboratively work together, allowing the child to lead while you safely guide. If you do this, the child views you as a working partner and is more trusting in following your guidance. Again, let him lead with your guidance.

The child will not initially trust your guidance and will resist. This is because he is used to people pushing and pressuring him into uncertainty. This is not a personal attack on you and do not see it as a power struggle. Remember, we must focus on "safety" first before teaching. When you see the defensive reaction, most likely the child is not feeling safe and is going to react with opposition to control. Allow the child to pace himself, and follow his lead at first. If he is too over-reactive, back off, regroup and respect the brain's sense of insecurity. Proceed cautiously while gauging the child's sense of safety. If you do this, the child will begin to trust that you will not push or pressure him into panic. This respect will teach the child that he can follow your lead.

Allowing the child to lead and knowing when to stretch is a balancing act that will vary from day to day and hour to hour based on the child's current level of anxiety.

On days when the anxiety is high, we need to back off as much as possible, not pressurize, and allow the brain to feel safe. On days of less anxiety, we can stretch a little further without overwhelming the brain. Over time, the brain will be less defensive and reactive and the child will gradually start to trust that he can follow your lead.

Working through resistance

It takes a patient and flexible adult to work with the very anxious child. The more rigid the child, the more flexible the adult needs to be. All hell breaks loose when a rigid and inflexible child meets a rigid and inflexible adult! The adult tries to control the child by commanding and demanding, using force when needed. This leads the child to feel even more insecure and fearful, driving him to be even more resistant to maintain precious control. Typical discipline strategies do not work with these children.

You must acknowledge and respect the child's fears and insecurities and be willing to give up initial control. You must bite your tongue, pick your battles wisely and let the child lead and control as much as possible. Remember, he needs that control to feel safe. You must keep reminding yourself of that. You must start where he is at, allow him to feel safe with you, and then gradually stretch his comfort zone.

Although you want to pick your battles, what boundaries you set must be clear, concrete and very consistent. The child may resist at first, but if you stay consistent, non-judgemental and in control of your own emotional reactivity, these boundaries will eventually help create a stronger sense of security. These absolute rules must be minimal and saved for those issues involving safety and respecting the rights of others.

Try to avoid "command and demand." Avoid directing the child. Instead, try to work with the child, let him lead if possible, and then slowly guide the child. The child must feel a sense of control over what he is doing and what you are doing to him. Give the child a voice in all decision making, allowing him to collaborate and negotiate with you. Yes, this may be hard at first, but it is essential in empowering the child to feel in control over his life. This will take time to develop and the adult may have to make most of the compromises at first. If you stay a working partner with the child, he will learn to feel safe and trust in following your lead.

When conflict arises, first acknowledge and validate the child's concerns (regardless of how exaggerated they are), "Wow, Jimmy you really look upset to me. I can understand how you might be upset if…happened." You do not have to agree with the child's behavior and may feel his response is over-exaggerated. However, it is important to look past the behavior and empathize with his feelings. This models respect and empathy and builds the foundation for negotiating. Once you have acknowledged and validated, then encourage the child to collaborate and negotiate a solution with you. Work together to try to find solutions that meet both of your needs.

The more oppositional, the more incompetent they feel!

Most children, both on and off the spectrum, will do the right thing if they can. If you look at children who are consistently oppositional, they are not usually happy children. It is not as if they feel good about being defiant. They are usually resistant because they feel insecure and incompetent, often with strong social and task performance anxiety. They usually have poor social skills, struggle with give-and-take reciprocal interaction, and only feel secure when controlling everything they do and what is occurring around them.

The more intellectually capable child who often appears competent may express defiance by calling everything stupid, too easy for him, he can do it better but just doesn't want to, and questioning/complaining about everything asked of him. That child often harbors very strong feelings of inadequacy, which he tries covering up with a "superiority complex." He takes an "I am better than all of this" attitude, so "I am not going to do it." This child tends to frustrate and irritate those around him, who often view him as intentionally oppositional.

Along with all the processing problems, sensory issues and social communication difficulties, oppositional behavior is often the result of ongoing failure to understand and meet expectations. Being defiant is a defense mechanism to escape and avoid any situation that makes the child feel inadequate and insecure. Unfortunately, once the child digs that hole, it becomes a predictable routine and provides a major avenue for dealing with the world. Being defiant allows the child to avoid feelings of insecurity and provides a strong sense of control and power. It gives the child a temporary false sense of security. In turn, it taxes not just him but everyone trying desperately to help him. This drive for control often comes from a rigid and inflexible thinking style.

Suggestions to increase responsiveness

1. Minimize all confrontations and struggles you can avoid. Pick your battles. If you think the child will be noncompliant, try not to ask or demand it. Can you work around it or rephrase it so that it is not a request (see discussion on declarative language in Chapter 6)? Avoid placing the child in situations where he will become defiant. At first you bite your tongue and minimize scolding, correcting, asking or demanding things of the child. If you do not have to ask it, then don't. If you pull back on 70 percent of the demands, you reduce 70 percent of noncompliance.

2. Focus on building competency in the following areas:

   i. Build feelings of competency by focusing on what the child does right and fostering his strengths and interests. Ask yourself, "What helps my child feel safe and competent?" and focus on these conditions. Create the conditions that help the child feel competent. This takes time, but builds the foundation to increase self-esteem and reduce the need to be oppositional.

   ii. Turn activities into "we-do" activities. Involve yourself in these activities, framing the event and working with the child to maximize success. Allow the child to lead and slowly add variations. Try using preferred activities that interest him, letting the child pace and lead the events. If possible, take photos of the two of you in these activities and together make one-page picture stories of the child successfully tackling these activities. We call these "ME books," a collection of events when the child felt competent engaging, and instilling memories of times when the child felt competent. Frequently sit down and review this book together.

iii. When engaging together, focus on sharing the experience, not on task performance. Focus on sharing positive emotions and reciprocal back-and-forth interaction—taking turns, helping each other out and so on. Take the pressure off and avoid focusing on performance. Minimize demands, directions and instructions. Simply share the pleasure of doing it together. Try to avoid specifically praising the child's performance. This will only increase his performance anxiety. Simply have fun and share pleasurable moments.

3. Although the child may be frequently resistant, he is not oppositional to everything. Take notes on every little request and activity when he is responsive. Even requests as simple as "give me five" are responsiveness trials. Make a list of all the little things that he currently feels comfortable with. Try and focus on increasing as many responsiveness trials as possible, drastically increasing the ratio of responsive to resistant requests—preferably a ratio of at least four responsiveness trials for every request that elicits resistance. These children are creatures of habit —the more resistant they are (the greater number of opportunities to be defiant), the more noncompliant they become. It will just become habit to immediately resist. Try to minimize the requests that will frequently elicit resistance, and drastically increase the requests that elicit responsiveness. Create a habit of responding!

4. The old phrase "catch them being good" is so important. We hyper-focus on their noncompliance, but we need to highlight all the times they are responsive. If you want to help them feel competent, highlight the times when they feel competent being good! Please remember not to praise these moments, just highlight them by drawing attention to them.

5. Probably the hardest suggestion to follow is to minimize your emotional reactions to the child's defiance. Do not yell, scold, coax, or plead with the child. These responses will only fuel the fire and create greater need to control. No matter what strategies you use, stay calm and matter of fact when reacting to your child's resistance.

Of course, there will be a small percentage of children who are driven by anxiety to be defiant to all requests, even if the requests are enjoyable to them. These techniques will work but take longer to establish.

It's all about trust

For the anxious, resistant child, we focus on their noncompliance and develop strategies to shape them to be more compliant. This is often perceived by the child as controlling and manipulative (because it is). We are missing the point. It is not about compliance, it is about trust. When the world is very threatening and the child feels helpless in the face of overwhelming anxiety, protecting one's "self" from external control is essential to survival. The need to control everything around them is the priority.

In normal development, children, through their attachment and relations with others, develop a strong sense of self in relation to the rest of the world; a stable and definite sense of self as separate, but interrelated, with others. This separation is established early in life through attachment to their caregivers who teach them that following the lead of others is safe and trustworthy. A strong sense of self develops out of safe relating with those around them.

For children with autism, this attachment, and sense of self that arises from it, is disrupted. Children develop a very fragile sense of self in relation to the world, which severely weakens their security, creates strong anxiety and drives a fear of giving up control (sense of self) to follow the lead of others. These children are not trying to make people unhappy, purposefully aggravating others or refusing to love others. It is not a conscious choice, but a defense mechanism to protect their fragile sense of self. To lessen this rigidity means to be engulfed in a spiral of losing their sense of self: "To succumb to the direction of others is to lose my very fragile sense of 'self'." Giving up control and following the lead of another is too threatening to even contemplate. Even if the event being offered is very inviting, giving up control to obtain it is too scary. Letting down their guard means possibly being swallowed up and losing their sense of self: "To protect my 'self' I will adamantly and forcefully resist any attempts to give up control and follow your lead. I cannot trust that following your lead is safe and will make me stronger. I will lose my 'self'."

How do we help? We must give up our own false sense of needing to control. As parents, teachers and professionals, we want to teach the child to respond and comply. This is very hard for us to give up. We need to forget about the power struggle and give up the notion of complying as the desired result. We need to reframe how we interact and relate with the child. Our focus needs to be on helping the child feel "safe and secure" with us, relating with us, with no threat or pressure; to be there with us, without directions, instructions, prompting; to first trust just allowing us to be at one with them; to share emotional experiences with no direction or pressure. This will help the child feel safe and that being with us is not a threat to their security, but makes their sense of security stronger.

How to do this will vary individually with each child. It requires including yourself unconditionally in what the child values, following his lead and sharing emotional experiences around his preferences. The secret is building numerous moments of positive "emotion sharing" in his safe world to establish a strong emotional bond. Once the child feels safe in these unconditional activities, then you can start to expand by adding little variations and elaborations to what the child is already doing. This teaches the child to feel safe and competent (to trust) in following your lead, in very small increments. Over time, the child starts to view you as a working partner with them and begins to trust in following your lead. The stretching must be very small, in tiny steps so as not to overwhelm the child. It must also be born out of the positive emotion sharing that is the glue to establishing the trust. By building this trust, the child will start to feel safer following your lead and learning from you.

Resist the focus on controlling the child and think instead of helping the child to feel safe. When they are noncompliant, they are feeling threatened or automatically resisting placing themselves in a position of feeling threatened. Keep your objective on first helping the child feel safe and building trust while you gently try to guide them. When resistance increases, respect their voice, back off and reduce the demands. Let them lead and pace the interaction, and become a working partner with them. Make sure to solidify the companionship by building in moments of strong "emotion sharing" to ingrain memories of sharing pleasurable moments. Feel good together, sharing the experience of doing it together. That is the glue to establishing security in relating.

Is this easy? By no means. It is very exhausting; it can take a long time to break through and build a strong sense of security and trust. You will initially feel as if you have failed at being a loving parent, but that is the furthest from the truth. This resistance is usually due to neurological vulnerabilities (e.g. sensory sensitivities) and has nothing to do with the loving care of the parent.

Do not question your love and parenting skills. However, the oppositional child will test every patience and regard that you have and frequently leave you feeling exhausted and defeated throughout this journey. All these frustrations and emotions you feel (often negative) are natural so try to avoid feeling guilty about them. They are temporary and will pass.

As a parent, and as a person, you will be tested and pressured by not just the child but by all those around you. People will see your child as defiant, oppositional, manipulative, a brat and spoiled, and they will question your parenting skills. If possible, try and find a support group (possibly online) of other families experiencing the same journey. By far, these children are the most difficult to parent and anyone who criticizes you does not have a clue about how to support you or these children. However, it is important that you seek out others who will help you feel safe and validated.

Anxiety and weak sense of self

Some children, especially those with PDA, often have severe anxiety related to a very weak sense of self. Not having a stable sense of self is very difficult for many non-autistics to understand, since it is often a sensation they have not experienced. Our sense of self develops very early in life as we begin to physically realize that we are physically and emotionally separate from the rest of the world we experience. Over time, we realize that our thoughts, feelings, experiences and perspectives are separate from others.

Developing a strong sense of self requires good sensory processing that provides us with consistent and reliable information about our own bodies as well as the world around us. For those with strong sensory defensiveness and integration problems, it is difficult to establish stable constructs about the world as separate from themselves. Their sensory experiences are threatening, inconsistent and unreliable. It is hard to feel secure in a world that is so threatening and overwhelming. Anxiety is constant in the face of chaos and uncertainty.

Regardless of how intelligent the children are, if they have a weak sense of self, they feel anxious and overwhelmed. They often feel disconnected from their bodies, that their bodies are separate objects they must manipulate. They report having poor control of their bodies and that they do not own their bodies. Also, they have very weak boundaries distinguishing them from the rest of the world. These individuals often report that they feel the emotions of others so strongly they cannot distinguish if the flood of emotion is theirs or from others. Both their sensations and feelings are confusing and frightening since they feel helpless in controlling them. It is as if their body and experiences are foreign intrusions they have little control over. The result is a very persistent sense of anxiety, insecurity and vulnerability.

When you cannot trust yourself, anxiety is constant

It is one thing to not be able to trust in following the lead of others, but when you have a weak sense of self you also cannot trust in following your own lead. Developmental theorists point to our sense of self unfolding from secure relationships with others. When sensory processing challenges make this social and emotional connectiveness difficult, some children with autism struggle to develop a strong self-identity; they are insecure in their ability to competently relate with others and in trusting their support. People are confusing and confronting, pulling them in chaotic directions. They cannot trust in following their lead and are continually defensive.

Since this weak sense of self is often born out of poor sensory processing (integrating the senses), it is crucial that these individuals receive a sensory integration evaluation from an occupational therapist highly experienced in working with autism. Through careful analysis of the processing challenges, the occupational therapist can provide therapy that will improve sensory integration and will help the children (or adults) feel more connected to their bodies. The more connected they feel both in their own body and in relation to the external world, the more secure they will feel. In addition, research is slowly starting to evaluate the effectiveness of using meditation and mindfulness to help these individuals become more connected with their bodies and reduce their anxiety.

Adding insult to injury, when you have a weak sense of self you also do not have confidence in following your own lead. We talk about parents and teachers trying to avoid directing the child and letting the child lead so that he feels safe controlling the pace and direction of activity. However, children with PDA or high anxiety also cannot trust in following their own lead. They do not feel competent trusting the expectations that they create for themselves. Because of their processing differences and own insecurities, they have difficulty appraising daily situations, what is needed and what they want. Because of weak executive functioning, they cannot adequately assess daily situations, appraise what is needed, organize a course of action and competently carry it out. So even if you allow them to control and lead, they cannot trust in following their own direction.

This means that all demands, those placed by others as well as self-imposed expectations, will create anxiety and agitation. The child freezes with emotional paralysis, not being able to pave his own way while also fearing the directions of others. There is no safe map, no trusted path, just scary uncertainty that risks ultimate danger. This innate insecurity and fear will create a "resistance at all cost" when placed with both external demands as well as many self-imposed demands. These children are forced to act out to escape and avoid all demands, all expectations and most attempts by others to help. They have an innate distrust in others as well as themselves and there is constant fear, anxiety and unhappiness.

How we can help

These children will never feel competent until they begin to feel safe engaging with others. We can withdraw all demands, provide indirect guidance and allow the children to lead, but this will only work so far. This will help the children feel safer engaging with you and, it is hoped, develop trust that you recognize what they need and that you will not press or push them into uncertainty. This is vitally important to developing a working partnership with them. They must feel safe and accepted, unconditionally, before trusting to follow your lead. You must become a safe, working partner before becoming a trusted guide.

For these children, trust comes from minimizing demands, allowing them to pace what is happening and respecting their need to escape when they feel overwhelmed. Once they feel safe engaging with you, then the next step is to build trust in your guidance. This trust can be assisted with the following guidelines:

1. Allow the children to control and pace what is happening, make their own choices and lead the action.

2. Teach the children to feel safe, allowing you to engage with them, sharing the experience without prompting or directing. This is non-demanding engagement, being there unconditionally, following their lead and becoming a partner in sharing the experience. No demands, no structured learning, no direction or instruction. You are simply relating for the joy of sharing the experience together.

3. Since they often struggle with feeling safe and following their own lead, assist them by not directing, but helping to scaffold the activity to make it more successful. By doing the task together, you allow the children to lead, but provide indirect support to assist them through it. They feel more competent doing it with you than by doing it by themselves. You do not verbally direct them, but frame the materials and your own role to minimize errors and provide the needed assistance to help the children's choices and actions be successful. This helps them feel safe engaging in reciprocal interaction and feel safe with your help: doing together, becoming more competent together.

4. Focus on engaging and relating together, not on task performance. The type of activity and how well it is done is not important. The task is just a vehicle to engage around, to create a "we-do" activity to relate together, sharing the experience and joy of doing together, helping each other out and interacting for the sake of relating. There is minimal verbal attention to performance, how well the child is doing or what the outcome looks like. The goal is using the activity to create an avenue to share pleasurable moments engaging together.

5. When doing with the child, engaging together, side by side, minimize all verbal directions or instructions. Support with gestures, demonstration and physically doing it together while using your verbal statements only to share the experience. "Wow, this is fun!" "Look at how pretty these flowers are!" Talk to share your thoughts, feelings and experiences, not to question, prompt or instruct.

6. Minimize all verbal praise and external reinforcers. Two aspects become the motivators: (1) the joy of emotionally sharing a fun experience together, and (2) the internal joy of mastering a challenge together, feeling more competent. Minimize directly reinforcing the child's performance. Celebrate doing it together, "We rock!" This will help the child feel safe, competent and confident in following the lead of others. Focus on the relating, becoming competent together, rather than throwing the performance attention on the child.

7. Most importantly, have fun "doing it together" with no worry about how well it is done, what specific skill is learned or how compliant the child is.

This sounds so easy, but as adults we are so used to prompting, directing, instructing and praising good performance and correcting errors, all of which create anxiety and avoidance of learning.

Negative side effects of positive reinforcement

Many parents and specialists have found that for some children on the spectrum, especially those with PDA, the use of both positive and negative consequences often results in more oppositional defiance. Usually this is because of the child's severe anxiety and strong need to control all interaction and activity around him. For the child, the fear of uncertainty and strong need for predictability means his security is tied to controlling all that occurs to and for him. He cannot give up that control and follow the lead of others. This leaves him too vulnerable to expectations and performance anxiety. This leads to radically different responses to typical positive rewards and punishments used to motivate other children. There are two main negative side effects of using positive and negative consequences.

1. Any attempt to reinforce positive behavior leads to the realization that the desired behavior is now an expectation to occur in the future. With positive reinforcement comes great expectation to perform again and, therefore, stronger performance anxiety. Task performance anxiety is severe when expectations are placed on

the child. Meeting the expectations and the resultant reinforcement leads to greater anxiety. Hence, resist and defy.

2. As can be expected, when they see us trying to manipulate their behavior by reinforcing or punishing it, they immediately sense that we are trying to control them (which we are). They are hyper-sensitive to control and immediately resist any sense that we are manipulating them. They do not trust in following our lead because we are trying to manipulate them.

For these children, it is all about the lack of trust in following our lead and doing anything that meets our expectations. To be compliant means to lose one's sense of control and security. Even when punishment is applied, or very strong desirable consequences are offered, nothing is more important than maintaining the control.

Where does that leave us? As adults, we must give up our preconceived notions that we are in control and the child must do what we want. We need to stop trying to direct and change their behavior. We must start by giving up the control and following the lead of the child until he sees us as a working partner with him and feels safe that we will not pressure him to comply. It is about building trust by being a non-threatening partner with no demands or expectations. We follow the child's lead rather than trying to direct and instruct him, helping him feel safe and secure engaging with us. Once this trust is established, then you can start to stretch the child's comfort zone by gradually building in variations and elaborations in what you are doing together, while still letting him dictate how and when we do that.

Avoid direct praise for good performance. Let the primary reinforcement be the feeling of mastery (becoming competent) by successfully tackling new challenges (with you). Praising can backfire by showing your approval of the child's performance, trying to shape or change their behavior. The need to control is the driving force and hence the positive reinforcement. However, do not try to hold the control as a contingent reinforcer because these children can sense the manipulation and you will lose all trust. We must become a true working partner with them to become a trusted guide. Stop trying to manipulate, shape and control by applying and holding back contingent reinforcement.

From trust to collaboration

The typical parenting and teaching role of the adult unilaterally directing the child will not work in establishing trust and responsiveness from these children. It is about the adults giving up the unilateral control and respecting the child's need to pace what, when and how they do things. To feel in control! Becoming a mentor for these kids involves giving up our insecure need to control and manipulate, meeting children where they are at and working collaboratively together. This is not just a recommendation, it's a must! These children see all demands, directions and reinforcement as manipulation, which they react violently against.

To effectively parent these children, you must give up your need to control, respecting their thoughts, feelings and opinions, and allow them to steer themselves through life.

They must feel that they are in the driver's seat, not sitting in the backseat allowing the adults to guide and direct. You have a complete collaborative role, taking their lead, following their preferences and letting them pick, choose, direct and pace the action.

This is a very unnatural role for adults with children. We are used to being in control, dictating what, when and how things will be done. It is not easy by any means, but is an essential shift if you want to develop a responsive relationship.

To collaborate you must provide your thoughts, feelings and perspectives without trying to direct the child. Do activities together in the "we-do" framework discussed earlier (see Chapter 6, Autism and Anxiety). Talk about what needs to be done, letting the child's perspective lead the way while you provide an informative narrative: "That sounds great! I wonder what would happen if we did…?" rather than, "We must to do it this way." Look at different ways to do things, highlighting options, collaborating together, but allowing the child to choose, direct and pace the action. Help the child feel competent tackling uncertainty with you as a collaborative guide, rather than instructor. Let him experience the challenge to feel the mastery. Over time, the more competent the child feels, mastering new learning with your non-directive collaboration, the more confident he will feel learning from you. Eventually, the child will begin feeling safe with your thoughts, feelings and perspectives and take them into consideration.

Negotiate and collaborate

It is important to teach children to problem solve and collaborate to meet their needs and keep themselves regulated. Children often go from 0 to 100 when they reach a road block, going into panic mode because they see the world as "all or nothing" or "yes or no." No means never, and snags mean disaster! It is important to also get them considering the viewpoints and concerns of others (which does not come naturally for them).

The Collaborative Problem Solving (CPS) strategy described here was developed by Dr. Ross Greene, author of *The Explosive Child*, and has been highly successful in working with children who have rigid and inflexible thinking and poor emotional regulation. In this sequence of steps, it is important to first acknowledge and validate the child's concerns and importance, "Wow, Johnny, you really look upset to me!, I can understand how you would feel angry if Julie took your favorite toy!"

Once you have validated the child's concern then you can concretely define your concerns. Then, together, collaborate on a solution that will meet everyone's concerns. It is very important to concretely define each person's concerns so that the compromise can meet both party's needs. When learning this, it is important to frequently practice this process. If the child is too upset to do it during the heat of the moment, then review it once everyone has calmed down. It is also good to use this before entering potentially problematic events, using it proactively to hold off problems.

This procedure is good for more cognitively capable children on the spectrum because it helps the adult learn to define (investigate) what the true problem is and teach the child that others have a different perspective. Once the two concerns are identified then the objective is to find an agreed solution that will meet both concerns. For most of our kids, teaching this problem solving and collaborating will take a long time. These children don't naturally see the perspectives of others and don't have a clue that negotiating can get them where they want to go. Patience and persistence are the key. However, the pay-off is beneficial.

Steps to collaborative problem solving (CPS)

1. *Empathy* (*plus reassurance*)

    i.   Stay calm.

    ii. Acknowledge that the child has a legitimate concern.

    iii. Engage in reflective listening: "I've noticed that…", "You seem really upset by…."

    iv. Clarify the problem: "What's up?" Specifically define what the concern is.

    v.   Ensure that the child feels his concern is heard and considered.

2. *Define the problem*

    i.   Define your (adult's) concern(s).

    ii. Specifically define concerns: child's and adult's.

    iii. Do not state your concern as an imposed solution: "You are not going to…!"

    iv. Do not state your concern as if it is more important. Both concerns need to be specified so the solutions meet the needs of each party.

    v.   State both concerns concretely to allow the child to understand the other person has a different perspective.

3. *Invitation*

    i.   Invite the child to collaboratively identify possible solutions. Solutions must be mutually satisfying.

    ii. Ensure that the invitation makes it clear that both parties will do it together: Key word: "let's." "Let's see how we can solve that problem." "Let's see what we can do about that."

    iii. Brainstorm solutions that will address both concerns.

    iv. Try to give the child the first crack at it: "Do you have any ideas?"

    v.   If the solution only addresses the child's concern, suggest, "That might make you happy, but it doesn't make me happy. Let's find a solution that makes both of us happy."

    vi. Ensure that both parties recognize each other's concerns and that the solution satisfies both of them.

Ways of using CPS

There are three primary ways you can use CPS: (1) at the time of a conflict to negotiate a solution, (2) after the person has calmed down to debrief and identify alternative ways of handling the conflict, and (3) prior to an unsettling event to reduce the conflict ahead of time.

1. *Reactive problem solving.* Do CPS at the time of the problem. When the problem arises, use CPS to work through the problem, try to defuse the conflict and work on a solution. You need to catch the child before he is too overwhelmed to calmly reason and negotiate. The more you use this technique, the better you both will get at it.

   It is a great tool for pulling the child out of the emotionally reactive center of the brain and into the thinking part of the brain. Over time, this can inhibit the immediate impulse to panic and react emotionally and redirect the child's attention away from his panic and into thinking about concrete solutions. Unfortunately, as the person reaches overload, his thinking, reasoning and communication skills start to deteriorate. Once that occurs, CPS will only further agitate the person. It must occur at the early stages of conflict when reasoning and communication skills are still good.

2. *After-the-fact problem solving.* For people who are too overwhelmed to collaborate, CPS can be used later following, the explosion, once everyone has calmed down, regrouped and is willing to collaborate. At this time, it is a good tool for finding out what happened, validating the child's emotions and brainstorming what would work best in the future.

3. *Proactive problem solving.* For common, reoccurring problems, do CPS beforehand, in preparation of upcoming events to anticipate possible problems and brainstorm how to respond. It drastically reduces anxiety when children are prepared in advance on what to expect, what may go wrong and how to react if it does.

Using CPS before, during and after conflict provides numerous benefits. Through your collaboration your child begins to view you as a supportive working partner with them, begins to use the thinking part of his brain to reason through situations and starts to feel more confident tackling situations that often overwhelm him.

What if my child refuses to collaborate?

Effective collaborating will take time to develop, for both of you. Many children with extreme anxiety and possible PDA will see negotiating as either too overwhelming or as a ploy to manipulate them, setting off a severe defensive reaction. Effective collaborating involves the two parties playing equal roles and considering each other's perspectives. For the very rigid, anxious autistic child, expecting them to talk and collaborate, especially in the heat of the moment, is too overwhelming.

For children who actively fight negotiating, at first you may need to forgo your perspective and concerns. Simply listen to and acknowledge the child's concerns and then validate the feelings behind them. You do not have to agree or say anything about the child's behavior. Simply listen, acknowledge and validate. Help him to define exactly what the issue is and what he feels he needs. Let the child see that you understand and validate his concerns.

Here is where you may have to forgo presenting your perspective and concerns, since the child is not ready to take the perspective of others. Skip this step and guide the child into brainstorming how he can get his needs met. Attempt to guide his thinking toward different options, without instructing or dictating an option. If the child is calm enough to converse with you, help him to consider what the consequences of the different options are: "I wonder what will happen if we did…? Would it get you what you need? For the very resistant child, you may not be able to offer suggestions, but it may help to steer the child's thinking to look at different options and consider possible consequences. The secret is not to dictate, diminish or actively reject any of the options the child projects, regardless of how unreasonable they may seem to you.

By removing your concerns from the table, you are not doing collaborative problem solving, but first establishing yourself as a working partner and trusted guide, willing to listen, learn, understand and validate. You realize that the anxious child is very rigid, but vulnerable. First, you need to identify and define what his concerns and feelings are before beginning to introduce your concerns.

Once the child becomes comfortable with your validating support, slowly work in the discussion of your perspective without requiring any need or demand for the child to meet your concerns. Trying to get the child to both understand your perspective and consider meeting your needs will probably be too much for him to accept. Especially for the child with PDA. Start with presenting your perspective without demanding equal consideration or that your concern should be met. Just let him hear your perspective and concern. As the child becomes more comfortable unconditionally hearing your concerns, then and only then can you begin helping the child to include your concerns in the negotiations. Notice I am asking the child if they have any ideas on how my concern could also be met, not instructing the child to negotiate with me. Over time, the child becomes more comfortable with collaborating and begins to see that he can negotiate effectively to meet everyone's concerns. This is a very effective coping tool that will last him the rest of his life.

Are you directing?

We discussed the need for the adults to avoid demanding, instructing and directing. This sets off an immediate defensive reaction in the child, blocking all forward movement. This is hard for us to do because we are so conditioned to prompt, instruct and direct. After all, we are the knowledgeable adult, we know what is best. This posture dictates the type of language we use, how we direct the child and how we demand compliance. For the very anxious, resistant children (especially those with PDA), this will not work and will only make matters worse. You cannot manipulate, demand or control these children.

Avoiding manipulation is a survival need for them and they will fight to the end, tearing apart whatever working relationship you have established.

You must learn how to redefine your role as supporting the child's lead: being a trusted assistant rather than an instructor; teaching by doing with the child, side by side; letting the child lead while you gently guide with support; biting your tongue, avoiding directives and validating the child's attempts at finding his own path. You will often catch yourself jumping in and trying to direct the interaction, but you will see the change of posture in your child. When you see the child freeze, pull back and resist, most likely you inadvertently tried to direct him. Please do not beat yourself over the head for this. It is very natural. Changing the way you parent, teach and guide is very difficult. At these times, simply step back and look at what you have just presented. Most likely you will see what little demand you placed on the child.

Becoming a non-demanding mentor, instead of an instructor, takes a lot of time and practice. You will also get a lot of complaints and suggestions from other adults that you are too lenient and not a good parent or teacher for giving in to the child. They will want you to be sterner with the child, demanding that he responds, and forcing him to comply. They will not understand that these very rigid, anxious children cannot be taught the same way as other children. You must be a respectful, non-demanding, truly collaborative mentor. Stick with it and you will see the positive results over time. You will repeatedly stumble, catch yourself directing and lose your path. Simply pull back, regroup and move forward, changing your guidance. You will be rewarded over time.

Naughty or nice!

I hate the word "naughty!" I am assuming that if kids are being naughty, it means that they are doing the behavior on purpose to get what they want, to get out of doing something, or simply to piss you off! It assumes that the child has the skills to do what is right and instead chooses to do something wrong. People often use it to mean that the child is somehow finding joy in making others miserable. It's not that this cannot occur in children with autism or other special needs, but it is an assumption that should not be used until you investigate why the child should be naughty in the first place. I never assume that a child simply likes to be naughty and it is fun for him…even if he is laughing (not a good indicator). Using that word for any child with special needs usually signifies to me that the professional doesn't know how to deal with the problem. It places blame on the child.

Dr. Ross Greene probably has one of the best sayings of all, "Children do well when they can." This means that if a child is not doing well, assume that the demands of the situation outweigh his current skills for dealing with them. Usually there is a need or lack of skill that is involved in why kids do poorly. If the child is not doing well, we should first look at what demands are too overwhelming for the child, reduce the demands, make them simpler or provide greater assistance. If the child is not doing well, assume the adult needs to be the one to make changes, not the child. This is not stripping the child of any responsibility, it just reflects that the child is probably not capable of successfully handling the situation.

I also hate the word, "manipulate!" Again, another word that is used with no specific meaning except that the child knows he is doing wrong, knows what and how to do it right and chooses to do it wrong. ALL BEHAVIOR IS MANIPULATION! All social behavior is to manipulate the behavior of someone else. We are doing it all the time, whether it's with a friend, spouse, co-worker or whoever. Believe me, every meeting I have with parents and schools is to figure out how to manipulate the child. We prompt, reward, punish, set up strategies and blame each other, all in an attempt to manipulate. All behavior is to either manipulate our way out of something or to get something. It also assumes that the child with autism can read the mental states of others, which is required to manipulate what they are thinking. If only they were so lucky!

Worst of all is the psychiatrist who labels the child a "behavior disorder." What the hell does that mean? This diagnosis usually implies purposeful intent to manipulate on the part of the child, simply being naughty. It has no prescriptive or meaningful treatment intent. Oh, it must be behavioral, meaning I don't have a clue how to help you. Let's blame the child. Punish and discipline! Ok, not much we can do…it is behavioral. Oh, yes, it means that if the parent would do better at parenting, the child would not be a brat.

When we are clueless and feeling inadequate (it happens to us all), we like to throw out these labels and place the blame on either the child, parent or teacher. Just remember, when you hear these three words "naughty," "manipulate" or "behavioral," then chuckle to yourself that this person probably is feeling lost and inadequate. Don't place the blame on the children; they are doing the best that they can given the situation they are in and their abilities to deal with it.

Chapter 10

SHUTDOWNS AND MELTDOWNS

Meltdowns occur when the brain becomes overwhelmed by too many processing demands, from sensory, cognitive, social or emotional overload. Too much information/stimulation is coming in too fast, or is too intense for the brain's processing skills to cope. All functional processing and coping systems of the brain break down and collapse. When this occurs, the brain panics, losing all ability to reason, problem solve and organize adaptive responses. The overwhelming surge of stress chemicals (cortisol and adrenalin) press the brain to act to escape and avoid the overwhelming stimulation and release the overflowing stress chemicals. This is when the brain's fight or flight response sets off. The brain begins to shut down and minimize the amount of stimulation, information and demands coming in to avoid overload. It presses the person to run to escape the situation, or physically act out (scream, hit or bite self, head bang, body slam and possibly attack others when they intervene). Once the person hits boiling point, he loses all reasoning ability and self-control, and impulsively acts to end the overwhelming chaos and release the painful stress chemicals. The most important thing to remember is that, in a meltdown, the person does not have control over his behavior and has no intent to do harm or negatively act out. The person is helpless in the face of the brain functions collapsing due to the surge of stress chemicals.

What happens when the brain becomes overwhelmed?

I have talked to hundreds of people on the spectrum about what it is like when they start to become overwhelmed. Processing becomes more impaired. All levels of processing start to deteriorate. The ability to register and integrate all information starts to fall apart as stress chemicals accumulate. Everything becomes confusing and unpredictable. They often report that their body experiences actual pain and engulfs them in panic. They quickly lose the ability to think, communicate and problem solve. The ability to use language, both receptively and expressively, weakens. They cannot think through the situation or problem solve. The more we talk, the more overwhelmed they become. They often lose their ability to speak. Trying to reason with them requires too much thinking, which they cannot do at that point.

In addition to deteriorating processing skills, their sensory sensitivities become heightened, adding more fuel to the fire. Strong emotions begin to flood the brain and the brain begins to panic! They report that intense emotions come on like tidal waves and overpower their ability to process. Every part of their body hurts and all coping skills collapse. Their brain starts to shut down or reaches fight or flight mode. If the overload is occurring slowly enough, the brain may start to shut down to avoid being overwhelmed.

However, if the overload is occurring too quickly for escape to be immediate, the stress sets off the fight or flight response, which is usually expressed as a meltdown.

Emotional overload resulting in meltdowns

Figure 10.1 shows the relationship between the pathways connecting the brain stem at the base of the brain, the limbic system that is the emotion center and the frontal cortex which is our thinking center of the brain. For the purpose of a brief, non-technical description of the brain, this is a very simple summary of how the process unfolds, since all experiences include communications between numerous complex networks all over the brain.

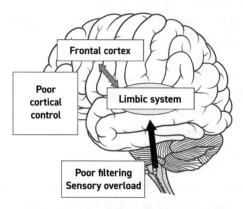

Figure 10.1: Emotional overload from poor sensory filtering and weak cortical control of impulses of overwhelmed limbic system

The black arrow shows the path of stimulation coming up into the brain through the brain stem. The brain stem acts as a filter to help block out information that is irrelevant, turn down the intensity of the stimulation and help direct the information to important areas of the brain. As we have mentioned earlier, many people with autism have poor filtering throughout the brain, and are often bombarded with too much stimulation or stimulation that is too intense for them to process. This intense stimulation comes in and overwhelms the limbic system, which is the center of our raw emotions, causing panic.

The gray arrow shows the neural pathways connecting the limbic system to the pre-frontal cortex, which is our thinking part of the brain. This is the center that allows us to inhibit our emotional responses long enough to appraise the level of threat and determine an adaptive emotional response. It allows us to think before we act.

So here the weak neural pathways between the frontal cortex and limbic system make it hard for the thinking part of the brain to override and inhibit the emotional flood coming from the limbic system. Consequently, the emotions overwhelm the cortex before it has a chance to inhibit them, leaving it helpless in controlling the surge of emotions. As a result, processing, thinking and problem-solving skills fall apart in the middle of a meltdown.

So, the poor brain has a double whammy. The limbic system is being bombarded with too much stimulation from the poor filtering system, and the weak connections with the frontal cortex render the thinking center unable to rapidly check the strong emotions before they overwhelm it. So, consequently we often see very strong emotional reactions from those on the spectrum. We must keep in mind that this is a brain wiring challenge, not a willful behavior problem. The person does not have control over this flood of emotions and inability to regulate them.

Shutdown or meltdown

As the brain starts becoming overwhelmed with stress chemicals, it has two primary ways of responding. If the stimulation/demands build up gradually, then the brain may begin to shut down and block out stimulation in order to avoid overload. This is a protective, defensive mechanism that helps the brain cope with overwhelming stimulation. However, if the accumulation of stress chemicals, stimulation and/or demands are occurring too fast or are too intense to block out, then a meltdown is probable.

Let's look first at how the shutdown process may occur. If the stress chemicals are accumulating gradually, the brain will start to shut down to protect it from being overwhelmed and to help it rebound. Many adults with autism report that this often starts with one or more senses closing down and not registering stimulation. This may also include not hearing others, feeling numb physically, a narrowing of vision and withdrawing from the external world. Along with the blocking out of stimulation, the person also starts to lose judgement and reasoning as well as communication skills.

As the brain starts to shut down, the child may become lethargic, limp or unresponsive or he may stare, put his head down or close his eyes. Because of the devastating consequences of melting down, many children will learn to start shutting down more readily to avoid putting themselves in situations of acting out. This defensive, protective, shutdown response can become an automatic strategy for avoiding emotional meltdowns that elicit negative social ridicule and punishment. Research has shown that ongoing exposure to overwhelming stress has deteriorating effects on the brain. Shutdown can be a good coping skill to protect the brain from becoming overwhelmed.

Unfortunately, when the child is shutting down others often misread it as daydreaming or, worse still, being noncompliant. Parents and teachers at this point often increase the level of prompting to get the child to respond, which will often push the child into a meltdown. Then, unfortunately, the child is labeled as aggressive and oppositional. To teach compliance, adults will often force the issue, which only fuels the fire and results in further confrontation. For a research article that details of physiology of the shutdown process, please refer to "Shutdown States and Stress Instability in Autism", (Loos and Loos Miller 2004).

The ability to recover from shutdown states can vary from minutes to hours, or in some cases, days if the person is subject to long periods of stress. The degree and length of shutdown will depend on the degree of stress and the length of exposure. Many adults with autism have reported that these shutdown states can put them in a stupor for days, sometimes in almost catatonic-type states, unable to function in their daily routine, requiring total isolation from others until they have fully recovered. Most shutdowns occur under social stress, where the person is required to perform under social pressure. One lady, whose job required her to periodically attend social parties, reported that it usually took two to three days of not leaving her house and minimizing all activity before she could recover.

Meltdowns

On the other side of the flight or fight response are meltdowns. With meltdowns, the stress chemicals reach boiling point, coping skills collapse and the person acts out to escape the situation and reduce anxiety. The brain is exploding with emotions and must find some way to release the stress chemicals. You may see hitting, kicking, pushing, throwing, slamming, biting self, head banging, and so on, all to provide proprioception, which releases stress chemicals. Proprioception, which is resistance to joints and tendons that comes from physical exertion, is thought to release stress chemicals from the nervous system and helps organize the chemistry in the nervous system. This is the same reason that people who have anger control issues will physically lash out or break things. All the acting out behaviors provide strong proprioception. Biting oneself, hitting or banging the head all provide strong proprioception in the jaw, head and spine. Therefore, these behaviors are often seen in children during stress.

What will determine if a child will go into shutdown or directly to meltdown? If stress chemicals increase gradually, shutdown is likely. If the stress chemicals build quickly or the child is not allowed to shut down, then meltdown may occur. Also, a lot depends on the temperament of the child. Some children may explode and run to escape the overwhelming stimulation, often with no awareness of the potential dangers involved. Trying to block them may trigger aggression, not to intentionally harm others, but to push past them to escape. Remember, the brain is swirling in painful confusion and only wants to escape the pain and release the stress chemicals.

Many individuals, both children and adults, will tend to direct their aggression to themselves in the form of hitting or biting themselves, or head banging. The sudden explosions of emotion drive them to seek out strong tactile and proprioceptive stimulation to release the surge of stress chemicals. It is much safer to take it out on oneself than to act out against property or others. Usually, the individual is not trying to harm others, only to escape the internal turmoil. However, aggression toward others may occur if they continue to present demands, block the individual from leaving or try to stop the child from hurting himself (biting, hitting, head banging). If the child is forced to stay in the overwhelming situation or is not allowed to physically release the stress chemicals, he may strike out at those trying to help or control him.

Those with more impulse control may try to hold it together and tend to shut down, while others will panic and immediately start acting out. A lot depends on the age of the child, their current state of emotional control and how quickly we interrupt the chain of events leading up to the meltdown. It is much easier to prevent meltdowns by (1) identifying and avoiding situations that trigger them, (2) knowing the early signs that the child is getting stressed, and (3) backing off and letting the child escape and rebound before overload occurs. Over time, we can work on teaching better coping skills for handling stress, but this vulnerability is always there. We must teach others around the person not to pressure, command and demand during these situations and to help the individual escape and feel safe.

Meltdowns! What do they feel like, what do they look like?

The best way to understand what emotional or sensory overload looks like is from direct reports from those who experience them. Only from those sharing these experiences do we understand how frightening and debilitating overload can be. This can best be represented by looking at how it affects the person physically, mentally and emotionally. As we will see, the build-up can occur from accumulated stress chemicals over time or from a sudden jolt of expectancy. As discussed in previous chapters, these stress chemicals can become overwhelming from too many sensory, cognitive, social and emotional demands, or these demands coming too fast. The environmental demands become too overwhelming for the processing abilities of the nervous system.

The surge of stress chemicals elicits an adrenalin rush that overwhelms every system in the body. Every system starts to break down, leaving the person helpless in coping with the tidal wave of chaos. Although we will look at these systems individually, all these variables are experienced together and augment each other.

Physically

There isn't much that affects us cognitively and emotionally that doesn't simultaneously affect us physically. Since many meltdowns occur from sensory overload, it is not surprising that the sensory system is often the first to break down during overload. We have already seen how fragile the sensory system is for many of those with autism. From sensory sensitivities, fragmented sensations and difficulty integrating sensations, their nervous system is often bombarded by chaotic, overwhelming sensations. As the person begins to experience overload, the sensory systems become even more sensitive. Sounds become more amplified, light and color become more intense, smells become more nauseating, and touch can become extremely painful. Those on the spectrum report sharp throbbing pain from sources of light, needles piercing the skin, strong throbbing pain throughout the head, and stomach cramps and nausea.

Those with cross-sensations (synesthesia), strong sensations in one sense (e.g. sound) can trigger sensations in other senses (e.g. color, physical pain). Noise may trigger strong sensations of color, light may elicit tactile sensations, smell may trigger strong taste. Whether the stress is coming from sensory, social, cognitive or emotional overload, the nervous system is compromised, and the sensory system becomes hyper-alert and begins to break down. Noise, light, smells and physical touch become intense, chaotic and unrecognizable. Many report that their ability to integrate and understand their sensations breaks down. Stimulation becomes mixed and distorted and often unrecognizable. They cannot understand what people are saying, what they are seeing, or what is going on around them. There is a swirl of sensations, chaotic and confusing. The nervous system becomes frightened, increasing its hyper-sensitivity, spiraling it to panic and breakdown. Noise, light, smells and touch become painful and unbearable.

As the nervous system becomes overwhelmed, it must act to somehow reduce or escape the overwhelming rush of sensation. How the person reacts to this sensory bombardment varies. For some, to prevent overload, often the nervous system starts to shut down processing to avoid being overwhelmed. For many, the sensory system will try and protect itself by reducing the amount of stimulation coming in. One or more senses may shut down part, or all, of that sensory track. The person may not be able to hear, see or feel the stimulation. Everything becomes a blur, fading in the distance or scrambling together. This might happen to only one sense or all of them together. The person may no longer respond to those trying to communicate with him. He may not hear you or be able to respond to you. He may initially be hyper-sensitive to touch, then become completely numb to it, essentially blocking it out altogether and becoming detached from the sensation.

This disruption of processing can lead to loss of physical functioning. People report being unable to physically act, to control their movements or their bodily functions. They become paralyzed, unable to move or react. The ability to speak can totally break down and they become unable to communicate. Their interoception (ability to sense internal bodily sensations) can become heightened (e.g. overwhelmed by their heartbeat) or become numb to all internal sensations. Even though they may want to escape the situation, they are unable to physically get up and move with intent. The inability to act leaves them feeling very vulnerable and helpless.

Others report being propelled into a rage of action, all the way from uncontrolled shaking to running, screaming, hitting/biting/digging at themselves, head banging and becoming aggressive if others try and intervene. The adrenaline rush activates a surge of energy that sets off the fight or flight panic response. Most of the physical actions seem to serve two primary purposes: (1) to escape the unbearable stimulation that is overwhelming the brain, to get it to stop, and (2) the acting out (hitting, biting, slamming, head banging, etc.) provides strong proprioceptive stimulation (to the joints and tendons), which releases stress chemicals from the nervous system. The body is exploding with stress chemicals demanding to be released in order to return to homeostasis (a stable equilibrium). Any strong jarring, slamming, pushing, hitting of the joints and tendons when we hit, kick, push, bite and so on will help release these stress chemicals. Both children and adults report that their bodies will explode and drive them to hit, bite, head bang and harm themselves involuntarily in order to release the exploding stress chemicals. Otherwise calm and passive individuals can be driven to explosive behavior in times of overwhelming stress.

Cognitively

As the brain becomes taxed and overwhelmed with emotion, the ability to process information, think, contemplate and problem solve breaks down. The thinking part of the brain becomes overwhelmed by the sensory and emotional centers, collapsing the executive functioning (attention, organization, impulse control, problem solving, etc.). Communication, reasoning and ability to initiate constructive action collapse. Trying to talk to and reason with the person only adds more fuel to the fire, further compromising the nervous system. The person cannot process information, understand questions or organize and physically produce the words to respond. Ongoing interactions (talking and demanding action) add more chaos to the madness. Once totally overwhelmed, the person is not capable of organized thoughts, reciprocal communication or focused attention. The brain is in a swirl of intense sensations and emotions.

Without the ability to focus, problem solve, organize actions and control emotional impulses, the person is left helpless to the explosive actions (running, screaming, flailing, hitting/biting self, lashing out, etc.), all primitive attempts of fight or flight, in an attempt to escape the situation, reduce the stimulation/demands and release the overwhelming stress chemicals. Hitting, head banging, biting, body slamming, throwing, pushing and so on all provide proprioception that helps release stress chemicals from the nervous system. The body must respond to escape the stimulation and release the overwhelming stress chemicals.

Emotionally

As can be expected, along with the breakdown of thinking, reasoning, communication skills and physical functioning, the build-up of stress chemicals presents a tidal wave of intense emotions. The build-up of emotions can gradually accumulate from anxiety, fear and panic or can be an immediate surge of intense emotion that overwhelms the person. This explosion of emotion totally overwhelms the thinking part of the brain (pre-frontal cortex, executive functioning), rendering the person incapable of controlling it. At this stage, the person feels overcome with uncontrollable emotion that totally clouds all reasoning and coping skills, leaving the person helpless in combating the painful stimulation. This is often seen in sensory overload, where the overwhelming sensory assault over-activates the limbic system (emotion centers). The intense raw emotion overwhelms the pre-frontal cortex, which is responsible for helping to inhibit our emotional responses. The raw emotion has no bearings, with no judgement or reasoning; it is simply intense, raw emotion that elicits panic in the brain.

Since the processing challenges that people on the spectrum experience already tax and drain the nervous system, it leaves the nervous system vulnerable to overload. It takes the fragile nervous system so much energy to process normal daily activity in our social culture, which leaves the individual taxed and vulnerable to breakdown under increased stress. This explains why sometimes the trigger of a meltdown can appear insignificant on the surface, but is often just the tipping point from a build-up of stress chemicals, compromising the coping skills as the day goes on. As the brain becomes taxed, the executive functions (attention, planning, organization, problem solving, impulse control) all get weaker, leaving the individual less capable of coping with little snags or ongoing stimulation. As the nervous system becomes more stressed, the ability to process and cope with daily stressors begins to collapse. When the surge of anxiety activates intense emotions and collapses all judgement and reasoning abilities, the brain panics out of fear and the individual loses all sense of self-control. This is very scary for the person, who feels completely helpless in the face of overwhelming stimulation.

Meltdowns are not temper tantrums

In the blue book, *The Autism Discussion Page on the Core Challenges of Autism* (Nason 2014a), I summarize the differences between temper tantrums and meltdowns.

It is very important for parents and teachers to understand the differences between tantrums and meltdowns. Although they can consist of similar behavior (yelling, screaming, crying, dropping to the floor, flailing, hitting or biting self, etc.), it is important to distinguish between the two. Why? Because it has major implications for how we interpret the behavior and how we intervene to help the child.

TANTRUMS

With tantrums, the child usually:

1. has some control over the behavior

2. chooses to engage in the behavior

3. wants something or wishes to escape something he doesn't want

4. can end it quickly once he gets what he wants

5. can focus on others around him, often looking at them, yelling at them, and drawing their attention to him

6. looks for reactions from others when being disruptive

7. has the ability to talk and negotiate, despite yelling and demanding

8. if aggression is displayed, will seek out others to hit or kick or get up and seek out property to disrupt.

Usually, the behavior is a means to an end (the child wants something or to avoid something) and the child acts out to get a specific reaction from others. Although tantrums can lead to the child being overwhelmed, they usually start under the control of the child. Tantrums often occur in nonverbal children when they lack other ways of communicating and getting needs met. The child will often calm down once he gets what he wants or feels that he needs.

MELTDOWNS

Meltdowns usually occur when the child's brain is overwhelmed with stress chemicals and has reached the panic, flight or fight stress reaction. The stress builds up to the point that the brain is overwhelmed and loses the ability to cope. With meltdowns, the child usually:

1. appears to be in panic mode

2. does not appear to have control over his behavior

3. cannot talk or problem solve—loses the ability to negotiate or reason

4. cannot follow directions or argue—is too overwhelmed to engage

5. feels unsafe and appears to be reacting out of deep fear

6. finds it difficult to identify the cause of emotion, or obvious want or demand

7. is experiencing sensory overload, too much cognitive stress, or ongoing social demands that tax and drain the brain

8. is trying to flee or escape the situation around him, rather than seeking out attention. He is seeking to escape what is overwhelming him, not seeking to gain something

9. does not hit, kick, or bite unless others approach and attempt to calm or redirect him. Aggression often subsides when others back away, give him space, remove demands and withdraw all interactions

10. takes a while to calm down (rather than calming immediately when he gets what he wants); needs time to escape and rebound

11. expresses remorse for actions afterwards.

The child in a meltdown is reacting out of fright and fear. The fight or flight panic reaction is set off, and the child is trying to escape the source of stress, and seeking proprioception (hitting, kicking, biting self, head banging, etc.) to release stress chemicals. He often does not want to interact with others, is not seeking their attention, and wants to withdraw and isolate. However, if the child does not feel safe, he may take it out on property or others to get people to back off, or to release stress chemicals. (pp.312–314)

It is important to remember that when in meltdown, the brain cannot respond to commands, demands, pressure and discipline. Attempts to scold, counsel, command and demand only fuel the fury and further overwhelm the person. The child has no control over his emotional turmoil nor how he responds, especially if we pressure or punish him. The brain is in a hyper-reactive, flight or fight state, for which the child has little control. The immediate need is to help the brain feel safe. The best way to do this is to (1) immediately acknowledge and briefly reassure the person he is safe, (2) pull away all demands, (3) reduce as much stimulation as possible (move the person to a quiet area if possible), and (4) give the person plenty of time to calm down and regroup. Be present, but as quiet as possible. We must respect the need for the brain to escape the crisis, release the stress chemicals and feel safe.

Tantrums, Emotional Dysregulation and Meltdowns: The three emotional outbursts!

Many people often mislabel all emotional control problems as "meltdowns." This is understandable since the three can look very similar and the child often has difficulty controlling them. We distinguished above between tantrums and meltdowns. With tantrums the child usually has some control and tries to use the behavior to manipulate an outcome (gain something he wants, stop something he doesn't want, etc.) and can usually stop after obtaining what he wants.

With emotional dysregulation the child has trouble controlling his emotional reactions and these responses are usually exaggerated. The child goes from 0–100 quickly and often has trouble calming himself down even if the adult "gives in" and allows the child to have or escape something. With emotional dysregulation, the child feels a natural emotion (frustration, anger, fear, etc.) but has trouble gauging and regulating the intensity of his reactions. It is an exaggerated response to a normal emotional reaction. For this child they may use aggression and property disruption to let off steam and to gain some control over his environment. It is important to teach the child to identify and label his emotional reactions and to teach him alternative ways to express and control his reactions.

When the child is having a meltdown, his brain is overwhelmed with too much stimulation, too many cognitive demands, or a very sudden change in routine or expectation that throws him into panic. A meltdown is a true panic, a fight or flight response to the brain being overwhelmed, not just frustrated or mad about not getting his or her way. Most of the time when the child is in a meltdown, if you pull away demands and stimulation and allow them to escape, they will usually not seek out others to aggress against. If he becomes aggressive it is usually because the adults are not backing off and are pushing him into further overload. In meltdown, the brain is trying to survive by escaping the overload and rebounding. Helping the brain do this will allow the brain to calm, organize and rebound. So, if the child is seeking out or chasing others to hit, kick and destroy things, it is likely not a meltdown but an emotional dysregulation issue. This is not always the case (some meltdowns can stimulate aggression to release stress chemicals) but usually it is because the child is cornered, and the adult is pressing and not allowing the child to escape and rebound. He is not usually running around hitting, kicking and throwing things because he is mad! These are emotional regulation problems.

Now, where does that leave the adult? Yes, we must expect many kids on the spectrum to have difficulty regulating their emotions. All children need strong boundaries, expectations and consequences. These help the child make sense of the world and pattern his reactions in the heat of the moment. Without clear boundaries and expectations that have immediate consequences, the child is left in a confusing, chaotic world. If the child is having difficulty regulating his emotional reactions (not meltdown) we must put limits on how he can express them. For example, in starting out with teaching emotional regulation, we acknowledge and validate that the child is very upset, allow him to yell, scream, slap himself if not causing injuries, etc., but try to create boundaries—no attacking others or destroying property. I let the child know that it is ok to get upset, help him feel safe being upset, but he cannot aggress against others or destroy property. We identify, define, role play and practice allowable emotional reactions so the child can still let off steam, protest and communicate frustration.

All children have individual differences and aggression occurs in different forms and for a variety of reasons. Emotional dysregulation in some children can lead into a full meltdown as they become overloaded with emotion. So, the boundaries, expectations and consequences need to be tailored to the child. For children who are very aggressive, I strongly recommend that you seek out a behavior specialist who can do a functional behavior assessment and help you design strategies that match the child's emotional needs.

Consistently inconsistent

Before we get into the common causes of meltdowns, it is important to understand why they are often not predictable and can come on suddenly or sometimes in clusters. We have already discussed how fragile and vulnerable the nervous system is to common stressors. There are so many variables that can tax and drain the nervous system (lack of sleep, hunger, illness and discomfort, social activity, sensory sensitivities, anticipatory anxiety, too much activity, etc.) that a mild stressor may trigger a meltdown one moment that would commonly not bother the person at other times. Often when the nervous system is taxed and fragile, the person may seem generally irritable for no apparent reason, and the least little snag sets him off. Parents will often report that during these states of irritability, nothing seems to satisfy the child. Everything seems to set off a tidal wave of emotions.

Many people do not realize that what occurred yesterday, or the day before, can still be taxing the nervous system, leaving it vulnerable to overload the next day. How the child starts the day often depends on how his day went yesterday, what social activity he had the night before, the quality of sleep he had that night, if he ate breakfast before rushing out of the house and if he ran into any snags that morning. Events that can tax very organized nervous systems will often be amplified for those with autism. When working with parents, I ask them to keep a journal of daily activity, along with any known sources of stress for the child. Often, they will pick up on patterns, like if the child had a social event one evening, he may be irritable, oppositional and prone to emotional outbursts the next morning. Or, if the child is engaging in a highly interesting activity, he may have problems later that night. In other words, the reasons for the meltdown may not be immediately obvious, and are often related to events that happened over the past couple of days.

To avoid meltdowns, we need to be aware of how taxed the nervous system is and how much mental energy the child has. As discussed in Chapters 3 and 4, we need to know what common events overly stress the child, and the variables (sensory and social pressures, uncertainty, etc.) within these events, that are challenging for the child and we must be aware of the child's current energy level in order to keep him from becoming too drained. Also, as they get older these children need to understand their own nervous system, what taxes it, how to assess upcoming events for processing demands and how to recognize when they are hitting the danger zone for being overloaded.

Common causes of meltdowns

There are many variables that can lead to a meltdown. However, usually it is under conditions when the demands (sensory, social, physical, emotional, cognitive) of the situations are too strong for the brain to process and cope with. Listed below are common triggers for many kids (as well as adults). However, whether a meltdown will occur is often determined by the current state of the nervous system when these triggers occur. These triggers may produce a meltdown one moment, but not at other times. Why? It depends on how taxed and drained the person's nervous system is at the time of the trigger. If the person has already had a stressful day, is hungry, tired, ill, in discomfort or has had multiple events without a break, then each potential event may have greater likelihood of triggering a meltdown. If the brain is already drained and disorganized, then a mild event could trigger a meltdown. At times when the nervous system is rested and more organized, the child may handle these events better. This makes meltdowns very unpredictable.

Sensory overload

Probably the greatest trigger of meltdowns is sensory overload. This can occur when there is too much sensory stimulation or it is too intense and it bombards the nervous system, sending it into fight or flight. Remember, the brains of autistic people often have difficulty filtering out stimulation, so can get overwhelmed easily. Most parents are aware of their child's sensory sensitivities, what stimulation to avoid and how much he can handle. However, we often do not realize that the child doesn't have to be overly sensitive to any specific sense, but that the accumulation and integration of all the sensory input occurring around the child can overwhelm him. The more activity, noise, bright lighting and visual distractions, the greater the risk of overload.

Unfortunately, the more taxed the nervous system becomes, the more fragile it is to sensory stimulation. Stimulation becomes intensified, more jumbled and sometimes painful, only compounding the stress the person is experiencing. When assessing what factors may have led to a meltdown, always consider the sensory demands of the current and recent activities. Also, once the person is emotionally collapsing, always assume there are sensory stressors and immediately reduce the amount of noise, light and activity around them (as far as possible). Once the brain is compromised, sensory demands continue to fuel the fire. The brain is actively trying to escape most or all sensory stimulation to calm down and rebound. Even others talking to the child can present too much stimulation. It is imperative that we recognize this overload and immediately reduce all demands and as much stimulation as possible, giving the brain the time to regroup.

Information overload

We have discussed how the autistic brain has problems rapidly processing multiple information simultaneously, so it can get overwhelmed when the information is coming in too fast and in too great a quantity at one time. If the child is resisting, blanking out, stimming more or becoming emotional, look at what cognitive demands are being placed on him. How much information is expected to be processed and does the child have time to process it all before moving on to more? This is where it is important to understand the processing skills of the child.

Does the child have delayed processing needs, need written (or pictorial) directions, rather than verbal, or need information broken into small chunks or presented concretely and a method to clarify and verify understanding. Also, be aware that the longer the person stays in events that require lots of processing, especially new information, the more vulnerable the brain will become to overload.

Emotional overload

Any sudden, unexpected and intense emotions can set off a meltdown. Emotions come on like a tidal wave and overwhelm the person. The child often cannot gauge the intensity of the emotion so any amount of anxiety may set off panic in him. We have all experienced a child going from calm and happy to fury over a sudden jolt in emotion. Many children are hyper-sensitive to the emotions of others, so when others around them are emotional, they often panic and emotionally break down. Although they feel the emotion strongly, they cannot identify what the emotion is and how to respond to it. The brain simply panics.

Many adults report that they are very sensitive to the emotional auras of others and can become overwhelmed by the multiple auras of others when in a group of people. This sensitivity to emotions can come on very strongly, scaring the person (especially a child) and setting off panic. Also, multiple emotions (feeling happy but anxious, or excited and frightened at the same time) can set off a panic response. The emotional reactions of children, and some adults, can be impulsive, all or nothing and very intense, causing fear and panic.

In addition, their temporal sense of emotions is weak and in the heat of the moment they feel as if the intense emotions will last forever. They do not realize that the intense emotion will subside soon, and everything will be ok. It literally feels as if the world is going to end. It is very important that in the heat of the moment, we stay calm and reassure the individual that he is safe, and the emotion will end soon. When others around the person become anxious, excited or demanding, it will only add more intense emotion to the fire.

Social overload

Interacting with others, even for those with strong social interest, is very draining for those on the spectrum. Even when they become more skilled in conversing, interacting is still very taxing. Having to relate with another for too long or being in a group situation that requires them to coordinate interaction with many people can cause overload. Difficulty understanding the unwritten social rules, social context, nonverbal communication and social expectations can overwhelm almost all individuals with autism. All these variables lead to confusion in the midst of trying to stay connected and coordinated within the social event.

Even if the child loves the social activity, it is still building stress chemicals. The worst part about these situations is that the child will want to stay in the activity even when it is best for him to exit before becoming overwhelmed. Often the child will become so hyper-focused on the excitement that he will not recognize he is getting overwhelmed or will not want to pull away from the highly stimulating event. This frequently occurs for the highly social child with Asperger's syndrome but can happen to adults also. Remember, just because the event is fun and exciting does not mean it is not stressful.

Variables that may influence how overwhelming a social event is include:

- How familiar the social event is for the person.

- Number of participants in the activity.

- Familiarity with the other participants.

- Amount of socializing expected of the person.

- How structured the event is (predictable events)—less structure, greater stress.

- Overall noise and activity in the event.

- Length of time spent in the activity.

All people with autism experience strong social vulnerabilities to varying degrees. It is important that parents, teachers and other support people are aware of what the child's limits are and do not put too much social pressure on him. Adults also must be aware of how much social stimulation these children can successfully handle and pattern their social life accordingly.

Because of their difficulties reading social expectations, being out of sync when relating and the negative feedback they get from others, those with autism have high social anxiety. If you cannot read what is expected of you, what you are doing wrong or how people react to you, social anxiety is likely to be high, and you will feel continually apprehensive and ambivalent when relating. When the child becomes stressed, overwhelmed and starts losing control, the fear of how others around him will react further increases the anxiety and resultant panic. The supporting adults must remain calm, immediately reassure him and move everyone away from the person (or give the person a way of escaping.)

Task performance demands

Task performance anxiety can also be very high in those with autism. Because of difficulty processing and understanding what is expected, not being able to gauge what is "good enough," high expectation levels for themselves (perfectionism) and the need to hyper-focus on a task until it is completed, expectations to perform can significantly increase anxiety. Unless expectations are very concretely defined, the person often is left confused on what is expected or misinterprets what is needed. This often leaves the person guessing, and frequently guessing wrong. Hence, the ongoing failures and negative feedback leave the person feeling anxious about new expectations. It is very important that we provide a clear vision of what is expected (exactly as needed), clarify and verify that they understand and provide visual steps (picture sequence, written checklist, etc.) if possible. Do not assume that the person knows what to do unless it is a routine task—spell it out.

Trying to judge when performance is "good enough" can be very difficult for autistics. With the all-or-nothing thinking style, this lack of gauging "good enough" leaves the child feeling anxious about performing. The child will have trouble identifying what is good enough and adequately assessing if he has the skills necessary to do it. This child will dive into the task without adequately judging what is needed and automatically thinks he has the skills necessary to be successful. Also, once fully engaged, the child impulsively acts without the ability to monitor how well he is performing. He does not have the ability to think about what he is doing while doing it. Thinking he can do it, he impulsively and enthusiastically jumps in, begins to struggle and then panics, resulting in a meltdown. As a consequence, enthusiasm and excitement turn into intense frustration when things start going wrong.

This difficulty judging what is "good enough," paired with the all-or-nothing thinking style, often drives perfectionism, where the only acceptable performance is perfection. Anything other than perfect is a failure. Again, the child often melts down and destroys what he has completed. The need for perfection and the frequent inability to meet that expectation usually lead to a strong fear of failure. Over time, the continual failure to meet the perfect performance frequently leads the child to refuse to perform for fear of failing. This child is often labeled oppositional, frequently refusing to follow the requests or lead of others. If he cannot do it perfectly at first, he doesn't want to try. Any and all failure can elicit panic.

Too many demands or demands that are too hard may push the person into panic. When the expectations are greater than the abilities of the child, frustration becomes intense and meltdown may occur. The expectations need to be previewed ahead of time, made literal and concrete and be presented one step at a time; they must be within the current abilities of the person. Unfortunately, for those with good verbal and cognitive skills, their differences are more difficult to see, thus leading others to expect greater performance. These hidden vulnerabilities put the person under ongoing stress to meet expectations that are above his skill level.

Multi-tasking and juggling several projects simultaneously is a requirement of many jobs. Multi-tasking is often a weakness for those on the spectrum. They are better at hyper-focusing on a single project until it is complete than juggling multiple tasks simultaneously. Whether a child at school or an adult at work, if they are thrown too many expectations too fast, the brain may panic, increasing the chances of a meltdown.

Finally, with the above challenges that can slow down the processing and performance and tax and drain the nervous system, ongoing prompting, instructing and pressuring to work faster will overwhelm the person. When the teacher, parent or boss continues to prompt, instruct and pressure faster performance, meltdown can occur. We need to allow the individual to pace himself according to his processing abilities. Pressing him to work faster will only spike anxiety, compromise his abilities and create panic for his brain. We need to understand what the person's processing abilities are, respect the need to accommodate for these differences and back off if the person starts to become overwhelmed.

Sudden changes or shifts in expectations!

Once the child has an expectation set (expects things to be a certain way or occur a specific way), sudden snags or changes can set off immediate fright! Remember, uncertainty is very scary for many children with autism. They like to have a clear mindset of what is going to happen in order to feel safe and secure. When there is a sudden snag or change in that mental map, their sense of security collapses and they panic. Flexibility (ability to go with the flow, shift gears and change course as a situation warrants) is often hampered in autism. It is very important for them to have a very clear vision (mental map) and predictable path to minimize uncertainty and lessen anxiety. This may be experienced when a store is out of a desired item, road construction requires an alternative route, or a work project is halted or delayed. You may also see this in children when adults demand that they stop in the middle of a preferred activity. Immediately shifting gears unexpectedly can set off panic.

Transitions from one event to another, even when planned and expected, can still increase anxiety and leave them vulnerable. The inability of the brain to shift gears, move from one activity or issue to another, can cause intense anxiety, especially when the change is initiated by others and not under the control of the individual. Even transitions that are common and part of the daily routine (e.g. coming home from school or work) can cause anxiety. The more predictable the change and the more time the person has to make the transition, the less stressful it is. Also, the more control the person has during the transition, the less anxiety it provokes. Unfortunately, adults frequently present transitions unexpectedly, give little notice without preparation and allow the children minimal voice or control in the matter. Hence, their world collapses with intense anxiety and meltdown occurs.

There are four strategies I use to help support children to prepare the brain for transitions:

1. Use a visual schedule to provide predictability, giving the child a mental map of what is coming up.

2. Prepare the child by previewing what will happen and what is expected of him.

3. Bridge the transition by always telling the child what is coming up next, and preparing the brain for the transition ("Once the television show is over it is time for your bath.").

4. Ease the transition by giving reminders near the time of transition ("In a couple of minutes, we will need to put things away and then use the bathroom").

Also, if possible, I try to collaborate with the child, so he has a voice and some control. These strategies prepare the brain for the upcoming transition and ease the shock.

Whether or not a transition will result in an emotional outburst will often be determined by how unfamiliar the transition is, whether it was expected, and the current state of the child's nervous system at the time of the transition. If the child has experienced a lot of stress build-up in the current event, then the transition may bring on a release of those stress chemicals. Therefore, some children frequently melt down once they get out of school. They hold back the stress chemicals that build up at school and then it all comes out once home in their safe setting. You can also expect this emotional reaction if the child is leaving a very exciting event, since even if highly preferred, exciting events also build up high amounts of stress chemicals. Parents are often confounded by children going from being extremely excited during the activity to emotional outbursts when they leave the activity.

Intense frustration

Closely related to shifting gears is poor frustration tolerance. Being blocked from getting something that they want or interrupting something they are currently doing may create a sudden burst of anxiety, leading to meltdown. There is a rigid need to have what they want, when they want it. A want is perceived as a must, a need! If the expected outcome does not occur, they become overwhelmed with emotion. This is not just a child upset about not getting his way. The emotion is intensified because of his either/or, all-or-nothing thinking that makes it hard for him to appraise the urgency, see alternatives, or understand a temporary delay. "No" means "never" and that is catastrophic! There is an immediate burst of anxiety with very poor ability to block it. The emotional center of the brain surges and overwhelms the thinking center's ability to inhibit the rage. This child simply loses emotional control and acts out of impulse.

Lack of communication skills

For nonverbal children, or those with limited verbal skills, the immediate frustration of not being able to communicate what they want or need can set off intense rage. It is natural to see more meltdowns in the early years before the children develop language to communicate what they want and to protest what they do not like. This frustration of not being able to immediately communicate naturally can send them into intense frustration and meltdowns. The more we help the children communicate their wants, needs and frustration, through any means (words, gestures, manual signing, pictures, etc.), the less prone they are to meltdowns.

Even with typically good verbal skills, for many, as they start to become overwhelmed, they lose their communication skills and cannot adequately express their needs. They literally cannot formulate what they want to say, find the right words or speak articulately. As their communication skills break down, frustration increases and anxiety becomes greater.

In addition, frustration often occurs for many verbal children if they either do not know how or do not feel safe to ask for help. Just because a child can talk does not mean he can adequately formulate what he needs to say, find the right words and express his needs, especially in social situations that already create strong anxiety. Unfortunately, we often assume that verbal children can adequately express their needs and we place greater expectations on them.

Combination of factors

Although each one of these precipitating events can trigger emotional overload, usually the outbursts are a combination of several conditions (e.g. sensory irritants, social stress and additional task performance demands). An event can host a variety of challenges, each adding accumulating stress. An analysis of an event must look at what sensory, cognitive, social and task performance demands it entails. These are important to identify if we are to help the individual handle these events in the future.

In addition to the multiple variables within an event, there is often accumulated stress that the person already brings with him into the event. Frequently, the immediate event is the apparent trigger, but the underlying reason may have been too many stressors accumulating earlier in the day. The person did not get good sleep the night before, refused to eat breakfast, was bullied at school and became overwhelmed when riding home on the bus. When looking at what produced the meltdown, it is important to look at what the individual has endured over the current day or even the last few days. The major reason for eventual overload is often not the most immediate trigger, but an accumulation of a variety of stressors experienced recently.

The delayed effect

It can be very confusing for those supporting the person, if meltdowns occur after the stressful conditions have ended and the person is in a safer and accepting setting. I often call this "the delayed effect." Many parents experience this when their child first gets home from school or is on the way home. The child holds it together all day long at school and then lets it all out as soon as he reaches home. The teachers may report that the child is usually very good, experiencing minimal problems at school, often quiet, passive and compliant. The school staff do not recognize that the child is stressed but holding it together to avoid melting down. When parents bring this up at school, the staff are surprised and think that the parent is doing something wrong, but these children need the same supports to reduce the stressors at school as children who frequently act out in class. Unfortunately, the school often responds by saying that the child is doing fine at school and does not need the extra accommodations or support. Whether a child passively shuts down or acts out often is determined by his general temperament and ability to block out and cope with the build-up of stress.

Adults experience the same thing at work. If in a job that has too many stressful sensory, social and task performance demands, the person may find ways to cope at work, hold it together, but still be very vulnerable to a minor stressor (traffic jam on the way home) once out of work.

For both the child and adult, we must look at what variables in the setting are causing the stress, accommodate and reduce the stressors and design coping strategies for the person to better deal with the stress. This is a combination of structuring work assignments to match processing skills, using sensory tools to help regulate the nervous system, giving regular breaks to regroup and recognizing the early signs, respecting and backing off demands when the person starts to become drained.

For the child getting out of school, it will be important that he has a break to rebound and regroup before any demands are placed on him. Each child is different. Some need physical activity to regroup, some need time alone to sleep and others engage in a preferred activity.

"The child was having fun!"

Parents are frequently surprised when their child gets upset at home after having a fun day in the community. Any exciting event, especially social events, can present an ongoing build-up of stress chemicals that will come out once the child begins to relax. This effect is augmented if the person has bounced from one exciting event to another over the course of the day. "What happened? We just spent all afternoon going to the playground, eating at McDonald's and shopping at the mall." Try to remember that any exciting event, especially if you string them together without a break, accumulates stress, drains the nervous system and overloads the child.

Another common problem is when children are very excited by an event and do not want to pull themselves away in time to avoid being overloaded. They either do not recognize that they are becoming disorganized or are too hyper-focused on the fun they are having to pull away. They frequently put themselves in situations that demand more than they can handle, become excited and meltdown when things go wrong, or parents try to pull them away from the activity.

I see this a lot with the highly social child who wants so badly to go to the party or other social event but becomes overwhelmed early into the event. Or the child who is hyper-focused on an exciting activity (e.g. video game) and either cannot pull himself away to rebound, acts out when things start to go wrong (game becomes too challenging) or melts down when parents try to have him take a break. Trying to pull away from a very engaging activity, especially if it isn't completed yet, is so difficult for these children.

This chapter was designed to give the reader a good understanding of what shutdowns and meltdowns are, how they are experienced and when and why they occur. Although very individualized for each person, both shutdowns and meltdowns are common for many people with autism. The next two chapters will look at how to prevent meltdowns and how to proactively respond to them.

Chapter 11

PREVENTING MELTDOWNS

We all agree that meltdowns can be traumatic for the individual as well as those supporting the person. The horror of painful sensory overload, surge of anxiety, flood of overwhelming emotions and losing control of all coping skills leaves the individual in a state of fear and panic. For parents, seeing their child or loved one in a state of distress is heartbreaking. Feeling helpless in stopping the terror leaves them feeling frustrated and guilty, not being able to protect their child from the trauma. In addition, the negative feedback parents get from others witnessing the meltdown creates a complex mixture of embarrassment, shame and anger. In most public situations, a meltdown can bring a host of negative reactions from store owners, bystanders, security and law enforcers that only fuel the fire and augment the distress. All parties end up feeling hurt, incompetent, frustrated and angry.

The number one strategy for reducing meltdowns is to prevent them from occurring. Once the volcano erupts, it is too late to stop it. No amount of scolding, threatening, demanding or commanding is going to lessen the overload, only add to it. In most situations, the person is simply reacting to the overwhelming demands (sensory, cognitive, social, emotional) that we are placing on them or pressuring them into—situations they cannot handle. The responsibility is ours, not theirs. When the environmental demands overwhelm the person's ability to cope, fight or flight sets in and meltdowns become likely.

The best ways to prevent meltdowns are to identify and reduce the demands to better match the person's abilities, provide greater assistance to support the person's struggles and help teach better coping skills for handling these challenges. This requires us to:

- identify, respect and support the person's processing needs
- identify the conditions that frequently trigger overload
- make accommodations and provide supports for reducing these overwhelming stressors
- recognize the early signs of overload
- give the person an out to escape situations before overload occurs.

In addition, we need to not blame the person and to help him feel safe and accepted regardless of the meltdowns. Placing blame on the individual will only heighten his anxiety in stressful situations, increasing the likelihood of future meltdowns.

Fourteen proactive strategies for preventing shutdowns and meltdowns

1. Respect neurological differences.

2. Identify and support the processing challenges (sensory, social, emotional, etc.).

3. Respect comfort zones (what the child can tolerate—sensory, cognitive and social).

4. Monitor mental energy reserve and avoid mental drain.

5. Back off during states of reactivity.

6. Give the child an active role in planning and guiding the situation.

7. Allow the child to pace the activity.

8. Give frequent breaks to rebound.

9. Provide sensory tools to help regulate stress.

10. Identify and minimize conditions triggering meltdowns.

11. Have a plan and preview it ahead of stressful events.

12. Always have an escape plan out of the stressful situation.

13. Recognize early signs of distress.

14. Teach coping skills for stress (relaxation, counting, exercise).

1 Respect neurological differences

Autistics have differences in neurology that represent different ways of processing information, integrating sensory input, relating socially, thinking and communicating. These processes represent differences in how information is gathered, interpreted and assimilated into adaptive responses. For those with autism, their concrete, detailed, literal processing is great when dealing with objects, physical science, mathematics, computer sciences, engineering and other static areas. However, when they are placed in our dynamic social world of vague rules, hidden meanings, complex contexts and fluctuating expectations, these processing differences put their nervous system at a disadvantage. They are frequently met with environmental demands that do not match their processing needs, and thus continually tax their nervous system. When your system does not match the cultural demands, it will have to work harder, longer and expend more energy. Hence, simply regulating the typical daily routine (especially at school or work) takes more effort, taxes processing skills and drains mental reserves. These ongoing daily challenges compromise an already vulnerable nervous system, rendering it less capable of coping.

These neurological differences are real and must be respected if we want to lower stress and anxiety for autistics. The more we continually ignore these differences and pressure people to process and act differently (ignore their autism), the more stress, anxiety and overload they experience. In computer analogy, we have different operating systems. Expecting one to process like the other will not work. Essentially, expecting an autistic person to be "normal" (neurotypical) will create ongoing stress and compromise both processing and coping skills. This creates a higher level of stress chemicals and greater risk of emotional overload.

We need to understand and respect these processing differences, not pressure these people to be something they are not, and focus on developing their strengths and preferences. If, when in school, a child arrives at the correct answers to math problems using a different processing style, then the teacher should not require him to do it a different way. Because of poor fine motor skills, if the child struggles at writing, do not pressure him to write the answers. Let him type or verbally present the information. If he must use all his concentration on writing the correct letters, he cannot focus on what he wants to say. If the child is more introverted and struggles socially, do not force him into complex social groups. He will become stressed, overwhelmed and emotionally dysregulated (or shutdown). Continued stress will erode his processing abilities and over time lead to burnout.

2 Identify and support the processing challenges

Given the child's neurology, our first approach should be to understand his unique processing challenges and then build in accommodations to support these vulnerabilities. These often include the following areas:

- *Sensory challenges:* including stimulation the person is sensitive to (light, noise, touch, etc.), problems processing and integrating multiple sensations and any sensory attractions and distractions. We need to understand what sensory demands an event will place on the child and how we can make accommodations or adaptations. Autistic adults often report that sensory overload is the number one cause of their meltdowns. It is important that once we understand the sensory challenges we help reduce sensory assaults by avoiding or reducing the stimulation in the setting (turning down the lights, noise, activity, etc.), providing tools to mask or block out stimulation (sunglasses, wide-rim hats, headphones, etc.) and providing a means to escape the stimulation before it becomes overwhelming.

- *Cognitive challenges:* problems processing multiple information simultaneously, delayed information processing, difficulty attending, planning and organizing, and challenges with abstract, multiple meanings. Understanding how the person takes in and processes information and then matching how we present information to those abilities will reduce stress and mental drain. People directing, instructing or prompting need to consider the best way to present information (visual, concrete, broken down into steps, etc.) and make it easy for the person to understand. Match the presentation to the processing style of the person.

- *Social challenges:* Difficulty navigating social rules and expectations, interpreting social context and reading the thoughts, feeling and intentions of others. Navigating social interaction (especially groups) is so draining and overwhelming, resulting in much confusion and frustration for autistics. What are the child's social strengths and weaknesses? Try to know ahead of time what social demands an event will place on the child and what supports you can put in place to limit those challenges.

- *Emotional regulation challenges:* Difficulty identifying and labeling emotions, poor impulse control, over-exaggerated reactions, and intense sensitivity to the emotions of others. This can make any challenging situation an emotional nightmare. Often, accumulated stress and unexpected challenges will trigger panic and emotional overload. Emotions are scary for many children and can surge out of panic. Understanding how the child handles the emotions of others as well as themselves will help identify what situations to avoid and how to support him in these situations.

- *Task performance challenges:* Difficulty multi-tasking, problems attending, planning and organizing, and poor ability to monitor performance. As with attention deficit hyperactivity disorder (ADHD), executive functioning skills are often impaired. If they are placed in situations that require them to assess what is needed, organize a plan of action and implement that plan, this can be overwhelming for them. Multi-tasking or multi-step tasks can overwhelm their organizational skills. Understanding how to accommodate for their weaknesses and utilize their strengths (detailed thinking, hyper-focus on interests, concrete guidelines, etc.) can make work, school and home demands much easier.

- *Communication challenges:* Difficulty formulating what to say, how to say it and physically saying it. Often understanding what is meant by others and formulating how to respond is very impaired, even if their ability to speak is good. Remembering to speak literally, clarify understanding and avoid vague, ambiguous language can make daily communication much easier.

Chapters 13–16 will provide more detailed suggestions on how to make accommodations for supporting these challenges. For a more in-depth analysis of these core challenges, please refer to the blue book, *The Autism Discussion Page on the Core Challenges of Autism* (Nason 2014a). Once we understand these challenges we can identify and build in supports to lessen them. Parents should make everyone relating with their child (teachers, professionals, employers, etc.) a brief, written profile of the child's vulnerabilities and how to accommodate for them, as well as strengths in these areas.

As noted, when the environmental demands are greater than the person's ability to handle them, problems will occur. We must find ways to modify and reduce these demands and provide added supports to make the demands manageable. This is essential for the person to feel safe, accepted and competent in tackling his daily demands.

The more discrepancy between these demands and personal skills, the more stress, anxiety and extensive drain on his ability to cope.

3 Respect comfort zones

Given the profile of strengths and vulnerabilities, as well as emotional sensitivities, it is important to identify what conditions the person feels safe and comfortable with. As much of the world moves too fast, too intensively and is too confusing for these children, we must know what conditions (sensory, social, academic, etc.) they feel safe and competent in handling. Given their fears, confidence and anxiety level, in all major life activities, what are these children willing to tolerate and what can they effectively handle? How much and what kind of socializing can they tolerate, what types of sensory environments should be avoided or kept short, and under what conditions do the children do their best?

What activities and interaction styles do they best respond to? What interests and preferences can we engage? What activities/events and interaction styles overwhelm them? How receptive are they with trying new things, stretching comfort zones and trusting those who are providing guidance? How much can we gradually stretch these comfort zones without overwhelming them? Comfort zones allow us to understand what level of engagement will be safe and how to accommodate the child's tolerance levels.

For many children, these comfort zones can be very rigid. They serve to buffer and protect the child from the chaotic, confusing world around him. They provide predictability, minimizing uncertainty and anxiety. People need to understand these comfort zones and respect the importance they have for the person's sense of safety and security. Pressing the person outside these comfort zones can elicit strong fear, panic and emotional turmoil. Many meltdowns occur because adults pressure the children to step outside their comfort zones, without respecting these needs, providing necessary support and slowly stretching these conditions. The more anxious the child, the more rigid the comfort zones and the more active resistance you can expect when stepping out of these comfort zones.

It is very important that we understand the child, what helps him feel safe and competent, how much he can safely risk, and how to help him feel safe stretching these comfort zones. Stretching presents "uncertainty" and each child has a level of uncertainty that they can tolerate. We need to identify just how much uncertainty the child can experience without being overwhelmed. This is called the "just right" challenge— the quantity of new learning or risk that may create a little anxiety, but not enough to overwhelm him. This band of risk will depend on the how much trust the child has that the adult will (1) move slowly to keep him safe and not overwhelm him, (2) provide support to maximize success, (3) respect his voice or early signs that he is becoming overwhelmed, and (4) immediately allow him to pull back if we are stretching too fast.

We must be a working partner with the child to become a trusted guide for him. Not understanding and respecting these comfort zones will often facilitate conditions for emotional meltdowns.

4 Monitor mental energy reserve and avoid mental drain

Just like all of us, if our nervous systems are well rested and organized, we can handle stressful events more easily. If we have had little sleep, are hungry and have already had a stress-filled day, we are more likely to explode over little snags. For those with autism, their fragile nervous systems are more vulnerable to both mental and physical drain. Research shows that, even in a resting state, the level of stress chemicals (anxiety) in the nervous system is much higher for those with autism. So, given their sensory challenges and processing differences, their nervous systems must work much harder to navigate their daily routine.

Whether or not a common stressor will trigger a meltdown is often determined by the state of the nervous system when the child enters the event. If the child is relatively calm and organized and not mentally drained, he may be able to handle the event at that time. However, if the child has had minimal sleep, eaten poorly or had an active day, the chances are that his mental energy is drained and his ability to handle stressors will be compromised. We must be cognizant of how organized the child is, how much stress he has already experienced and how much mental energy he has available to handle a presenting event. We often press children into situations when they do not have the resources (cognitive and emotional) to effectively deal with them. When pressed above their operating level, the children will panic and meltdowns are likely. The more drained they are, the more compromised their coping skills and the greater likelihood of becoming overwhelmed.

We need to be conscious of how much sleep the person had, if he is experiencing any physical discomfort, has been eating well, and how busy his day has already been. Has the child had adequate breaks to rebound or has he been bouncing from one activity to another? At the other end, we need to be aware of how much processing drain (sensory, cognitive, social challenges) an upcoming event will present. How long will the activity be, what sensory challenges will arise, is there ongoing pressure to socialize and are there task performance expectations? Emotionally, if the child is very excited or anxious about the event there is a greater chance of becoming overwhelmed if things are not going well. All these variables will help determine if an event is going to present greater processing challenges than the child can handle.

We can help the child extensively if we continually monitor where he is at, what he has done and what are we asking of him. For many children, with their already fragile nervous systems and numerous processing challenges, their energy reserve will vary significantly from day to day and moment to moment. They will have good days when they are more organized and capable of tackling routine challenges, and other days, or moments, when their nervous systems are more fragile, easily drained and less capable of handling many challenges. We must be able to adjust their schedules and arrange daily demands to match their present abilities. The number one strategy for preventing meltdowns is not pressing the child into situations that he is unable to handle.

5 Back off during states of reactivity

Almost all parents are aware when their children are more organized, relaxed and receptive. In turn, parents are often keen to help when the children are anxious, on high alert and very emotionally reactive. We have discussed how the neurological pathways connecting the emotional center of the brain (limbic system) with the thinking part of the brain (pre-frontal lobes) are weak, with poor communication between the two centers. If the child's emotional centers are on high alert and overpowering the thinking centers of the brain, the child is going to be anxious, on guard, impulsive and emotionally reactive. How this will look will be different for each child. However, usually the child is more anxious, more resistant and easily upset. His emotion center is on high alert and hypervigilant to demands. His stress chemicals are elevated. He will perceive even minimal demands as negative and react impulsively.

Of course, whether a child can handle a set of demands will be dependent on how receptive his nervous system is at that moment. If the child is already in an anxious, reactive emotional state the likelihood of overwhelming him is much higher and meltdowns much greater. Unfortunately, we might be pressured for time and emotionally reactive ourselves and press the child into events that will trigger panic (fight or flight response). It is difficult to shift gears and rearrange everything to match the child's state of receptiveness. Also, some adults can be very controlling and try to command and demand that the child performs. This rarely works, escalates the emotional reactivity of both the child and adult, and usually pushes the child into a meltdown.

We must be observant and flexible enough to recognize when the child is in a more anxious, reactive state and be able to back off, reduce or modify our demands. If the child is having difficulty regulating simple, routine expectations, it may be too overwhelming to expect him to handle more challenging events (especially social activity). We may even have to withdraw all demands, no matter how small, temporarily until the child becomes more receptive. Although this may not always be possible, be aware that the child is very vulnerable to becoming overwhelmed and having a meltdown.

6 Give the child an active role in planning and guiding the situation

Because the world is often chaotic and confusing for the child, uncertainty is scary. This often drives an intense need to control everything around him to make the world predictable. The more anxious the child, the more resistant he may be to follow the lead of others. Being pressed into situations of uncertainty and having no control will often elicit panic and meltdowns. Adults like to be in control and expect the children to respond. Unfortunately, trying to assert control and command the child to engage will only elicit emotional outbursts.

We can lessen a lot of stress, while reducing the uncertainty, by giving the child an active role in planning and guiding the activity. Be a working partner with the child and collaborate with him. Once the activity is agreed on, work together on how it will evolve. Preview what the child can expect, what will be expected of him and how we can respond if problems arise. This lessens the uncertainty, provides a mental map of what is expected, makes it more predictable and gives the child some sense of control. This lessens many of the variables that can easily overwhelm the child once pressed into an activity. In addition, once in the event, give the child a voice in guiding through the activity. Essentially, try to be a working partner, working hand in hand, rather than pulling the child from behind.

7 Allow the child to pace the activity

We all have a processing speed and pace at which we do things. For many autistics, because of processing challenges, their processing speed is slower. Take a computer with different processing speeds—we cannot expect it to perform faster than it can process. Because of delayed information processing, it takes longer for expectations to be processed, a plan of action to be formulated and responses executed. Unfortunately, many of us tend to move at a faster pace and expect the child to also do so; we push the child along to match our pace. Pressing the brain to process and respond faster than it can will make it anxious, work harder and possibly panic (melt down). Most parents have learned that this just doesn't work, creates bigger problems and results in frequent meltdowns.

In many cases, the child may shut down, freeze and stop responding. If the child has delayed processing, it will take time for directions to be processed. If we give an instruction, we expect the child to respond immediately. However, if the child has delayed processing, he may need 10–30 seconds, even longer, to process what is requested. Not recognizing this processing delay, we restate the prompt, sometimes several times. However, each time we do this, the child must restart the processing all over again. This leads to increased frustration and emotional overload. If we continue to prompt, instruct and demand, the child may melt down. Unfortunately, this delay in processing and responding often leads others to perceive the child as resistant and oppositional. This sets up a pattern of ongoing attempts to pressure the child into responding.

One of the best ways to protect from overloading the brain is letting the child pace the activity. Work with them, letting them guide you in how much and how fast they do things. Learn what the processing speed is for the person and adjust expectations accordingly. Of course, since processing speed can vary from day to day, and moment to moment, this pace may also vary. Allowing the child to pace the activity will tell you how fast the processing is at that moment. Matching our expectations to the pace of the child will help maximize his ability to process and perform.

8 Give frequent breaks to rebound

With all the processing differences, autistic brains must work harder to process the ongoing events of the day. This is especially true for our social world, which requires intense concentration to identify what is expected, decipher vague social rules, read nonverbal communication and navigate social situations. Paired with sensory sensitivities and academic/work expectations, this means that the nervous system is continually taxed and drained. We do not realize how draining the average daily routine is for autistics. What we take for granted is very taxing for them.

Even if we make accommodations to lessen stress and let the children pace the flow to their advantage, stress chemicals continue to accumulate throughout the day. The next best support we can provide is giving the child occasional breaks throughout the day to escape and regroup. For some, breaks can be going off by themselves to a quiet area to rest, others need physical activity to release stress chemicals, and some desire engagement in a preferred activity such as reading or listening to music.

The number of breaks needed and the length of each break will vary extensively from child to child. At school, usually the breaks last from 10 to 20 minutes and occur at least twice a day. However, adults have reported that for long, very draining activities (parties, concerts, etc.), they may need several hours or even a couple of days to rebound. In addition to scheduled breaks at school, children often have a card that they can present if they feel they need a break. Adults at work often find ways to take breaks (go for a walk, go to the bathroom, etc.) at work to escape and regroup.

Both parents and teachers need to be cognizant of how draining the schedule of activity is for the child. Parents need to make sure that breaks are frequently scheduled between draining activities, especially community outings and social events. Try not to string several activities together, which may drain the child and possibly lead to overload. Space out the activity and give the child time to rebound. Teach the child to understand his own energy reserve, make a list of preferred breaks (e.g. sleeping, stimming, playing outside). The more the individual is aware of his own needs and how to meet them, the better equipped he is.

9 Provide sensory tools to help regulate stress

Almost all of us use sensory stimulation to alert our nervous systems when under-aroused and to calm it when over-aroused. When the nervous system feels anxious and disorganized it will seek out stimulation to optimize it. Since the nervous system of those with autism is more sensitive and fragile it is continually vacillating between being over- or under-aroused and fighting to maintain organization. Sensory stimulation is a great tool to help individuals provide their nervous system's adaptive input. There are three main avenues for sensory regulation:

- *Sensory diet.* Providing structured sensory activities at intervals throughout the day helps to release stress chemicals and organize the nervous system. Frequent movement (vestibular) and physical exertion (proprioception) help alert and organize the nervous system. Proprioception (tension and resistance to the joints and tendons) helps release stress chemicals and calm and organize the nervous system. It has a double benefit of releasing stress chemicals and maintaining optimal arousal level.

- *Sensory tools.* In addition to structured activities, sensory tools such as fidget toys, weighted backpacks, deep pressure vests, chair cushions to sit on, and gum to chew can be used to help reduce anxiety and regulate arousal level. Deep pressure and proprioception can also be good tools for calming over-arousal.

- *Self-stimulation.* A major tool for autistics is their self-stimulation (repetitive actions—hand flapping, rocking, flipping material, rubbing fabric with their fingers, etc.). The repetitive, rhythmic actions can be used to block out unwanted stimulation as well as regulate arousal level (calm or alert). This helps minimize anxiety.

Both sensory sensitivity/overload and using sensory preferences to help modulate the nervous system should be assessed for anyone who experiences ongoing emotional regulation problems. It is best to receive an evaluation by an occupational therapist trained in sensory processing treatment. See Chapter 13, Sensory Overload, for more ideas.

10 Identify and minimize conditions triggering meltdowns

A primary step for reducing meltdowns is identifying the conditions (antecedents) that give rise to them and either avoiding them or finding ways to minimize their impact on the person. If we know that loud, noisy settings can overload a child, we can avoid certain activities and provide adaptive supports such as sound-canceling headphones to help block out the noise, or turning down the noise. We can find ways to avoid or modify the conditions or provide greater support to help the child through them.

By keeping a journal of each occurrence of meltdown, we can pick up common patterns (conditions) that frequently present in meltdowns. Usually, the journal notes when, where, with whom and what activity/demands are presented, how the child reacts and how others respond to the child. Once we identify when and what conditions elicit the behavior, we must figure out why these conditions cause such problems, to decide how to best support the child and lessen the stress. For example, a child may have frequent meltdowns when pressured to do homework. This may be because he cannot attend that long, the homework is too hard, or he needs more time after coming home from school before starting the homework. Knowing why can help us determine if we need to shorten the amount of time doing homework (breaking it up into sessions), wait until later to do it or make the homework easier. If necessary, we can eliminate homework altogether.

Some events will have more than one variable causing the problem. For example, if the child has difficulty handling parties or family gatherings, it could be the combination of too much activity, too much noise, the uncertainty of what will occur, too many people, expectations to relate with everyone and so on. This is where knowing the child's processing challenges, sensory sensitivities and social struggles can help identify why a given event frequently triggers meltdowns. For these antecedent conditions, we need to find ways to reduce each one of these variables if we are going to expect the child to frequently engage in these activities.

11 Have a plan and preview it ahead of stressful events

We often drag children into events with little preparation, either for the child or ourselves. Walking into uncertainty is very anxiety provoking for these children and once in the event the anticipatory anxiety can escalate into panic. Not knowing what to expect and how to handle it can produce immediate panic, resulting in meltdowns. Get used to sitting down together and previewing with the child what you can expect to happen (sequence of events, who will be there, what activity is going on, etc.) and what will be expected of him. Talk over what challenges he may experience and what strategies can be used to minimize those challenges. Giving the child a mental map of what to expect and how to tackle and minimize challenges will reduce the uncertainty and give him predictable scripts for navigating the event. Previewing ahead of time and collaborating with the child will help empower him by being an active agent in tackling his challenges. Knowing what to expect and how to act will also drastically reduce the anticipatory anxiety of not knowing and then melting down from fear.

12 Always have an escape plan out of the stressful situation

Before entering events, discuss with the person what the plan is if things become too overwhelming. People often walk into events with no forethought given to what conditions might overwhelm them and how to quickly escape the situation once it become too much. Just planning this out ahead of time will reduce the anxiety going into the event. If the child knows what to expect, what barriers may occur and how to quickly escape if needed, this can drastically reduce his anticipatory anxiety. This may be temporarily finding a quiet area, taking a break, doing calming strategies, going back to the car and returning once calm, or leaving the event entirely. Having a plan, collaborating together and practicing it, can help reduce the anxiety of going into potentially stressful situations.

13 Recognize early signs of distress

It is extremely important that we know the early signs that the children are becoming overwhelmed so that we can act quickly to support them. Individuals with autism often do not feel their bodies' cues that they are getting stressed until it is too late, and they are falling apart. It is important that people around them identify and watch closely for these early signs of agitation. This can be changes in physical appearance (e.g. flushed skin, dilated pupils) or changes in behavior (becoming more or less active, more or less vocal, an increase in self-stimulation, becoming giddy or argumentative, withdrawing, etc.). Knowing these early signs gives us a chance to recognize that the person is becoming compromised and needs immediate help. Again, often the individuals themselves are not aware of their early signs. Over time, we must teach them these early signs, so they can begin to recognize for themselves that they are getting stressed.

During events, we need to monitor the child closely for these early signs so that we can intervene quickly and use the designated coping skills (pull away for a break, deep breathing, putting on headphones, any practiced coping skill) to calm the nervous system. Too often, I see parents pressing their children into activities without previewing the potential barriers or having a prepared plan and then not monitoring the child for early signs of distress. Even if we have a plan of action, unless we monitor the child closely for early signs, it is often too late once the meltdown begins. We have missed the window of opportunity for catching the child before he becomes overwhelmed. Once the fire begins, it is fueled quickly and the emotions of everyone escalate. It can be difficult for everyone, but even more traumatic for the child. Pre-planning the support upfront is the only way to successfully deal with emotional overload.

14 Teach coping skills for stress (relaxation, counting, exercise)

High stress and anxiety levels are common for autism and will last a lifetime. Coping with anxiety will always be a central issue for many on the spectrum. Learning to manage stress and anxiety usually consists of three main areas:

- *Exercise and relaxation.* As with everyone who experiences high anxiety, daily exercise does wonders for reducing anxiety and regulating emotions. Running, resistance weight training and swimming are good activities for reducing overall stress levels, as they help to release stress chemicals and keep the nervous system regulated. Relaxation exercises, meditation and mindfulness training can also have good implications for reducing the overall levels of stress and anxiety. These increase the individual's awareness of internal body sensations of both stress and anxiety, even when they are calm and organized. All three also have calming effects on the autonomic nervous system, which helps reduce stress and anxiety. A calm and organized nervous system is better prepared to handle the increased stress that autistics experience.

- *In the moment coping skills.* Techniques that can be used in the moment to manage stress and anxiety will be important to teach over time. Techniques such as deep breathing, muscle relaxation, positive self-statements and sensory tools can be used by the individual to minimize stress (see Chapter 7, Coping Skills).

- *Medications and supplements for reducing anxiety.* When anxiety is severe and resistant to these other proactive supports, medication may help to reduce generalized anxiety. Anti-anxiety and anti-depressant medications have been used with moderate success with anxiety. However, many autistics are sensitive to medications and results are very individual. Adults report that usually low doses work better than high doses. Use of medications with children need to be considered only as a last resort and monitored very carefully. All medications come with potential negative side effects and possible adverse reactions. Also, medications should not be a substitute for teaching better copings skills. It is very important that medications are prescribed by physicians who have experience with autism. Some families have used supplements to help reduce anxiety, to avoid side effects of medications. A discussion of medications and supplements is beyond the scope of this book.

Developing a comprehensive plan of proactive supports

Minimizing processing strain, avoiding overload and reducing chances of meltdowns usually requires developing a comprehensive plan using a mixture of the strategies mentioned above. Supporting the nervous system, modifying demands with accommodations, understanding the triggering conditions, teaching coping skills and so forth all need to be incorporated into a comprehensive plan that matches the needs of the individual. These comprehensive plans often need collaboration between settings (parents and teachers) and may include psychologist, occupational therapist, counselor or social worker and other support staff.

Reducing challenges at school

For most autistic children, school represents a stressful environment that can be very draining and emotionally overwhelming. Many children become drained and shut down during the day at school to avoid being overwhelmed and melting down. As mentioned earlier, these kids may be able to hold it together while at school, but frequently melt down soon after leaving school. Even if the child is behaving well at school, there are numerous variables at school that need to be carefully looked at and that together present overwhelming stress for these children. Below is just a summary of some of the major challenges.

1. *Sensory challenges.* Bright florescent lights; nauseating smells of markers, paints, pastes, laboratory chemicals, perfume and deodorant of teachers and other students; distracting visual array of classroom walls cluttered with colorful posters/pictures; other students bumping into them; hard unbearable seats; too much competing stimulation to integrate; transition buzzers, fire alarms, assemblages.

2. *Cognitive/academic challenges.* Too much information coming too fast; poor working memory and attention problems; listening and writing simultaneously; multi-step academic demands; task performance anxiety; poor ability to organize, initiate and complete work, work too hard or too much, difficulty asking for help.

3. *Social challenges.* Difficulty understanding and relating with peers; problems understanding hidden social rules and expectations; difficulty navigating unstructured social contexts like lunch, recess, locker room, halls, bathrooms, bus; teasing and bullying.

4. *Communication challenges.* Difficulty understanding directions and expectations; problems reading nonverbal communication and hidden meanings; difficulty processing more than one person talking at a time; problems formulating what they want to say and how to say it.

5. *Suppression of autistic needs.* Pressed to act normally and blend in, lack of resources to support processing needs, pressured into active social situations they cannot navigate; lack of sensory tools to regulate the nervous system; pressured to suppress self-stimulation; lack of breaks to rebound; lack of understanding, accepting and respecting their differences; forced to comply, conform and fit into a highly demanding neurotypical environment.

These are just some of the challenges that children with autism experience at school. The numerous sensory, social, academic and emotional challenges present an ongoing accumulation of stress chemicals throughout the day, taxing and draining mental energy and coping skills. Many of the children are forced to shut down part of their processing skills to block out stimulation that is overwhelming them. Some children can shut down and block out effectively enough that their struggles escape notice: "Your child is a perfect angel at school; never a problem, passive and quiet." However, this constant demand to comply, suppress and process overwhelming demands continually taxes and drains the nervous system and creates ongoing stress and anxiety. For those who have difficulty emotionally coping with the stress, frequent emotional outbursts and problem behavior may occur. Those better able to cope and hold it together may explode once out of school, especially at home where they are safe to release the stress.

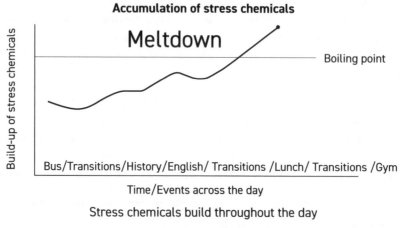

Accumulation of stress chemicals

Meltdown

Boiling point

Build-up of stress chemicals

Bus/Transitions/History/English/ Transitions /Lunch/ Transitions /Gym

Time/Events across the day

Stress chemicals build throughout the day

Figure 11.1: Accumulated build-up of stress chemicals leading to meltdowns

Figure 11.1 represents the accumulation of stress chemicals as the child goes through the day at school. With all the cognitive, sensory, social and emotional processing challenges that the child is experiencing each day, it takes considerable ability to hold it together while at school. Simply regulating the sensory, social and academic demands of the normal school day is very taxing and overwhelming for the child with autism. Much of what the typical child's nervous system processes with ease can be very taxing for the nervous system of those with autism.

The simple event of riding the bus to school can be overwhelming for many children. The sensory issues, as well as social challenges, with many children on the bus can be very challenging. The child may sit still and say nothing, but stress chemicals are accumulating. Transitions from one class to another, especially regulating in the noisy and crowded hallways, can be very stressful, adding more accumulation of stress chemicals. Then there are the social, communicative, sensory and task performance demands of the classroom that continue to add to the stress and overload. Stress chemicals continue to accumulate as the child moves through the day. Remember, as the stress chemicals rise, anxiety heightens, and coping skills begin to deteriorate. Eventually, the child begins to shut down to hold it together or reaches boiling point where the stress chemicals explode and must release. This is when meltdowns are likely to occur. The teachers or parents may not know what triggered the outburst, or why the meltdown occurred, because the child can look completely fine until he reaches boiling point.

It is important to realize that all these transitions, social interaction, processing of the sensory stimulation and task performance demands are accumulating and adding stress chemicals across the day. We need to be cognizant of these stressors so that we can build in strategies to help support the child in dealing with them.

Most of us can feel when we are getting stressed and often pull back or engage in coping strategies to lower the stress chemicals. Our brains can sense the build-up of stress chemicals, telling us that we need to pull back and take a break so that we do not reach overload. Many autistics often have poor internal body awareness and do not feel the stress chemicals build up. Consequently, they may be unaware that they are getting stressed until they hit boiling point. Unfortunately, by that time their coping skills have often collapsed.

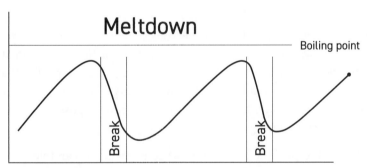

- Provide accommodations to reduce sensory, social and task demands (e.g. sensory diets, visual schedules, minimize demands)
- Allow periodic breaks in daily routine to regroup
- Provide a "safe area" for rebounding
- Provide a sensory diet to keep the nervous system calm and organized
- Identify and respect the child's comfort zones (which he can tolerate)
- Help the child understand when he starts to become overloaded
- Teach alternative replacement behavior (coping skills)
- Become a supportive partner for the child (safe and accepted)

Figure 11.2: How proactive strategies can minimize meltdowns

Figure 11.2 displays our goal, which is to keep the child calm and organized by providing proactive supports to lower the overall stressful challenges during the day, provide periodic breaks to escape and rebound and provide coping tools for tackling the stress. Since every child is unique and requires different supports, these following strategies will help lower the stress level and provide outlets for releasing the stress so that it doesn't accumulate to overload. A good proactive plan may consist of the following:

- Provide accommodations to reduce sensory, social and task demands (e.g. sensory diets, visual schedules, minimize demands). As just mentioned, identify what the child's core vulnerabilities are in each main domain (sensory, social, task demands) and build in supports to help minimize the stress. The better we can match the sensory, social and task performance demands to the child's processing skills, the less chance of overload.

- Allow periodic breaks in daily routine to regroup. This is very important. As Figure 11.1 shows, the stress chemicals accumulate as the child moves through the day. Periodic breaks can include going to a quiet area, doing physical exercise, relaxing in a tent with bean bags, or rocking in a sky swing—strategies that will release the stress chemicals that have been building up and allow the child to regroup before entering the demands again. How long each child can go before a break is needed and how much of a break the child may need will vary significantly.

- Provide a "safe area" for rebounding. The safe areas are often small areas away from the classroom or in an isolated area within the classroom for children to withdraw to when feeling stressed (see Chapter 12, Supporting Meltdowns). Schools often use break cards for the child to present when needing to escape, or the teacher may give the card to the child to remind him that he needs to take a break and go to the safe area.

- Provide a sensory diet to keep the nervous system calm and organized. Keeping the nervous system regulated is very important for minimizing meltdowns. In school, the occupational therapist should design a sensory diet that includes (1) periodic calming and organizing sensory activities to maximize arousal level, (2) sensory coping skills to minimize overload, and (3) possible sensory tools for calming the child during a meltdown.

- Identify and respect the child's comfort zones (what he can tolerate). This takes us back to assessing and identifying the vulnerabilities and challenges that compromise the child, defining what his comfort zones are (what helps him feel safe, accepted and competent) and then respecting those comfort zones.

- Help the child understand when he starts to become overloaded. It is important to identify the early signs that he is becoming stressed and the common triggers, so he knows when he needs to pull back and take a break.

- Teach alternative replacement behavior (coping skills). Over time, it is important to teach the child a few coping skills that he can use to reduce the anxiety when starting to feel anxious. We need to work with the child to identify what will help him and then practice and role-play the strategies.

- Become a supportive partner for the child (safe and accepted). It is important for the child to feel as if the adults around him are working partners with him, are listening to him and respecting his vulnerabilities and supporting him when he feels overwhelmed. Just knowing that the teacher and parents understand and respect his needs greatly reduces anxiety and helps the child manage the stress better. It is important for the child to have a go-to support person (counselor, social worker) when he has problems or the classroom becomes too overwhelming. When the demands become great, the child may not feel safe approaching the teacher. He may need somebody outside the classroom who he can talk to about his problems, get support with social issues and discuss fears and classroom conflicts. Since the teacher may be part of the conflict, or perceived so by the child, a neutral, safe person is important.

As you can see, developing a comprehensive support plan for children at school can be a complex endeavor. Such plans need to be developed by an interdisciplinary team, consisting of teachers, teacher's assistant, occupational therapist, speech and language specialist, psychologist, counselor, social worker and parents. A good plan will consist of several proactive preventative strategies for reducing the stressful challenges, rather than simply outlining how to intervene during meltdowns.

Chapter 12

SUPPORTING MELTDOWNS

Even with the best intentions and the most comprehensive supports, you cannot eliminate the inevitable meltdowns, especially for younger children, but also occasionally
for adults. At times the world is simply too chaotic and overwhelming for them. As
discussed earlier, their fragile nervous systems are vulnerable and easily compromised
by stress and anxiety. Even with the best of plans and accommodations we cannot shield
them from unexpected snags, sensory overload and being overwhelmed by too many
processing demands taxing their abilities.

It is very important that those people around the person understand how to help him
feel safe and accepted through the emotional turmoil. When the brain is overwhelmed
it cannot function adaptively. Like a volcano erupting, the surge of stress chemicals
overloads the brain and seeks release. The control systems of the brain collapse, and
emotional/behavioral outbursts are the result. The person must react to release the stress
chemicals. The brain panics and the person reacts helplessly. Screaming, stomping,
running, hitting and biting self, body flailing, head banging, throwing property, all
provide physical release of the stress chemicals that are boiling over. By this time, the
individual has lost self-control and is held captive by an emotional tidal wave.

This does not mean that there is nothing we can do to support the child, help calm
the fury, keep others safe and respect the self-esteem of the person. In all phases of
intervention, the primary aims are to keep everyone safe, avoid fueling the fire, and communicate reassurance and acceptance. Empathy, compassion, acceptance and validation
are important to minimize the trauma during the episode, and the embarrassment, guilt
and remorse following the incident. Once the rage is occurring, the responsibility is
totally on those around the person to help calm the fury and keep everyone safe.

Three stages of meltdowns

Brenda Smith Myles, in her book *Asperger Syndrome and Difficult Moments* (Myles
and Southwick 2005), uses a three-stage model to describe meltdowns: the three Rs
of meltdowns—rumbling, rage and recovery stages. I will use these three stages to
categorize the strategies for helping support individuals during meltdowns.

The rumbling stage is when the individual is first starting to get agitated. The stress
chemicals are building, the nervous system is draining and coping skills are waning.
However, although the brain is compromised, we still have a window of opportunity to
intervene and help de-escalate the emotional overload. We can redirect that turmoil.
Once the individual escalates into the rage stage, he is too far gone to use judgement and

reasoning to calm the fury. The control centers of the brain are totally overwhelmed and non-functional. It is about keeping everyone safe, avoiding fueling the fire, and letting the meltdown play out. The last stage is the recovery phase when the brain is coming down from the turmoil, it is completely drained and is trying to regroup and stabilize. This is a fragile time and how we respond can drastically affect how the child rebounds.

The rumbling stage

As we have already discussed, prevention is the best way of reducing meltdowns, but we cannot control all variables that lead to stress build-up. The early, rumbling stage is our last chance for holding off a full-blown meltdown. The stress chemicals are building, the person starts to become distressed and judgement and reasoning skills start to wane. This is where it is vitally important that we identify the early signs of distress, understand the child's vulnerabilities, what helps the person feel safe and what helps him feel calm. It is also very important that we stay calm, supportive and validating. Any emotional reactions from us or trying to pressure, command and demand compliance from the child will only fuel the fire and escalate the chances of a meltdown.

What is it like?

The individual may not realize at first that he is becoming stressed. Those who know the person well can usually identify the early signs before the individual begins to feel disorganized. Many autistics have poor sensation of their internal cues and do not initially feel the build-up of stress. Or, they are so hyper-focused on the excitement of what they are doing that they are too distracted. Often, they do not recognize they are becoming distressed until it is too late. As the autistics age, they can become more capable of recognizing these internal cues, as well as their disorganized behavior.

What does it feel like for the person? It varies extensively. Some become more excited and active, while others may withdraw and pull inward. Often their senses become more sensitive (noise and light intensify), distorted and fragmented and their body starts to hurt (headache, chest pain, achy joints, etc.). Their ability to focus becomes impaired and confusion starts to set in. Some can become giddy and hyperactive, while others may become passive and withdrawn. They might begin to lose their ability to communicate, becoming either nonverbal or less coherent. Their ability to formulate what to say and how to say it becomes compromised. The children will frequently tell me that their brain is spinning, people's voices become confusing and any request, instruction or direction can elicit resistance. Their ability to reason becomes compromised and questions from others become difficult to process. Pressure from others to control and force compliance will frequently push the person into the rage stage.

This is where it is important to understand their vulnerabilities, the early signs of overload and how best to help guide them to safer ground. They may rely on you to identify the early signs and help support them out of the turmoil before they become overwhelmed. This is also where being a working, empathic partner with the child is so important to maintaining the person's emotional stability.

Know the early signs of distress

Most people will show early physical and behavioral signs that they are starting to get agitated. Although not always obvious, usually there are at least subtle changes in behavior, facial expression and body posture that signal the child is starting to become overwhelmed. We cannot over-emphasize the need to understand these early signs. They may be obvious, like complaining, arguing and refusing to engage, or subtle, with flushed skin and dilated pupils, becoming passive, withdrawn and minimally responsive (shutdown). Changes in speech, becoming more, or less, verbal, rapid and pressured speech, demanding attention and bouncing from one person to another may indicate that the child is becoming overwhelmed. It is important that others around the child understand that this behavior means that he is struggling and they should not interpret the behavior as intentional, well-controlled behavior. The child is communicating to us and we need to receptively listen and immediately begin to back off and support the person. Ignoring these signs, pressing for control and demanding compliance will not only escalate the emotional rollercoaster but also compromise the child's trust that others keep him safe.

Whereas some children may become hyper-verbal, others may shut down, become less responsive or even nonverbal. In addition, the more we say, the more confused they become. It is important not to read this behavior as noncompliance and increase our level of prompting. The more we prompt, the more overwhelmed and agitated they become. Another common cue is an increase in self-stimulation, either frequency or intensity. Increased body rocking, hand flapping, foot tapping, twirling, moving, humming, self-mumbling, flicking objects all represent the person trying to regulate his nervous system, lessen anxiety and block out overwhelming demands. Changes in body language (head down, hands over ears, looking away, blank stare), changes in mood (irritable or giddy) and increased repetitive behavior are all possible signs that overload is coming.

By knowing what triggers your child's meltdowns and identifying the early signs of possible overload, you can help to intervene early in situations to prevent them happening.

What to do?

1. *Intervene and provide immediate support.* Once you see the early signs of agitation, it is important to provide quick support. Remember, at this time the child is trying to hold it together, but can quickly lose all coping and reasoning skills if you do not act fast and provide support. As discussed earlier, when the stress chemicals are building, children start to lose their ability to think and communicate. Their emotions start to heighten and overwhelm the thinking part of the brain. They lose their words and have difficulty comprehending what others are saying.

Listed here are several common strategies that are often used to help immediately reduce the stressors, pull back and allow the child to rebound.

2. *Pull back on demands.* Usually when a meltdown is brewing, the demands of the event, be they sensory, social, cognitive or performance demands, are too strong for the current skills that the child has for dealing with them. The event is simply too overwhelming for the child and we need to immediately pull back to avoid overloading the child. The demands are either too much, too complex or too intense for the moment and the child starts to decompensate. This is not the time to command and demand, pressure or force the child to perform. Doing so will result in an immediate meltdown.

3. *Reduce stimulation.* Often the triggering circumstance is sensory overload, but even when it is not, the child's sensory sensitivities become heightened during the rumbling stage of stress. It is very important to try and reduce the noise, lighting and activity around the child. Try to lighten the load that the brain is trying to integrate and process. This also includes the speed and volume of your voice. Talk quietly and provide short but clear instructions. Slow yourself down and soften your voice and actions.

4. *Provide greater support.* Stay calm, validating and supportive. If the child is responsive, offer your help. Lower the task demands, simplify expectations or provide assistance to help navigate the demands. Acknowledge the child's struggles, validate his concern and reassure him that he is safe. However, children's reactions during this stage can vary significantly. Some children will welcome the support from a trusted person and others will adamantly refuse any assistance and only escalate if you try. This is where knowing the child's vulnerabilities, temperament and predictable reactions is important.

5. *Remove to a quieter area.* If possible, try to move the child to a quieter area. This immediately allows the child to escape the overwhelming demands to give the brain a chance to escape and rebound. Allow the child to temporarily regroup while the situation is assessed and greater support is provided. Sometimes, the child can return to the situation with added support. This helps the child learn that when times get tough, he can pull back, reassess and return to tackle the challenge. Pulling away to a quiet area will allow the brain to recover enough to regroup. However, if the event is simply too overwhelming, then it may be better to end the event entirely. It is important to plan ahead and have an escape route identified and preview this with the child. Knowing this ahead of time can lower the child's anticipatory anxiety of entering challenging situations.

6. *Give a break.* When understanding that an event may be challenging, give children occasional breaks. Allow them to pace the activity and take breaks so as to avoid overload. Giving frequent breaks is not only a great preventative tool, but also a good tool to use once children start to become overwhelmed.

7. *Distract attention.* Sometimes you cannot reduce the stimulation or remove the child from the situation. Or, once you do reduce stimulation, the child still needs help maintaining emotional control. Distraction can be a good tool. Giving the child something to occupy his attention can help mask the demands by redirecting attention. Sometimes humor can help, or talking about their favorite subject. Using their favorite electronics or other preferred activity can also be a good source of distraction. Getting the child to focus on something more familiar, predictable and under his control can help avoid meltdowns.

8. *Provide calming strategies.* Knowing what soothes a child can help during these times. For some children, engaging in a soothing activity (music, self-stimulation, physical activity, etc.) can help calm and organize the nervous system. This is best used once you remove the child from the overwhelming event, but can also be used as a coping tool during the event. For example, using headphones to listen to calming music not only helps mask the noise and distract from the overload, but also helps soothe the nervous system. This can be used during the event itself or if the child requires a temporary break.

9. *Self-stimulation.* Self-stimulation (rocking, hand flapping, etc.) is often the person's go-to tool for distracting, soothing and regulating their arousal level. Self-stimulation can be a very effective tool for blocking out overwhelming stimulation as well as soothing the overly aroused nervous system. This is not the time to try and interrupt and suppress the repetitive behavior.

10. *Teach coping skills.* Teach the child to identify and practice coping strategies (see Chapter 7, Coping Skills). It is important to teach, practice and role-play two or three coping skills that can be quickly used in times of stress. Techniques such as counting, deep breathing, positive self-talk, isometric resistance and deep pressure can be used to help regulate the stress and provide tools to tackling challenging situations. They not only help calm the nervous system, but also act to distract attention away from the overwhelming demands.

11. *Listen and respect their voice.* No matter what their communication skills, it is important that we listen to their behavior, understand they are struggling and help them feel as safe and accepted as possible. Bombarding them with questions, directions and commands will overwhelm the already compromised brain. Some adults will try and force compliance with threats and controlling language. This will spike anxiety and elicit panic. Some, in desperation to help, will push their assistance on the person, which may also overwhelm him. Bombarding the person with questions and offering suggestions may also be too much to process. As the person's processing skills start to slide, ongoing questioning, reasoning and expectation of coherent responses puts the brain on the spot, requires the person to process what is being expected, think about how to respond and formulate how to say it. This is too much, too fast, pushing the person further toward boiling point. Instead, assume the person is struggling to process, is not

capable of ongoing dialogue and so you need to minimize questions, expectations and threats. Acknowledge that the child is struggling, validate his emotions and reassure him; minimize language, let him pace the action and try to avoid fueling the fire.

12. *Prepare for challenging events.* Knowing the person's early signs and past challenging situations, you can better prepare for upcoming events and make them easier to navigate. If you know that an upcoming event could present some possible challenges, discuss these possibilities ahead of time and create a plan of action for when they occur. Discuss how to minimize the challenges; for example, wear headphones if the setting is going to be noisy, take a break (go to quiet area to regroup) if the event becomes stressful and have an escape plan if you need to exit quickly. While in the event, by knowing the early signs of stress build-up, both you and the child can implement your agreed on coping strategies. Knowing what may happen and how to deal with it will significantly lower both the child's anxiety and your own.

The importance of self-stimulation

In Chapter 13 on sensory overload, we discuss the important functions that self-stimulatory behavior provides. For many years, professionals have focused on suppressing self-stimulation without considering the importance it has for autistic people—often a main coping skill. It helps calm them when over-aroused, alert them when under-aroused and allows them to block out overpowering stimulation. It provides repetitive, rhythmic, self-controlled, predictable stimulation that helps regulate the overwhelmed nervous system; it is a very important tool, especially in the heat of the moment. Self-stimulation provides them with a way of holding themselves together when anxious or over-stimulated. It helps calm and organize their nervous system. Increased stimming also is an important sign for recognizing that the child is becoming overwhelmed and indicating that we need to back off or increase support.

Window of opportunity

What if we do not recognize the early signs? We may be so busy that we forget to recognize the fragile cues the child is expressing. With pressing responsibilities and time constraints, we get distracted, plow forward and miss the early signs.

Many children may show a freeze response just before reaching the point of no return. They may temporarily freeze, look away, get a glazed look, appear dazed or zone out. This is often our last opportunity to recognize, respect and immediately support them before meltdown occurs. The children may also shut their eyes, put their head down and cover their ears, or simply become non-responsive. We have all seen that look—the glazed-over eyes, the staring into space or looking straight through you. The brain is trying to shut down and block out stimulation to avoid overload. It is a defense mechanism for shutting down incoming stimulation.

This freeze moment means back off demands, lower stimulation and give the child time to rebound. This last window of opportunity can be brief, so we must act quickly. Immediately stop all demands, briefly reassure the child he is safe and give him time to rebound. No questioning, pushing interaction or forcing assistance on them. Stop the action and let him regroup. Stay close and let him determine when he is ready. Let him initiate the interaction and approach you when ready. That is often the best support you can give in the waning moments.

Have a pre-planned routine

It is very important to develop a pre-planned routine for supporting the child when he becomes overwhelmed. Remember, once the stress chemicals start to build, children start to lose their ability to think and communicate. It is best to have a safe, familiar, predictable intervention routine that can be implemented in times of distress. For children, knowing how people will respond, what they will do and that they will be safe, makes them more trusting when they become distressed. This plan should be reviewed and practiced frequently and previewed before entering potentially challenging situations. "While we are at the mall, remember all the noise and people may upset us. When we start to get upset, we can take a break and go to the car to calm down. Then we can decide if we want to go back to the mall or go home." It tends to reduce both the child and adult's anxiety about what may happen and how to respond.

Using a pre-planned routine

1. Once you see the early signs, act quickly to support the child. This should include a predetermined, predictable routine to calm and organize the child. (e.g. withdraw and isolate, rock, music, deep pressure, counting, physical activity, deep breathing).

2. Parents, teachers and child should develop the routine together. It is important that you include the child in designing this routine if possible. You want to be a working partner with him, allowing him to determine what techniques help him feel safe and calm. Also, try and include the teacher since it is best if everyone implements a similar routine.

3. Practice when calm, role-play if possible. It is important to first practice and role-play this routine when everyone is calm until it starts to become automatic. This way the child will be more responsive to using it in the heat of the moment. Remember, no new learning occurs if the person is overwhelmed. Do not try and implement something new and unpredictable when the child is already overwhelmed. Practice, preview it ahead of challenges, coach the child to use it during the heat of the moment and then review how well it worked once the situation is over. No matter how awful the meltdown was, always try and focus on what worked and how the child attempted to implement the plan.

4. Always use the routine as consistently as possible. The person must trust that we will act according to plan. Trust and predictability are vital when the child is overwhelmed.

5. Before going into events, preview the routine. "When you feel overwhelmed, we will go for a walk together." This way it is fresh in their head—what to expect and what to do.

6. Write this routine on a laminated card and hand it out to others when he loses his voice. This "routine card" can be important when parents are trying to implement the routine in a public place or when they need to provide a babysitter, or when support staff need instructions for challenging situations. This is also important for adults on the spectrum to carry with them, to hand to authorities during times of crisis, when they need support but are unable to communicate. For example, the card may state that they are emotionally overwhelmed, not able to communicate and reason, may hit or bite themselves. It may give simple instructions in how to help them calm. This is important for teens and adults who may encounter law officers.

The rage stage

Regardless of how observant and prepared we are, eventually there will be times when meltdowns are inevitable. We cannot control for every variable or be continually observant for early signs, and sometimes a quick snag, unexpected frustration or sensory assault will bolt the nervous system into fight or flight panic. At this stage, all reasoning and most communication abilities deteriorate, and coping skills fall apart. Lights, sounds, smells and touch become amplified and painful, their body hurts and they have headaches. Painful emotions are stirring, overwhelming the brain with stress chemicals. Panic sets in and fight or flight is activated. Screaming, crying, yelling/hitting/biting self, body flailing, running, disrupting property and even assaulting others may happen. The bottled-up stress chemicals are screaming to be released and the brain is struggling to escape the overwhelming event. It is a dreadful experience for both the child and those trying to help him.

To help we often try to reason with the person, bombard him with repeated questions, instruct him in what to do or physically try to direct him. Most often, all these responses will only fuel the fire and escalate the moment. Our anxiety and emotional reactions further overload the person. As adults, we feel it is our responsibility to make it end, to take charge and make things better. When this doesn't happen, our own frustrations can also become overwhelming. A child in meltdown makes us all feel helpless, vulnerable and incompetent.

How we can help

At this stage the volcano erupted, emotions have hit boiling point, adrenaline is surging, and the body is reacting violently. The brain is in a state of panic and responding with reactive fight or flight. The person has very little cortical control over his actions, is confused, often with little awareness. The person can act violently (hitting, biting self, running aimlessly) and may be putting himself in danger. He has very little awareness of danger and minimal impulse control. Often the best we can do is (1) immediately back off all demands, (2) maintain the safety of everyone involved, (3) reassure the person that he is safe, and (4) let the meltdown run its course. At the same time, we need to reassure the person we are there to keep him safe, remind him that it will pass soon, and not scold, threaten or condemn him for something over which he has no control.

General guidelines

In the heat of the moment, once a meltdown begins these are the common strategies that work the best. Again, the major objective is helping the individual feel safe.

1. *Remove demands and lower stimulation.* The brain is overwhelmed, and we need to immediately back off any demands (including questions, reasoning and interaction) and reduce the overall stimulation if possible. Stop activity, remove others from around the person, reduce noise, confusion and light if possible. At this moment, the brain is hyper-reactive to all stimulation.

2. *Slow down and lower your voice.* The world is spinning too fast and we need to slow it down. The more upset the child, the calmer and quieter you become. Use brief clear statements, talk slowly and lower your voice. By doing this, you minimize fueling the fire and help yourself stay calm. The more emotionally reactive you are, the more panic the child will experience.

3. *Ask very few questions, minimize language.* Questions, even as simple as "What's wrong?" or "Are you alright?" require the brain to think, when it has lost all power to do so. Asking questions is pressing the brain to figure out what is wrong and how to communicate it. Both thinking and communication skills are compromised. The brain is completely overwhelmed and literally cannot think or problem solve.

4. *Reassure, "It's ok, you are safe".* Communicating acceptance and safety is essential. Fear is at a maximum and reassuring the person that he is safe is important. "I am here, we are safe." The person may be swearing at you or lashing out, if you intervene. Please do not take this personally. It is an impulsive reaction based on confusion and fear.

5. *Remind the person that the emotion is temporary.* Adults have told me that in the heat of the moment they think that the emotional surge will last forever. The brain panics in the tidal wave of emotion. It is very important to reassure the person that the emotion will not last long, that he is safe and it will end soon. Knowing that it is only temporary helps ease the fear.

6. *If possible, remove the person to a "safe area."* This is not always possible. Sometimes the person is too upset to move, and some may lash out at others if directed to move. However, if they are responsive, it is often best to move them to a quiet

area where there is less stimulation, no demands and they are out of the way of others so that they can rebound and regroup. If this is not possible, move others away and give the person lots of space to calm down.

7. *If receptive, calm with deep pressure or rhythmic patterns.* If you have discussed and practiced a calming routine, such as counting, deep breathing, deep pressure, the child may allow you to help soothe him. Often, any interaction will escalate the emotion and he will resist your help. Do not force your assistance. Respect his voice and do not touch him, unless as a last resort to protect everyone from physical harm.

8. *If resistant, give space and time.* Back off and allow the person to calm and rebound. Give the person space to regroup. Stay close, communicate "safety." Staying nearby while saying nothing still gives the child a sense of safety, which is important.

9. *Rebounding will be gradual.* Immediately following the rage, the person is still vulnerable to overload. Each child is different. Some children require several hours to regroup, while others can rebound shortly. However, even if the person is calm enough to talk, it doesn't mean that he is not still distressed. Once the rage starts to subside, the stress chemicals are often still high and can boil over again if demands are placed too early. Let the person pace the speed and intensity of stimulation and demands.

It is all about feeling safe! When the emotions are flying, the number one objective is to help the child feel safe. This lowers the fright and panic. This is noted by autistic adults when describing what is most important for us to remember. When overwhelmed with emotion and losing control, fear and panic set in.

Feeling safe means both physically and socially. Strong negative reactions from others only escalate the panic. When the brain is in fight or flight mode, it feels threatened and responds out of fear. Helping the person feel safe (physically, emotionally and socially) is vital.

Sometimes it is better to say nothing at all

Many autistics report that when upset, their auditory processing skills collapse: words become jumbled, confusing and irritating. Questioning, reasoning, trying to problem solve or engage the person in conversation can overwhelm them, further escalating the intense emotions. Talking adds fuel to the fire. The more we talk, the more agitated they become. We need to minimize what we say or say nothing at all.

This is where we need to understand the person well. However, when in doubt, assume that language processing is strained and seeking ongoing conversation with the person will further overwhelm him. Briefly acknowledge that you see he is in distress and reassure him you will help keep him safe, "Sam, you look upset to me. It is ok, you are safe." These are declarative statements that do not call for the person to respond.

Assure the person that you recognize his struggles and will keep everyone safe, with no pressure to act or respond.

Sometimes a child will have a favorite nursery rhyme or repetitive chant, "I'm ok, you're ok, we're ok together," that helps soothe them. These are declarative statements that are familiar, predictable and soothing. There is no demand to process words or instructions, simply a familiar, repetitive chant. There is no demand to respond, only reassuring chants.

For those who can still process some language, give a concrete statement of what to do, "Johnnie, lie down on your bed." This is short and concrete, requiring little processing. It works well if you have identified and practiced a predetermined strategy for calming. This action should be discussed and practiced ahead of time, so it is familiar and predictable. A clear, concise statement will often remind the child of what to do; it should be short, concrete and simple to understand. Since it is practiced ahead of time, it requires little processing. For those who lose language processing, use pictures or objects to prompt a coping skill. Show them a picture of the coping strategy, such as swing, lie down, deep breathing, deep pressure.

If processing totally collapses, say nothing at all. Briefly reassure them that they are safe, then say nothing else. Some children want you to stay nearby, others may need you to leave them alone. Respect their need for space. Many adults report that they prefer the support person to stay nearby to maintain safety. They will calm on their own if others leave them alone. Wait for them to initiate interaction.

Avoid touch

As much as possible, try to avoid touching the person. Many autistics are tactile defensive and sensitive to touch, and most will immediately react negatively to others touching them. When the brain is overwhelmed, touch is perceived as a threat and will escalate panic. Many adults warn us that touching them may elicit an attacking response from them. It is the number one factor that will turn emotional turmoil into physically lashing out. Laying hands on the person will initiate a struggle, increasing chances of injury to oneself or others. Even getting close to the individual may increase anticipation of others touching them and result in lashing out. There are only two exceptions to this rule: (1) if their behavior represents great potential for causing injury to themselves and others, and avoidance techniques have failed, and (2) if touch is part of a calming strategy, repeatedly practiced and under the control of the individual (discussed below).

Safe hands

Touch can be used to establish greater trust with a person when respecting their needs. It can be used to express affection, guide a response, initiate safe interaction and calm the child. However, touch should only be used when either initiated or welcomed by the individual and under the control of the person. Never forced. As discussed above, touch should be avoided when the person is upset unless it is part of an established calming routine.

For those I work with, I always initiate interaction with what I call "safe hands." Throughout the day, when approaching the children, I initiate the interaction by putting out the palms of my hands for them to touch. I invite them to reach out and touch my hands (like giving ten). I open the invite and allow them the control to reciprocate. Even for those who are sensitive to touch, since they are the one controlling the touch, it is much safer. "Safe hands" represents, "I'm ok, you're ok." It establishes my touch as safe. In addition, I frequently use this technique to "give ten" when celebrating things we are doing together. I always initiate it, allowing them the control of touching.

This "safe hands" technique, used frequently throughout the day, represents trust and safety. When the child starts to become upset, I always approach with my hands out, inviting "safe hands." This allows my initial interaction to be a routine, trusted response that is familiar, predictable and supportive. It automatically means I am a working partner, there to support. Often when a person is upset, someone approaching is interpreted as a threat, someone who is going to control. This "safe hands" immediately signals safety. If the child is too agitated and doesn't reach out and touch my hands, then I know he doesn't feel safe enough and I am not going to push interaction, especially further touch. It is a good test to see just where the child is at with your support.

Have a script (routine)

As mentioned earlier, it is important to have a pre-planned, scripted routine to help calm the individual during rage. This is important and empowering for both the child and those supporting him. Knowing how others will respond and support you lessens the uncertainty, provides familiarity and predictability and reduces processing strain and anxiety. Autistic adults have reported that in the heat of the moment when they are struggling, it is so comforting to know exactly how others are going to support and how they are expected to respond. Negotiate the plan ahead of time, role-play and practice it. Such a scripted routine provides familiarity and predictability in the middle of chaos. It also respects the processing needs and vulnerabilities of the person, and is individualized to match the needs of the person.

In working with parents, teachers and support staff, I see the advantages of having a set, practiced routine detailing how everyone will respond when the child is in distress.

EXAMPLE 1

For this young girl, rocking was a preferred form of self-stimulation she used to regulate her nervous system—a familiar, soothing response. From practice, she learned to wrap a blanket tightly around her to provide pressure and warmth, that also soothed her. She controlled the blanket, not staff or her parents. When a blanket was not available, she wrapped her arms around herself and squeezed, while rocking back and forth. Both the rocking and wrap provided sensory tools for calming. This routine was practiced at least once a day, with parents and staff too. This established the procedure as safe, comforting and accepted by both parties. The routine was also practiced when everyone was calm, as new learning can occur during the heat of the moment. Knowing that she was safe, accepted and not pressured by others was predictable and very reassuring.

The following routine was established (for supporting person and child):

- *Support from others.* When upset, acknowledge, reassure, provide reminder to sit, self-hug (or blanket) and rock. Back away, reassure, give space and keep others away. Wait for her to calm and initiate interaction. Allow her to determine when ready to move and re-engage in activity.

- *Child* (*practiced routine*). Sit down on floor or chair, wrap blanket around herself (or arms in self-hug) and rock to self-soothe.

Over several weeks, this strategy became a familiar routine that felt safe. Practicing when calm established the routine as both familiar and predictable for both the child and those supporting her. Knowing what to do and what to expect lowered the stress and anxiety of both parties.

EXAMPLE 2

This young boy was very attracted to and soothed by deep pressure. Usually we avoid touching the person during meltdowns, but this child soothed with deep pressure and was not able to give it to himself. The child welcomed it and felt safe with it.

The child and adult sat on the floor. The adult sat behind the child, wrapped their arms around the child (facing away from the adult) and pulled the child tightly into them. While rocking side to side the adult provided pulsating deep pressure hugs to the child and quietly chanted, "I'm ok, you're ok, we're ok together." They practiced this procedure at least once a day, when everyone was calm, to establish it as safe, familiar, predictable and under the control of the child. We never forced the child or used it if he resisted. He learned to enjoy the deep pressure stimulation. We encouraged the child to ask for it when he felt the need. We would use it when he was excited (over-aroused) as well as when he was upset. Since it was used frequently as a positive, proactive support, the child welcomed the support during meltdowns. However, a word of caution—this should not be used unless the child welcomes it, doesn't resist and can determine when it is being used. Do not force it on the child. This can be very intrusive for many children.

EXAMPLE 3

This young adult woman loved singing her favorite hymn. The words and rhythm were comforting to her. Also, when she went to bed at night, she found it relaxing to lie on her stomach, with arms folded underneath her and roll back and forth until she fell asleep. After she was consulted, it was decided to help her use these two tools to help calm herself during meltdowns.

At home, she would lie on her bed, roll and sing her hymn, often starting out as yelling the words. The movement, deep pressure and chanting would eventually calm her. This lady needed minimal interaction. Interaction and further attempts to intervene only resulted in self-hitting/biting and acting out if needed. Away from the home, she would sit down, wrap her arms around herself for pressure, rock and sing. Again, this routine was practiced with staff during times when everyone was calm. Staff reassured her that they would remind her to use it when she was upset but would then back off and leave her alone if she was safe.

EXAMPLE 4

This highly anxious young man, when distressed would self-restrain his hands and arms with his shirt. He would place his arms up and under his shirt and apply pressure to the material. He would do this frequently throughout the day as a calming, regulating self-stimulation. During meltdowns, this behavior would intensify, and he would frequently end up destroying his shirt, wrapping his arms in the shirt, twisting and tearing the material. Trying to stop him only irritated him more and resulted in aggressive behavior.

He was using deep pressure, proprioceptive resistance (twisting, pulling, resistance to wrists and arms) to help regulate his anxiety, but he needed another way of providing this stimulation. He learned to use a small hand towel to wrap around his hands and then twist and pull to provide pressure and resistance to his hands, wrists and arms. This worked well throughout the day when he needed strong input to stay regulated. When he was upset and trying to self-restrain in his shirt, staff would calmly redirect him to use his towel. Again, staff would then reassure, back off and minimize engagement until he calmed and initiated interaction. This technique was practiced together with staff and provided as a sensory tool throughout the day.

For many people, the scripted routine may simply be acknowledging and reassuring the person, backing off all demands and interaction, keeping others away and letting the person calm on their own. It is a way to respect their need to back away, give them space and let them recover and regroup on their own. There are no pressures, no interaction and minimal processing. All routines should be designed in collaboration with the person, under their control, and practiced until they become almost automatic. They should be individualized to respect the preferences, vulnerabilities and needs of the person.

In summary

- A scripted routine is a predetermined sequence of events that will be predictable in times of rage and confusion. It provides predictability in the height of uncertainty. This is important for helping the child feel safe when he knows exactly how others are going to react. It helps ease the panic.

- Scripts can be identifiable strategies for acting—as simple as pulling back from the situation, seeking out help, relaxation/coping strategies. They should be designed collaboratively with the person, allowing him to help guide us in what will work for him.

- Practice and role-play the routine. Do not expect a strategy to work in the heat of the moment unless it has been practiced repeatedly to become almost automatic. Role-play situations when calm.

- Implement it consistently so the person feels safe during times of rage. It should go without saying that it is important for all parties to implement this strategy consistently during times of rage so the person will trust that we will respond predictably.

For more independent adults who do not rely on parents or support staff, it is important that they carry with them a card that briefly describes what others need to do when they become overwhelmed and melt down. It should briefly state that they are emotionally distraught, cannot think or talk and what others need to specifically do to help them feel safe. When the person is too upset to talk, he can hand out the card. These cards are often good for parents to hand out when the child is melting down in public.

Stuck in a sea of emotions!

For many on the spectrum, intense emotion comes on like a tidal wave and spins them into a whirlpool of emotions that overwhelms them to the point of getting stuck in a cycle they find hard to get out of. They lose all ability to think, reason and communicate what is going on. Their brain is in a panic attack mode. Trying to talk, reason or counsel them in the heat of the moment only adds fuel to the flames.

This is where establishing a "behavior script" (routine) can be a good tool to redirect the child out of the whirlpool. This is a scripted routine that you practice ahead of time and that parents can redirect children to when they are upset. This pulls their attention into a "behavior pattern" and away from the emotional centers of the brain (seas of emotions). Often these routines can be rhythmic sensory motor patterns or auditory patterns like repeating numbers or letters.

Loss of temporal sense

When the child is responding reactively in fight or flight, the thinking part of the brain diminishes, leaving the raw emotions overwhelming the child. The child loses the rational ability to evaluate how threatening the event is and how long it will last (temporal sense). Panic sets in, often over-exaggerating the immediate threat, under-estimating their ability to deal with it and feeling as if it will last forever. Raw emotion elicits impulsive reactions to escape the threat and lessen the emotional tidal wave. Therefore, it is important to:

- reassure the child he is safe, and you will ensure that is the case

- reassure the child that the emotion will not last long and will end soon. It is very important to be reminded of this

- if possible, try to engage the child in a simple coping/calming technique (counting, deep breathing, chanting, etc.) that has been predetermined and practiced extensively. This routine must be very set and not require any cognitive reasoning.

If the child allows this, the intensity will diminish and redirecting attention into a prescribed routine (calming routine) will bring the child gradually out of the reactive center of the brain. However, once the child is in peak meltdown, all interaction becomes overwhelming and all you can do is say little and protect, until the child calms on his own. The sooner the support, the better.

Calming tools

As part of the reaction plan, learning a few coping tools can be very beneficial. The type of calming tools will vary from person to person. They can be used in all three stages of meltdowns. Unfortunately, once in the rage stage, the child is often too resistant to follow the lead of others. Therefore, you need to put these tools together and repeatedly practice them when calm; at first, use them frequently during the day when the child becomes a little disorganized. Over time, these tools become routine and easier to use in the heat of the moment. I always have the parents or teachers practice them along with the child, so they become working partners with the children as they start using them in the heat of the moment. As can be expected, all these strategies should not be forced or pressured on the child. Only use if the child receptively engages in the routine and stop if he starts to actively resist. Respecting the child's voice during these times is essential to maintaining trust. The most important factor in helping the individual is that he feels safe and respected and that you are a working partner with him.

Most of the tools at this stage are helping the nervous system calm. For children, adults often must apply or engage the child in the techniques. As they get older, they will need to learn techniques that they can implement themselves. If the children will allow you to help them calm, these are some common tools for calming the nervous system. Many of these strategies use sensory input to calm and organize the nervous system. Three of the most common calming strategies include deep pressure, proprioception and slow, rhythmic movement. Often, I try to combine two or all three together for maximum effect.

DEEP PRESSURE TECHNIQUES

Some children crave deep pressure stimulation and for them deep pressure can be a welcomed soothing strategy. Supposedly it helps increase the effectiveness of dopamine, the feel-good chemical in the nervous system. However, many kids do not want to be touched during a meltdown and for them this will not work. Do not implement it if they are resistant.

Many of these strategies require the child to allow the adult to touch them. That is why it is so important to teach that our touch is safe and pleasant. As mentioned above, I teach "safe hands" and always approach with "safe hands" first. If the child is responsive then, and only then, do we move on to using the practiced calming technique. When working with children, I always condition my hands as "feel-good hands." Throughout the day, I use my hands to provide preferred sensory input (deep massage, movement, simple hand games). This way the child perceives my hands as providing supportive touch, not to be feared. This is the only way I can be trusted to implement hands-on calming strategies when the child is upset.

Here are some types of deep pressure massage:

1. *Hand hugs.* Pulsating squeezes to palm of hand, with deep pressure across fingers. Cup both of your hands around one hand of the child—one hand in the palm and the other over the top of the hand. Place the fingers of your upper hand on top of the child's fingers. Provide pulsating massage to the palm of the hand while providing pressure down into the child's fingers. If the child is responsive, he will like this procedure. This is nice in that it is very portable and can be implemented anywhere. Since it is only working with one hand, it is not very intrusive. I always start by initiating "safe hands" first. If the child is responsive, then I move to hand hugs.

2. *Arm squeezes.* Cup your hands around the child's arm and provide deep pressure with squeezes up and down the arms. When applying deep pressure, work with the palms of your hands, not just your fingertips. Try not to lift your touch off the arm as you move to the next stop. Gradually work your way up and down the arm.

3. *Deep pressure thigh stroking.* When the child is sitting in a chair, provide rhythmic deep pressure stroking to thighs. Providing deep pressure massage to the large muscles of the thighs can be very calming. Use this technique with caution if either the child or others perceive this as having a sexual connotation. We also teach the child to firmly rub their own thighs.

4. *Neutral warmth/wrap.* This is often a favorite for small children, but also can be used with larger children if they enjoy it. Sit down with the child facing away from you. Wrap your arms around the child and pull him into you (his back against your front), in a firm bear hug. Slowly rock side to side while providing pulsating, firm squeezes. Place a pillow in front of the child for added deep pressure to the chest. The child gets deep pressure from being squeezed into you: deep pressure into his back from being pressed into your chest and into his chest from your arms and the pillow. Use a gentle, calming chant with the rocking. Pairing slow movement with deep pressure and rhythmic chanting can be very calming. Again, only use this technique if the child welcomes it and does not struggle. It should not be perceived as a restraint.

5. *Pillow press/sandwiching.* With pillow press, lie the child down, on his back, on a soft surface such as a bed, couch or bean bag. Then take another bean bag or large pillow and apply gentle pressure across his torso and legs. Usually I apply pressure by leaning with my arms and rocking slowly back and forth to provide a calming,

pulsating pressure. Since the bean bag or large pillow molds around the body, it makes it easier to spread the deep pressure across the whole body, especially if the child is lying on a soft surface, gaining deep pressure up through his back. Make sure not to cover the face, head or neck. Keep pressure gentle so as not to cut off breathing or hurt the chest. Again, this procedure must be practiced when calm before using it when the child is upset.

6. *Shoulder/arms deep pressure stroking.* Usually I provide this following neutral warmth (see above), since I am already sitting behind the child. With the palm of one hand on each shoulder, provide firm pressure and slowly move hands down each arm in rhythmic fashion. While seated behind the child, cup the palms of your hands on top of the child's shoulders. Slowly provide deep pressure strokes down the arms and back up to the shoulders again, in a continuous flow. Continue in slow, rhythmic strokes.

7. *Self-applied deep pressure.* This involves deep pressure techniques that do not require others providing touch: sandwiching between bean bags or couch cushions (sit on one with other on the lap); cocooning with blankets, body pillows and sleeping bags; snuggling under weighted blankets. Simply sitting on large stuff pillows or bean bags in a quiet area can be soothing.

PROPRIOCEPTION

Proprioception is any resistance or exertion to joints, tendons and muscles. Many individuals during meltdowns will seek proprioceptive input by hitting or biting self, banging wrists/ankles on solid surfaces, head banging, throwing things, jumping up and down and so on. Strong jarring/exertion into the joints releases stress chemicals and helps calm and organize the nervous system. Providing other, less injurious, forms of strong input into the joints and tendons can help the person calm.

1. *Hand wringing towel.* As described earlier in an example, teach the person to wrap a towel around both hands, twist and pull, providing strong resistance to hands, wrists and arms. This is a good technique to occupy the hands, especially for individuals who hit themselves.

2. *Hitting/slamming.* Provide children with something soft (e.g. a pillow) to hit or throw around. For those who need to body slam and head bang, place them on a cushioned mat to soften the blows while allowing them the strong input. This needs to be done under close supervision to ensure they are not hurting themselves.

3. *Hand hug, forearm rub, wrist compression.* While one hand provides pulsating squeezes to the palm of the hand, use the other hand to provide deep pressure rubs to the forearm. Add wrist compressions while doing this. This is an extension of the hand hugs. Take your upper hand and move it to the forearm, a few inches from the wrist. In sync with the palm squeezes, provide joint compression to the wrist while using a deep pressure rub to the forearm.

4. *Playful wrestling.* For those using neutral warmth (see above), where you are already sitting behind the child with him in a firm arm wrap, have the child playfully squirm out of your hold. In addition to the bear hug, I usually wrap my legs around his, requiring the child to use his legs to get himself out. Actively struggling to get out will provide great input into the joints, tendons and muscles. Again, this must be practiced frequently, seen as fun and not as a restraint, and under the child's control. Stop if the child is complaining or negatively resisting.

5. *Finger squeezes.* The person provides this to himself by placing one hand around the fingers of the other hand. While squeezing the fingers together, twist the fingers back and forth. This provides good input into all the joints of the fingers.

6. *Biting chewery/tubing.* The teeth and jaw provide strong proprioception. That is why some individuals bite themselves. The strong input from biting releases stress chemicals from the nervous system. Provide hard rubber items (chewery or tubing) to bite on. There is a variety of small items that individuals can chew and bite on to provide strong input into the teeth and jaw.

7. *Rocking on solid, stationary chairs.* Intense rocking, back and forth, on stationary furniture can provide resistance and jarring into the joints that releases stress chemicals. Again, make sure to monitor closely for safety and ensure it is very solid furniture that can take the beating.

8. *Jumping, crashing.* Jumping (trampoline, mattress, etc.) provides good proprioceptive jarring of the legs and spine. Also, jumping and crashing on a bed, large pillows or bean bags provides strong input into the body.

Again, all these activities need to be monitored closely to ensure the individual is not harming himself. Stop any activity that appears injurious. There are many other activities that can provide strong proprioceptive input. I recommend consulting with an occupational therapist to design strategies specific for your child.

REGULATORY PATTERNS

Regulatory patterns are often repetitive, rhythmic sensory activities that help calm the child: slow rhythmic rocking, swaying back and forth, bouncing, soft rhythmic chanting, rocking or bouncing on an exercise ball while singing a favorite nursery rhyme, cuddling and deep pressure while chanting a calming statement and so on. Although most often used in either the rumbling or recovery stage, sometimes regulatory patterns that are very familiar and predictable can be used at this stage. Most often the window of opportunity has lapsed, and the person is too upset to cooperate in such activities. If they are cooperative, such sensory patterns can shorten the length of the rage cycle.

Safe areas

The number one recommendation during meltdowns is providing the person with a quiet area where they can avoid all interaction/stimulation and let their brain calm.

Most adults tell us the number one thing people can do is simply back off and leave them alone. All interaction and attempts to help just escalate their turmoil. It is simply too much stimulation for the brain to handle when overwhelmed. Both at home and at school, children can benefit from having a safe area to escape to when needing to withdraw and rebound. Adults also need a safe area where they can escape to regroup. Safe areas should never be used as time out or punishment. They need to be perceived as a safe area where children can isolate, avoid other people and calm themselves down.

At home, the safe area can be the children's bedroom, closet or other area of the home where they can calm themselves—an area where others will respect their need to engage in whatever activity they use to calm. The area should include favorite sensory tools, if the child will use them to calm. It should be an area where the child is safe to shout and scream, throw soft items around, or body crash on a bed or pad.

At school, these areas should consist of:

- an area with reduced stimulation and demands, very little if any noise, soft lighting, away from any activity

- a small space that isolates the person away from activity, for example a large closet, pup tents, a small partitioned area in corner of room. This area needs to be designated as a safe area, so children can trust that people will leave them alone to regroup and rebound.

Include items that tend to calm and organize, such as large pillows, bean bags, stuffed animals, favorite toys, soft lighting—all typical tools for calming the nervous system. The purpose is to allow the person to escape and withdraw from stimulation and demands so their nervous system can rebound. Some children are slow to rebound. Once overwhelmed, they may need anywhere from 30– 90 minutes to rebound. If the safe area is used regularly as a preventative approach, approximately 20–30 minutes might be good. Never use the safe area as time out or punishment. Never scold or counsel the child while using the safe area. It must be associated as a positive support.

These safe areas must be available at any time. They can be used simply to give the child a break when a little overwhelmed or to recover from meltdowns.

It doesn't work for us!

It often takes time and hard work to teach children to use the scripted routines during the heat of the moment. At first, the child may be fine practicing the routines but refuse to use them when melting down. Stay patient. It takes a lot of practice and role-playing situations before the child feels safe enough to use them during the rage stage.

Each child is different, has different needs and preferences and needs repeated practice over time. The routine may need to be tweaked occasionally. If you work with the child, listen to him and give him an active role in developing the routines. Most importantly, if you are persistent and consistent, you have a good chance at succeeding. Unfortunately, it does take time, persistence and sometimes professional assistance, but over time the child will learn to use these routines in the heat of the moment.

The recovery stage

Once the rage subsides, it doesn't mean that the episode is over. The person is often exhausted, scared, confused and still swirling in emotions. The stress chemicals are still high, and the person is still vulnerable. The child has entered the recovery stage but needs time to calm down. It takes time for the nervous system to regroup and rebound. The emotional and physical discharge from the meltdown leaves him very fragile and vulnerable. He is still on high alert, anxious and prone to rage again if not allowed to safely escape and regroup.

The mistake that parents and teachers make is assuming that the child is fine and ready to return to activity as soon as he stops acting out. We need to back off and give the child time to escape and regroup. This usually consists of some of the same strategies we use in the rumbling stage. Reassure the child that he is safe and accepted, give him time and space to rest and do not bombard him with questions, counseling or demands. Let him know that you are nearby if he needs you, and give him any sensory tools (blanket, pillows, favorite music, etc.) that help him soothe.

How do I know when they enter the recovery stage?

Every child is different. Frequently the screaming, shouting and acting out will subside. However, this may be a temporary lag and the rage can return if people press engagement too soon. Often the child may cry as a release from all the swirling emotions he feels. He is still confused and disoriented and the brain is still scared and on high alert. Simply reassure the person that he is safe, everything is ok and he can take time to relax and calm. Again, reassure him you are close by in case he needs you. Try not to ask any questions that require the child to respond. The brain has a high need to feel safe, protected and accepted. Give him space and keep others away. If he is not pressured and you provide reassurance that he is safe, the child will start to calm down and gradually recover. Following five to ten minutes of calm behavior, again reassure him, but make no demands. Let the child rest and regroup. Wait until he initiates interaction or becomes active again. Let the child pace the recovery, allowing his processing to return.

How long does it take?

This varies extensively depending on how exhausted the nervous system is, how much stress chemicals are still accumulated and how safe the person feels with those around him. We must respect that the incident of rage has been exhausting for the child, so allow time for him to regroup and rejoin when ready. If we do not give him that time, the child is at high risk of melting down again if redirected too soon. It can take anywhere from minutes to hours, and longer for some. It can also vary for the same person from one event to another, depending on the state of their nervous system before and after the meltdown. Respect the person's need to withdraw from the demands and give him a quiet area to recover. You can check on him periodically with brief interaction to gauge where he is at or simply wait until he approaches you to engage. Usually this is the best.

Trying to push the child back into the daily routine too fast will only risk overwhelming him again.

Should I comfort him?

Again, this depends on the person. Remember, when the person is confused and disorganized, interacting with others can be very demanding and taxing. Avoid questioning, counseling or trying to reason with the person during this stage. All questioning, thinking, reasoning and coping skills are compromised, and pressuring interaction can overwhelm the person. He can also begin to feel embarrassed, guilty and regretful for being disruptive. He may fear the negative reactions from others. He often needs reassurance that he is safe and accepted and that we understand the pain that he experiences. Some individuals, children especially, may welcome soothing deep pressure, firm hugging, slow rocking or soft singing to help them feel safe and calm and to regroup. However, this varies extensively, should not be forced on them and only be under their control. This is where we must know the child, understand his vulnerabilities and respect his needs. If you do not know the child well, back off, simply reassure and wait for him to initiate interaction.

Just like in all three stages, having a pre-planned recovery routine can help. If the person has some favorite sensory tools or calming activities (like those used in the rumbling stage), the child may feel secure in these familiar and predictable activities. Repetitive, rhythmic patterns (singing, rocking, deep pressure, etc.) can help soothe the nervous system, help it feel safe and recover quicker. Again, these must be discussed and practiced previously before offering them to the person. Also, they must be under the control of the person, never forced on him.

When is it safe to re-engage?

The best-case scenario is to let the child totally escape the event and allow him as much time as he needs before placing daily demands on him. Letting him rest and pace himself, and waiting for him to initiate activity is usually the best. However, that may not always be possible when outside the home. We need to be prepared to end the event and leave once the child is prepared to move.

Usually it is best to let the child determine when he is ready, either by backing off and waiting for him to initiate engagement or gauging readiness with brief interaction once every 20–30 minutes. The interaction needs to be brief, supportive and void of demands—a brief initiation to measure the level of responsiveness. As stated above, this is where I use "safe hands" to initiate a safe approach. If the child is not willing to reach out to complete the contact, he is not ready to re-engage. Acknowledge that, reassure and back off for another 20–30 minutes. This will help establish trust that you are respecting him.

If the child is responsive to your approach, ask if you can sit with him. Continue with non-demanding, simple conversation and/or soothing activity with the child. Once the child is receptive to interacting with you, initiate a simple, preferred activity with him. Again, use a simple, very familiar, predictable activity for the child. This helps measure if the child is ready to engage in activity. If the child is not responsive to this activity, then he is not ready to re-engage in his daily routine. You might need to work in short intervals (a few minutes) several times before the child feels safe enough to re-engage in his routine. However, be aware that the child's processing skills may not have returned to normal and could still be easily overwhelmed. Watch the child closely, provide greater support and be willing to allow more time to rebound.

Some children have poor awareness of their own stress level. If it was a fun activity that initially overwhelmed them, they may want to return to that activity too soon. They may feel that they are ready, but you can see by their behavior that they have not regrouped enough to re-enter the activity. This is where you need to know them and structure their return based on what you see and not what they report.

Remorse

It is very common for the person to be remorseful, feel embarrassed and guilty for how they behaved. It is very important to validate and reassure the person that he is still safe and accepted by you, to acknowledge and validate how he may feel embarrassed and possibly remorseful. Let him apologize if he wants to, and do accept the apology. Allowing the child to correct any wrongdoing can help bring closure for him. However, do this only if he initiates it. Many kids may only escalate again if this is mentioned. It is too upsetting for them to discuss their emotional reactions.

Debriefing

Many parents and teachers want to discuss the episode during the recovering phase. Most children are not ready to discuss such an emotionally sensitive issue that soon. Many children cannot process what and why it happened. They cannot process what went wrong, what overwhelmed them, what they could have done differently and how they can avoid it in the future. Frequently, adults want so badly to discuss the situation and provide counseling. Often the child is too embarrassed, remorseful or cannot accept what his actions did to others. Forcing the issue will only tax his processing and ignite another meltdown. There is no need to make this happen, especially here and now. Do not put the person on the spot, make him process what just happened, relive the experience and expect him to learn from it. It is best to debrief and strategize with other supportive adults and not with the child at this time.

It might take hours, or days, before the person might be ready to discuss the situation. This is determined by the age, processing skills and responsiveness of the person. I often use the following activity to teach children to use coping skills and scripted routines. Together we make a list of stressful events that often trigger meltdowns for that person. On index cards, I write out a brief description of the event on one side and then the coping skills or scripted routine on the other side of the card. Then from the deck of cards, each day we will pick one or two situations to role-play and practice. This helps instill what to do, when to do it and how to do it when these situations arise.

Don't punish meltdowns!

Many people mistakenly see these children as oppositional and purposely acting out. Consequently, they feel they need to punish them for acting out. This only adds more shame and anxiety. The children will feel more anxious in stressful situations, fearing the ramifications, rendering them more likely to have a meltdown. In true meltdowns, children lose self-control and are not being oppositional. Their brain is overwhelmed and exploding emotionally. These are not purposeful acts of manipulation.

Punishment works if the child has some degree of control over the behavior. That is the difference between a tantrum and a meltdown. There are three conditions for punishment to work: (1) the child knows that what they are doing is wrong, (2) the child knows what to do right and can do it in the heat of the moment, and (3) the child intentionally chooses to do the wrong thing rather than the desired response. This is not the case in meltdowns. In a meltdown, children's judgement and reasoning abilities fall apart and their brains are reacting to the fight or flight panic. There is no ability to appraise alternative options and evaluate the effects of their behavior. Punishing them for being overwhelmed will not help, only make matters worse.

No, that doesn't mean that learning cannot occur over time and better coping skills cannot be taught. They can learn, but it takes creating a scripted routine (what to do) and a lot of practice. The brain will still go into fight or flight but can have a more desirable way of reacting behaviorally. This is not learned in the heat of the moment, but only when practiced when calm and coached during the rumbling stage of meltdowns.

Summary of stages

1. *Rumbling (early build-up) stage*

    i. Identify the triggers and early signs of overload.

    ii. Provide quick support:

        - Pull back on demands

        - Provide greater support

        - Reduce stimulation

        - Remove to quieter area

        - Give a break

        - Distract

        - Allow for soothing activity (music, self-stimulation, physical activity, etc.).

iii. Teach the child to recognize and practice coping strategies.

iv. Develop a pre-planned routine.

2. *Rage (heat of the moment) stage*

   i. Remove demands and lower stimulation.

   ii. Slow down and lower your voice.

   iii. Ask few questions, minimize language.

   iv. Reassure, "It's ok, you are safe."

   v. Remind that it is temporary.

   vi. If possible, remove the child to a "safe area."

   vii. If receptive, calm with deep pressure, or rhythmic patterns.

   viii. If not, back off and allow the child to rebound. Give the child space to regroup. Stay close, communicate "safety."

   ix. Remember that rebounding will be gradual. Immediately following, the child is still vulnerable to meltdown.

3. *Recovery stage*

   i. Note that once the individual is calm, he will still need time to recover and rebound. Just because the storm is over, it doesn't mean he does not still have a strong build-up of stress chemicals.

   ii. Allow as much time to regroup as necessary. The person can be exhausted and is at high risk of melting down again if redirected too soon.

   iii. Let them pace their recovery and determine when they are ready. This is where knowing the child is very important.

   iv. Remember to validate and reassure acceptance. The person is often highly remorseful following meltdowns. Do not punish meltdowns.

4. *Developing a plan together*

   i. Be a working partner with the child. Develop a plan.

   ii. Help the child to feel safe talking about the episodes.

   iii. This plan would need to include a comprehensive plan for avoiding and handling meltdowns.

   iv. Develop a laminated instruction card to give others.

   v. Practice your routine.

In conclusion, it is very important to develop a comprehensive plan for both preventing and avoiding meltdowns as well as how to react during the meltdown. This plan should consist of preventative strategies to avoid meltdowns, recognizing triggers and supporting when early signs of distress appear, how to keep everyone safe and support the child during the rage stage, and how to assist during recovery. Be a working partner with the child, including him in all phases of developing and modifying the plan. Review the plan frequently and practice the strategies so they become familiar, predictable and routine. Continually work together on the plan to prevent and safely handle meltdowns. This helps children feel safe and builds trust that others are supporting them through these meltdowns. It gives them a voice and empowers them to feel more in control. It also helps them understand their vulnerabilities, what overwhelms them, what accommodations they need and how to advocate for those needs. Remember, children become adults and they will need to be able to appraise new situations for problems, identify what supports they need and advocate for those supports. This comprehensive plan may well be needed throughout their lives.

Chapter 13

SENSORY OVERLOAD

Just imagine!

Just imagine that what you are seeing, hearing, touching and smelling all comes in frag-mented and cannot be integrated. Each sense is competing for attention and not working together. This is a world where you must block out all other senses to concentrate on one, or where you use your peripheral vision only because looking directly at something is too overwhelming. Just imagine that you must hum to yourself to filter out stimulation so you can attend and think. Just imagine!

Just imagine that you cannot sort out the relevant from the irrelevant details to focus your attention on what matters, and then when one detail is changed, the whole picture falls apart. Nothing is familiar because it is continually changing. There is never predictability to build stability. When a person changes her glasses, hairstyle or perfume, you no longer recognize her. Imagine that you cannot distinguish faces and must recognize others by how they smell or move, where one day you know who you are talking to and the next day you don't. When you walk into a room, you do not recognize it because one piece of furniture has been moved or replaced. How can you begin to feel safe and secure? Just imagine!

Just imagine sitting in a classroom where the flicking and humming of the fluorescent lights are giving you a headache, the smell of the markers and paste are making you nauseous, the scratching and screeching of the pencils around you assault your ears and the hardness of the chair you are sitting on hurts your body. Just imagine sitting in each class anxiously waiting for the bell to ring and send your brain into panic. The sound of congested breathing from the person behind you is overpowering what the teacher is saying. You continually tap on the desk, fidget and hum to yourself to stay organized. Just imagine!

Just imagine that you cannot concentrate on the person you are talking to because her perfume is overwhelming, or the reflections bouncing off her necklace are calling your attention. Just imagine that you can hear the words but cannot see the faces you are talking to. Or that you try to join a group of friends, but the multiple voices drown each other out in a mix of jumbled sounds. When you finally grasp and understand what was said, the conversation has moved on before you can respond. You know what you want to say, but cannot find the right words, or get your mouth to say them.

Just imagine that you cannot understand the thoughts, feelings and perspectives of those around you. You cannot read the expressions, gestures and actions simultaneously to understand meaning. You cannot read the invisible cues and unwritten social rules that help provide the backdrop for understanding what is expected. You are always out of sync with others because you cannot listen, think and act simultaneously. The words are coming too fast, too loud and there are too many for you to process. The facial expressions do not seem to match the words you are hearing. You guess wrongly at what is expected and are confused by the negative reactions this elicits. You continually try to fit in, but always fail. Just imagine!

Just imagine that you do not feel connected to your body, cannot walk without looking at your feet, or lose the feeling of your body unless you are moving or tapping parts of your body against objects. You do not feel pain or are hyper-sensitive to any soft touch. The clothes you are wearing feel scratchy and they hurt. You feel off balance when walking and have difficulty coordinating your movements. Just imagine that you cannot sense your internal body cues to tell you that you are hungry, stressed or need to use the bathroom. You feel as if your body is not part of you, but is an object that you must manipulate—a body that can be a friend or enemy based on the continuous, confusing feedback. Just imagine!

Just imagine that your emotions are too strong and overwhelming for you to identify, label and control. The emotions come on like a tidal wave with little warning and you have no ability to control them. Your thoughts and feelings are not connected enough for you to make sense of them or anticipate when they are going to happen. Just imagine that you are so sensitive to the emotional auras of those around you that you cannot identify if the emotions belong to you or others. You cannot identify, label or control, not just the emotions, but also your reactions to them. You interpret all emotion as fear and panic at first notice. You are scared to feel. Just imagine!

Just imagine that the world is so unpredictable, confusing and overwhelming that you are constantly on high alert and anxious all the time. You are on guard for the next unpredictable sensory assault or unexpected social demand. The physical, social and task demands of your immediate environment are coming too fast and there are too many. Your brain starts to shut down, you lose the ability to speak and act purposely, and your body begins to hurt with pain. The panic overwhelms you with the need to escape. You scream, run or lash out in uncontrolled fear and rage. Just imagine!

You try to intervene, discipline or support what you see from me, but please take a moment to "just imagine" what it is like to be me in that moment. Once you can imagine, you can begin to understand and learn how to support me. It is so important for my safety and security and to my emotional survival. Just imagine!

Sensory processing challenges

In the blue book, *The Autism Discussion Page on the Core Challenges of Autism* (Nason 2014a), I discuss in detail many of the sensory processing differences (fragmented/distorted perception, hyper-/hypo-sensitivities, sensory defensiveness, mono-processing, poor sensory integration, etc.) commonly found in autism, both strengths and challenges. It is not my intent to reiterate this information here, for many of you have already read that book. In this book, I will only focus on sensory defensiveness and sensory overload, since they present the most difficulties for those on the spectrum. For a more detail discussion on the wide variety of sensory challenges in autism, I refer you to the blue book.

Sensory defensiveness

Sensory defensiveness is one of the most challenging sensory issues in autism. Those with sensory defensiveness experience hyper-sensitivity in one or more senses: touch, sounds, light, smells, taste or movement. Normal daily touch, sound, noise and lights that we process comfortably can be more intense, uncomfortable and even painful for those with autism. Common sounds, like the vacuum, a baby crying, the school buzzer or phone ringing, can be experienced as very loud and painful. Bright lights, sunshine and an array of artificial lighting can be painful and overwhelming. Many common smells, especially foods cooking, perfumes and gasoline, produce nausea.

For those who are sensitive to touch (tactile defensiveness), light touch can be painful and alarming. Wearing certain clothing can be irritating, touching specific textures can be tormenting, light touch can be piercing, and personal hygiene (bathing, tooth brushing, washing hair) can be painful. Even being close to others can make one defensive, since they may be unexpectedly touched. Many of the common sensory experiences we encounter every day can be painful and tormenting for these individuals.

For those with sensory defensiveness, their nervous system is on "high alert" and on guard, anticipating when the next sensory assault may occur. At any moment, someone might brush up against them setting off panic, a sudden loud noise might send a pain through their head, or a strong smell might send them running to the bathroom. Most people usually try to avoid or escape stimulation that they are sensitive to. They can become overwhelmed easily when confronted with aversive stimulation, resist entering settings with the painful stimulation, freeze or shut down once in the situation, or act out to get out of the stimulation. The child is usually overwhelmed and anxious when around the offensive stimulation.

When the nervous system is overwhelmed, the brain may go into panic mode, setting off the fight or flight response that results in melting down or acting out to escape the stimulation. Sensitivity can be heightened by stress, fatigue, hunger, illness and lack of sleep. The more taxed the nervous system, the more sensitive it is to stimulation. When it is overloaded, sensitivity heightens, and the person may shut down or panic and melt down if not allowed to escape the overwhelming stimulation. Figure 13.1 shows how the normal sensory demands at school can become overwhelming for kids with sensory sensitivities.

When the brain is forced to hyper-focus on painful stimulation, it cannot concentrate on learning or being productive. The brain is in a reactive, defensive mode, and is not receptive to learning. When you have sensory vulnerabilities, even normal daily activities become very demanding and stressful.

Figure 13.1 displays some of the sensitivities that a child may experience in a classroom. Most children will not experience all these sensitivities, but the irritants can distract and overwhelm the child in the typical classroom. The fluorescent lighting, the breathing of others, the screeching of pencils and chalk, the humming of the lights, smells of pastes, felt pens and other school supplies, people touching them, others sitting too close, the seat being too hard, clothes irritating them and trying to block out these competing stimuli in order to focus on what is expected can become very overwhelming for the child. The brain is not receptive to learning when it is in the reactive, protective mode.

Bright light gives me
a headache

Smell of materials
is awful

Humming of lights is
distracting

Kids' breathing is
annoying

People are laughing,
talking too loud

The kid next to me is too
close

Seat is too hard

Clothes are irritating

Teacher's words are too fast and
confusing

I can't listen and write at the
same time

The sound of the bell is horrifying

I CAN'T THINK OR FOCUS!
GET ME OUT OF HERE!!!

*Figure 13.1: The sensory demands at school can be
overwhelming for those with sensory sensitivities*

If the child must transition between classes, navigating the crowd in the hallways can be very anxiety provoking. The noise is chaotic and bombarding, people touching and bumping into the child are threatening, the smells of perfume and cologne are overwhelming and the weaving in and out of scattered movement is confusing. Trying to keep their focus on finding their locker or the right classroom can be very draining. These transitions leave them exhausted by the time they get seated in their classroom. These same challenges follow the children into the cafeteria for lunch, recess and gym class (especially the locker room). The brain spends most of its energy defending itself from the onslaught of sensory bombardment. It begins to shut down, withdraw to minimize stimulation and protect itself from becoming overwhelmed. The brain is in survival mode, and not in any condition for learning.

Sensory overload

In the blue book, *The Autism Discussion Page on the Core Challenges of Autism* (Nason 2014a), I define sensory overload as:

> Sensory overload occurs when the nervous system is bombarded by too much, or too intense stimulation for it to process effectively. Although sensory defensiveness can influence sensory overload directly, sensory overload can also occur from the inability of the brain to filter, or turn down, the stimulation coming into the brain. For many of us who do not have sensory processing problems, our brain stems filter out much of the stimulation bombarding the nervous system. It filters out much of the background noise (sensory distraction) that is irrelevant for us to be aware of, so we can concentrate on the task at hand. This allows our brains to comfortably integrate the important information, so we can process it smoothly and effectively. We can attend to what we need to because we block out what is irrelevant.

However, for some people with sensory processing problems, this filter does not function effectively, and allows too much stimulation into the brain, taxing and overloading it. The individual is not able to block out the background noise (feels their clothes scratching them, the sound of the refrigerator turning on and off, the smell of the perfume or deodorant of people near them, the flickering of sunlight coming through the blinds, a conversation going on nearby, the scratching sound of the pencil, etc.). Their nervous system is unable to filter out, or tone down the stimulation. Too much stimulation coming into the brain, at too high a level of intensity, results in sensory overload. Rather than necessarily being defensive to one sense, as in sensory defensiveness, overload can come from too much stimulation bombarding the brain at one time.

For these children, the average day at school can be full of sensory assaults. They cannot adequately filter out all the conflicting sensory stimulation. The bright lights may give them a headache or the humming of the lights distracts them. Their seat may be too hard, and they cannot avoid attending to it. Their clothes may irritate them, the sound of the chalk on the board screeches in their head, the whispering of other students distracts them, smells of the markers and glue may be nauseating, and the sound of the buzzer is overwhelming. With all these sensory distractions and irritations, the nervous system is in an escape/avoidance mode, making learning almost impossible. When the brain feels insecure, it goes into survival mode, focusing on protection, not learning. If the stress chemicals build slowly, the brain will often start to shut down to avoid being overwhelmed. During shutdown, the child may look "out of it," unresponsive, and sometimes lie his head down and fall asleep. This shutdown is the way the brain protects itself from sensory overload. If the stress chemicals build too fast, the child may melt down, acting out to escape and avoid the assaulting stimulation, as well as releasing the stress chemicals. Either response is the result of the fight or flight stress reaction kicking in. The brain is in survival mode, not in a learning readiness mode. (pp.138–139)

With these neurological differences, it is no wonder that our world is so overwhelming. With the difficulties filtering, integrating and modulating stimulation, sensory overload is always a possibility, especially in our world of intense chemical smells, artificial lighting, synthetic fabrics and loud noises. Sensory overload can result in two primary ways:

- *Sensory defensiveness.* The person is highly sensitive to stimulation and experiences normal levels as too intense, uncomfortable and even painful, setting off the person's fight or flight response.

- *Poor sensory filtering and integration of multiple stimulation.* From too much stimulation rather than being over-sensitive to any specific stimuli. Sensory overload in this case would be more likely as the environment around the individual becomes "busier" with multiple stimulation (noise, lights, people interacting, activity, smells, etc.). For example, a person might be able to handle shopping in a small specialty store but become overwhelmed in a busy shopping center. He is not necessarily over-sensitive to any one stimulation but overwhelmed by too many stimuli to integrate successfully.

Many people on the spectrum experience both problems—too much and too intense. Since the brain has problems integrating the incoming information, the world is often confusing, overwhelming and scary.

The brain becomes hyper-aroused, on guard and very defensive, never knowing when the world will bombard and overwhelm it. The child may be oppositional, easily irritated, explosive and need to control everything around him. The child needs to control all stimulation around him to feel safe.

Sensory filtering and sensory overload

From what I can decipher from the research on neural connectivity, there are two primary differences in the brain wiring of people with autism. The first is that the long-range neuro-pathways that connect the different brains centers, allowing them to simultaneously communicate with each other, are underdeveloped. This means the person will have a difficult time rapidly processing multiple information simultaneously. What the neurotypical brain processes simultaneously and subconsciously, many on the spectrum need to process sequentially and consciously. In other words, what we pick up intuitively (with minimal thought), those on the spectrum need to consciously think through. As you can imagine, this slows down the processing and becomes very exhausting, leading to the brain becoming overly taxed and drained. Much of our dynamic world, especially the social world, moves way too fast for their processing speed.

Second, whereas the long-range neuro-pathways that connect the different brain centers are underdeveloped, the short-range neuro-connections within individual brain centers are often overdeveloped, with too many, poorly integrated, but intensively reactive neuro-connections. This leads to taking in too much information that is often intense and overwhelming. The typical brain goes through stages of "pruning," whereby the pathways that are used frequently are strengthened and the rarely used connections fade away. This allows for more refined filtering of unneeded stimulation and more selective attention to meaningful stimuli. Our brain filters out a lot of the irrelevant stimulation hitting our nervous system, so we do not become overwhelmed and can focus on what stimuli are needed to adapt to environmental demands.

For many on the spectrum, this pruning has not occurred correctly and there is an over-abundance of highly reactive neurons that are not integrated together and take in too much information (poor filtering) that overwhelms the brain, causing it to be anxious, on high alert and defensive. Whereas the neurotypical brain has a volume control (turns down the stimulation), people on the spectrum often just have an "on/off" switch and cannot turn down the stimulation. The person becomes hyper-sensitive, hyper-attentive, and hyper-reactive. The world is often too loud, too bright, too much. Many on the spectrum must shut down (processing starts to turn off) to avoid being overwhelmed. This leads to detaching themselves from what is going on around them.

When the filtering system is not working properly, too much stimulation floods the brain, overwhelming the brain centers and making it difficult to sort out and attend to what is relevant. Three main challenges can occur: (1) too much information coming in, (2) lack of ability to turn down the intensity (volume) of stimulation, and (3) distorting of the stimulation, making it difficult to identify what it is (e.g. hear it but cannot understand it). The brain becomes overwhelmed, panics and sets off its fight or flight response. When overwhelmed, the brain loses its ability to function, it becomes disorganized, coping skills decompensate and panic sets in. If overload occurs slowly, the brain may start to shut down to avoid the overload, or if the brain becomes overwhelmed too quickly it will panic and melt down. Everyone is different in how this plays out for them, but for many it is a scary, helpless tidal wave of panic.

When you combine the underdeveloped long-range connections between the brain centers with the overdeveloped, but poorly integrated, short-range connections within the brain centers, you essentially have a brain that has delayed processing due to poor communication between the brain centers and over-sensitivity to sensory stimulation. The neurotypical world moves way too fast and the information is too much (too loud, too bright, no filtering). The brain becomes hyper-aroused and hyper-reactive, making the world chaotic, confusing and overwhelming.

Given this, how do we help? Although this book offers many strategies, there are a few main principles to remember:

1. *Slow the world down!* Slow yourself and the world down, giving the child time to adequately process what is expected. Try to match the flow of information to the processing speed of the individual. Allow the child to pace the speed of information. If the child starts to freeze, blank out, increases stimming or becomes oppositional, then the chances are the expectations are too hard, too much or coming too fast for the child.

2. *Turn the world down!* Remember that the brain is not filtering stimulation well; it takes in much more than it needs, cannot turn it down, is hyper-sensitive and has difficulty integrating multiple stimulation simultaneously. Assume that our world is simply too loud and overwhelming for the child, causing him to be on high alert, defensive and hyper-reactive. We must be very aware of how much (noise, visual stimulation, smells, busy activity, etc.) and how intense (loud, bright, etc.) the stimulation is that surrounds the person. Then, try to turn it down or provide filters (sunglasses, ear plugs, etc.) to block out the intensity of stimulation.

3. *Simplify information and expectations.* Break tasks and projects down into simple, sequential steps and make expectations clear, concise and concrete (literal). Use visual strategies if possible and plenty of demonstration, repetition and guided participation.

4. *When in doubt, change our expectations.* When things are not going well, and the child is pulling away, being oppositional, or shutting down, assume that our expectations and information are either too fast, too hard, or too confusing for the child. The demands are stronger than his current abilities to handle them.

This places responsibility for change on us, not the child. Back up, break it down, slow it down and offer assistance as needed to match the demands to the processing abilities of the child. Learning will not only become possible, but also fun. The world will be less scary and more comfortable to handle. The child will begin to feel safe, accepted and competent.

Unfiltered perception

Neurotypical people, for the most part, can attend to what is important and selectively filter out all other irrelevant information. The important information pops out at us, so we can focus on it. Our nervous system blocks out the background stimulation so that we can focus on the important details. This allows us to be at a party with multiple conversations going on around us and still focus on the conversation we are engaged in. It allows us to block out the noise of the fan humming, the air conditioner going on and off, the traffic noise occurring in the background and other noises that are irrelevant to our task at hand. If during a football game we need to focus our vision on the running back carrying the football, we can selectively filter out the people moving around us, the cheerleaders jumping along the sidelines, the band grouping for half time and all the players who are not in the immediate play. At any time, our perception is continually directed to what is important by the context of what we are doing and what is expected. We immediately and subconsciously filter out all the information irrelevant to that objective.

Many individuals on the spectrum have poor sensory filtering. They take in every detail, all the background noise, sights, smells and so forth. They hear every voice in the room, see every detail and become overwhelmed by there being too much information to sort out. They do not have the ability to automatically isolate what is important to attend to and then filter out the rest. They take in everything, which distracts their attention. What we do intuitively and subconsciously, they must think through, piece together what is needed, and consciously try to block out what is irrelevant. Essentially, they attend to everything and must work hard to focus on any one thing. This not only overwhelms the brain but also delays its processing because it takes longer to sort out what is important to attend to. This frequently results in sensory overload and cognitive strain.

This problem varies extensively throughout the spectrum. For some people, this is only a mild problem in one or two senses but for others it is severely disabling, making the world very confusing and overwhelming. Defense mechanisms to help reduce this overload may include mono-perception where the individuals shut down all senses except for one sense so that they can focus on that specific information. They essentially filter out stimulation by shutting down one of more senses to minimize overload. Some people use peripheral perception, looking at the world through their peripheral vision to lessen the intensity of information. Many will use self-stimulation, giving them a predictable, repetitive pattern to block out unwanted stimulation. Another tool is to hyper-focus on one detail extensively to help filter out information. All these strategies avoid overload, but can interfere with what is expected of them.

How we can help

First, it is important in learning environments to minimize background sensory clutter that can distract and overwhelm. Many classrooms like to have every inch of the walls covered with bright, colorful posters, decorations and visual learning tools. This can be very overwhelming. The blander the environment, the fewer stimuli there are to process. Effective classrooms need to minimize the noise, sources of light and visual clutter. The child may also need to be seated near the front of the room to minimize distraction from the other students, or it may be possible to use a portable partition to minimize background vision. Listening to music via headphones can help block out all the whispering, sounds of pencils writing, labored breathing of others and so on.

Understanding the child's sensory strengths and vulnerabilities allows us to build in accommodations to facilitate learning, especially accommodations to help highlight what is important to attend to. Preview learning so the child knows what is important, and highlight essential information to focus the child's attention on what is relevant. Using overlays to block out or narrow down the information on a page can help focus attention.

Most importantly, remember when you see the child spacing out, looking away with glazed eyes, putting his head down or engulfed in repetitive self-stimming, assume that he may be overwhelmed and shutting down. Do not force participation and try to give the child a break away from all the stimulation. Identify a safe place with minimal stimulation where he can escape to and rebound. Always be conscious of the amount of stimulation occurring around the child and be tolerant if his responses are delayed.

When you cannot adequately filter stimulation, your brain becomes distracted by all the details and it becomes mentally taxing to sort out what is important and a mental strain to focus on what is relevant. Expect much longer time to process and let the child pace the speed of performance. Always be cognizant and respectful that our sensory world is so chaotic, confusing and overwhelming for these children. Be patient, give extra time to process and respond, and assume that any resistance or tuning out is a protective response to being overwhelmed. Assume processing overload whenever the child is oppositional or not acting as expected.

The brain's sensory coping mechanisms

As the brain is being overwhelmed with stimulation, it tries to fight back with mechanisms to block out stimulation to avoid overload. The reports from autistic adults have revealed four main ways to help cope with sensory bombardment:

1. Sensory stimulation

2. Mono-processing

3. Peripheral senses

4. Sensory shutdown.

Sensory stimulation

One of the common characteristics of autistics that stands out is their frequent attraction to self-stimulation. This usually consists of rhythmic, repetitive sensory patterns, often in the form of motor movements (hand flapping, rocking, jumping, twirling in circles, etc.), vocal patterns (humming, chanting, repetitive vocal noises, etc.) and tactile seeking (rubbing self, hand wringing, finger twisting, chewing shirt, biting finger, etc.) Self-stimulation can help block out overwhelming stimulation, provides self-control sensory feedback to distract and helps the person regulate the increasing anxiety he experiences under sensory bombardment. Self-stimulation is the one important tool that autistics have for minimizing, filtering and modulating the sensory input to their nervous system. It also helps regulate the emotional charge associated with sensory stress. Self-stimulation is a very powerful, adaptive tool for protecting the brain from being overwhelmed.

Mono (single channel) processing

Those who have a hard time integrating their senses can only process one sense at a time. They often have a dominant sense that they use to interpret their world. If touch is their primary sense, they may need to touch and manipulate everything they are processing; if it is the olfactory sense, they may need to smell everything that they engage in (food, people, objects, etc.). For mono-processing, the person often tunes out the other competing senses, so they do not overwhelm the dominant sense. The person who is a visual processor may frequently cover his ears to block out noise so that he can focus on his vision. This helps filter out and turn down the amount of stimulation bombarding the nervous system and is a coping tool to avoid sensory overload.

Many autistics have difficulty looking at people while listening to what they are saying. If they are looking at you, they cannot hear what you are saying. "I can listen to you or look at you, but not both." There is too much stimulation to process. Forcing the person to look at them is too overwhelming.

As can be expected, the dominant sense can develop into a highly sensitive strength. We need to identify what sense (vision, hearing, or touching/manipulating) the child primarily uses to explore his world, and then use that sense for engaging and teaching. For example, if the child uses smell as the dominant sense, we can use smells to identify, label and categorize people and objects, or if he is visually tuned, then teach by using visual strategies instead of verbal instructions.

Peripheral senses

Many individuals on the spectrum tone down stimulation by using their peripheral senses. The most common is peripheral vision. These individuals experience direct vision as too overwhelming, so they focus their attention on their peripheral vision. They look off to the side using their peripheral vision to observe. Peripheral vision is less intense and easier to process. Unfortunately, people often interpret this as not attending and prompt the person to look directly at the target. This can be overwhelming and anxiety provoking.

Sensory shutdown

Another coping skill that the brain can use is the ability to shut down when it feels itself being overwhelmed. This is a defense mechanism that the brain can use to avoid overload. If the stimulus overload is coming too fast or is too intense to shut down, then the individual runs the risk of melting down or acting out to escape the stressor and release the stress chemicals.

Many adults with autism report that when overwhelmed with stimulation their brains will start to shut down one or more senses to avoid overload. Often individuals may look as if they are tuning or spacing out, they may stare off into space, get a glazed look, or put their heads down and fall asleep. Their systems start to shut down, become a blur and are unresponsive. This can be frightening for them. They can withdraw and lose contact with their immediate surroundings. Over time, shutting off sensory channels can become the brain's primary response to sensory overload to avoid painful stimulation. The person may seem to be deaf, daydreaming or simply unresponsive to attempts to engage them. Sensory shutdown is often involuntary but can become a voluntary tool when used frequently.

This sensory shutdown can be very scary when it occurs while in the community. When the setting becomes overwhelming, the person starts to lose focus, voices become muffled and incoherent, and vision becomes blurred and images unrecognizable. The person becomes frightened and starts to panic or may withdraw into his own world to avoid the stimulation. Fear of how he might react and how others will respond to him adds significantly to the anxiety. It is important to help the person move away from the setting, helping him feel safe and reassure him that this will soon pass. Minimize speech since it will further overwhelm the person, and give him time and space to regroup.

Many adults with autism report sensory overload as feeling like a tidal wave of painful stimulation and strong emotions raging over them. Their thinking and reasoning skills start to shut down and their coping skills deteriorate. Their brain starts to panic, and they often lose their ability to comprehend and use language. Their body often hurts, and they may feel compelled to hit, slap, or bite themselves. Fear often overcomes them while they lose their ability to act rationally. They report that people trying to help can add to the confusion by asking them questions.

Since they are losing their ability to process language and speak, asking questions can further overwhelm them. Usually the best we can do is pull back all demands. Lower stimulation or take the person to a quiet area, reassure him that he is safe and let him rebound and regroup. Give him quiet space, with minimal demands to process, and allow him to withdraw until he can rebound and regroup. Let his brain cool down, regroup and gain cognitive and communication skills again.

Emotional response to sensory overload

If the brain is too overwhelmed with sensory overload to shut down, then the result is often a meltdown. Figure 13.2 displays how poorly filtered sensory stimulation overwhelms the limbic system (emotional centers). In addition, the weak neuro-connections between the frontal cortex (thinking centers) and limbic system make it hard to inhibit emotional impulses. Consequently, strong, impulsive, emotional reactions occur.

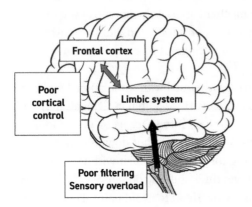

Poor filtering

Poor sensory filtering floods limbic system

Very raw emotions (limbic system) with little cortical control

Limited frustration tolerance

Poor impulse control

Poor emotional regulation (overreacts, mood swings)

Often anxious, easily upset

Unpredictable emotional outbursts

"I feel scared, overwhelmed and insecure!"

Figure 13.2: Sensory stimulation overwhelms the limbic system, resulting in meltdowns

When the brain cannot adequately filter out stimulation, there is a massive amount of stimulation flooding the limbic system. This is a very primitive part of the brain, which generates our raw emotions. For most of us, these emotions are held in check, tapered down and modulated by the thinking part of the brain in the frontal cortex. We might get an immediate impulse, but check it long enough for our thinking part of the brain to appraise the situation and tell us how much threat the stimulation is.

For those on the spectrum, especially children, the neurological pathways connecting the frontal cortex to the limbic system are not well developed, rendering the thinking part of the brain weak in controlling the emotional centers. Consequently, the flood of emotion overwhelms the cortex before it has a chance to inhibit it; hence they experience poor frustration tolerance, weak impulse control and limited ability to control their emotional reactions. The tidal wave of emotions simply floods over the cortical control. For these individuals, their emotions can be very unpredictable and scary, which leaves them feeling insecure and vulnerable.

The negative effects of sensory overload can help explain many of the behavior challenges that we experience with autism. The constant anxiety and irritability can leave the nervous system defensive and on high alert. So, to summarize, sensory overload can result in meltdowns, shutdown where the child is withdrawn and unresponsive, self-stimulation to block out stimulation and calm the nervous system, ritualistic and compulsive behaviors to control the stimulation around them, oppositional and defiant behavior to minimize uncertainty and a host of disorganized, hyperactive behaviors (see Figure 13.3).

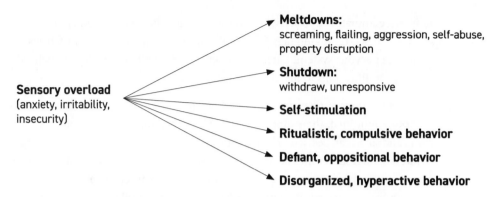

Figure 13.3: Behaviors associated with sensory overload

Children often need to control everything around them to reduce uncertainty and obtain predictability. They can be highly resistant to following the lead of others, very apprehensive in situations that they are not controlling and may act out to avoid or escape any of these situations. Unfortunately, adults often read these children as oppositional, defiant, noncompliant and manipulative, without understanding why they are driven to such resistance. We tend to command and demand respect and compliance, which only overwhelms the child even more. Adults often take it personally and try to use techniques (command and demand, pressure, scolding, punishment, etc.) that may work with typical children but for those on the spectrum only increase the fear and overload, sending the brain into further panic.

Supporting sensory defensiveness and sensory overload

In the blue book, *The Autism Discussion Page on the Core Challenges of Autism* (Nason 2014a), I summarize strategies for minimizing defensiveness and overload.

1. *Modify the environment to minimize overload.* Turn down the lights, reduce the noise, avoid unexpected touch and scratchy clothes and minimize foods and smells that are not tolerable. Parents need to get used to scanning the immediate environment to appraise for sensory threats to the child. It is up to us to monitor and modify the child's environments to reduce the amount of sensory bombardment. Whether it be at school, at home or in the community, it is important to think ahead about the type of stimulation that may assault the child's nervous system. Florescent lights, mechanical noises, chemical smells, scratchy materials and so on may all need to be modified to match what the nervous system can handle. As children get older, they need to understand their own sensitivities, be able to appraise situations for level of sensory threat and build in modifications and coping skills for dealing with sensory overload. We may need to build in accommodations and adaptations into the school IEP, as well as at home to minimize defensive overload. Some common accommodations may include: changing to unscented soaps and detergents at home, building in special

air filters, eliminating florescent lighting at home and in the classroom, purchasing seamless socks, removing tags from clothes, and eliminating certain fabrics to pacify the nervous system. Each child's sensitivities will be very individualized, needing modifications to match his sensory needs.

2. *Using adaptations to filter down the level of stimulation.* When the environment cannot be modified, then sunglasses, ear plugs, headphones, MP3 players, sun visors and so on can be used to help filter the stimulation. If the stimulation cannot be filtered, then sometimes favorite activities, such as Gameboys, hand computer games, music, reading, can be used to temporarily distract the nervous system and minimize overload. Parents often carry around a toolbox of sensory filters and temporary distracters for times when they cannot modify the environment to tone down the stimulation. It is important to use these filters to prevent overload, rather than waiting for the child to get overwhelmed before using them. Once they are overwhelmed, such adaptations often will not work.

3. *Allow the child to control the stimulation.* When the child is defensive, reduce anxiety tremendously by allowing the child to control the type and intensity of stimulation. If the child is reactive to the sound of a vacuum cleaner, let him run the vacuum and show him how to turn it on and off. If the radio is too overwhelming or the song playing is irritating, let the child control the volume or choose the music. Usually when it is predictable and under their control, they can dictate the intensity of stimulation they can handle. Let them control the pace and intensity of interaction, the activity, and the stimulation around them to feel safe and secure.

4. *Give frequent breaks to rebound and regroup.* To keep the stress chemicals from overloading the child, give him frequent breaks during the day to unwind, release stress chemicals, and re-energize. Some children need to go to a quiet area to regroup, some prefer to engage in solitary activity like listening to music or reading, and others prefer physical activity to release the stress chemicals and re-organize. Know what your child can handle. We often keep them in events too long or jump from one event to another without giving them time to rebound. Gauge how much and how long the child can handle the stimulation. This is especially true in fun, highly stimulating activities. Parents and teachers often think if the child likes it, he can handle the stimulation, but this is not true. Spending the day engaged in fun, ongoing, highly stimulating activities (especially if it requires socializing with others) can be just as stressful as an activity that is not enjoyable. Like most children, they will not want to stop the preferred activity when they start to become disorganized. We need to know what they can handle, arrange for the activity to be as sensory friendly as possible, and only expose the children for short periods at a time.

5. *Preview events ahead of time; have a plan.* Predictability reduces anxiety and lessens sensory overload. Get used to previewing with the child before entering events what he can expect to happen, what is expected of him and what sensory stressors might occur. Next, discuss what coping skills (sunglasses, earplugs, distractors, etc.) might be used to reduce sensory overload, as well as an exit plan to escape the situation if it becomes overwhelming. This helps the child feel more comfortable knowing what he is stepping into, that you understand and respect his sensory needs, and he trusts that you will help support him if he must escape the situation.

6. *When overwhelmed, back off and let them escape.* When the brain is in sensory overload, we must immediately remove all stimulation if possible. Let the child go to a quiet area, remove all demands, and talk very little. Some children will allow an adult to use deep pressure strategies to help sooth them, but often they need you to back off and give them time to rebound. Children may appear calm before their nervous systems are ready to engage again; give them plenty of time. When returning to the normal routine, be aware that overload can occur again very easily. Evaluate the situation to determine what stimulation/activity may have resulted in overload. Often it is ongoing participation in a highly stimulating/demanding activity.

7. *Sensory diet to keep the nervous system calm and organized.* A sensory diet includes controlled presentation of sensory stimulation throughout the day to keep the child calm, alert and organized. Usually an occupational therapist can evaluate the child and recommend sensory activities that can help him process stimulation better, help alert him, and soothe him when overwhelmed. This may include chewing gum or drinking water through a straw to help the child focus and stay calm and alert in class. It also may include sitting on an air cushion or therapy ball to keep the child alert and organized, or giving the child physical activity periodically throughout the day to release stress chemicals and regulate the nervous system. (pp.139–142).

Modifications/Adaptations

Usually, the quickest and easiest step for helping the child is to modify or adapt the environment to reduce sensory overload. This includes analyzing the immediate setting to reduce the amount and intensity of sensory pollution. First, identify what stimulation the person is sensitive to and then modify or filter down the stimulation. Modifications are when you make changes in the environment to reduce the stimulation and adaptations are tools that we can use to filter/mask the stimulation that we cannot change. Figure 13.4 provides examples of modifications and adaptations.

	Modifications	*Adaptions*
Auditory	Turn down volume Eliminate unwanted noise Avoid crowded, noisy events	Headphones Earplugs MP3 player
Visual	Eliminate visual clutter Soften lighting Avoid flickering lights Minimize bright colors	Tinted glass Brim hats Sit in shade Use umbrella
Tactile	Avoid light touch Warn before touching Sit child away from others Modify tasks using sensitive items (finger paints, etc.)	Choose clothes child tolerates Spandex clothing

Figure 13.4: Examples of modifications and adaptations for auditory, visual and tactile senses

With modifications, you can either avoid or eliminate the stimulation or attempt to turn it down. The person can either avoid situations that are too overwhelming or we can make modifications in the setting to reduce the level of stimulation. Often, we are thrown into situations where we cannot avoid things or make changes to the activity and stimulation. Keeping a toolbox of filters and distractors (sunglasses, ear plugs, MP3 player, fidget toys) with us can help navigate such events. Lastly, I always recommend that we give the child frequent breaks from sensory noisy settings and always have a quick escape route for when the child starts to become overwhelmed. Watch the child closely for early signs of sensory overload, give frequent breaks and end the event if they start to become overwhelmed.

Parents need to be aware of their child's sensory sensitivities and be able to appraise situations for sensory challenges before leading the child into events. What challenges does the child have, what challenges does the activity present, how can we accommodate for these challenges and what is our plan if the child becomes overwhelmed? Try to avoid situations that are overwhelming, make modifications to the setting if possible and provide sensory tools (sunglasses, headphones, fidget toys, etc.) for masking stimulation or distracting attention away from it. I also recommend that you design these strategies with the child, discussing the sensory stressors and accommodating strategies as well as devising an escape route before entering situations. Preparing the child ahead of time reduces anxiety of the unexpected and helps the child feel sure that we respect his sensory needs. As the child becomes older (late teens and adulthood), he will have to learn how to do these things himself.

Coping with sensory defensiveness and overload often requires major modifications in their daily living. Avoid situations that overwhelm them, modify settings as you can, and build in sensory tools to reduce the sensory bombardment.

Importance of self-stimulation

The stereotype of the boy sitting in the corner rocking and flapping his hands was once considered to be the hallmark of autism. Since then, many therapists, teachers and parents have gone to major efforts to stop self-stimulatory behavior. It looks too autistic. If they do not rock and flap, they do not "look" autistic. Little consideration was given to why this behavior was occurring and what important functions self-stimulation provided for the individual. It just looked weird, therefore it had to be extinguished. Once we stopped all "weird" behavior, the child was no longer autistic. This was a very disrespectful stance to take. As we listened more to those with autism describing their experiences, we learned how important stimming is for them, the functions stimming serves and the coping mechanisms it provides.

Self-stimulation is usually a rhythmic, repetitive sensory pattern. Common forms of stimulation include rocking, hand flapping, twirling, pacing, jumping, vocalizing, flicking or flapping objects. This behavior often serves to help children regulate their arousal level, taper anxiety, release stress chemicals and maintain focus. Self-stimulation (stimming) can be a great tool for coping with sensory overload. Sensory stimulation serves multiple functions, usually to regulate the nervous system by reducing outside stimulation when overwhelmed, or increasing stimulation when under-aroused. However, these functional purposes can be broken down into the following areas:

1. *Mask.* The person can hyper-focus on stimming to help block out uncomfortable stimulation (too much noise, chaotic activity, etc.). Often, this is the only self-controlled, immediate coping skill the individual has for dealing with uncomfortable stimulation.

2. *Soothe.* When anxious or overwhelmed, self-stimulation can be used to soothe and calm the nervous system. Rhythmic, repetitive sensory patterns (rocking, deep pressure, humming, pacing, etc.) that the child controls can be very calming to the nervous system. Stimming is an important tool for regulating anxiety. This tool should be supported, not discouraged.

3. *Alert and organize.* Sensory stimulation helps modulate sensory input to keep the nervous system calm and alert. To keep their nervous system organized and regulated, children will use self-stimulation to calm themselves when over-aroused and alert themselves when under-aroused (more on this in a moment).

4. *Stay connected.* If hypo-sensitive, meaning that the person has difficulty registering the stimulation, he may seek out intense stimulation to stay connected with that sense. He may hum, sing and make loud vocalizations to stimulate his hearing, or continually bang his ankles or wrists on objects to feel connected to his body when having difficulty registering proprioception (stimulation to joints, muscles and tendons). Children who have difficulty registering vestibular movement may seek out intense swinging and spinning to wake up that sense.

5. *Feels good!* Children can engage in sensory stimulation simply because it feels good! It releases feel-good chemistry (dopamine). The sensory stimulation can feel very good to the nervous system and is self-reinforcing.

Self-stimulation occurs in many forms, but usually consists of repetitive, rhythmic sensory patterns to one of more of the senses. Examples of these include:

- *Movement.* Rocking, pacing, head rolling, spinning, swinging.

- *Proprioception.* Hand flapping, tapping body parts, crashing, bumping into things, twisting limbs, cracking fingers, head banging, biting self.

- *Tactile.* Fidget toys, rubbing self, licking self, smearing, scratching, biting self, touching everything.

- *Visual.* Staring at fans, reflections, light sources, visual patterns (waves, leaves, falling sand, flicking light switches, etc.).

- *Auditory.* Banging objects, tapping, drumming, vocalizing, scripting, singing, listening to repetitive noises.

- *Olfactory.* Smelling items before playing with them, smelling hair, smelling food before eating, body odors.

Self-stimulatory behavior is a common way to screen out unwanted stimulation when over-aroused or block stimulation that overwhelms. Hence, you often will see an increase in children's self-stimulatory, repetitive behavior when they start to become overwhelmed. It is a tool they use to block out and turn down stimulation, as well as distract the nervous system to calming activity. Most self-stimulation consists of self-controlled, rhythmic, repetitive patterns that soothe and organize. Rhythmic, sensory patterns have a strong calming effect on the nervous system. Never try to stop self-stimulation when children are trying to "hold it together." It is their main tool for coping with the overwhelming sensory demands.

It used to be thought that sensory stimulation needed to be interrupted, because it either didn't "look normal" or distracted the child from learning. Without evaluating what purpose the behavior provided, it was labeled as bad, "autistic" and needed to be stopped. However, now that many autistic adults tell us the various functions that stimming provides them and how important it is to regulating their nervous systems, we realize that self-stimulation is a vital coping skill for them.

We all use self-stimulation to regulate our nervous system. We bite our nails, twirl our hair, rock, hum, crack our knuckles, tap our feet, chew gum, doodle and a host of other self-stimulatory behaviors. Smoking cigarettes is a sensory stimulation behavior pattern. We use these behaviors to alert us when under-aroused and calm us when over-aroused. What type of self-stimming do you do? It helps to become aware of your own behavior and how it serves you to get a good idea of why these behaviors are important for those on the spectrum. The only difference is that children with autism usually have much more fragile and disorganized nervous systems and have a greater need for self-stimulation.

So, to answer the "not normal" argument, self-stimulation is important for all of us. It is "normal." However, it is usually much more important for those on the spectrum. The type and intensity of self-stimulation (rocking, hand flapping, vocal noises, etc.) may be different and make them stand out in public. The child may flap his hands when excited or when anxious, which makes him stand out, or he may pace in circles when in a chaotic setting to cope with the chaos, but trying to get him to stop leaves him helpless in coping with his disorganized nervous system. Since most self-stimming does not hurt anyone, it is more of an acceptance problem than a behavior that needs to be extinguished. Most of us feel that self-stimulation should be accepted and respected, but many people, even some of those on the spectrum themselves, would like to "not stand out." If the individual chooses to stop such self-stimulatory behavior, he should be encouraged to substitute less obvious forms of stimming that can serve the same function.

Let's also look at the argument that self-stimulation distracts the child from learning. We have already learned that for the child to focus and learn, his nervous system must be in a state of optimum arousal (state of readiness to learn). If the child is anxious and over-aroused, or under-aroused and cannot focus, he may need to use self-stimulation to organize his nervous system, so he can focus and learn. We have found over the years that a child doodling, rocking, fidgeting and so on can still be listening and taking in information. People have been surprised to find out that the child who appears to be detached in his own world of self-stimulation is listening and learning the whole time. In fact, it is the self-stimulation that allows him to keep himself regulated, focused and attentive. To stop his self-stimulation dysregulates his nervous system.

One more important matter that autistics want us to know is that consciously trying to inhibit stimming is so distracting and mentally exhausting that it inhibits their ability to focus and mentally drains them. Trying to intentionally suppress the actions takes enormous conscious effort. Not only does the nervous system become dysregulated, but also the person becomes more anxious, since he is intensively trying to suppress the tool he is using to cope with the anxiety. This is not only very intrusive and invalidating to the child, but also makes it more difficult for him to focus and learn.

Sensory diet and arousal problems

When your nervous system is hyper-alert, strained and disorganized, sensory sensitivities are heightened, and sensory overload is more likely. The state of the nervous system going into activities will help determine the impact that sensory stimulation has on the person. A calm organized nervous system can cope with the stimulation much better than a tired, drained or disorganized system.

Keeping your nervous system calm, alert, and organized

In addition to sensory sensitivities and sensory defensiveness, another sensory impairment is difficulty maintaining an "optimal state of arousal," meaning keeping the nervous system calm, alert and organized. Our nervous system has a built-in filtering system that allows us to modulate the amount and intensity of sensory stimulation to stay optimally aroused to meet the demands of the moment. Our arousal level affects our ability to attend, concentrate, motivate and activate. When we need to focus, learn or perform, we must be alert, organized and ready to act. When it is time for us to rest and sleep, we need to lower our arousal so that we become relaxed and drowsy. Our nervous system gets good at modulating the amount of stimulation coming in to match the arousal level needed for the situation (rest or action)—what we call our "optimum level of arousal." When we need to focus, we may chew gum, tap our feet, twirl our hair, or splash water over our face to increase our arousal. If we need to calm and relax before going to bed, we might take a warm bath, read a book, snuggle with pillows or listen to calming music.

Our nervous systems need a certain level of stimulation to stay calm, alert and aroused. Our brains have a system that modulates how much stimulation is coming in and how much is filtered out. If that filtering system is working well, we stay calm, organized, alert and productive. However, if our filtering system is not working well, we are either under-aroused (slow and sluggish) or over-aroused (overwhelmed, scattered and disorganized). When over-aroused, the person is even more sensitive to stimulation and prone to sensory overload.

Many children with autism have difficulty with their filtering system and staying in the optimum level of arousal. Their filtering system is either filtering too much (under-registering) or not filtering out enough (over-registering) stimulation, making it difficult for them to attend, focus, act and learn. If the person is in an over-aroused, over-stimulated state, he is hyper-alert, anxious and on guard. He may be defensive, oppositional and become easily overwhelmed. Over-arousal will often activate the child's fight or flight response and he may either shut down to reduce overload, or melt down.

If the person is in an under-aroused state, he might be slow and sluggish, unmotivated and lack initiative and effort. Simply getting him up and moving and interested will be an ongoing problem. Alternatively, he can be over-active (hyperactive), seeking out constant stimulation to stay aroused. This is often the hyperactive child who is seeking more intense stimulation to stay alert. Regardless of their state of arousal, these individuals often have a hard time attending, listening, understanding and acting as expected. The brain is not in a state of "readiness" for attending, learning and performing. The brain must focus on meeting its needs rather than focusing on what is expected.

Staying optimally aroused

The nervous system is continually trying to keep itself calm, alert and organized. For many with autism and sensory processing disorder, their nervous system has difficulty maintaining this optimal state of arousal. They are often fluctuating between being over- and under-aroused, frequently feeling anxious and disorganized. Figure 13.5 shows how a person's arousal level can fluctuate based on how well the brain is filtering stimulation. If too much stimulation is filtered then the nervous system may become under-aroused. If the brain is not filtering enough, the nervous system may become over-aroused.

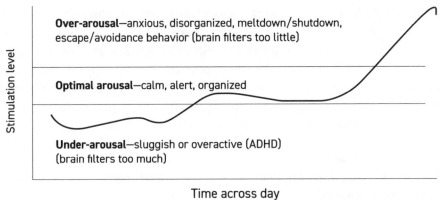

Figure 13.5: Arousal levels fluctuate based on how well the brain filters stimulation

In a very simple way, we can look at regulation in terms of three levels of arousal. The nervous system tries to maintain an optimal level of arousal, where it is relaxed, alert and focused. The person feels safe, secure and ready to meet daily expectations. He can focus, learn, act and adapt.

When over-aroused, the brain is being overwhelmed with too much stimulation, making it scattered, disorganized, hyper-alert and defensive. At this time, the person may be shutting down in an attempt to avoid being overwhelmed, or become over-active, giddy, agitated and combative. He is very sensitive to stimulation and sensory overload.

However, if under-aroused, the brain stem is filtering out too much information to stay aroused and alert. The child may zone out, become slow and sluggish, difficult to motivate and require constant prompting and supervision to perform.

Or, as already mentioned, the brain will become anxious and seek out more intense stimulation to bring itself into an optimal level of alertness. This person may have difficulty sitting still, be constantly moving, talking, or engaging in other highly stimulating activity.

Sensory diets

The field of occupational therapy has introduced us to the benefits of using sensory diets to help calm, alert and organize the nervous system. Sensory diets allow the child to stay regulated within the optimum level of arousal. Although there is not much research and scientific evidence that verifies these benefits, anecdotal information, clinical reports and personal testimony have led to the popularity of using sensory diets to help regulate the nervous system. Clinical experience has demonstrated numerous times that a well-designed sensory diet can help many autistics stay calm and organized, reduce anxiety and minimize sensory overload.

A sensory diet is a carefully scheduled routine of sensory activities that is implemented periodically throughout the day to help keep the nervous system calm, organized and focused. This lowers anxiety, increases focus and maximizes the child's ability to learn and adapt to daily demands. Usually the sensory diet helps to calm and organize the nervous system when over-aroused and alert the nervous system when under-aroused. When the child is over-aroused, calming and organizing activities are given to stabilize the nervous system. When the child is under-aroused, alerting activities are given to increase the arousal level. Once the nervous system is in the optimal range of arousal, then a steady dose of organizing stimulation can maintain that state of readiness. Figures 13.6 and 13.7 provide examples of calming and alerting activities.

- Deep pressure massage
- Sitting on bean bags, large body pillow
- Sandwiching, pillow press
- Lap pads
- Deep pressure or weighted vest
- Bear hugs, neutral warmth
- Slow rocking
- Lotion rubs
- Soft lighting
- Soft, slow music
- Joint compressions
- Stretching
- Chewing gum
- Sucking
- Figdet toys
- Calm, rhythmic movement patterns
- Physical relaxation exercises

Figure 13.6: Examples of calming activities

- Brisk rubbing
- Tickling
- Chewing gum, chewy food
- Any push/pull, run, skip, jump, heavy lifting
- Fast, irregular movement (swing, trampoline, therapy ball)
- Kick, bounce, throw a ball
- Strong tastes and odors (peppermint, perfume)
- Bright lighting
- Loud, fast music
- Cold water play
- Fidget toys
- Drinking carbonated drinks
- Sitting on a T-stool or air cushion
- Physical exercise
- Dancing

Figure 13.7: Examples of alerting activities

In designing a sensory diet, as part of the evaluation, the occupational therapist develops an inventory of sensory preferences and sensitivities. From this profile, the therapist identifies what stimulation calms the child (e.g. deep pressure, slow rocking, etc.), what stimulation alerts the child (e.g. jumping, swinging, chewing crunchy snacks), what stimulation the child seeks out (preferences) and what he avoids (sensitivities).

From this profile, the therapist can design a schedule of activities for the child's daily routine that will calm and organize the nervous system. Often, a set of activities is recommended to be used on a set schedule each day (frequently every couple of hours) as standard practice to keep the child organized. Calming or alerting activities are suggested as needed based on the child's arousal level.

For a more detailed discussion on developing and implementing sensory diets, refer to the blue book, *The Autism Discussion Page on the Core Challenges of Autism* (Nason 2014a).

Corrective therapies

There are a variety of direct therapies that can be used to reduce sensory sensitivities and sensory defensiveness. This discussion is to give you an awareness of what is out there, not to recommend any specific strategy. There has been little conclusive evidence for any one of these strategies, so I recommend you research any strategy here you might be more interested in.

The Wilbarger Protocol

The Wilbarger Protocol is a popular technique used by occupational therapists, consisting of sensory brushing and joint compressions to decrease tactile (touch) defensiveness, as well as overall sensory defensiveness. The Wilbarger Protocol, named after the founder, Patricia Wilbarger, is designed to decrease tactile defensiveness specifically and overall sensory defensiveness in general. The strategy consists of two steps:

1. *Deep pressure brushing with a soft, specific brush (e.g. surgical brush).* By firm and quick brushing across arms, hands, shoulder, back and legs, the brushing floods the tactile system with deep pressure stimulation to reset the fight or flight threshold, increasing tolerance to tactile stimulation. Avoid brushing the face, chest and stomach. This procedure can also help decrease defensiveness in senses other than the tactile system.

2. *Joint compressions.* Immediately following the brushing, joint compressions are implemented to the shoulders, elbows, wrists, fingers, hip, knees and ankles. Joint compressions consist of compressing the joints together for approximately ten repetitions.

This procedure only takes a few minutes. To work effectively, the procedure should be implemented approximately once every 1.5 to 2 hours throughout the day. Usually, the child will see results within a few weeks. The Wilbarger Protocol should be designed, trained and monitored by an occupational therapist or other specialist trained in this technique.

Auditory integration therapy (AIT)

Auditory integration therapy, developed by Guy Bernard, is designed to help desensitize auditory sensitivity to noise and lead to better integration of auditory stimulation. AIT consists of listening to different sound frequencies during 30-minute music sessions via headphones, to retrain the ear and areas of the brain responsible for auditory processing. After an assessment is completed to determine what sound frequencies the person is sensitive to, an individualized program is designed where selected sound frequencies are filtered out until these frequencies are normalized. Treatment usually consists of two 30-minute sessions a day, for ten days. AIT claims to decrease hyperactivity, auditory defensiveness, social isolation and anxiety. AIT may also help with concentration, attention, comprehension and auditory processing.[1]

Therapeutic listening

Another listening program, developed by Sheila Frick, is based on the early AIT principles. It consists of a selection of modulated music CDs that modify sound waves to help reset structural parts of the ear and build stronger sensory pathways in the brain. The person listens to CDs while often engaged in movement activities for 30-minute training sessions. It is claimed to decrease auditory defensiveness, reduce anxiety, increase modulation, improve emotional regulation, attention, concentration and learning, improve integration of senses, and develop greater motor planning. Therapeutic listening is often incorporated with other sensory integration procedures and used along a sensory diet.[2]

Visual integration therapies

Visual integration therapy includes Irlen lens to correct visual defensiveness and special lenses, prisms and corrective therapies to increase visual integration. There are two primary therapies for visual processing dysfunction.

Helen Irlen has developed two methods for treating visual processing disorders. Her theories claim that visual distortions can be reduced by using tinted colored lenses that filter out the light frequencies that the person is sensitive to. These lenses also slow down the rate of processing to avoid visual overload. The second method developed by Helen is the use of colored overlays that correct visual distortions of printed text. Distortion of printed text (print jumping off the page, moving or distorting) can be corrected by placing colored overlays over the page. Helen's methods have been quite successful and there are many studies showing positive results.

Vision therapy (or behavioral optometry)

Vision therapy uses special lenses, or prisms, to correct visual distortions by retraining the eye coordination with the brain. The therapy usually consists of doing daily activities at home with the specialized lenses, and weekly visits to the optometrist for four to six months.

Sensory integration therapy

Probably the most popular work related to autism has been sensory integration therapy in the field of occupational therapy. Many of today's strategies are based on the early work of Jean Ayres. The therapy often consists of three main areas.

---

1   See www.aitinstitute.org
2   See www.vitallinks.net

After a thorough sensory processing assessment has been completed, therapeutic strategies are designed to:

- increase overall integration of all sensory input by normalizing sensory registration and integration of senses. Usually this consists of a variety of sensory-based activities designed to improve adaptive functioning during daily living activities (motor coordination, performance of normal daily care, sleeping and eating habits, etc.)

- desensitize sensory sensitivities and defensiveness. Once sensory sensitivities are identified, graded exposure to the sensory input is provided to decrease sensitivity

- maximize arousal level, keeping the nervous system calm, alert and organized. This utilizes a sensory diet of daily activities of tactile, vestibular and proprioception.

Sensory desensitization

In the field of behavior psychology, systematic desensitization procedures have been used to reduce sensory sensitivities. Desensitization usually starts with an assessment of the sensory sensitivity to determine a hierarchy of least-to-most aversive stimulation, both in quality and intensity. This hierarchy starts with stimulation that presents very mild negative reaction and gradually works up to stimulation that provides the most aversive stimulation.

Once a hierarchy is established, therapy starts with the first step of the hierarchy, providing repeated exposure until the person no longer finds that stimulation uncomfortable, then gradually moves up the hierarchy as each previous step is mastered. The child is often taught to rate the level of discomfort and determines himself when he is ready to move to the next level.

To help cope with the anxiety of exposure, the child may be taught relaxation procedures, provided with distracting activities or taught other coping skills to help tolerate the exposure. Desensitization is based on providing repeated, non-punishing exposure to the stimulation, gradually increasing the frequency, intensity and duration of stimulation.

Let's look at an example of using desensitization to reduce sensitivity to touch.

First, we need to develop a hierarchy of least to most sensitive stimulation. An assessment would be needed to determine what type of touch (deep pressure, light touch, different textures, etc.) the child is most sensitive to and what parts of the body are the most sensitive. For example, people are usually more sensitive to light touch than to deep pressure touch, and many people are more sensitive to their face, hands and feet and less sensitive on the back and shoulders. So, the hierarchy may start with providing deep pressure to the back and shoulders, gradually lightening the touch as tolerated, and then moving on to more sensitive areas of the body.

- Work up the hierarchy providing graded exposure to the stimulation.

- Start off with brief exposure to the most tolerated touch and gradually increase frequency, intensity, and duration of stimulation.

- Provide frequent, non-punishing trials to stimulation throughout the day.

- Keep it simple, build gradually, maximize success.

If needed, give the child support in tolerating the stimulation by providing a distraction. For example, sneak in the touching while engaging the child in a preferred activity (e.g. rubbing his arm while playing a video game). Another technique is to use deep pressure to relax while providing more arousing touch. For example, I might use firm shoulder massage when I first start providing deep pressure touch to the child's arm. Since deep pressure rubbing to the shoulders is calming, I use that stimulation to relax the child while providing touch that may be more alarming for him. As the child becomes more tolerant of the touch, I gradually reduce the shoulder massage.

Find ways to sneak tactile stimulation into the daily routine. Often, I work in conjunction with an occupational therapist to build a sensory diet of tactile activities throughout the day. This may consist of lotion rubs, water play, sand/rice play, finger painting, shaving cream play and so on; again, gradually exposing the child to a greater variety of tactile stimulation, providing gradual exposure and ensuring tolerance.

Planning for generalization includes expanding the tolerance to tactile stimulation across activities, across different settings and across different people.

In seeking out and using corrective therapies it is very important that you find a therapist who will (1) seek out your input and listen to your concerns, (2) understand your child's strengths and vulnerabilities, (3) tailor the therapy to your child's specific needs, (4) let your child drive the therapy (respect their needs, feelings and desires), and (5) listen to the child and back off at any moment when he is overwhelmed or resistant. At no time should the therapy be designed to "cure" autism or change the child, only to help alleviate some of the co-occurring sensory sensitivities that are causing distress.

Chapter 14

SOCIAL CHALLENGES

Difficulty relating with others is probably the most well-known struggle for people on the spectrum. They live in a very social world that requires rapid processing of multiple information simultaneously. Their difficulties reading social cues and the invisible social rules leave them stumbling through social situations. What comes intuitively for us does not come easily for them. What we come by naturally, they must learn through repeated practice. Even then, their social skills are often scripted and mechanical and do not fit smoothly into ongoing interactions. Some of the common struggles include the following:

- Difficulty reading and interpreting social cues.
- Impaired ability to read the thoughts, feelings, perspectives and intentions of others.
- Difficulty understanding unwritten social rules.
- Problems reading social context.
- Difficulty processing the rapid flow of conversations.
- Difficulty co-regulating, back and forth, reciprocal interaction.
- Problems understanding vague language with hidden meanings.
- Difficulty rapidly formulating what they want to say and how to say it.
- Social responses that are often out of sync with others.
- Poor awareness of how their behavior affects others.
- Often misinterpreted, viewed as rude, indifferent or oppositional.
- Difficulty establishing and maintaining relationships.
- Strong social anxiety.

In the blue book, *The Autism Discussion Page on the Core Challenges of Autism* (Nason 2014a), I discuss many of these social struggles in depth and provide a variety of strategies for supporting these challenges: how to read nonverbal communication and mental states of others, understanding the social context, becoming a social detective, when, where and how to use copying, making social events more understandable, teaching relating skills, facilitating play dates, and many other social relating skills. The toolbox of strategies is comprehensive, user friendly and easy to understand.

It is not the purpose of this book to repeat what is provided in the blue book. This chapter will highlight the two main social processing functions that provide the backdrop for many of the other struggles:

1. Difficulty interpreting social context, which provides the hidden meaning to social events.

2. Problems reading the thoughts, feelings, perspectives and intentions of others.

The impact of these two weaknesses leaves the individual with autism at a huge disadvantage when relating with neurotypicals. The first, interpreting social context, is important to the development of the second, reading the mental states of others. Underlying these two functions are four main processing weaknesses. Like most differences, these processing challenges are weaknesses only when trying to relate in the neurotypical world. They are social processing styles utilized by neurotypical people when socializing. Because of these differences, the two processing styles relate on different planes. However, since many of the struggles that autistics encounter are associated with relating in the neurotypical world, these processes are important to understand.

Four main cognitive weaknesses behind social struggles

Many of the social deficits that people with autism struggle with come from the differences in how they cognitively process information. There are four primary cognitive differences that lead to many of their social struggles.

1. *Information processing differences.* Relating with others requires very rapid processing of multiple information simultaneously. It requires the simultaneous referencing of people for information: listening to what they are saying, reading their facial expressions, thinking about their perspective, figuring out how to respond and checking whether the person is understanding what we are saying. Neurotypical people process all this information intuitively, with little conscious thought. As we have discussed extensively throughout this book, people on the spectrum have great difficulty rapidly processing multiple information simultaneously. Hence, our social world moves way too fast for their processing style.

2. *Difficultly reading social context.* Autistic people have difficulty immediately seeing the "big picture" behind social interaction in our social world. Neurotypicals pick up on a few details and immediately infer what the overall intent and expectations are. Most autistics do not immediately infer the underlying meaning but must piece the puzzle together from their concrete observations. This leads to difficulty grasping the "gist" of what is going on. They have a hard time understanding the social context that gives meaning and direction while relating.

3. *Weak theory of mind.* Theory of mind is our natural ability to read the mental states of others, allowing us to share common experiences with them, take their perspective and use this information to predict their behavior. This requires the ability to read the nonverbal social cues that allow us to understand the thoughts, feelings, perspectives and intentions of others. This allows us to stay connected and coordinated with the person we are relating with. Because of the first two cognitive deficits, people on the spectrum have great difficulty reading the mental states of others.

4. *Cognitive inflexibility.* Navigating in our social world requires a great deal of cognitive flexibility—being able to bend our expectations and modify our behavior as situations change. What is socially acceptable in one situation may not be in another. The rules of the game change based on the context of the situation. Since people on the spectrum find it difficult to read these invisible social rules, they do not have the needed flexibility to make subtle adjustments to these rules based on the context of the situation. What was socially appropriate on one day and place, should stay the same the next day and place. Since expectations change across settings, people and time, these variations catch them off guard and create major stress for them.

When you combine these four challenges, it helps explain most of the above social struggles autistics experience. Much social skills training is focused on teaching concrete social scripts without considering the importance of reading the invisible social context that provides meaning to how these skills are applied in different situations. The inability to intuitively read social context makes it hard to modify and adapt social scripts across settings and situations.

What is context?

Everything we perceive is interpreted by the context in which it is occurring. The context is the background that provides meaning to the object or event we are experiencing. We interpret individual details in relation to the overall picture. Take for example, how we interpret what we see. If we walk into a room and see a table with a chair on the far side, we cannot see the entire chair, only the back of it that is not being hidden by the table in front. We only know it is a chair because of its relationship with the table. If we just saw the cutout of the back of the chair, we might not interpret it as a chair. Seeing it in relation with the table, plus our past experiences of seeing chairs around a table, our minds infer it as a chair. Almost everything we perceive is inferred by the background (context) in which it is viewed. The meaning of an object changes based on the background information. A knife sitting on the kitchen table next to a plate is interpreted as an eating utensil. A knife lying next to a dead body is immediately interpreted as a murder weapon. Everything that we experience is significantly influenced by the context of the event.

Literal processing and context processing

Literal and context processing are two different processing styles. People with autism are much better at literal processing—processing concrete details and facts. They have a very unbiased perception of details and events; what you see is what you get. Neurotypical processing is more influenced by the context of the event (invisible relationships between the parts that provide meaning to the whole). Neurotypicals see a few details and immediately infer meaning to the overall picture. We gloss over the details and look for the overall meaning (relationships between the parts that define the context).

Research has shown that the neurotypical brain looks for context (overall meaning) first, before interpreting any details. This processing occurs in a millisecond, perceiving context before interpreting the individual details. It immediately looks past the details to infer overall meaning of what we are experiencing. This speeds up the processing, since we do not have to piece all the details together to extract the overall meaning. Unfortunately, it leaves us open to misinterpretation, because we may infer incorrectly, thus biasing our perception of what is occurring. We size things up immediately and make judgements based on limited information, often missing important details.

People with autism tend to focus more on the concrete details first and extract the context by piecing together the details. They stay truer to what they perceive, with fewer biased interpretations. When the context is mostly concrete details (what you see, hear, touch, etc.), autistic processing is very accurate, more so than the quick inference processing of neurotypicals. However, when the context includes a lot of hidden, invisible meaning (social norms, hidden expectations, perspectives and intentions of others, etc.), then processing of context becomes difficult for people on the spectrum.

We immediately gloss over the details and infer overall meaning whereas someone on the spectrum will be attracted to the facts and details. People with autism are more content thinkers and we are more context thinkers; both have strengths and weaknesses.

Social context

Unfortunately, for autistics, our social world is heavily based on context thinking. The rapid pace of relating requires us to quickly infer the gist of what is occurring to grasp the overall meaning of the interaction. We immediately size up a social situation to understand what is happening and what is expected. This helps us read what the situation entails, the perspectives and intentions of others and how we should respond. This context processing occurs so fast that it is often below our awareness. It occurs "intuitively", rather than us having to think it through. It simply happens with little forethought.

Social context includes four main variables, set out in Figure 14.1.

Situational context

What's happening, the event, rules and expectations

Personal variables

Thoughts, feelings and perspectives Relationship variables, status

Past experiences

Memories of past experiences in this situation

Physical variables

Structures and objects, arrangement of setting, weather, etc.

Figure 14.1: Breakdown of four main variables in social context

1. *Situational variables.* What is happening? What is the event and the unwritten rules and expectations? What can we expect to happen and what is expected of us? Every common social event comes with a host of invisible social rules, norms and hidden expectations. Usually we grasp the gist of these expectations immediately on entering social situations.

2. *Personal variables.* This includes basic qualities of the people involved, such as their age, sex and nationality, as well as the relationship you have with them. Are they relatives, friends, acquaintances or strangers? Are we talking to a police officer, minister or neighbor next door? They are all assuming different expectations. Also, personal variables include the ability to read the thoughts, feelings, perspectives and intentions of those involved and how they are reacting to our behavior (are they accepting, interested, annoyed or angry?).

3. *Past experiences.* How we size up a situation will also be determined by our past experiences with similar events—our memories of what occurred, what was expected and how we acted influences entering these events again. Every time we walk into a library, we carry with us the memories of what we can expect to happen and how we are expected to act.

4. *Physical variables.* Sometimes our expectations change based on the physical setting, number of people and the arrangement of objects in the setting. For example:

    • Two kids may be safe running around playing tag in the backyard, but not in the house or in a busy street.

    • How we read the body language of someone standing stiff, with arms crossed and a tense facial expression, when outside in bad weather (person is cold), will be different from in the same stance and look of a person in the office (boss is upset).

- If we are in a friend's home, we may feel comfortable picking up a figurine to closely examine it, but not so much in an expensive store where the items have great worth.

- The amount of space we must navigate, the noise, activity and arrangement of furniture all affect how we behave, often without us being aware of it.

Most of us do not consciously assess each one of these variables, then connect the dots to define the hidden norms and expectations. As you can see, reading context requires us to rapidly process multiple information simultaneously, often subconsciously and intuitively. We establish a mental map that helps us smoothly navigate the social event. For events that are familiar to us, we interpret social context immediately, which patterns our actions. If we are entering a church, school, library or a concert, we bring with us a host of norms and expectations that are common to these settings. We then immediately pick up on individual differences for that event and use this information to pattern our behavior.

When we are in new, unfamiliar situations, we may need to do all this processing at a conscious, "think it through" level, such as if we were in a social gathering that is novel to us. We need to consciously figure out the hidden customs or norms (etiquette, invisible rules and expectations) of the group, what common objectives bring them together, in what style everyone is relating (formal, relaxed, personable, etc.), how I should act, what I should say, and how I can fit in. We initially stand back and observe what others are doing and apply meaning to the context for which we are entering. Once we get the gist of what is going on, we start to pattern our actions and interactions to this perceived context.

Mental map

Reading social context is very difficult for most people with autism. Since most of the contextual information is unwritten, invisible and hidden, they are left without a mental map of how to smoothly navigate their day in the social world. They are amazed at how neurotypicals can intuitively grasp the gist of events and smoothly navigate through them. We understand the unwritten rules, invisible relationships and abstract contexts that provide automatic meaning and direction. People on the spectrum do not have this "mental map" and are lost without it. Consequently, our world is vague, confusing and unpredictable for them. This creates strong insecurity and anxiety.

Yes, autistics can learn to construct social meaning by piecing together common traits as they accumulate experiences over time. We can teach them all the numerous social norms, rules and expectations that are common to events, which significantly helps them to adapt. However, each situation comes with its unique configuration of expectations that must be appraised in order to fit in. Not all schools, libraries, churches, parties, concerts or friendly gatherings are the same. There are common norms, but also expectations that are unique to the event.

Autistics may have fragmented pieces of the mental map but are left guessing at the overall picture, leaving the person stumbling along, missing valuable information and out of step with everyone else. Plus, trying to "connect the dots to define the plots," is very laborious and exhausting. Trying to simultaneously define the plot while acting in the play is almost impossible to navigate successfully.

Seeing the big picture

How does contextual processing affect our daily lives? As discussed, the brains of neurotypical people are wired to immediately read the "overall picture" (social context) as to provide meaning to what is experienced. This allows us to easily grasp the gist of what is going on, interpret what is expected and pattern our behavior accordingly. The context helps define for us what people may be thinking, feeling and intending. It allows us to pattern our behavior to meet the common social expectations. Let's look at how single behaviors have different meanings depending on the social context (see Figure 14.2).

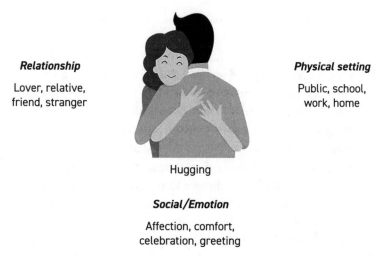

Relationship

Lover, relative,
friend, stranger

Physical setting

Public, school,
work, home

Hugging

Social/Emotion

Affection, comfort,
celebration, greeting

Figure 14.2: Variables to consider when hugging

When it is appropriate to hug others can be very complex based on the situation, people involved, cultural and personal attitudes and variables. Hugging is usually more acceptable at home than at school, but not always. Giving a hug is often appropriate when greeting others or saying goodbye, but this may vary depending if the others are friends, acquaintances or strangers. Also, some people may be uncomfortable with hugging or it may be against their cultural norms. Then there is the intent of the hug; to say goodbye, express affection, comfort someone, celebrate a positive event, etc. Lastly, there is the type of hug you will give (full hug, shoulder hug, etc.), the degree of firmness and the length of the hug. Consequently, when and how you hug will vary depending on the people and social context of your situation.

This illustrates how a simple behavior can have numerous contextual factors that must be considered in patterning our actions. A misread of contextual meaning can be disastrous when our actions offend others. For example, a teenage boy inappropriately hugging girls in the hallway at school may get very negative reactions and find himself in trouble.

Contextual processing underlies all our social interactions, usually without our awareness. We automatically use it to define what is expected and pattern our actions. Let's look at a common experience for children—rough-housing (see Figure 14.3).

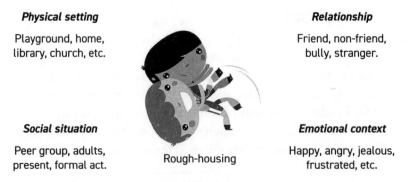

Physical setting

Playground, home, library, church, etc.

Relationship

Friend, non-friend, bully, stranger.

Social situation

Peer group, adults, present, formal act.

Rough-housing

Emotional context

Happy, angry, jealous, frustrated, etc.

Figure 14.3: Different contextual variables surrounding rough-housing

For a child on the spectrum, rough-housing or teasing can be a difficult behavior to judge. He may learn that it is a good way of having fun with a peer. However, it may be more acceptable in the playground or at home, than in the library, school or church. It also may work well with a close friend, but have a different meaning if they try it with a classmate at school who is not a close friend, or worse yet, the classroom bully. Even with a friend, it may not be a good action to do if the friend is frustrated or upset.

When others push and shove them, does it mean they want to play, they are teasing, or picking a fight? Even if both friends love to rough-house, it is still not appropriate to do during basketball practice or at the dinner table. Again, the appropriateness and meaning of an action will change given the context in which it is occurring. We often must process many variables to judge what to expect and what is expected of us.

Contextual processing allows us to adapt our responses to the unique variables of the situation. As variables change (time, place, people, expectations), we flexibly adapt our responses. The child's behavior will need to flexibly adapt when moving from the hallways at school to the library, and when alone with friends to being in the presence of the peer's parents. Or, it's ok to tease with close friends but not with those less familiar. Whether it is physical setting factors (hallway versus library) or people variables (alone with peers or with adults) we need to process that information quickly and adjust flexibly. Social rules and expectations change across many variables.

Reading context also allows us to generalize and adapt our responses to "same but different" situations. Typically, our social expectations when shopping are similar across most stores; however, whereas we usually can pick up and examine the merchandise in most stores, some stores that have fragile, breakable items often frown at handling the items.

Immediately reading the context allows us to process quickly and rapidly infer what is needed to stay in sync with expectations. Such processing allows us to flexibly change with different expectations and read when change is needed. Within a given event, the variables may change throughout the event, requiring us to adjust our behavior to the expectations.

Perspective taking: reading the mental states of others

In addition to the situational context, the other major struggle for those with autism is reading the thoughts, feelings, perspectives and intentions of others. This is commonly called "theory of mind" in the literature. In the neurotypical world, relating with others is often dependent on people reading the thoughts, feelings, perspectives and intentions of others so they stay coordinated in back and forth, reciprocal interaction.

When we relate, we are often sharing mental and emotional experiences. We intuitively read the facial expressions, tone and intonation of voice, gestures and body language to help grasp what the other is thinking and feeling. This allows us to pattern how to respond and to predict how the other will behave. By doing so, we try to meet both the needs and expectations of the other as well as ourselves. This perspective taking allows us to share common mental and emotional experiences together. This requires processing of multiple information simultaneously. For neurotypicals, the complex dance of sharing mental experiences with others usually occurs intuitively, with minimal conscious effort. This process often is lost for many autistics. It simply requires too much processing of vague, fleeting and fluent information.

How can we help teach strategies for compensating for this difficulty in perspective taking? Since this does not come intuitively for those on the spectrum, it can be constructed cognitively by figuring it out. In the blue book, *The Autism Discussion Page on the Core Challenges of Autism* (Nason 2014a), I outline some simple strategies that can help children to look past the spoken words to read the perspectives of others.

> To effectively relate with others, we must look past the spoken words and "think" about how others are "thinking." Next, based on this appraisal we (1) predict what the person will do, and (2) pattern how we will respond. Ongoing interaction consists of continually thinking about how the other is thinking, predicting his behavior and then patterning our behavior based on this assessment. This ongoing appraising is essential for staying coordinated with others in interaction.
>
> Since children on the spectrum do not think about how others are thinking (or are weak at doing so), they are not using this information to add meaning to what they are saying and doing. They are reacting to what others do literally (say and do), rather than appraising, predicting and projecting what will happen in the interaction.
>
> Teaching the child to look past the literal:
>
> 1. First start with thinking about how others are thinking. Think out loud to model this thinking process for the child. Later, this process can extend to thinking about how others are feeling as well as thinking; connecting how the person may be feeling based on what he is thinking. "I bet Johnny is sad because he thinks Jenny doesn't like him." Many children do not make the connection between their thoughts and feelings. However, this comes later when the child has a good knowledge and language base for identifying and labeling emotions. Unless the child has gained that knowledge, only start with what the other is "thinking."

2. During the day, together watch what others are doing and talk about what is literal (what you see and hear happening); then talk about what the people are thinking. Help the child learn to look at the body language and facial expressions, and what is going on in the situation, that helps us determine what the person is thinking. Do it together, mentoring how you do it. Then talk about what evidence led you to the guess (body language, facial expression, situational factors, etc.). Practice "watch, listen, think (about what they are thinking), and then predict (how they will respond)." Use this "watch, listen, think, predict" model for practicing together.

3. There are numerous ways of practicing this. Go to the mall or park and watch others interacting. First, list what you see and hear (literal), then guess at what they are thinking. From this assessment, predict how they will act based on what they are thinking. You can also do this while watching TV or movies, and while reading stories together. Use picture books so you can discuss how the characters are thinking and use this information to predict how they might respond.

4. Keep it simple at first. Just focus on what the person is thinking. Once they get used to that, then you can move onto what the person is feeling. From there, you can start guessing at what the person's perspectives and intentions are. The final goal, over the long term, is for the child to think about the other person's thoughts, feelings, perspectives, and intentions, and use this appraisal to (1) predict what the person will do, and (2) pattern how they will respond. This process will take years to develop, but each step in that direction is valuable.

5. When making these appraisals, make sure to discuss what evidence they are using to make the guess (facial expressions, body language, actions, situational factors, etc.) This way, when in doubt, they will have a few tools to use to make an appraisal.

6. As the child gets older and more skillful, the appraisals can also include how others think and feel about you and your behavior. "Jim, when you let Johnny borrow your toy truck, how do you think that made him feel?" "Jess, what do you think Tommy was feeling (or thinking) when you took his ball?" This way they can get better at monitoring how others are responding to their actions. This requires more abstract reasoning and can only be mastered after first learning to appraise the perspectives of others.

Make sure to have fun doing this! Get used to "thinking out loud," as you evaluate social situations during the day. The "thinking out loud" strategies can be used to teach the child that people have different thoughts, feelings, and perspectives. (pp.212–214)

I often hear parents report, "My child refuses to see the view of others or listen to what I have to say." One reason is because we do not teach at the best of times. We wait until the heat of the moment, when everyone is upset, to try and teach this (more like talking the kids into it). You cannot teach new learning in the heat of the moment.

Even neurotypical people have difficulty seeing the issue from a different viewpoint when they are emotionally involved in the conflict at the time.

Teaching should begin with situations that do not directly involve the children, so they can observe and learn without direct involvement. Again, this is best taught by either (1) you "thinking out loud' for events you, yourself, are experiencing and/or (2) discussing it together while observing others who are interacting (either in real life or on TV/video.) This way the child is not personally involved and is observing the process as a third person, where there is no emotional investment. This takes many months, if not years, to teach and cannot begin to be used in the heat of the moment.

We think we are teaching when we are scolding, lecturing or even rationally trying to convince the child. These are the times that we think about doing it. However, these are the worst times to try teaching any new learning. Start when the child is not directly involved and gradually build as the skill becomes more instilled. You both will be more patient and happier with the results.

Social context and emotions

Context is very important to interpreting emotions. Crying is a good example. Is she crying because she is sad, happy, frustrated or angry? This is important to know so we can interpret what she is thinking and feeling and pattern how we should respond and predict how she will react. We can only determine this by the situational context that the person is in and the events occurring in that situation. If something really exciting happened to her, we may infer that she is happy. If she is at a funeral, we would most likely infer that she is sad. However, if she is upset because she messed up an important project, crying may be expression of frustration. So, the emotional expression of crying can have very different meanings based on the context in which it is occurring. Without the situational context, we would be left guessing at why the person is crying.

Emotions are very complex and difficult to accurately read for many on the spectrum. This is often interpreted as lack of empathy, but we need to distinguish between emotional empathy and cognitive empathy to get a true understanding.

Three phases of empathy

Empathy is often misunderstood because it is a complex integration of several processes. In a simple form, there are three primary processes to empathy.

1. *Affective empathy.* This is the raw sensory perception of the emotional states of others, often called "emotional auras." This varies individually, but can be very strong for some with autism, much more so than for most neurotypicals. This is thought to be due to the very keen sensory perception of those on the spectrum. Like many animals with this keen sense, many autistics can sense the emotional aura of others, often so strongly that it overwhelms them, especially in groups of people with many emotional auras bombarding them. Sometimes the emotions

are so intense that the person cannot tell if the emotions are coming from others or from within. However, even though they can intensively feel the emotions of others, they often cannot label what the emotion is or why the individual is feeling that way. Since they cannot label and connect the emotions, these intense experiences are often scary and overwhelming.

2. *Cognitive empathy.* Cognitive empathy includes identifying and labeling the emotion, connecting the emotion to the external or internal cause, and gauging the intensity of the emotion. This requires "theory of mind," the ability to infer the thoughts, feelings, perspectives and what the person is experiencing. The two functions that are necessary for this are (1) the ability to read nonverbal cues, especially facial expressions and fluctuations of voice, and (2) the ability to immediately read social context (social event, invisible social norms, interactions with others, time, place, etc.) These two functions are thought to be weaknesses for those on the spectrum.

    Consequentially, those on the spectrum may be over-sensitive to feeling the emotions of others, but unable to identify, label and connect the reason for these emotions unless this is spelled out for them. A lot depends on how obvious the concrete facts are. For example, if someone physically gets a severe cut, this may be easy to cognitively understand, whereas someone having their feelings hurt may be much harder to interpret without being able to read the nonverbal communication and social context.

3. *Sympathy.* Sympathy is the amount of compassion and desire to help the person once they understand what they are experiencing. This is a by-product of combining affective and cognitive empathy. The result is the extent of compassion you feel both for the subjective experiences and external consequences this person is experiencing.

    Feeling sympathy for others varies extensively across all individuals, both on and off the spectrum, but can be much stronger for those with autism. However, they may require someone else to cognitively interpret what the other is mentally experiencing. In other words, once someone explains what the person is mentally experiencing, then those on the spectrum can show strong sympathy. The weak link will be in the cognitive empathy function. People on the spectrum can have strong affective empathy and strong sympathy. The weak link will be in cognitive empathy.

This problem with empathy goes both ways. People on the spectrum have difficulty with cognitive empathy of neurotypical people, primarily because we process and experience the world differently. However, neurotypical people have just as many problems empathizing with people with autism, because they do not understand the mental states and experiences of those on the spectrum. Strong cognitive empathy requires "like" worlds.

Context blindness

Peter Vermeulen, in his book *Autism as Context Blindness* (Vermeulen 2012) does a great job of explaining the importance of being able to read context to understand the thoughts, feelings and actions of others. Social and personal meaning varies based on the context in which the events occur. Therefore, the same response can have different meanings based on the context in which it is occurring. Also, a specific response may be appropriate and successful in one situation, but not in another. Actions of others have different meanings depending on the situations in which they occur. Being able to read the context (surrounding variables that give meaning to a situation) allows us to modify and adapt a response to ever-changing events. No two situations are alike, so flexibility of responding (to match behavior to situational demands) is dependent on rapidly reading the context to guide us in how to respond.

This ability to read context is the brain immediately seeking the overall meaning (central coherence) of a situation to direct our attention to the relevant details. The process of reading context happens in a fraction of a second (instantaneously), before we even recognize any details. It also happens subconsciously, without being aware of the process. Context includes the external (perceptional) characteristics of the situation, as well as the internal context, which is our knowledge from past experiences of similar situations and people involved.

With our example of crying, our interpretation of the emotions of others is not just about reading the facial expression of others. It requires us to intuitively understand the context to give meaning for what we see. Crying can mean different things based on the context. A person can cry when they have just won an Olympic gold medal, when they see something sad happening to another, when fearful, when physically hurt, when angry or simply when cutting an onion. Usually, we instantaneously and intuitively pick up on the context to give immediate meaning to the crying that we are seeing. We never see things literally (in isolation of context).

Another example is a child seeing others smiling at him. If it is a good friend, it will usually mean they enjoy doing things together; if it is the school bully who is cornering him in the hallway, it may represent a threat; and if it is a girl smiling while staring at him in class, it may mean she really "likes" him! These physical smiles have different meanings based on the context (people and situations) for which they occur.

In Peter Vermeulen's book, he summarizes numerous research studies that demonstrate that people on the spectrum have difficulty intuitively reading context, making it difficult to read social situations and the thoughts, feelings and perspectives of others. People with autism can learn to read context but must do so consciously (must think it out). Their brains are not wired to instantaneously perceive the context and immediate meaning of events. Their brains tend to focus on all the details and only by piecing the details into an overall whole does the meaning of the context occur. They can see the overall perceptual picture (concrete image) but not the contextual meaning.

These studies also show that people on the spectrum show good empathy and theory of mind when the context is pointed out to them. This demonstrates how important being able to read context is to understanding social meaning and the thoughts, feelings and perspectives of others. The two primary factors are that people on the spectrum are not wired to instantaneously perceive the meaning of context, and if they learn to look for it, they must consciously figure it out or have it pointed out for them. This results in delayed processing and often the contextual meaning has changed by that time. This important processing difference is what makes it so hard for people on the spectrum living in the neurotypical world. The ability to instantaneously and subconsciously read context allows us to smoothly move through the day, easily adapting our actions to ever-changing social situations. For people on the spectrum, this inability to intuitively read context also explains why navigating social situations is so difficult and exhausting.

With repeated experiences, people on the spectrum can get better at consciously recognizing common contexts, but since each situation is different, they will always be a little out of sync with us.

How can we help?

Where do we go from here? How can we help? With children, parents need to fill in the blanks, connect the dots, so the children better see the big picture. We need to make the abstract, concrete and the invisible, concrete and visible. We need to prepare children before going into events on what they can expect to happen, what is expected of them and then help define both the invisible context (social norms and expectations, purpose of the event, etc.) and the perspectives of others (thoughts, feelings, perspectives and intentions). We must literally describe what we intuitively assume. Pretend that we are the social interpreter for an alien stranger who has no idea of our customs or how we relate. We must paint the big picture, define the plot and provide the hidden meaning behind what we are doing.

Parents need to be social interpreters and coaches for their children. People with autism need to learn how to analytically define what we process intuitively, like "social scientists," consciously observing and analyzing the facts to define underlying meaning. They need to learn how to ask, "What is the purpose of this event?" "What are the prescribed norms, expectations and social rules for this event?" "From what people are saying and doing, what are the perspectives of the people participating (or person they are talking to)?" What we do intuitively, they need to literally define before jumping in and participating.

Prepare by previewing

Until the child becomes more competent socially, we must define the social context for him. Before entering social events, we need to preview (1) what the child can expect to happen, (2) what is expected of him, (3) any specific dos and don'ts, and (4) discuss any specific challenges (sensory, social, emotional) that may arise. We must define the context of each situation, what is going to happen, what the common goals are of the event (why we are here) and any specific dos and don'ts for that event. Define any social norms or unwritten rules and why they exist. Children hate stepping into uncertainty.

It makes them very anxious. The more we prepare them for what to expect and what is expected of them (say, do, not do), the better mental map they have to guide them. Without this mental map, they are either anxious and apprehensive, or have their own expectations that often fail once in the event. Without this mental map, children begin to struggle, become confused and angry, and are likely to respond negatively.

Ways to preview

1. *Visual strategies.* For younger children and those with limited communication skills, we can assist understanding by using pictures to help define the sequence of events. This works especially well for common, reoccurring events. For example, if the child is going to a family holiday gathering, a one-page picture sequence of four to six photos outlining the order of events can assist parents in previewing the outing before attending. The child or parent can also carry it with them to refer to during the event. Parents will need to call ahead to gain knowledge of what is expected to happen.

2. *Videos.* There are numerous YouTube videos that provide good tutorials of events, anything from going to the dentist, birthday parties, grocery shopping, flying in an airplane and interacting with authorities. The parents and child can watch them together, going over details, social norms, expectations and concerns of the child. One family was very concerned about taking their child to Disney World. They outlined the schedule of events they would attend each day and were able to find YouTube videos of each ride and event. Watching these ahead of time and downloading some to take with them gave their child a clear image of what to expect. This lowered his anxiety and the vacation was a success.

3. *Social stories.* Social stories are short narratives, sometimes including pictures that are great for teaching social context, hidden meanings and the thoughts, feelings and perspectives of others. The following is a simple story used to teach a child that teachers talk to and help other children, not just her. She was becoming distracted by the teacher attending to others and tried to interrupt and monopolize the teacher's attention.

> My teacher talks to many people.
>
> Sometimes she talks to me.
>
> She gives me directions and helps me with my work.
>
> Sometimes she talks to other people.
>
> She might talk to other children about their work.
>
> She might talk to another adult.
>
> It is ok when she talks to other people.

When my teacher talks to other people I should keep working or playing.

This will make my teacher happy.

I will try to keep working or playing when my teacher talks to other people.

Social stories are non-threatening and good for teaching specific social behavior and situational context. The child also learns how others may be thinking and reacting to his behavior. There are numerous resources (online and books), that provide large stocks of social stories for most situations and social rules. Simply Google social stories and the topic you are interested in.

4. *Previewing worksheet.* As children get older, it becomes important to teach them how to preview in preparation for going to events. Using a simple worksheet can help outline what the context of the event is, what to expect and what may be expected of them.

Define the event (party, concert, dance, etc.).

What can be expected to happen (sequence of events, people who will be there, etc.)?

What is expected of me (sit quietly, interact, dance, take turns, etc.)?

Common do's and don'ts (rules and boundaries)?

Any anticipated challenges (sensory, communication, social, etc.)? How to cope?

At first, do the outline with the child to assist and pinpoint areas that need to be defined. As the child becomes older and more competent, play less of a role as he begins to preview events naturally on his own.

It helps to know what types of conversations may arise, and preview what topics to build conversation around. For social events with common rituals (birthday parties, church, family gatherings, etc.), practice by rehearsing and role-playing possible interactions that may occur. If the event is new, and you have time, it helps to visit the setting to provide a visual of the physical context. If the situation is a re-occurring event, such as dance lessons, scouts, sports, take the child to observe once or twice before participating. Talk about what everyone is doing, the norms of the activities and what will be expected. Of course, such preparation is not possible for every social event, but the more preparation that can occur, the better.

Once a mental map is outlined, then try to discuss what problems may arise and possible ways of handling them. Having pre-planned strategies for possible challenges helps reduce anxiety and can aid when struggles occur. These might consist of pulling oneself away when overwhelmed, using sensory tools to minimize overload and setting scripts to excuse oneself for a short break.

Autistic adults also need to prepare themselves before entering social situations. Many visit the settings ahead of time to get an idea of what the setting looks like, talk to people to define what to expect and what will be expected of them, and rehearse what they will say and do before going. This can be exhausting, but is a needed tool until events become familiar for them. Most adults learn to stay within familiar settings (same grocery store, gas station, post office, etc.) where they have compiled working contexts they can more easily navigate.

Good preparation and previewing are so important for autistics to connect the dots and piece together social context and expectations, especially for events that are not familiar. Without that mental map, they are often confused and lost in social situations. Get them started early in life by collaborating with them to prepare for events, previewing the context, what they can expect and what is expected of them.

Navigating in events

Once in events, we need to teach children how to analytically read situations. They must learn to be social scientists: What is happening? What do we see and hear? What do we already know from past experiences (social rules, expectations from similar situations)? What can we infer and predict will happen? Be a social interpreter and help them learn to "size up" situations. Make the invisible, visible. When first entering events, spend some time standing back, analyzing the situation. Discuss what you see happening, what others are doing and what the common goals and norms are. As a social scientist, teach them to look at the facts (what they see and hear), piece them together with what we already know and then predict what will happen. Do it together, modeling how it is done, and helping them paint a mental picture.

Together, observe what is happening, guess what people are thinking and feeling, what is intended and predict what will happen. Have fun collecting facts, inferring meaning, making predictions and then sitting back to see what occurs. Pretend that you are strangers in a strange land and learn to observe, figure out and predict what is happening. From what you observe from the interactions (what is said, body language, facial expressions, context, etc.), try to predict the thoughts, feelings, perspectives and intentions of others in the setting.

Becoming a social interpreter

The social world will always be a mystery for most people on the spectrum. As they become older, they must learn to be skillful investigators. However, until then, parents and other mentors need to be their social interpreters and trusted guides. Social learning is a lifelong endeavor, an accumulation of thousands of learning experiences. What we process intuitively, they must learn concretely through accumulated experiences. Together, help them interpret:

- social norms and unwritten rules

- thoughts, feelings, perspectives and intentions of others

- what to expect of others, and what is expected of them

- social context that defines expectations

- how behavior can be appropriate in one setting, but not another

- the effect their behavior has on others.

Stay with the children and provide coaching and guided participation during social events. Help them learn to observe and analyze first, then participate. Then when they are engaging, provide cues on how others are reacting and how to respond. Make it fun, take notes, compare findings and allow the child to "figure it out" with your guidance.

You can practice these skills in several different learning situations: (1) being passive observers in real-life situations, standing off to one side, analyzing without participating, (2) watching television, movies or YouTube videos, and (3) reading stories together while discussing what is occurring, inferring perspectives of others, predicting what will happen. Everyday community activities (shopping, library, post office, social gatherings, recreational activities, etc.) become platforms for observing, inferring and predicting what happens. Make sure to have fun doing it, laugh when wrong and congratulate yourself when guessing right.

In summary, navigating social situations requires the ability to read the invisible context that provides meaning to the event and defines what is expected, and the ability to read the thoughts, feelings, perspectives and intentions of those participating. Context and perspective taking are the two processes that are intuitive for us, but not for people with autism. What we infer intuitively, they need to literally think through and figure out. This can be time consuming and exhausting. Over time, with repeated experiences in common situations, they become better at observing, inferring and predicting— connecting the dots to define the plots. However, always be cognizant of how exhausting this is. Keep socializing brief, never pressure engagement and allow the person plenty of time to recover. Adults on the spectrum need to balance how much socializing they can comfortably handle and provide themselves with as much isolation as needed to regroup and rebound. Respect their comfort zones and stay within their tolerance levels.

This chapter was not meant to provide a toolbox of strategies for all the common social challenges autistics face. For those who are looking for such step-by-step guidelines, please refer to the blue book, *The Autism Discussion Page on the Core Challenges of Autism* (Nason 2014a).

Chapter 15

THE COSTS OF FITTING IN

Socializing is exhausting!

In Chapter 2, we discussed in detail how many on the spectrum have difficulty rapidly processing multiple information simultaneously, especially when it applies to fleeting information that is continually changing. This processing difference underlies many of the struggles socializing has for people with autism. The social processing of our neurotypical world requires integrating multiple information simultaneously, information that is often vague and fleeting.

The simple act of interacting with another requires simultaneously processing the following:

- Listening to and interpreting the spoken words (what are they saying?).

- Interpreting nonverbal communication (facial expressions, body language, voice fluctuations, etc.).

- Reading thoughts, feelings, perspectives and intentions of others (what do they mean, what do they want?).

- Understanding the context and social expectations of the situation (social rules, norms, etc.).

- Deciding how to respond (what do I want to say, how to say it, does it apply?).

- Referencing the other's feedback to our response (did they understand me, are they interested, am I offending them?).

- Staying coordinated in the back and forth flow of interaction (knowing how to initiate, coordinate, maintain and expand on the rapid shifting during conversations).

All relating consists of simultaneously processing all this information, much of which is rapidly changing as the conversation flows. For neurotypical people, most of this information is processed subconsciously with minimal thought. We intuitively pick up and assimilate the information without thinking of it, requiring minimal mental energy.

For autistics, much of this information is not processed intuitively or simultaneously. They must consciously process and interpret this information sequentially—thinking it through, connecting the dots. What did he say? What does he mean? How do I respond? What words do I use? Did he understand me? They must think it through, consciously connecting the dots. This can be very draining and exhausting. It takes a lot of concentration and mental energy. Since conversations often move very quickly, for many autistics, by the time they have it adequately processed and have formulated an answer, the conversation has moved on to a different topic.

Even if these people can process and interpret some of the information, it is often not enough to successfully grasp the meaning, leaving them out of sync or off kilter from the ebb and flow of the conversation and having to guess at what is expected, often guessing wrongly.

It becomes obvious that socializing would be very taxing if we did not process all this information intuitively and simultaneously. For many on the spectrum, trying to join in and regulate and maintain conversations renders socializing very draining. It simply taxes all their mental energy.

For some, moving from simple one-on-one interaction to group events can be very difficult to regulate. Parties, family gatherings and other group events are not just exhausting but overwhelming. Trying to navigate the sensory and social demands of group gatherings can be so overwhelming that the person emotionally crumbles. Many autistics are very sensitive to the emotional aura of others, so the swirl of emotions emitted in group settings can overwhelm and incapacitate them. They report being so hyper-sensitive to the emotions emitted by others that they cannot concentrate and feel smothered and frightened. They often cannot distinguish between their own emotions and the emotional swirl in the room. It is overwhelming and sometimes very frightening.

Since interaction can be chaotic and confusing, and they do not want to stand out or offend, interacting can create intense anxiety, which inhibits their processing even further. When you often misinterpret, unintentionally offend, and frequently miscue, you're left feeling anxious and insecure. Social anxiety is very high for many autistics.

Many autistic adults report continually worrying about offending others. Because the actions of autistics are often interpreted as rude, controlling or indifferent, others are confused or offended. The autistic adult often picks up on the negative reactions but does not understand why or how to improve it. This ongoing negative feedback creates strong social anxiety. For many, it is often easier not to socialize, so they avoid trying to fit in and isolate themselves, if not because of the anxiety, then for the simple fact that socializing is too exhausting. It's just not worth it.

Because it is so hard to relate spontaneously, many people prepare ahead of time what to expect and what will be asked and expected of them, rehearsing what to say and anticipating what troubles may arise. Some spend hours to days preparing for an upcoming social event—what topics might come up, how to introduce and initiate conversations and how to navigate the event without standing out or offending others. Their strong social anxiety drives a greater need to anticipate and prepare for all possible scenarios, to role-play and practice social scripts for interactions they might encounter and to figure out how to mask their autistic tendencies. This can be emotionally draining.

What can we do to help?

In the blue book, *The Autism Discussion Page on the Core Challenges of Autism* (Nason 2014a), I provide a wide variety of strategies to help people with autism navigate our social world. In this chapter, the primary purpose is to emphasize how stressful and exhausting socializing can be, which significantly adds to the daily mental and emotional drain. Given the taxing nature of socializing, we need to be cognizant of what people with autism experience and learn to balance social exposure to the person's tolerance level. Socializing is a great source of mental drain but is a manageable one if we respect the processing needs of the individual. The following recommendations can help lessen the drain, and all require us to respect the person's social interest, preferences and tolerance for socializing.

1. *Match exposure to social interest.* The greatest mistake many parents make is pushing socializing too much and too fast. Because they highly value friends and socializing, they want their children to have friends and be social. The amount of social exposure should be, in part, driven by the child's social interest. Some children have a strong social interest, but weak relating skills. These children want to be frequently socializing, even if it overwhelms them. They need frequent social exposure but keep it simple and brief so as not to extend their processing abilities. In turn, there are many kids on the spectrum who are more introverted and have a low interest in having friends and socializing. Do not force these children into social activities. Keep socializing light and focus around preferred interests and daily community activities. As they get older, many will enjoy communicating with others online. The internet has provided many teens and adults with a social network that they feel safe with. Always work with the individual to stay within their comfort zones. They may choose to expand their social interests as they feel safer and more competent socializing.

2. *Keep it simple, keep it brief.* The next mistake parents often make is throwing the children into unstructured play situations (playground, parties, etc.) with little support and facilitation. For most children, regulating the sensory and social interaction is far too overwhelming for them. For young children, keep socializing to individual play dates with adult supervision to facilitate cooperative play. Try to have the school avoid pressing the child into multiple peer activities without an adult facilitating the interaction. As the child's relating skills increase, gradually expand the size, length and complexity of the socializing. Observe and listen to the child. Does he appear to be having fun or is he withdrawn and avoiding his peers? Is he regulating the back and forth play effectively? How are his peers responding? Keep the complexity of socializing to the child's current skill level.

   Also remember that family events, holiday gatherings, birthday parties and other large social gatherings can be very taxing and overwhelming for the child. Do not pressure the child into lengthy events because we wish to socialize longer. Keep exposure brief with minimal demands and allow the child to leave early. Respect his tolerance level.

3. *Peer training.* We make the mistake of thinking that autistic children are the only ones who need to learn how to relate. We also need to teach their neurotypical peers how to play with the child as much as teaching the child how to play with them. Socializing is a two-way street. The child's peers need a general awareness of how to understand the autistic child and how to help facilitate interaction. I was surprised to see how little training this requires. Children just need to know why the child with autism is acting in certain ways and how to help include the child. This will require an adult facilitating and coaching everyone involved. Successful integration requires everyone to learn.

4. *Minimize the need to mask or suppress autistic mannerisms.* As we will discuss below, feeling pressured to suppress your natural mannerisms (e.g. self-stimulation, avoiding eye contact, repetitive behaviors), is very draining. These behaviors are used to regulate arousal level and reduce anxiety. They are part of who the person is. When providing peer training, make sure to explain why the unique mannerisms are important for your child so that peers understand why he does them. Kids are a lot more tolerant when they understand the need for behavior differences. We want the child to feel safe with his own natural mechanisms for regulating. This will drastically minimize the drain.

5. *Tailor socializing around common interests.* Many children with autism have very strong, fixated interests. Socializing is much easier when it is focused around the person's favorite interest. It gives them a topic they feel competent socializing with. They can tailor the socializing around what they know. Of course, adult facilitation is often needed to coach the kids along, since the autistic child may dominate the conversation and activity. Video games, Lego projects, photography, animation, trains and so forth are common interests that many kids enjoy. There are many clubs tailored around these common interests.

6. *Balance social events with down time.* Socializing is draining, even if they are having fun. Remember to provide plenty of time to relax and regroup following social events. The longer and more complex the social demands, the greater the amount of downtime needed. Work with your child to let him pace how much socializing and downtime are needed. It is important to both minimize the duration of socializing to avoid over-tasking the child, as well as provide enough downtime for him to regroup and rebound.

7. *Minimize unstructured social events.* If possible, try to keep early socializing to structured activities, with well-defined topics, concrete rules and predictable interactions. Having a clear goal, set guidelines and predictable interactions can make socializing much easier. Free play situations (playground, recess, unstructured playgroups, etc.) are too chaotic and confusing for young children to regulate. They have no rules or guidelines on how to regulate on-the-fly interactions; it is simply too much to process.

8. *Peer mentors.* Many school districts have started peer mentor programs, beginning in middle school. Neurotypical peers are paired with the children with autism to help them navigate socializing at school. The peer mentors model age-appropriate social skills, help interpret the unwritten social norms, facilitate inclusion at school events (dances, sporting events, assemblies, etc.), and help protect the children from bullies. The best peer mentor usually includes two to three friends who know each other and hang out together; this is great learning for all participants.

9. *Don't forget autistic friends.* It is a mistake to only involve neurotypical children when looking for friends and social groups. The children should have ongoing exposure to other children with autism (especially with similar interests), as well as autistic adult role models. They relate on the same level, there is less needing to pretend or suppress their autism, and the socializing is less draining. Look for local recreational and leisure clubs for autistic children and ask the teachers at school for kids who could connect as friends. Children with autism should not be isolated from each other and can develop strong support groups. This helps facilitate friends who can last a lifetime.

10. *Prepare before events.* Before entering events, prepare by previewing what the child can expect to happen, what is expected of him and any anticipated challenges that may arise. This makes socializing more predictable and less stressful. Discuss the implied norms of the event. You can also rehearse and practice any common interactions as well as discuss what problems might arise. This should be done even if there will be an adult available to facilitate.

11. *Identify an escape route.* Always have a planned means of escape if the situation starts to become overwhelming. Work with the child to plan how to handle situations that may overwhelm them (pull back, withdraw to the bathroom or quiet area, go for a walk, etc.) and identify a plan of escape if things become overwhelming and they must leave.

12. *Develop good self-care skills.* As these children age, it is important for them to know what their vulnerabilities are, what activities tax them, how to monitor their energy drain and how to advocate for accommodations they need. These self-care skills are necessary for older children to begin to monitor their own physical, social and emotional needs.

With the above considerations, socializing can be safe and fun for autistic children. We must respect their wishes, identify their comfort zones (what type of socializing, for how long and with what supports) and allow them a voice in all social exposure. This will help reduce the anxiety, lower stress and maximize success. Parents must be aware of what types of relating their child feels comfortable with, how long he can safely socialize and how to balance socializing with downtime. In turn, autistic adults need to define their comfort zones, identify accommodations to better navigate social situations, not over-extend themselves and allow plenty of recovery time.

The price of conforming

If you talk to adults on the spectrum, they will tell you that the number one stressor and greatest drain is pressure to conform to our social norms. The pressure to "appear neurotypical" and suppress their autistic tendencies can have disastrous effects. First, it is exhausting to suppress the very mannerisms that help them regulate, deny what they need to feel safe, act in ways that are counter to their nature and pretend to be interested in the small talk and interpersonal topics that many neurotypicals find interesting. Second, the constant worry of fitting in and not offending others (that comes from years of negative reactions and rejection) intensifies anxiety and greatly inhibits any enjoyment from socializing. Third, the social invalidation and pretending to be neurotypical is demeaning to their very nature. Fourth, in the midst of denying their autism and pretending to be neurotypical, many autistics lose their self-identity and their sense of self-worth. According to adult autistics, this pressure to fit in, conform, suppress their autism and pretend to be neurotypical is the number one factor resulting in burnout in later years.

Autistic adults have coined the word, "masking" to refer to the need to suppress their autistic tendencies (mannerisms, preferences, sensory vulnerabilities, etc.) and pretend to be normal (copying the actions and social scripts of non-autistics). Not only is this stressful and draining, it is also oppressive and demeaning.

Copying, mimicking, masking, all to conform! Many use the phrase, "Fake it to make it." Faking who you are, masking what you do, pretending to be what you are not, all take their toll over time. This is invalidating, demeaning and self-harming, especially when the child internalizes, "I am bad, broken, unworthy, of no value as I am! I must suppress 'me' and pretend to be 'them.'"

Actor without a script

In the blue book, *The Autism Discussion Page on the Core Challenges of Autism* (Nason 2014a), I make an analogy of an actor without a script.

Autism is like being an actor in a play, with no prepared script!

Adults with autism learn how to be effective actors, often living in pretense in an effort to fit in, or at least not stand out. When it is difficult to grasp the unwritten social rules around you, understand the thoughts, feelings, and perspectives of those you are with, and rapidly process the conversation occurring around you, you often must "pretend" to understand, fit in, and blend in with others.

For many people on the spectrum, to be successful they learn to "imitate" those around them. When entering a social event, they immediately scan those around them to see how they are acting. From this they learn to copy their behavior after what they see others doing, so they can blend in. If the conversation is with one person only, they may be able to regulate it well, but if the conversation is between several people, the children get lost very quickly. For people on the spectrum to be successful in such situations, they must become very clever social scientists, often copying behavior which they don't understand. As years go by, they accumulate a lot of "scripts," which they can adapt to many situations. They learn scripts for introducing themselves, topics for small talk, being pleasant, etc. The older they get, the more situations they experience, the better they get at it.

However, this "social acting" takes its toll over time. Socially, the person cannot be himself; he must fake it! Since we develop a sense of self from our relations with others, masking (not being yourself) tears at their self-identity and self-esteem. When you must pretend all the time, you get anxious, angry, and depressed. It is also very draining. Even for those who are good at it, trying to "copy" others requires extensive mental energy and can only be done for short periods of time. (pp. 206–207)

Difference between copying and masking

Copying is a learning tool by which we observe others engaging in a behavior and learn to copy that action. We match our behavior to that of a model. Copying (imitation) is a great social learning tool for acquiring new social skills that help all of us fit into our society. We watch those who are socializing successfully and try to copy those behaviors and characteristics that seem to work well for them. Copying is also used very frequently by children with autism, but the difference is they do not always understand the meaning behind the behaviors, when to effectively use them and which behaviors to imitate (often copying negative behaviors that they see peers getting attention for). Copying is a good strategy, but the child must learn how, when and with whom to use it. In the blue book, *The Autism Discussion Page on the Core Challenges of Autism* (Nason 2014a), I go into detail about how to use copying effectively and how to protect the child from imitating the wrong behaviors.

It is important to distinguish between copying, as a learning tool, and "masking." With masking, the person is suppressing his autistic tendencies (mannerisms, interests, coping skills) plus pretending to be someone he is not. He is pretending by not just copying behavior but internalizing the values that his autism is deficient and defective and that being neurotypical is the goal, feeling the pressure to conform and pretending to be neurotypical to avoid scorn and self-depreciation. In some cases, children learn to despise their own autism and mask it at all costs. This is dangerous and traumatic. Over time, through masking and pretending, they lose their own sense of self (self-identity), become depressed and burn out.

Do not feel that copying is bad and to be discouraged. Encourage its use as a good learning tool; however, continually discuss with these children how they are using it, how to use it effectively and when and what to copy. Make sure to distinguish that copying is a way to learn new skills, not to become someone different. Teach them to value their unique differences, processing style and preferences, allowing them to feel good about themselves and their differences. Learning social behaviors that help them co-exist in our social world is good, if they do not feel the need to suppress and deny their own identity and unique qualities.

Fitting in

To summarize, trying to fit in to our social world is one of the biggest stressors for many on the spectrum. Trying to appraise what is needed, copy and imitate others, understand hidden social context, guess at what others want, and still be out of sync with others is exhausting and often invalidating. When you cannot adequately appraise social context, read the thoughts, feelings and intentions of others, and understand the invisible social rules, you are always left guessing, responding haphazardly and often missing the mark. Then the looks, scorn, disgust and rude remarks of others are invalidating and discouraging. You try and try to fit in, but don't quite "get it." You can beat your head against the wall only so long before you become exhausted and worn out. You try so hard learning to "act like them" that you lose your own sense of self. You give up and isolate yourself, while depression and despair set in.

Not only do you struggle to "fit in" with others, but you must adapt to a sensory world of fast-paced activity, strong insulting noises, intense smells and glaring lights that overload your vulnerable nervous system. You are stuck in our fast-paced culture that requires multi-tasking, overwhelming information and activities. You push yourself into events that leave you exhausted and feeling defeated. You feel angry and inadequate at the same time, screaming for the world to slow down, recognize your challenges and bend a little bit. Many adults eventually become so taxed and drained that it affects their mental, emotional and physical health, and they suffer extreme burnout!

Finding the right balance (adults and children)

When you experience autism, you are always out of sync with the world around you. Every day takes more mental and physical energy to simply regulate normal daily demands than it does for neurotypical people. Dealing with the sensory assaults, task demands and social challenges requires constant multi-tasking that your nervous system is often incapable of. It is inevitable and will continue for the rest of your life. If you try too hard to "fit in," you will become exhausted and eventually burn out. Both your mental and physical health will suffer. You must find a balance between "fitting in" and maintaining personal stability. To do this, you have to understand what your skills and vulnerabilities are (sensory, social, emotional, etc.) and what you truly desire and value (not what society wants you to value). You must know yourself (strengths and weaknesses) and know what you want (preferences and desires). From there, you must find the "just right" balance between fitting in enough to meet daily social and work demands, and maximizing your strengths, accommodating for your vulnerabilities and protecting your preferences and desires.

What does all this mean? Socially, just like all of us, people on the spectrum have widely different levels of social interest. Some crave friends and social connections and others are more introverted and not really interested in relationships other than common acquaintances they experience in their daily routines. If you are not that interested in relationships, then be true to that. Learn enough social rules to maintain and regulate through your daily routine, until you can escape to your world patterned around your own needs and desires. Even if you desire a lot of social contact, realize how draining it will be and hold yourself to what you can realistically handle. Be true to your nervous system (physical, mental and emotional needs). Do not push yourself to stay in social situations, and regulate group events if they totally exhaust you. Not only will your coping skills deteriorate the more you become taxed, but your emotional stability will also suffer. Pace yourself and keep true to both your desires and your capabilities.

If you are not socially driven, then learn the needed social graces for getting by. Realize that others may think that you appear cold and indifferent, but that is inevitable and simply a fact of life. Go to work, shop, meet your community needs as necessary, and then pattern your home life to match your basic nature. When choosing work, make sure you pick jobs that match your strengths and desires, while accommodating for your vulnerabilities. Do not put yourself in work environments that challenge all your vulnerabilities and minimize your strengths. Know what you can handle and match your work around that. Advocate for what you need and build in supports to help you get there. It often requires changing jobs several times until you find a match that you can handle.

Identify what types of social contacts (close friends, social events, love and marriage, etc.) you desire and how much contact you can handle. If you don't desire a lot of social contact, do not do it! Don't push yourself past this. It is not worth it. If all you can handle is brief one-on-one contact, and no group events, then limit yourself to what you desire and can handle. You don't have to be a social butterfly to have quality of life. Quality of life is not defined by others but by what you desire. In addition, although you can choose how much to disclose about your condition and vulnerabilities in the roles you play, make sure your close friends, spouse and family understand exactly how you are and what you need. Do not hide your autism from people close to you. You need to feel safe and accepted for exactly who you are, with all your strengths and quirks. You need to be able to feel supported by those close to you and "be yourself." Do not hide yourself. This is so important for you to regroup and re-energize for the time spent regulating in the outside world, and to maintain your emotional and physical health.

Find that balance to what you can handle in the outside world to "make it," while maintaining your safety net at home. Be true to your personal needs and desires, while learning the basic social rules for making it through the daily demands outside your sanctuary. Only marry and have children if that is what you truly desire, and then be very up front with what you need to make it through these demands. They will be exhausting. Don't hide the support and help you will need, and build the required expectations up front, so everyone is clear. If others don't accept you for who you are, then reconsider how much contact you will have with them. I know this is not always possible but try to maintain some degree of support around you. When all else fails, always have your little "safe area" where you can escape to, self-isolate, and regroup. Always save time for your special interests that help you calm and organize.

Find the "just right" balance and your life will be more enjoyable!

Being yourself while fitting into society

Below, one mother from our Facebook page shares a concern common to many parents.

> As the mom of a little boy with autism—I am very pro stimming, letting him be himself, cope how he needs to cope while gently assisting him in the world around him. I don't want him to feel like he needs to fit into a certain box. Then I worry I'm not pushing him enough to prepare him for a world that doesn't understand him. Trying to find a balance. I always try to seek out experiences of other people with autism. Your thoughts please?

AUTISM DISCUSSION PAGE

Sure, you must play that balance, providing exposure and teaching skills to live in our society. That includes stretching comfort zones and playing roles with a public face. However, it is also about respecting the child's identity and allowing them to be themselves at home and to learn how to meet their own needs while fitting into society. You can do both. We all learn to play our daily roles and the social rules that go along with them. However, we also keep our own individual identities. Those on the spectrum are often unintentionally taught that they are broken and learn to suppress their individuality while taking on pretense all their life. It leads to burnout, despair and total exhaustion. So yes, provide safe exposure and teach social skills but also respect and teach the child that his individual differences are good and how to meet his own needs. This protects their self-esteem.

And yes, seeking out experiences of others on the spectrum is a great idea. Just be aware that there are many shades to autism and their experiences may not match the needs of your own child. Given that, they all can give you a good idea of the struggles and devastations they experience with trying to pretend to be neurotypical. There are many Facebook pages and internet blogs by autistic adults that can be of great benefit for both parents and the teens/young adults with autism. It is important for these kids to have role models, learn about their own identities, learn coping skills from those who live it and learn how to protect their autistic identity.

Protecting self-identity

For parents, here are some recommendations to help establish strong self-identities and foster positive self-esteem.

1. *Make home the safe-haven.* As with all children, we need to teach the basic social skills, norms and expectations so that they can comfortably co-exist in our social world. Being in the external world will inevitably be taxing and draining for them. However, once home they should feel free to be themselves with people who value their autism and who they are, as they are. Teach them that society will

not always understand, but that they are valued by those who love and respect them. Home should always be a safe-haven, a place where they feel safe, accepted and respected.

2. *Build a small network of supportive family and friends.* We all can handle adversity when we have at least a few close people who accept, value and respect us for who we are. Parents need to ensure that those who step inside the home accept and respect the child, differences and all. Those who do not should not be invited. Parents also need to feel this acceptance and respect. Your home is your fortress; only supportive people are invited. You and your child's preferences, sensitivities, and values are not to be questioned in your home. Next, try and find a few others (family members, friends, etc.) outside the home with whom you can safely socialize. Joining a local autism support group can often bring families together who are traveling the same journey.

3. *Teach your child about his own autism.* It is important that your child learns about his own autism. This includes learning about autism in general as well as how it is expressed in him. This includes all the sensitivities, weaknesses, strengths and preferences. There are many good books written to explain autism to children. Most families find it beneficial to read a few of these books with their children to facilitate a discussion about autism and their unique qualities. It is very important that they learn to appreciate and value their own strengths (fixated interests, eye for detail, warm acceptance of others, memory of facts, strong commitment to what they believe, etc.). Talk freely about autism, validating their frustrations, but focusing on their strengths.

4. *Compensate for weaknesses while fostering strengths and preferences.* Autism will usually require accommodations to help support any sensitivities and weaknesses. While doing that, turn the bulk of your attention to fostering the child's strengths and preferences. Many have strong fixated interests that should not be discouraged, but valued and fostered. Whether it is trains, faucets, baseball statistics, fans or video games, you can become involved with them, marvel at what they value and use these interests to build further skills. Regardless of how weird or insignificant an interest seems, it can be of great value to the child, a strong means for child and parent to bond around and a good tool for building learning experiences. A restrictive interest in faucets can be fun to research all the different types, functions, history of development, costs, companies who make them, categorize and experiment with different types. You will find it fun, validating for your child and it will foster his commitment to things that he values. Autism presents new ways of experiencing the world. We need to embrace these differences and grow with them.

5. *Find autistic role models.* Look for autistic adult role models who can help teach your child about the autism culture and to take pride in who they are. There are good books about autistics who are artists, scientists, engineers, computer

specialists and so on, as well as autistics who share how they navigate life and cope with their struggles. They are very good mentors for your children. Look in your area for any adult autistics who are mentors for children. As they get older, there are many adult blogs online that provide a supportive network for autistics. It is important not to isolate children from their own culture. This culture will be important for them as they mature into adulthood. More and more adults with autism are going into counseling and social work to help provide direction to both the children and their families; they make excellent guides.

6. *Include autistic peers.* As stated earlier, if possible, try to establish relationships with other kids on the spectrum. Look for peers at school, network with families from a local autism support group and join recreational activities or clubs for autistic children. It is important for the children to have some peers who relate on the same level, who accept and value their common traits and are compassionate about their favorite interests. Inclusion is good, but do not segregate them from their own peers.

7. *From an early age, be a working partner with your children.* Give them a voice, listen to their concerns, include them in the decision making and teach them to advocate for their needs. The more empowered they feel in what, when and how things go, the less anxious and more competent they feel. Yes, they need to learn that life is going to have some struggles, but also that they can take responsibility for understanding and advocating for what they need to protect their positive identity.

My intent in this chapter was not to discourage parents from encouraging their children to socialize, but to understand how draining it can be; to stay within the children's comfort zones and work together with them to build safe, social exposure; to teach them to value who they are and not to feel the need to deny their own autism; to learn how to "fit in" while protecting their self-identity.

Chapter 16

LIVING WITH EXECUTIVE DYSFUNCTION

Lost without a mental map!

How can I be so smart, yet so lost? How can I have a high intelligence, but lack the ability to organize my life and navigate my world? When I watch everyone around me, they are floating through their day, navigating the maze and never missing a beat. They know where they are going, how to get there, and how to navigate the daily snags and social distractions along the way. They seem to have an intuitive sense or mental map of how to get to and through their daily routine. They all seem to connect and relate with one another like they have a common goal, even though their frivolous small talk seems to have no purposeful meaning. People move so fast, bouncing from one thing to another, navigating through their invisible map. They know when to turn, when to brake, when to focus and when to chat. I am so lost in understanding how they navigate this. How do they shuffle through the maze, not getting lost and loving the chaos that engulfs their day?

Why do I not have this "mental map?" I can know what I want to do, but seem lost in getting it done. I can define a goal but can't seem to organize myself to get there. I solve complex computer problems, envision detailed mechanical designs, spit out impressive historical facts, but cannot clean my house, get to work on time or organize my work to make project deadlines. I have a hard time paying my bills, getting myself neatly dressed and remembering to make my doctor's appointment. I have no sense of time. Jobs I think will only take me an hour can take me a whole day to complete. I start many tasks without completing them and never seem to get back to them. I have good intentions but seem to get stuck before I get started. If I do plan, it completely falls apart as soon as an unexpected snag occurs.

I simply cannot connect the dots to define the plots that make up the lives of others. I can't keep up and I become overwhelmed by all the chaos and confusion around me. There is too much uncertainty that I cannot read or grasp to provide me with a vision. Somehow others have this mental map that guides them fluently through the day. Without this, I am lost and vulnerable. I am anxious and on guard. I fall apart easily and isolate to recover. Sometimes I crash and become almost immobile for days. I may not get out of bed when I need to escape. The mental and emotional drain of trying to navigate without a map is exhausting. It is so much easier to simply withdraw and avoid. But I can't; I will keep stumbling around until I find my way. I hope I will not get hurt in doing so. If I could only connect the dots to define the plots, life would be so much easier!

Executive dysfunction: the hidden disability

The inability to plan, organize, initiate, monitor and complete functional daily activities is one of the greatest disabilities in autism. No matter how bright, intelligent and seemingly capable someone appears, the inability to organize their skills to effectively navigate daily demands can be greatly hampered by an often-misunderstood brain wiring weakness called executive dysfunction. This is the area of the brain that helps organize all our brain functions to coordinate goal-oriented behavior. It is often called the conductor of our intentional actions. Just like an orchestra, it can be filled with very talented musicians, but that talent needs to be coordinated by the orchestra's conductor. It's the same with sports teams. A team can have numerous talented players but needs the coach to coordinate that talent into great team execution. Without the conductor or coach coordinating these splinter skills into collective, goal-oriented action, successful execution becomes difficult.

This characteristic of autism is less talked about but is probably the number one deficit that restricts independent living for otherwise very capable people. These brain functions are taken for granted by those with strong executive functions, so everyone assumes that very bright and capable autistic people should also have them. When these individuals cannot complete simple daily tasks, get lost trying to organize work or school activities, forget to change their clothes or take a shower, lose or forget things, they are often viewed as lazy, indifferent, or defiant. "Of course, they can, they're bright!" You can have all the skills in the world, but if you do not have the conductor to organize them into goal-oriented action, they become practically useless.

What is executive dysfunction?

In the blue book, *The Autism Discussion Page on the Core Challenges of Autism* (Nason 2014a), I summarize executive dysfunction problems as follows:

> The pre-frontal cortex of the brain holds what is called the executive functioning skills. These skills allow us to attend to what is important, inhibit our impulses, think before acting, and evaluate the consequences of our behavior. It also allows us to break a task down, evaluate options, plan and organize a course of action, monitor what we are doing as we do it, and evaluate the effectiveness of our actions. These skills also allow us to hold several things in our short-term memory so we multi-task several tasks at one time. The executive functions area of the brain is the "conductor," telling the rest of the brain how to work together to appraise, evaluate, and execute action. Without it we could not function effectively in our day-to-day living.
>
> There are many areas in the executive functions that people on the spectrum often struggle with. Listed below are some of the common challenges they experience:

WEAK EXECUTIVE FUNCTIONING SKILLS

Poor inhibition

- Poor ability to inhibit impulses.
- Often impulsive; acting without thinking; interrupting.

Attention problems

- Either difficulty focusing or hyper-focused on detail.
- Problems inhibiting/filtering out distracting stimuli; picking out relevant details.
- Difficulty maintaining attention, getting distracted off task.
- Difficulty shifting attention; gets stuck and has difficulty moving on.

Shifting gears

- Difficulty shifting from one mindset to another.
- Problems with unexpected changes.
- Difficulty with transitions.
- Rigidly adheres to viewpoint.

Planning and problem solving

- Difficulty planning: setting goals, predicting future outcomes and designing course of action.
- Difficulty following sequential steps.
- Problems judging how long it will take to do things, to organize a course of action.
- Poor problem solving.

Organization skills

- Problems organizing materials, turning in homework, bringing what is needed, and remembering to deliver messages.
- Forgetful, disorganized, messy.

Working memory (the ability to hold information in immediate memory while focusing on a task)

- Difficulty shifting attention between task and active memory.
- Difficulty with multi-step tasks and complex instructions.
- Often forgets directions once task is started.

Self-monitoring

- Poor ability to monitor and check work.

- Poor self-monitoring of behavior.

- Tends not to use past experiences to evaluate present actions.

As you read through the different functions, you will notice the difficulties that are common for your child. Poor impulse control, difficulty regulating emotions, trouble concentrating on topics of low interest, difficulty shifting gears, and little snags causing frustration are all very common for children on the spectrum.

Even though the children may be bright, they usually have problems organizing themselves, allowing enough time to do things, forgetting where they are at in the task, and problems completing assignments. They may complete homework and then forget to turn it in. If you tell the child to clean his room, he will freeze and become overwhelmed by the task, not knowing where to begin. These children have problems breaking things down into small parts, getting started and then sequentially completing all steps of the task.

These children have difficulty multi-tasking because they have problems holding information in their short-term memory and then shifting their attention from one task to the other. Also, while engaged in action, they have difficulty monitoring and evaluating their own behavior and assessing how their actions affect others. They cannot act and think about how they are acting, at the same time. This multi-tasking job of both acting and monitoring how we are doing is essential when interacting with others. (pp.85–87)

In this chapter, we will expand on these issues and provide further suggestions. First let's look at each function individually.

Poor inhibition

This area of the brain is responsible for checking our impulses to act so we can appraise what is needed and evaluate what the consequences of our actions will be before deciding to act. We check our impulse to act long enough to evaluate if this response will get a favorable result or if it needs to be modified. When this function is impaired, the individual will have poor ability to control his impulses, often acting without thinking. He will act out of impulse, with minimal forethought. He may be able to tell you he shouldn't have done it, but did it anyway. He could not inhibit the action long enough to appraise what to do. He can also be remorseful for what he did, but was unable to hold back. This can be frustrating and is often seen as intentional for children who are bright and appear able to control themselves.

These children may also have problems with blurting out answers in class and saying inappropriate statements to others without forethought of how they will be received by them. They will have problems waiting for their turn and often interrupt others. They simply have difficulty holding back. The desire overpowers the thinking part of the brain, thus they act impulsively. This often gets the child into trouble, even though there was no intention to do wrong. This doesn't stop with childhood. An adult may hyper-focus on an item of desire and impulsively spend all his money on something online. "Why, why, why did he do that? He knows better!"

Attention problems

With executive dysfunction, there can be a variety of problems concentrating, and initiating and maintaining attention. The neurotypical brain has a built-in filter that sorts out what is important to attend to from the background irrelevant information. The autistic brain tends to take in and attend to all the details, with little filtering. This presents problems deciding what is important to attend to and maintaining attention on this information in the midst of many distracting stimuli. Children can be distracted easily and lose their focus before completing activities. Or, they may become hyper-focused on an irrelevant detail and miss the main points. The child may have trouble concentrating on what the teacher is saying because his attention keeps being distracted by her large earrings, a small spot on her dress or the reflection of light coming from an item on her desk. Attention floats from one irrelevant detail to another, with an inability to filter out background information.

Some individuals may have problems shifting attention. They can be working, become stuck on a step and have problems moving on. Or, they may become hyper-focused on a preferred activity and be totally oblivious to what else is occurring around them. Some individuals will lose track of time and forget to eat or sleep. This difficulty in shifting attention may also be problematic for tasks that require the brain to multi-task and shift attention back and forth from one task to the next. Often these children can be bright but labeled as lazy, unmotivated and indifferent because they simply cannot stay focused long enough to meet expectations.

Shifting gears/transitions

Life often throws us snags and unexpected road blocks. People with executive functioning problems can have difficulty shifting from one mindset to another, problems with unexpected changes and difficulty transitioning from one activity to another. They can get stuck on one way of thinking, which they may rigidly adhere to and argue profusely for, even in the face of opposing evidence. Once they learn one way of doing something, it becomes difficult for them to shift gears and try a different way when their strategy is not working. We have all seen the child who melts down when faced with simple changes in routine or a minor snag in the way he is doing something. He will argue against trying an alternative strategy and adamantly resist trying a different way. He may also hyper-focus on something when he cannot handle moving on to something else. This can be very frustrating for both the adult and the child. These children are often labeled inflexible and oppositional.

Planning and problem solving

This is where daily living can be affected. Of prime importance, good executive functioning allows us to set goals, define what our objectives are, evaluate options, plan out a course of action, and then implement the sequential steps needed to complete the plan. Regardless of how bright the person is, he may have difficulty getting things done, even the simplest daily activities needed for independent living. He may have difficulty getting up and ready for work on time, completing basic self-care and household chores, or executing the steps necessary to cook a simple meal. He may know what he needs to do but cannot plan and carry out the course of action needed to complete it. This can be confusing for those who do not have this difficulty. Autistic people can be very bright but simply cannot connect the dots to make things happen. They may have graduate degrees but be incapable of holding down a job because they cannot regulate the steps needed to get to work, organize what is needed and maintain focus on doing it. Many very intelligent people on the spectrum are dependent on support staff or living with family members because they are not capable of executing the daily living tasks without help.

Organization skills

We have all known people who can never find what they need, lose things easily, start activities without first organizing what they need, and forget to hand in their work, even when completed. They usually are forgetful, disorganized and messy. They often have no organization skills regarding their belongings and the way the accomplish things. They may stay busy, but never complete activities, forget where they put things, and need others to help keep them organized. They might have trouble getting started because they cannot determine the necessary steps or cannot organize the materials to easily navigate the task. Often, they spend time looking for items, remembering where they are and losing them again in the clutter once beginning the task.

Big projects such as tidying their bedroom become overwhelming. They simply cannot figure out where to start and what to do. The longer they delay, the messier the room becomes and the harder it is to organize. They cannot find anything and become paralyzed in what to do. However, the more disorganized they become, the less motivated they are to do things. This spiral becomes self-depleting, feeding feelings of inadequacy and depression. Inactivity breeds further inactivity, which increases depression.

Working memory

Working memory is the ability to hold information in our short-term memory to help us execute an activity or task. For example, if the teacher gives the child directions on what to look for while reading a story, the child must hold these instructions in his working memory while reading the story, so he can remember what to reference while reading. This requires the child to shift focus back and forth between the task and his memory of the directions to complete the assignment. For autistics, once they start the activity, they lose the working memory of the instructions. At home, a parent may give their child a three- or four-step direction, such as, "Hang your coat up, take your books to your room and then feed the dog." Holding this information in his working memory while executing the tasks is too difficult. Once he starts the first task, he is likely to forget what comes next.

Before doing something, you might ask the child to repeat to you what you have asked. He might be able to do that fine, but then lose the information once focusing on the task. He simply cannot hold on to the directions while simultaneously completing the task. These children often need additional cues, such as checklists or visual sequence cards, to remind them of what they have completed and what comes next. Usually those with poor working memory will have difficulty multi-tasking. They will need to stick to one project, with written or pictorial directions to reference, since they cannot rely on their working memory.

Self-monitoring

The last executive function we will look at is self-monitoring. This is the ability to monitor what we are doing as we do it and to check our work as we go along. It requires multi-tasking and thinking about what we are doing as we are doing it. Good self-monitoring requires us to continually appraise how we are doing as we are doing it, and flexibly modify our performance accordingly. These individuals must plow ahead without being cognizant of how they are doing. They cannot monitor their own performance. Even though they can tell you what is needed before starting, they have difficulty monitoring their performance to stay within expectations. Another aspect of this deficit is a poor sense of time and how long something is taking. When planning to do something, they often misjudge how long it will take them and lose their sense of time while doing it. Often projects do not get done on time.

Even simple tasks such as personal care are affected. The person might dress himself, but look sloppy (shirt half tucked in, zipper unzipped, shoes untied, etc.) because of his inability to monitor how he is doing. His hair may not be well combed, not washed well enough, or he has brushed his teeth poorly. He may have completed all the steps to "getting ready," but was not able to monitor how well he was doing.

Putting all these functions together, it is amazing how complex many of these skills are. Also, confusing for some, the lack of these functions can still occur in people who otherwise seem very capable. Executive dysfunction is not just a characteristic of autism. It is common with ADHD, closed head injury and other psychiatric and neurological disorders. Executive dysfunction is characteristic across the autism spectrum, with severity of deficits varying greatly. People may have strengths in some of the functions and not in others, or be weak in all the areas.

For many autistics, these weaknesses inhibit their ability to use all their cognitive skills effectively and can be the biggest block to independent living. However, even though these deficits are due to brain wiring differences, many of these challenges can be bridged with simple supports, which we shall discuss shortly.

Steps needed to execute actions

Before we look at strategies for supporting problems with executive functioning, let's look at some of the executive functions that need to take place to execute daily activities. Since we complete most of these steps subconsciously and simultaneously, we are not very cognizant of what it takes to perform a simple act and where these simple acts can break down.

Ten steps for successful actions:

1. Be aware that action is needed.

2. Appraise what is needed or expected.

3. Identify and appraise the options available, reflecting on past experiences and forethought of future consequences.

4. Plan a course of action, understanding when your plan is good enough and doesn't need further attention.

5. Organize the materials and time needed to complete the task.

6. Start to execute the plan.

7. Monitor and appraise how well it is going and modify strategies as needed.

8. Maintain attention on where you are at and what still needs to be completed.

9. Judge and monitor how much time it is taking to do the task.

10. Evaluate your performance so you know when you have met the objective and completed the task, understanding when the performance is good enough.

Given that our brain must execute these ten steps to successfully execute our daily actions, it stands to reason that deficits in any of these areas will influence our ability to function successfully. Let's apply these steps to the simple act of getting dressed.

Getting dressed in the morning

1. *Be aware that action is needed.* Often on weekdays you may have a set routine that you do each morning (get out of bed, take a shower, get dressed, eat breakfast, etc.) to get up and out to work or school on time. Somewhere in that routine your brain is cued to get dressed (e.g. after showering). Like dressing, many routine behaviors are cued by following common routines or by the time of day (e.g. take medication at 5pm). Whether it is a certain time or following an event, your brain must recognize that it is time to get dressed.

2. *Appraise what is needed.* In this example, you must decide what to wear for that day: underwear, socks, shirt, pants, shoes, maybe a sweater if it is cold. What do your daily events require (tie, dress pants, simple t-shirt, school uniform, etc.)? You must appraise what you need to wear for the weather and type of activity you will be doing that day. That may require you to check outside or the weather report to adjust your clothing accordingly. If you forget and/or misjudge, you may freeze all day because you forgot to wear a sweater, or you go to an important meeting wearing a t-shirt and jeans.

3. *Appraise the options and make a choice.* What color do you want to wear, which shirt and pants, shoes? From the options you have available, what do you want to wear?

4. *Plan a course of action.* When it is a simple chain of actions like dressing, you often do it out of habit. You have a routine order in how you dress (e.g. put on underpants, pants, undershirt, shirt, belt, socks, shoes, etc.). Since you do the same chain of actions (dressing) each morning, you can usually do it with little forethought. You do it out of habit, without having to think it through. However, if there is a new event or one that is not habitual, you need to plan a course of action (e.g. make and pack your own lunch when mom usually does it for you). You need to break the task down into a sequence of steps (get out materials, make the sandwich, place items in baggies, place this in the lunch bag, etc.) from start to finish. For people on the spectrum with severe executive functioning difficulties, breaking these tasks down into steps can be difficult to do and remember. They may need a checklist or picture sequence chart to provide the planned steps.

5. *Organize the materials needed to complete the task.* Where are your shoes? They are not where they are supposed to be. You saw that shirt yesterday. It must be in the wash. Now you must shift gears and get something else! You must know where each thing is at and arrange them (lay out the clothes) so you can start your course of action. This can be very difficult if you are messy and disorganized. I personally have this trouble when it comes to doing a home project, since I never have my tools well organized. It takes me twice as long as is necessary to find the needed tools, because they are not well organized. This makes doing home chores frustrating.

6. *Start to execute the plan.* Now you have the materials and your course of action planned, you need to start initiating the plan. It is hoped that you know what to do and when to do it. You do this every day and usually out of habit. However, those with severe impairment often get confused about how to start and what steps to complete. It may take them three times longer than most of us to get dressed. They may not have an established habit of how and in what sequence to get dressed. How I get dressed always varies a little based on if my pants have a zipper, snap or button, and need a belt or not, or if it is a pullover or button-down shirt. Am I wearing the slip-on shoes or ones with laces? Each day may present a strategy that is a little different. Some people with executive dysfunction often eliminate a lot of these decisions by wearing slip on shoes, pants with a belt, button-down or pullover shirts. This makes the task less exhausting. Otherwise, they may forget to tie their shoes, not wear a belt and so on.

7. *Monitor progress.* To successfully execute a plan of action (e.g. dressing), it is important to monitor how you are doing as you are doing it. Did you remember to put your underwear on before putting on your pants? Are your pants on

backwards? Did you put the right shoe on the right foot? Did you get the shirt buttoned correctly? This ability to continually monitor or think about what you are doing, as you are doing it becomes more crucial for complex tasks that are not implemented automatically out of habit—especially if each step must be done successfully before moving on to the next step. One step done wrong may mean undoing a series of incorrect actions to correct the error (unbuttoning the whole shirt to correct one button out of sequence).

8. *Maintain attention (focus).* To complete even a simple task like dressing, you must be able to maintain your attention on the sequence of steps and shift attention from one step to the next. If you have an impairment in that area, you may get distracted and lose your concentration half way, become stuck on deciding what shirt to wear and forget where you are at in your sequence of dressing. For those having difficulty maintaining and shifting attention, a checklist helps them remember where they are at, what they have done (check off steps completed) and what is still needed to be completed. If they get distracted, they can reference the checklist to see what step they are on and what is next.

9. *Judge sense of time.* When doing tasks, you must estimate how much time it will take to accomplish something, when it needs to be completed and monitor the time as you are doing it. How long will it take you to get dressed, what time do you need to be ready to leave for school? Then you have to monitor the time accordingly as you are getting dressed. Parents sometimes complain about their children taking an hour or more to get dressed, and not being ready in time to catch the bus. Apparently, they have no sense of time or urgency. Problems misjudging how long it takes to do things and then not leaving enough time to complete them can be chronic for many with autism. This leaves both us and them very frustrated and anxious, since we are all on a schedule. For some autistics, who must keep on schedule to maintain security, not completing one task soon enough can set off panic, because now their schedule is off mark. For many, their sense of time and passage of time can be weak. Hours can go by like minutes, often without them noticing.

10. *Evaluate performance.* Finally, once you have finished getting dressed, you need to check your work to make sure it is neat and organized. Many with executive functioning issues forget to check their work to make sure it is completed correctly. Make sure your shirt is not inside out or on backwards, your zipper is zipped and pants snapped. Ensure your shirt is tucked in and buttons are done up in correct sequence. Is your collar straight? We all know individuals who have trouble in this area. They dress themselves, but their clothes are in disarray, shoes untied, collar turned up or shirt tail hanging out. They do not have a clue that they are not dressed to expectation.

As you can see, the simple actions in our daily routine can be laborious when we have problems with executive dysfunction. We take all these functions for granted and execute them with ease. But, when we have impairments in these areas, it inhibits our ability to live independently. There are many bright individuals on the spectrum who must rely on support staff for daily living because they cannot execute these daily activities without assistance.

Normal daily activity can be stressful, taxing and exhausting

For people with good executive skills, most of the functions described above occur smoothly, with minimal mental energy. They are the tools that organize goal-directed behavior, from the simplest daily activities to more complex work-related tasks. When these functions do not operate correctly, even simple daily activity becomes more labored, taxing and mentally draining. The individual strains to work past these challenges, disorganized from start to finish, continually backing up or starting over due to mishaps, frequently taking much longer than expected and often upsetting others who are pressing them to move faster.

Executive dysfunction adds significantly to the mental drain, stress and anxiety. It takes so much more mental energy to struggle through what for others is executed easily. This often leaves the person feeling inferior, inadequate and unworthy. Constantly taking one step forward and two steps backward leads to ongoing frustration. Even when people on the spectrum can effectively navigate these weaknesses, simply regulating their normal daily routine can be very draining, adding to the already taxing processing drain.

All these complex functions that go into goal-directed behavior use a lot of mental energy. Most people who have high stress jobs, requiring extensive thinking, problem solving, multi-tasking and supervising/directing others, feel the exhaustion of taxing their executive functions throughout the day. Any activity that requires ongoing thinking, planning and organizing action is going to drain mental energy. This will include navigating new situations, social events, multi-tasking and any task requiring new learning or planning. For autistics, all these situations present significant mental drain, which taxes and overwhelms them. Socializing in a group of people will be highly exhausting and they often require extended breaks of doing nothing to rebound.

Executive dysfunction and self-esteem

Poor executive functioning underlies many of the struggles that autistics have in navigating our world. Since this dysfunction can occur, even with otherwise very capable individuals, these deficits are often viewed as behavioral challenges. They are often labeled as lazy, unmotivated, indifferent and purposefully defiant. You often hear the reports, "He can do it if he wanted to!", as if he purposefully chooses not to meet expectations. "What is wrong with you?" "You just don't care." Since these functions occur smoothly and subconsciously for others, they cannot imagine what it is like to not be able to organize your thoughts and actions to successfully implement typical daily functions.

The individuals themselves do not understand what is wrong with them. They often internalize the negative feedback they get from others. "Why can't I get it?" "They are right, I am no good, simply lazy and unworthy." They get mixed up, forget what they are supposed to do, get frustrated easily and simply give up. You can imagine the feelings of inadequacy you would feel if you could not organize your thoughts and actions well enough to meet the daily expectations at school and work. The child at school is continually being pressured, prodded and reminded of how inadequate he is, if not by others, then by his awareness of his own inability to do the work. How can he stay motivated to do tasks which he continually struggles to complete or do successfully? The child gives up easily, often comes up with excuses of why he does not try or does not finish his work. He must hide or cover up for deficits that he himself does not understand. "I am just stupid, no good!" He eventually stops trying because the ongoing failure is too damaging.

Most teachers and support staff do not understand that these are brain wiring deficits, not behavior problems. Unfortunately, the more capable the child (highly verbal, bright, etc.), the more hidden the disorder. Teachers get frustrated when the kids cannot focus, complete their assignments and become frustrated, shutdown and uncooperative. It is a spiral of self-defeating thoughts and actions that eventually leaves the child depressed and helpless. These deficits need to be recognized early through assessments at school. By seeing these deficits as brain weaknesses, we can begin to provide the supports that will allow children to understand that it is not a character flaw, but the way their brains are wired, and we can provide supports that will help bridge these weaknesses and allow them to be successful. We can protect their self-esteem, praise their efforts and provide them tools for compensating for these weaknesses.

Compensating for weak executive functioning

As discussed so far, people with executive dysfunction usually have difficulties in the areas of attention, impulse control, working memory, planning and organizing, monitoring their actions and multi-tasking. Neuroscience is in the infancy stage in terms of understanding brain plasticity and strengthening the wiring in areas of the brain that have weak connections. So, for individuals with executive dysfunction, most strategies focus ways to compensate for those weaknesses and work around the issues. These usually include (1) changing the physical environment to help bridge these weaknesses, (2) making modifications in the activities to make them easier, and (3) teaching the individuals coping skills to assist them through the activities. For example, let's look at how these supports can assist a child with attention/concentration problems.

- *Modify environment.* This may consist of making modifications to the classroom to minimize distractions, such as sitting the child to face away from the activity that may distract, using partitions around his work area, taking the child to a quiet area for tests. It could include removing visual distractions, sitting the child in the front row to avoid distraction of others in the room and making changes to lighting.

- *Task modifications.* Next, we can make modifications to the activities to support attention. Break the task down into smaller parts and present only one portion at a time, reduce the amount of work on a single page (three math problems instead of 20), and provide page rulers/templates to aid reading, and written outlines to direct the child's attention. Writing notes in the margins can also highlight what is important to look for when reading.

- *Individual coping skills.* The child might sit on an exercise ball, chew gum and listen to music on a smartphone to facilitate attention. They may use visual schedules, to-do lists and written task sequence lists to keep concentration on what to do and when to do it. Simple alarms and auditory reminders can be programmed into smartphones to cue the child into what and when to do things.

Teaching automatic habits

Teaching automatic habits (a set sequence of actions) to compensate for weak executive skills is another strategy that bypasses the executive functioning centers of the brain. Many of our daily functions occur habitually, with little conscious thought. For example, most of us have a bathing routine, where we wash and rinse our body parts in the same sequence every day. Over time, the sequence becomes habit and we do it without thinking. Although an established habit doesn't bypass all executive functions, it can bridge the need to plan, monitor and "think through" what to do.

At school, the child can be taught a set sequence of actions for starting the day (hanging up his coat, getting his toolkit from the shelf and sitting down at his desk). He may need reminders and supervision to implement these steps until they become a habit and implemented automatically. Although this doesn't ensure that his attention will not get distracted, it does increase the likelihood that he executes the actions with minimal planning, forethought and monitoring. Establishing habits often requires building in external supports (pictures, verbal prompts, reminders, etc.) and supervision until an automatic routine (habit) is established. The habitual routine takes the place of the need for the cognitive thinking skill they lack.

When someone has good executive functioning, we assume they can inhibit their impulsive response long enough to use their thinking skills to appraise, evaluate and execute what is needed. When the brain does not do that naturally, we must provide that function externally (see the above strategies) until we establish a set routine that becomes automatic (habit). Here are some other examples of this:

- Use a picture routine to cue the child into doing his morning routine (picture schedule or written list of getting dressed, eating breakfast, brushing teeth, etc.), until it is repeated enough to become habit. Once the routine becomes automatic, the picture routine can be faded out. However, for every new routine, we may need to always begin with a visual schedule until the routine becomes habit. As the person becomes older, he learns to always set up a visual list (checklist, written steps) when starting new routines, until they become automatic habits. He may always have a need for the visual reminders, which is also fine.

- A child who impulsively blurts out comments while the teacher is talking can be taught (prompted and practice) to raise his hand before talking. The teacher must prompt, practice and reinforce the behavior until it becomes habit. We might also place a visual cue card for raising the hand (no talk, raise hand) on his desk to visually remind him. Once this behavior becomes habit, we can remove the cue card.

- A child who often rushes through tasks and does a sloppy job may be given a visual model, or photo, of the finished product to match his work to. Once he can complete the product accurately, we can fade out the visual cue card.

As you can see, in all these examples, we are not necessarily improving the executive functioning skills, but providing the missing function externally until it becomes a habit, which bypasses the need for the cognitive (thinking) mediation. We all need to develop strategies to compensate for our weaknesses. By focusing on developing our strengths and compensating for our weaknesses we grow stronger!

Strategies for executive dysfunction

At the beginning of the chapter, we listed the individual executive functions. Now we will look at each executive function individually. For each function, there will be a summary of the possible dysfunctions and suggested support strategies, followed by a discussion of each strategy.

Poor inhibition (impulse control)

INHIBITING IMPULSE

Poor ability to inhibit impulses

Often impulsive; acting without thinking; interrupting

Strategies

- *Sensory diet:* Sensory activities to calm and organize the nervous system
- *Shape alternative response:* Raise hand before talking, touch arm instead of hugging
- *Add visual cue:* Red/green light/card to signal when you can ask questions
- *Visual timers:* To stay on task
- *Specific black and white rules:* No hugging unless you ask; no comments about appearance (overweight, acne, clothing, etc.)
- *Define boundaries before event:* Hands on cart, stay with me, stay on sidewalk, etc.
- *Social referencing for pacing:* Pacing with another, walking side by side, staying coordinated by checking in and slowing down

Figure 16.1: Strategies for increasing impulse control

How can we help the child inhibit his impulses and think before acting? Let's take a closer look at the strategies in Figure 16.1:

1. *Sensory diet.* Many children with poor impulse control have problems regulating their excitement (arousal level). Trying to hold back an excited nervous system is too much for their weak ability to think before acting. These children can often benefit from having a sensory diet (calming and alerting activities) to help keep their nervous system calm and organized. The child is usually referred to an occupational therapist to assess and design a schedule of sensory activities to keep the child's energy level well regulated, so that he is less impulsive. The activities keep the child calm, alert and less overreactive.

2. *Shaping alternative behavior.* This is used to inhibit an undesirable behavior by substituting an alternative, more desirable behavior, such as teaching a child to raise his hand, instead of blurting out responses, or teaching a child to touch others on the arm to reduce hugging everyone for attention.

   When thinking of an alternative, replacement behavior, it is often best to choose one that is incompatible with the undesirable behavior. For example, a child, when grocery shopping with mom would frequently grab items off the shelves and inappropriately touch others with his hands. The parent was advised to give the child the role of pushing the cart while she shopped. By pushing the cart, the child was instructed to keep his hands on the grocery cart to minimize grabbing items off shelves and touching others. When his hands were on the cart, he could not grab items or inappropriately touch others with his hands. Keeping his hands on the cart was physically incompatible with both grabbing items and touching others. At first, the parent had to monitor the child continuously to ensure he kept his hands on the cart. When the child removed one or both hands, the parent "stopped the action" and redirected him to keep his hands on the cart. Once the habit was established, grabbing items off the shelves and touching others inappropriately decreased substantially.

   I once worked with a child who got so excited when chatting with me that he would end up hugging and climbing on me. To reduce this excitable behavior, I made the rule that we had to sit straight in our own chairs, with our backs touching the back of the chair for us to talk with each other. If his back was against the chair he could not lean over and in to me, climb on me, or touch me inappropriately. By keeping his back against the back of the chair, it physically interrupted the excitable behavior and helped him stay calm and organized. It was incompatible with leaning over and inappropriately touching or hanging on me. At first, I had to stay firm, "stopping the conversation" whenever his back left the chair and redirecting him back to expectation. It took a lot of redirection at first, but he learned quickly and all the inappropriate touching and climbing on me stopped. I did, however, realize that I needed to respect his need to regulate his excitement by tapping his feet, hand flapping, wiggling in his seat, or any other means of stimulation. This behavior allowed him to stay calm and focused on the conversation.

3. *Add visual cues to signal behavior.* Going back to the child who is constantly interrupting, asking questions and blurting answers in class, in addition to raising his hand to request permission before speaking, we might also put a red light/green light card on his desk to signal when it is appropriate to request permission to speak. When the red light is displayed, the child cannot ask questions, and when the green light is on, he can verbally engage. This makes the conditions very clear and concrete, visual and easy to understand. Between learning to raise his hand before speaking and using the red light/green light card to signal when he can ask for permission, the child learns not to blurt out.

4. *Visual timers.* Visual timers (Time Timers) are small plastic clocks that allow the child to see how much time is left. These are great for focusing attention, staying on task and transitioning to other activities. Children with impulse control often have trouble staying seated and on task. Using a visual timer can give them good cues on how long to stay on task or engage in the activity. They can also be used to delay an impulsive action. For example, if a child is constantly wanting to talk to the teacher, he may respond well to a visual timer to tell him when he can get up and talk to the teacher. Sensory tools (air cushion, fidget toy and bungy cord on the legs of the chair) can also be used to help calm his nervous system. Start with having the child sit for five minutes before approaching the teacher, then once he understands the conditions, gradually expand the time. By starting where he is at (getting up every five minutes to approach the teacher), giving him sensory tools to help stay calm and providing the visual timer to signal when he can approach the teacher, we can help the child to become more focused on his work and less fixated on approaching the teacher.

5. *Specific black and white rules.* Some impulsive behaviors can be interrupted by presenting very black and white, absolute rules to control the behavior. Many children with autism are very rule bound. Rules make the world easier to understand; for example, "No hugging without asking first" or "No making comments to others about their appearance (weight, acne, clothing, etc.)." Often, we need to begin with very black and white rules to stop an inappropriate behavior until we can go back later and teach when and where it is appropriate to hug, or what constitutes appropriate comments about appearances. At first, we need to make the boundaries and social rules concrete and consistent. Over time, we can teach variations and gray areas and introduce more flexibility.

6. *Define boundaries.* Most importantly, for those who have poor impulse control, be sure before going into events that you define the boundaries (rules and regulations). Define the path you want the child to stay on, the boundaries framing the activity, and then maintain focus on them. Keep to only a couple rules that are

simple and concrete, but minimize the impulsive behaviors. For example, for the child in the grocery store, they may be "Keep your hands on the cart and walk by my side." The parent needs to monitor these two rules closely. If the child takes a hand off or fades from their side, the parent needs to stop the action and calmly redirect the child back on path.

These behavior boundaries provide a mental map that keeps the child on the right path, giving him easy-to-see concrete boundaries. We often forget to do this, letting the child stretch the boundaries and then trying to reel him in. This often results in disaster. Define the boundaries, preview them before the event and remind the child throughout the activity. It is easier to keep the child from overstepping the boundaries, than reeling him back in after overstepping the boundaries.

7. *Teach social referencing to pace the child.* Many children with autism become distracted by what interests them and forget to reference the adult's instruction. For example, for two people walking together continually reference each other to stay coordinated in their actions—walking side by side, continually checking in with each other to stay "connected." Many kids with autism are poor at referencing others. The child may fall back or impulsively run forward with little or no reference to where the parent is. For impulsive children, it is very important that they learn to reference you to stay regulated in what they are doing. This helps keep them from acting impulsively.

    Staying with the grocery shopping example, remember one of the rules is staying side by side. To accomplish this, the child needs to learn to frequently reference the parent to stay alongside them. The parent can help teach this by stopping frequently to look at items, speeding up a little, slowing down, turning around. Instead of verbally prompting the child to stop and go, it is better to get him to visually check in with you. To do this, it is better to use silent, visual cues like nodding your head yes to signal go and shaking your head no for not yet. This way the child learns that he must visually reference your face to determine when to move and when to stay. You learn to use more nonverbal communications (gestures and facial expressions), instead of verbal directions.

    In social referencing, the child learns to reference the other person for information on what and when to do something, to stay coordinated in action with the person and for feedback on how to modify his actions. For the impulsive child, I call this pacing. The child learns to use the adult as a guide to slow himself down, stop and think. Start with simple activities, like walking together, passing a soccer ball back and forth, doing simple tasks together where the child must continually reference the parent to stay coordinated together. Essentially, the adult is then pacing the child to slow down, check in and stay coordinated in action. This teaches the child to model his actions on the adult to keep himself calm and regulated.

Attention/concentration problems

Difficulty focusing, concentrating

Problems inhibiting distracting stimuli; picking out relevant details

Suggestions:

- *Removing distractions* from area or shielding (partitions)
- *Sensory buffers:* Headphones, MP3 player, sunglasses, etc.
- *Sensory arousing tools:* Music, air cushions, leg (chair) bands, gum, fidget toys, etc.
- *Sensory breaks:* Up and moving, physical activity
- *Breaking tasks down* into simple steps, one step at a time
- *Highlighitng important details:* Previewing material, highlighting important points, outlines, graphic organizers (thinking maps, thought bubbles, etc.)
- *Visual strategies:* Task sequence boards, reinforcement puzzles, visual timers

Figure 16.2: Strategies for improving attention/concentration

There are a variety of issues that can occur with attention: problems distinguishing relevant from irrelevant details, initiating and maintaining attention, getting distracted easily, maintaining arousal to attend and so on. There are a variety of strategies that can help guide attention and maintain focus (see Figure 16.2).

1. *Removing distractions.* First, modify the environment to minimize distractions. Remove distracting stimulation such as bright lighting, unnecessary noise, number of people and amount of activity, and visual clutter such as bright items on the wall, unnecessary furniture, toys and items that may distract the child. Often this means eliminating distracting items from the area, sitting the child in the classroom facing away from the distractions, or using a partition to block out the distractions.

2. *Sensory accommodations or buffers.* When you cannot modify the environment to reduce the distractions (cannot change the lighting or noise level), the next best thing is to provide accommodations to help mask or filter the distractions. This includes sunglasses or tinted glasses to minimize lighting and headphones, ear plugs, or MP3 players to block out unwanted noise. The child who is touch sensitive might wear latex gloves when doing finger painting. When you cannot reduce the source of distraction, build in something to filter the impact.

3. *Sensory arousing tools.* Maintaining attention is often related to modulating arousal level. When under-aroused or over-aroused, the child cannot maintain focus. The child will often need to feed his nervous system stimulation to stay alert enough to attend and focus. Fidget toys, chewing gum, sitting on an air cushion, standing or moving, listening to music, drinking out of a straw, all can be built in to help provide stimulation to the pre-frontal cortex to stay alert and focused on the task at hand.

4. *Sensory breaks.* Another sensory tool is providing sensory breaks throughout the day to let the child engage in physical activity that will increase alertness or release unwanted energy, whichever is needed. This is good for all children, but very important for kids who have difficulty staying focused. To ask a child with attention problems to focus for a long time before getting up and moving will only cause problems. Providing brief movement breaks to do wall push-ups, jumping jacks, run an errand and so on can be valuable.

For strategies 1–4, please consult the occupational therapist at school to assess and develop strategies specific to your child.

5. *Breaking tasks down.* The next three strategies focus on the task itself. The first is to break the task down into simple, easy-to-understand steps, then provide only one step at a time to minimize multi-tasking. This allows the child to narrow the task down into a small step rather than looking at it as a massive task. The secret is to break the steps down into time frames that match the attention span of the child. Do it step by step, giving breaks as needed while eventually it accumulates in a completed project. It is important to keep each step short and simple to maximize success. The pace and speed of performance must match the attention level of the child, not some artificial standard.

6. *Highlighting important details.* Many children have difficulty picking out the important aspects of the task to focus on. For them, find ways to highlight or isolate important information so it is salient for them to see. This can be done in several ways. Often it is good to preview or pre-teach the important points or the big picture before the learning lesson begins.

   Next, highlighting important points helps to spotlight the most relevant information. Many textbooks now will put important points out in the margin, so they become obvious. Screening sheets can be used to block off parts of the page to minimize what the child can see from moment to moment. Only work on three math problems per page instead of overwhelming them with an array of 20. Using graphic organizers such as written outlines, Venn diagrams, thinking maps and thought bubbles can help organize information and narrow attention. All these strategies help the child attend to, organize and categorize important information.

7. *Visual strategies.* In addition to the graphic organizers, there are a host of visual strategies for organizing time and activities. Visual schedules allow the child to attend to what his routine will be for the day; checklists and task sequence boards help show steps of a task; visual timers help keep focus on how much time there is; and visual reinforcement puzzles help keep attention on what the child is working for. With these visual reinforcement puzzles, the teacher uses a picture of a preferred activity that the child earns for completing his work. The teacher cuts the picture into several pieces and the child earns one piece for each bit of work (or steps of work) completed. Once he earns all the pieces to complete the puzzle, he gets to participate in that preferred activity.

Shifting gears/handling transitions

Many children with autism have problems stopping one activity and moving on to another. Transitions can bring uncertainty and panic. These same children have difficulty shifting gears when something is not working and get upset with sudden, unexpected changes. This executive dysfunction often appears as an intentional behavior problem, rather than a brain wiring difference. Building in the following supports can help significantly (see Figure 16.3).

Difficulty shifting from one mindset to another
Problems with unexpected changes
Difficulty transitioning between activities

Suggestions:

• *Predictable routine:* Visual schedules, checklists, now and next, etc.
• *Preview events:* What he can expect, what is expected of him, how long, what is next
• *Prepare for changes:* Preview ahead of time, build into schedule, teach "routine" for asking for help
• *Plan Bs:* What ifs, alternative strategies for common snags
• *Transition warnings:* Visual timers, 5/3/1/ warnings, frontload what is next
• *Transition routines:* Putting things away, transition chants, listing transitions in visual routines

Figure 16.3: Strategies for increasing flexibility with shifting gears and transitions

When uncertainty is scary, and predictability is so important to your security, unexpected changes—having to quickly shift gears and transitioning between activities—can cause huge anxiety. There are several strategies which can help with this.

1. *Provide a predictable routine.* Reduce uncertainty by providing information on what is coming up, so the immediate future is predictable. Use picture or written schedules, daily planners, checklists, and now and next strategies (first we do this, then we do that), to provide predictability to the person's day. Lay out the day, step by step, including any possible changes and anticipated snags. This gives the children a mental map and allows them to collaborate and navigate their day. The more predictable the day, the less anxiety and the better the brain is prepared for what is coming up.

   Sit down with the child and map out the day, or next few hours, together. Make changes as needed, collaborate and negotiate, compromise and give the child a voice in what is coming his way. This teaches him to map out his day so as he gets older, he can build in more certainty and predictability to his life. This reduces anxiety, helps organize his time, keeps him on track and maximizes his completion of activities.

2. *Preview events.* Preparing the child by previewing events ahead of time is crucial to providing predictability and minimizing anxiety. Previewing consists of highlighting important information, defining expectations and preparing for transitions. Preview (1) what the child can expect to happen, the sequence of events, (2) what is expected of him, (3) how long it will last, and (4) what will

come next. Also preview what problems may occur and how to deal with them. This helps provide a mental map for the child. Previewing what to expect and what is expected of them is one of the best overall strategies a parent can provide for their children. It creates a mental map of what to expect and helps guide their expectations and behavior. Autistic adults must learn to collect this information themselves, including what challenges given events will present them with, alternative plans (plan Bs) if snags occur and an early escape route if they need to exit fast.

3. *Prepare for changes.* When possible, try to anticipate changes and preview them ahead of time. If there are going to be changes to a consistent routine (substitute teacher the next day, taking bath at night instead of in the morning, etc.), discuss them ahead of time so the child is mentally prepared for them. You may also want to change up the routines a little periodically so that the child gets used to some variability.

4. *Plan Bs.* When previewing events and schedules, try to anticipate any changes or possible snags and develop plan Bs or alternative strategies for common snags. For example, if you are doing an activity outside, plan another activity to take its place in case it rains. Plan what to do if the event gets cancelled. For common activities, develop a list of "what ifs" that could happen and planned alternative strategies for when they happen. This helps prepare the children for the possible snags, plus gives them knowledge of what will occur instead.

5. *Transition warnings.* When children have trouble with shifting gears and transitioning from one activity to another, it is important to do two things. First, always let them know what is coming up next: "Once we are done painting, we will eat lunch." This way the brain is already prepared for what is coming up next. Second, give the brain time to make that shift as the event begins to end. One tool is to use a visual timer (Time Timer) so the child can see how much time is left as it counts down to the end of the activity. Another tool is to give five-minute, three-minute and one-minute reminders as time is ending: "In three minutes, we will finish painting and go to lunch." It is always best to remind the child with three-minute and then one-minute reminders that the current activity will end. If you can let the child know what comes next, either using a visual timer so they can monitor the time or giving reminders before transitioning, the brain is better prepared for the transition.

6. *Transition routines.* Teachers have found that using transition routines helps to build familiarity and predictability to the transitions. Common routines in school frequently end one activity with the putting away of materials to help bridge transitions between activities. Often, they will have a little chant or song that they sing as they put away materials for one activity and get out materials for the next. If the song is kept the same, and the transition is organized and consistent from day to day, this helps to reduce the anxiety of transitions. The routine lining up and walking from room to room can also help structure transitions.

Organization/Planning

Poor planning: developing goals, designing and following course of action, completing work, poor judge of "how long"

Poor organization: organizing materials, cluttered/messy, forgetting to turn work in or take home, etc.

Suggestions:

- *Visual strategies:* Visual schedules and task boards, checklists, flow charts, goal/objective/ steps planners, visual timers, etc.
- *Visual organizers:* Color code items, folder organizers, graphic organizers, concrete spots for everything, photo of completed work/area
- *Alarms, watches, timers, etc.:* Apps, alarms, schedules, to-do lists, smartphones, etc. to monitor time
- *Break projects down:* Small steps, concrete timelines, double time to complete

Figure 16.4: Strategies for improving planning and organizational skills

This weakness is often obvious because it usually results in children not completing something, doing it badly, being way behind schedule or forgetting to hand work in once it is completed (see Figure 16.4). They may know what they need to do but cannot plan an objective or course of action to get it done. They often seem lost as to what to do. They often have difficulty organizing what materials are needed, seem to lose things and are often disorganized and messy. They may be busy all the time, but rarely complete anything. Alternatively, out of frustration, they may shutdown and refuse to even try. It is better not to try than to appear inadequate. People often see them as lazy and lacking motivation. Unfortunately, even the individuals themselves feel inadequate because they do not understand why they have difficulty completing even simple projects. Seemingly very bright individuals can have difficulty completing projects on time. This can be very frustrating for both the person and those who support them.

Here are some suggestions for supporting these difficulties.

1. *Visual strategies.* We all benefit from using organizational tools such as schedules, calendars, appointment books and checklists. They help us plan and organize our time and remind us of what we need to do. Over the past several years, smartphone apps that help us schedule and plan and remind us have been instrumental tools for many of us, but especially for those with executive dysfunction.

   For young children, picture schedules are commonly used to provide structure and predictability to their daily routines. As the child gets older and obtains reading skills, written schedules often substitute for pictures and eventually electronic apps become the norm as portable schedulers with auditory reminders. They can also include a checklist for everything from items to take to school, instructions for what to do when lost in the community, steps for preparing a recipe or checking out a book at the library, and other important information to reference in the moment.

   To-do lists and task organizing worksheets create supports for planning and completing activities. They help organize what and when things need to be completed. For learning new tasks, picture boards or written checklists can be used to display each step of a given task. They concretely break the activity down into simple steps to be checked off when completed. Checking off the steps can also be helpful for those who get stuck or become confused about what steps they have completed and what needs to be done. Again, like most executive functioning assistance tools, these visual strategies provide external support for what the brain wiring lacks.

Visual organization worksheets can be used to assist individuals with breaking down a project, organizing what materials are required and planning out the steps that need to be done. These worksheets can be used for academic assignments, work projects or daily living activities. Visual timers can also be incorporated to help keep the individual on track as to when to start, stop and transition between activities. Time Timers (commercial visual timers) have a watch that can be used as a visual timer for those who cannot tell the time.

Problem-solving worksheets can be used to assist an individual with daily decision making. They usually include (1) defining what the problem/decision is, (2) listing the options, (3) weighing the pros and cons, and (4) evaluating the outcomes. Again, these worksheets simply provide external supports to compensate for what the brain is unable to do. They are great tools for allowing the individual to function more independently.

2. *Visual organizers.* Visual organization systems can also be used to structure the environment so the person can adequately find things. They help to minimize clutter, organize materials and facilitate completion of daily activities. For example, having structured areas in the classroom for each subject separated by visual boundaries helps signal where to go and what to do. Well-organized shelves with color-coded containers that are labeled can aid the student in obtaining and putting back materials. Having note books where subjects are color coded, with sections for homework (to take home and hand in) can help organize materials and remind the child what to take and bring to school.

At home, having set places where things belong, with areas labeled or color coded can help individuals remember where things are and where to put them. Placing items that need to go to school or work in a container right by the front door can assist children in remembering what to take when leaving in the morning. Laminating picture or written schedules and checklists and putting them on the wall in important areas of the house can assist the person in what to do and staying on track. Parents can place color-coded labels on clothes to assist children in picking clothes that match (e.g. all red-coded items go together). Placing a picture step board (pictures of each step for dressing) on the wall right next to a full-length mirror can assist the child in dressing. Also, getting the clothes out the night before, with a specific spot to place them, can help mornings go more smoothly. For those living on their own, having set containers for mail, bills and their keys, and labeled containers for food helps a lot. I have found that providing well-defined areas for things that are labeled and color coded is essential. Make sure to develop a written index of all things and where they can be found in case they forget.

3. *Alarms, watches, timers to cue.* The passage of time can be very difficult to judge for people with executive dysfunction. They forget when to do things, mistake how long tasks will take and when things must be completed. They often misjudge the time needed to do things. If they allotted only one hour to do something and it takes twice that long, their schedule is thrown off and panic sets in. They frequently have problems monitoring the passage of time while doing things, losing track of time. Often, if they get hyper-focused on a preferred activity, they can lose track of time, forget to eat and miss another activity. It is good to have watches or smartphones with alarms to signal when to do things, when things need to be completed by and when to move on to the next activity. For example, a college student uses an app on his smartphone when doing a workout routine at the gym. The phone shows a picture of each activity to be completed, with a built-in timer to signal when to start, finish and transition to the next activity. Without this app, he would be lost in remembering what to do, how long to do it for and when to transition.

4. *Break projects down.* Lastly, for those with planning and organizing deficits, it is important to break projects down into simple steps with concrete timelines for each step. For longer projects, the steps can be completed over a course of time, especially when attention and stamina are problematic. The individual may only be able to attend to a given task for 25 minutes or become overwhelmed if the activity (e.g. house cleaning) includes multiple steps (picking up, vacuum, dusting, etc.). A project can be broken down into smaller steps that can be briefly completed, with rests in between, or, as with house cleaning, do one short task a day (vacuum, dust, etc.), completing the housework a little at a time. Individuals should allow for twice as much time as anticipated, giving them plenty of time to compete things. For teachers and work assistants, although each person is different, a good starting point is to only expect half as much work, in twice the time.

As you can see, all these strategies are designed to help compensate for the lack of skills by providing external supports to bridge what the brain is weak at doing. By building in external executive functioning for lacking internal skills, we can compensate for many of these deficits and the individual to function more independently.

Working memory

Problems with working memory often result in people forgetting what needs to be done, getting lost in the middle of doing things and forgetting to hand their work in when completed (see Figure 16.5).

Hold information in immediate memory while shifting attention between task and active memory

Often forgets directions once task is started

Problems multi-tasking and multiple step instructions

Suggestions:

- *Visual instructions:* Written or picture steps/instructions, checklists, flow sheets/thinking maps, highlighters, etc.
- *Avoid multi-tasking:* One task at a time, with steps broken down
- *Preview before and during activities:* What he can expect, what is expected of him, any boundaries and rules, with reminders throughout
- *Smartphone apps:* Folder of common events with steps and checklists (shopping, banking, library, etc.)
- *Photo activity stories:* One-page photos of sequence of events

Figure 16.5: Strategies for supporting working memory

Working memory is our ability to hold information in our short-term memory that we then reference while doing activities. This allows us to complete multi-step directions, hold instructions in our head while doing things, and help us if we get stuck once doing it. Working memory also allows us to keep a mental picture of what the finished product should look like as we monitor our performance. Without working memory, we would forget directions that guide us through events, get lost in the middle of activities and not have a mental map of what we are doing.

Here are some suggestions for supporting difficulties with working memory.

1. *Visual instructions.* Write out the instructions for the children to reference rather than just telling them. Without good working memory, verbal instructions are fleeting, going in one ear and out the other. Even if they can repeat back to you what they need to do, children will often lose it once they start working. Highlighting important points, providing written instructions, graphic organizers, flow charts and thinking maps are useful strategies. We must put the memory into concrete, visual forms to reference. This way the person can continually reference the instructions as he is completing the task. This strategy removes the need to remember the information.

2. *Avoid multi-tasking.* Most people on the spectrum who struggle with executive dysfunction will have difficulty with multi-tasking. They cannot keep multiple information and multiple tasks simultaneously organized in their memory. In both work and school, the teacher and supervisor need to present one project at a time and to break it down into concrete steps with specific timelines. Let the person start and complete each task before moving on to the next. Do not expect several projects to be occurring at one time.

3. *Preview before and during activities.* Do not assume that individuals know what is expected without previewing it. Preview and clarify expectations. Preview what they can expect to happen, what is expected of them and clarify and verify

that they understand. Again, since they have difficulty keeping this information in their memory while in the activity, reminders or a written checklist may help keep them on track. Previewing should occur just prior to starting the activity. Reminding children to hand their homework in before going to school will not ensure they will remember to do it once at school. If you give instructions in what or what not to do before a lengthy activity, you may need to provide reminders periodically throughout the event.

4. *Smartphone apps.* There are smartphone or tablet apps that can provide an individualized library of common events the person regularly experiences. This library may include step-by-step instructions of what to do when shopping, going to the bank, navigating public transportation or when lost or needing help. These apps store important information for people to reference when they get stuck or run into a snag in their daily routine. It is common for autistics to freeze and panic when there is a snag, especially when in the community. Having instructions they can reference helps reduce anxiety and provides concrete directions when confused. These apps can list "what ifs" in common situations for when the person runs into snags. Apps can be tailored to the specific needs of the individual.

5. *Activity stories.* For those who cannot navigate apps and written checklists, photo stories can work well. Create a page with several photos sequencing the steps of an activity. The parent can preview it with the child ahead of time and use it during the activity to remind the child.

Self-monitoring

Poor ability to monitor and check work

Poor self-monitoring of behavior. Think about what he is doing as he is doing it

Poor ability to appraise effects of behavior and consequences

Suggestions:
- Teach to appraise (what is needed), act then evaluate (how did I do or how did it work out?)
- Visual task sequences to stop and check after each step. Checklist of steps
- Photo of completed work to check work

Example—Dressing: Full length mirror, visual sequence on one side, photo of completed task (neatly dressed and groomed) on other side

Figure 16.6: Strategies for improving self-monitoring

It is important to help these individuals monitor how they are performing as they are doing things and to check their work to make sure it is completed correctly (see Figure 16.6). Remember, people with good executive functioning can think about what they are doing as they are doing it. They can simultaneously monitor how well they are doing and make needed adjustments to ensure they are doing it correctly. This also includes monitoring how their behavior is affecting others simultaneously as they are engaging. We can judge when we are off course and modify our actions to stay on the correct path. We can also reflect on past learning as well as future consequences of our actions to determine how we do things. This self-monitoring is often weak for those on the spectrum. Whereas others can multi-task all these functions simultaneously, those with executive dysfunction usually must do them sequentially.

Here are some suggestions for supporting difficulties with self-monitoring.

1. *Appraise, act and evaluate.* It will always be difficult for those with executive dysfunction to simultaneously monitor how they are doing as they are doing it. They must do these functions sequentially. They must learn to "appraise, act and evaluate." When engaged in an activity or interacting with others, they must learn to first appraise what is needed, act on it, then check to see how it is working. Break the task down into simple steps. At the end of each step, evaluate how they are doing, adjust as needed to stay on course and then appraise what to do next. It is best to teach this process by "we-do" teaching or mentoring. Do the activity with the child, stopping at each step, check together how you are doing, what you need to change and what is needed next. The mentor thinks out loud, modeling this step, checking and modifying as needed, to keep each other on the correct path. Break the task or interaction down into short phases and appraise and evaluate at each phase. Through repetition, the child learns to slow down, pause frequently to appraise and evaluate, then adjust his behavior accordingly. He eventually learns to internalize this process.

2. *Visual strategies.* For individual tasks (like work tasks), this appraise, act and evaluate process can be signaled with a visual task sequence consisting of photos of all the steps, so that each step can be checked for accuracy. The photos give the person a visual model to continually check how well his work matches the photo. This allows him to appraise, act and then check the photo at each step to see if his work looks like the picture.

3. *Finished product.* Finally, it is important to give the person a model or picture of how the finished product should look when the task is completed. This allows him to check his work to make sure he has completed it successfully.

Let's look at an example. To teach a child to dress appropriately, I find it effective to put a full-size mirror on the back of the bedroom door. On one side of the mirror is a photo sequence of putting each article of clothing on in the order of how it occurs. This allows the child to go through each step, one at a time. On the other side of the mirror is a photo of the child completely and neatly dressed, shirt tucked in, shoes tied, zipper zipped. The child can reference this photo to see if he has completed dressing correctly (his image in the mirror should match the photo).

Many kids do tasks without monitoring or checking to see if they are done correctly. This is the child who will have all his clothes on but be sloppy—shirt may not be tucked in, or inside out, shoes on the wrong feet, or shirt buttoned incorrectly. To teach this process it would work well, as in step one above, for someone to dress alongside the child, modeling the appraise, act and evaluate process until the child learns to use the visual supports.

Executive issues in problem behavior

We have looked at how the executive functions impact goal-directed behavior and how to support weaknesses in these functions. Now let's look at how executive dysfunction often is behind problematic, challenging behaviors a child may display. People often view the misbehavior as intentional and purposeful, when the child does not understand what the expectations are, does not know how to meet them or cannot read how his behavior is affecting others. Some of the deficits can help explain the misbehavior we see from these children.

To understand this, let's first review what is needed to pattern our behavior to meet expectations. To behave as desired, the person must understand what is expected, know what to do and be able to do it, be able to read the invisible rules and boundaries, monitor what he is doing as he is doing it, understand when he is getting off course, be able to project what effect his behavior is having on others, and what consequences this behavior will have. That is a complex chain of processes that must be functional to meet expectations. When children have executive dysfunction, the following problems can occur:

1. *Not knowing what is expected.* They will have poor ability to see the big picture, read the invisible rules and understand what is intuitively expected. They may refuse to respond and appear noncompliant or oppositional. We often assume that they understand, because they either do not know that they misunderstand or cannot adequately tell us. Often, we either assume that they can read between the lines or the language we use is too vague for them to understand. When children are not meeting expectations, first assume that they do not understand or misinterpreted what we expect. Clarify and verify understanding. Always seek understanding before assuming that they choose to misbehave.

2. *Inability to meet expectations.* Even if they intellectually understand what is expected, children often do not know how to do what is needed. Sometimes, if they know how to do it, they may get stuck or lost in doing it. They may be able to tell you what they should do, but are not able to do it in the heat of the moment. This makes them appear even more oppositional, lazy or indifferent. Knowing what to do and being able to do it in the moment are two different processes. If your child has a good awareness of what he should do, do not consider it learned until he is able to do it in the context for which it is required. It often takes practice in the heat of the moment to instill new learning. If the child does not follow through with the correct action, even though he knows cognitively what to do, first assume this possible deficit.

3. *Poor inhibition (impulse control).* Many children have very poor impulse control and will often act without thinking, not being able to hold back. They simply act on impulse before the thinking part of the brain can step in, inhibit the response and appraise what is needed. The executive functioning part of the brain (frontal lobes) develops last and often is not fully developed until the late twenties. This is

the part of the brain that allows us to check our impulses until we can appraise what is needed and what the consequences will be. Since this area of the brain is weak, the child's impulses act before the thinking part of the brain can inhibit them. This is a brain wiring weakness, not an intentional behavior. Often these kids feel very badly about what they did after doing it.

4. *Not aware of boundaries.* Since many rules and expectations are invisible and assumed, many autistic children are not aware of the boundaries or when they are overstepping them. Since they have difficulty reading context (the big picture), they often do not know that they are stepping off the path and heading in the wrong direction. Therefore, it is very important to preview before entering events, what is expected and what the boundaries are. Provide a mental map so they have a concrete guide to navigate the confusion.

5. *Poor working memory.* Even if you preview the expectations, the children may not be able to hold these expectations in their memory during the act of doing the task. Remember, this is a brain wiring deficit where this information comes in but does not stick. Once attention is engaged in the activity, they often lose directions, rules and expectations, especially in new situations. Until these events become a learned habit, through repetition, children may need close supervision, monitoring and reminding to bridge this deficit. Also, it is good if you can write out a few of the rules so they have a concrete visual reminder to reference.

6. *Poor attention.* Ability to maintain attention and shift attention can often lead to misbehavior. Children may have a hard time discriminating between what is important to focus on and distracting background stimulation. They may become distracted by something attractive to them, which pulls their attention away from what is expected. When this happens, they become fixated on things that attract them, and cannot shift attention from them. In no time, they are wandering off course from what the expectations were.

7. *Poor monitoring skills.* The inability to monitor what you are doing while you are doing it is a major part of executive functions. A child with this problem is not capable of monitoring what he is doing to stay within the boundaries. He cannot perform the two functions (think about what he is doing, as he is doing it). This also makes it difficult for him to see that others are reacting unfavorably to his actions or to know why others are giving him negative feedback. It is so frustrating for the child when he is constantly out of line, but he either does not know it or cannot monitor his performance.

8. *Unaware of consequences.* These children often act in the moment, with little forethought about what the consequences will be. Again, this requires multi-tasking, reflecting on what has happened in the past while projecting what will be the result of their actions. Again, they act without forethought.

9. *Poor awareness of how their behavior affects others.* Lastly, autistic children have difficulty understanding how their behavior affects others and how others are responding to their behavior. Individuals on the spectrum have difficulty reading the thoughts, feelings and perspectives of others. They may not realize that others have different perspectives and expectations or understand what those perspectives are. They think others think and feel like them, so it is upsetting when others try to stop them from doing what they see as important for them.

10. *Poor emotional control.* Part of executive functioning is being able to regulate our emotions, match them to environmental demands and not emotionally overreact. Those with executive dysfunctions often overreact emotionally, panic easily, go from 0 to 100 quickly and have difficulty calming down once upset. For emotional control, the thinking part of the brain (frontal lobes) must keep the emotional centers of the brain in check. Essentially, the executive function centers of the brain inhibit our emotional impulses long enough to appraise what is needed, assess if the emotional impulse is adaptive and evaluate what the consequences will be. We then adjust our emotional responses to better match the immediate demands of the setting. For those with executive dysfunction, these emotional impulses overwhelm the weak executive functioning centers, resulting in intense, unregulated emotional responses.

It is amazing how many executive functions come into play that can result in children misbehaving. Since these deficits are common in autism, it is important that we step back before judging the intent of the children's misbehaving. They are often seen as oppositional, defiant and purposefully trying to upset or manipulate us, especially the very capable children who should "know better!" Most children will do good if they can. If they are not doing well, stop and assess if their misbehavior is not a reflection of these weaknesses. Do not blame the child, but seek ways to bridge these deficits.

As we discussed earlier in the chapter, since most of these functions are brain wiring differences, the best approach to helping the person is to provide external supports (accommodations) that help bridge the brain deficits in executive functioning. Let's look at an example of how external accommodations can be used to reduce severe behavior challenges in a classroom.

Tony

At school, Tony had frequent problems with remaining in his seat, finishing his work, and getting aggressive (hitting, kicking) when teachers tried to redirect or correct him. According to staff, Tony was unmotivated and oppositional and would act out to get his way. He would get bored quickly, refuse to work, and would get up and move about the room. When the teacher tried to redirect him, Tony would throw materials, tip over desks and physically attack the teacher. Aids would often physically restrain Tony to keep everyone safe, which only aggravated the problems.

Tony was a bright boy and had the knowledge to complete most of the tasks, which frustrated the staff even more. However, Tony would not complete his work, became negative about trying and resistant to everyone attempting to help him. Assessments revealed that Tony had strong executive functioning issues which might underlie his challenging behaviors. He seemed to have difficulty maintaining attention and staying focused and emotionally regulated. His working memory was weak, and he had poor organizational skills.

His sensory processing evaluation revealed he had sensory modulation difficulties resulting in an under-aroused nervous system (meaning he needed ongoing stimulation to stay aroused and alert). Tony needed frequent doses of movement and physical activity to stay aroused. Knowing that he liked playing basketball, the teacher tried using time in the gym shooting baskets to reward completion of work. This did not improve his performance or behavior, but just made Tony more frustrated. Since he could not complete his work, he often did not earn time playing basketball.

Assuming that Tony would do good if he could, staff started looking at which accommodations would help him successfully complete his work, allow him to frequently earn basketball time (which was also important to keep his nervous system aroused and alert) and allow him to build self-esteem through experiencing success. Instead of trying to force Tony into complying, it was assumed that it was difficult for him to meet expectations and staff focused on bridging these deficits. The following accommodations were added:

- Tony's desk was moved to the front of the classroom, close to the teacher. This minimized distractions and allowed the teacher to provide easy monitoring and assistance.

- Tony could sit on an exercise ball and chew gum to arouse his nervous system. If he chose to, he could stand while working. The teacher also gave Tony some up and moving activities (erase the board, take items to office, sharpen pencils, do wall push-ups, etc.) at least once an hour to alert his nervous system. He enjoyed helping the teacher and being up and moving. This helped keep Tony aroused and alert and gave him short breaks from sitting.

- Tony would become overwhelmed and freeze if given a lot of work at one time. Academic tasks were shortened or broken down into smaller steps; for example, 20 math problems were reduced to ten.

- To help with working memory, for both the directions for the task as well as the reward he was working for (basketball), on one side of the desk was placed an index card with written directions to reference. In the middle of the desk was a photo of a basketball to remind him that he could play once the task was completed. On the other side of the desk was a break card that he could use when losing focus and needing to get up and move.

- To help with emotional regulation, Tony had a written menu of activities (wall push-ups, jumping on a mini-trampoline, getting a drink of water, going to the bathroom, etc.) he could use to take a break and escape demands when he started to become overwhelmed. If he got tired, he could go to a mat and lie down.

- At all times, if Tony raised his hand, the teacher or aid would assist him. They also monitored him closely to offer assistance and remind him to take breaks when he started to lose focus.

All these strategies were about supporting Tony's executive functioning problems, not treating his challenges as intentional behavior. He was given choices, allowed to pace his work, his voice was respected when he needed help or movement breaks, and he was given assistance as needed. Staff did not pressure, demand or continually prompt Tony. He was provided with the tools to be successful and this gave him the control to pace himself. There were no time constraints or ongoing prompting to stay on task. All attention was focused on what Tony was doing right, even when he was struggling.

Tony began to see staff as working partners with him, instead of people instructing, directing and policing him. As Tony developed greater feelings of competence and trust in staff, perceptions and attitudes of staff toward Tony became more positive as they saw him succeed. Tony was given a voice and felt respected and valued. He was not seen as unmotivated, indifferent and oppositional. Staff saw that with the right supports, Tony was successful and happy. The more Tony felt safe, accepted and competent, the more successful he was. Staff learned that when Tony was struggling, they needed to pause, look closely for what deficit was presenting the challenge and, with him, design accommodations for bridging the problem.

Executive dysfunction and independent living: connecting the dots

We briefly touched on how executive dysfunction interferes with adult daily living. Here is where I would like to emphasize the need for structure and daily routines. Many adults on the spectrum often feel lost without a set routine. Keeping routines the same allows them to follow a script and get things done. One individual presented a very accurate analogy. He stated that most of us (non-autistics) have a mental map that helps us navigate through the day, connecting the dots to provide predictability and security. This mental map is the context of our day and of each situation that provides the backdrop (map) for connecting what to do, when to do it, how to get there, what to expect and what is expected of us. This context allows us to connect the dots to see the whole picture that provides the glue to our day. Many autistics do not have this mental map to piece together the context that provides continuity from one activity to the next and enables them to navigate the invisible expectations within the day. Unless the daily activity is very structured, concrete and predictable, their mental map collapses and everything falls apart.

Once they map out what they are going to do, if there are any snags their map falls apart and anxiety and panic set in. Trying to flexibly navigate through the multiple, unexpected variations in their day often does not match what their mental map says. Anxiety increases and their mapping skills deteriorate. One lady related that navigating her day at work can be very anxiety provoking. Before leaving her home in the morning she tries to plan out her day. Like many, her temporal sense (passage of time) is weak, which makes it hard to determine how to schedule her day. If she allows 30 minutes to get to work and she runs into a road block and is late, this throws off her whole schedule, collapsing her mental map for the day. She needs frequent recovery breaks at work to avoid mental drain. She tries to plan in these recovery breaks between meetings and other job responsibilities. If meetings run over or tasks take longer than expected (which occurs frequently with her poor sense of time), she gets off schedule, misses her breaks, is often late for meetings and does not complete tasks in time. Figuring out how long it will take to do things, remembering what to do and getting hyper-focused to the point of forgetting to move on create enormous anxiety and insecurity. Even though she has someone to schedule her appointments, she is often off track. At least her boss and co-workers understand her challenges and help bridge her lack of organization (help remind her to move on, avoid having her multi-task, allow her extra time to complete things and to excuse herself to take a break and regroup).

Like most characteristics of autism, there are wide variances in how executive functions play out. Some are much more severe than others. Usually, most individuals need to use schedules, checklists, auditory reminders, and keep their setting very structured and consistent to maintain continuity in their lives. They often use a whiteboard, centrally located in their house, to map out their immediate day, or try and rely on calendars, smartphone schedulers with auditory reminders and checklists to remember what to do, when to do it and how to do things. The better they get at using these organizing tools, the less confused and anxious they are. It is best to start using these tools early in life so that they become skilled at keeping their daily lives organized.

At least at home, autistics can arrange their environment to match their neurology (sensory sensitivities, predictable routines, set places to put things, written schedules and checklists, etc.)—unless they are married with children, which presents a host of irregularities and uncertainties. Organizing their lives so they get things done (house cleaning, paying bills, doing laundry, keeping medical appointments, etc.) can vary from difficult to doable (with strong structure) to haphazardly getting by with a messy, disorganized life.

Some adults are compulsively organized to keep their mental map together, while others cannot begin to map out and follow a consistent routine. They give up expecting to keep things organized, picked up and clean, and may forget to eat, take medications or even to go to bed on time. They forget to do things, lose track of time, get lost in what they are doing and become stifled with anxiety. They forget where they put things, often losing items and miss appointments if they remembered to make them.

Executive dysfunction can also interfere with completing self-care needs. I had a co-worker who struggled with dressing and grooming. He would show up to work with his clothes in disarray, shoes often untied, shirt tails out, shirt buttoned incorrectly, hair a mess and often without brushing his teeth. He relied on the secretaries to straighten him up once he came in. He also kept a toothbrush and deodorant in his desk in case he forgot to use them at home. Many autistics report that this disorganization becomes worse with anxiety. When they are preoccupied or fixated on a worry, they forget to complete daily tasks, or they miss an important event. This can be very frustrating for them, as well as those around them.

Some autistics report that they have difficulty completing daily tasks because they "fog out" and forget what they are doing in the middle of tasks. For simple tasks like dressing, they may fog out and forget what they have done and what still needs to be completed. This becomes problematic for tasks like cooking, when they may forget to turn off the burner. This can make independent living difficult. We can, however, build in accommodations to bridge such problems. In this case of cooking, the person cooks most of her meals on Sunday afternoon for the rest of the week, while her friend is there to help monitor. Throughout the week, she warms up her meals in the microwave and avoids using the stove. With most executive dysfunction issues, we can usually find a way to adapt, accommodate and work around the problems. However, many adults still need some type of assistance and supervision for living.

Many very capable adults do not drive because they cannot multi-task all the processing that driving demands. Some of those who do drive, only drive to routine places near home and avoid driving unfamiliar routes. Many get confused trying to navigate congested highways, lose track of where they are going and get very anxious and overwhelmed from all the navigating driving takes.

Navigating the community can be very confusing when you do not have an adequate mental map. All the sensory bombardment can make shopping very difficult. Handling all the sounds, smells and people can be overwhelming. They often shop in off hours to avoid the people, or at stores that will gather the items for them, or order as much as possible online. Remembering what to buy, how much it costs and bringing enough money can be difficult. Often impulse buying throws their checklist off course, rendering them without enough money to cover everything. They may spend way too much money at the store and not have enough left to pay their bills. When they use delivery services, family and friends are frequently needed to manage these events. Taking cash instead of a credit card can help avoid overspending. Mapping out the store aisles for common items, then grouping the checklist by aisle number can greatly assist finding things. Unfortunately, if the store rearranges its aisles, the whole map falls apart. If a person shops at the same store frequently and gets to know staff, often they can help the individual navigate these situations. Having familiar people working at frequently visited stores, banks, gas stations, post office and so on can provide great support when the individual needs assistance.

In this chapter, I summarized executive dysfunctions and how they affect daily living. Although these weaknesses will remain for a lifetime, there are many strategies for modifying the environment, changing task requirements and accommodating the lack of abilities so that more independent functioning is possible. Simply look closely at what aspects of living are challenging and then modify the environment, change what is required or build in adaptations to override the weakness. More independent living is always possible.

References

Loos, H.G. and Loos Miller, I.M. (2004) *Shutdown States and Stress Instability in Autism.* Online access at www.researchgate.net/publication/228890735_Shutdown_States_and_Stress_Instability_in_Autism.

Greene, R.W. (2010) *The Explosive Child: A New Approach for Understanding and Parenting Easily Frustrated, Chronically Inflexible Children.* New York, NY: HarperCollins Publishers.

Groden, J. Weidenman L. and Diller A. (2016) *Relaxation: A Comprehensive Manual for Children and Adults with Autism and Other Developmental Disabilities, Second Edition.* Champaign, IL: Research Press Publishers.

Myles, B. and Southwick, J. (2005) *Asperger Syndrome and Difficult Moments: Practical Solutions for Reducing Tantrums, Rage, and Meltdowns.* Shawnee Mission, KS: AAPC Publishing.

Nason, B. (2014a) *The Autism Discussion Page on the Core Challenges of Autism: A Toolbox for Helping Children with Autism Feel Safe, Accepted, and Competent.* London: Jessica Kingsley Publishers.

Nason, B. (2014b) *Autism Discussion Page on Anxiety, Behavior, School, and Parenting Strategies: A Toolbox for Helping Children with Autism Feel Safe, Accepted, and Competent.* London: Jessica Kingsley Publishers.

Vermeulen, P. (2012) *Autism as Context Blindness.* Shawnee Mission, KS: AAPC Publishing.

From the same author

The Autism Discussion Page on the core challenges of autism
A toolbox for helping children with autism feel safe, accepted, and competent
Bill Nason

Paperback
ISBN: 978 1 84905 994 7
eISBN: 978 0 85700 924 5
384 pages

The Autism Discussion Page blue book focuses on the core challenges associated with autism (cognitive, sensory, social, and emotional) and provides concise, accessible information and simple tools for supporting children with these vulnerabilities.

Based on posts on the popular online community page and organised by subject for ease of reference, this book offers an excellent understanding of how children with autism process and experience the world and effective strategies for coping with the challenges.

The Autism Discussion Page on anxiety, behavior, school, and parenting strategies
A toolbox for helping children with autism feel safe, accepted, and competent
Bill Nason

Paperback
ISBN: 978 1 84905 995 4
eISBN: 978 0 85700 943 2
336 pages

The Autism Discussion Page green book covers anxiety and stress, challenging behaviors, stretching comfort zones, discipline, and school issues. It also provides more general teaching and mentoring strategies for coaching children on the autism spectrum in basic daily living strategies to improve their day-to-day lives.

Based on posts on the popular online community page and organised by subject for ease of reference, this book offers an excellent understanding of how children with autism process and experience the world and effective strategies for coping with the challenges.